Fashion Marketing

THEORY, PRINCIPLES, & PRACTICE

Fashion Marketing

THEORY, PRINCIPLES, & PRACTICE

Marianne C. Bickle
UNIVERSITY OF SOUTH CAROLINA

FAIRCHILD BOOKS
NEW YORK

Vice President & General Manager, Fairchild
Education & Conference Division: Elizabeth Tighe
Executive Editor: Olga T. Kontzias
Assistant Acquisitions Editor: Amanda Breccia
Editorial Development Director: Jennifer Crane
Development Editor: Rob Phelps
Creative Director: Carolyn Eckert
Production Director: Ginger Hillman
Production Editor: Jessica Rozler
Copyeditor: Rayhané Sanders
Ancillaries Editor: Noah Schwartzberg
Cover Design: Carolyn Eckert
Cover Art: *Front cover: Black store Interior: The new Versace store in Dallas, Texas. COPYRIGHT ©2009 FAIRCHILD FASHION GROUP. ALL RIGHTS RESERVED; Green/Yellow store interior: Interior shot of new Miu Miu store on Rodeo Drive, Beverly Hills, California. COPYRIGHT ©2009 FAIRCHILD FASHION GROUP. ALL RIGHTS RESERVED; Manolo Blahnik shoe and Chanel bag: Stephen Mark Sullivan; Back cover: Stephen Mark Sullivan.*
Text Design: Carolyn Eckert
Composition: Andrew Katz and SR Desktop Services, Ridge, NY
Director, Sales & Marketing: Brian Normoyle

Library of Congress Catalog Card Number: 2009931522
ISBN: 978-1-56367-738-0
GST R 133004424

Printed in the United States of America

TP08

I dedicate this volume to

Diane Claudia and William Charles Bousquette.

They continually demonstrate commitment to family and friends,
live life to the fullest, are grateful for all life's experiences,
and look at the glass seven-eighths full.

Thank you for inviting me to the party.

Contents

Extended Contents

Preface

Since I received my bachelor of science in Textiles and Clothing in 1980 from Michigan State University, undergraduates in textiles and clothing, retail management, fashion merchandising, and related programs have been required to complete a marketing course. There is excellent justification for this course requirement. Professionals in the fashion industry conduct some of the most elaborate and expensive marketing campaigns throughout the globe. Throughout the years of teaching, my students have frequently commented that they would like a marketing textbook that featured fashion-related examples. After all, while Kodak, for example, does indeed market its product, most of our students don't work for Kodak. They work for Nordstrom, Neiman Marcus, and Bloomingdale's. While a course on the principles of marketing taught in a different college provides our students with the concepts, the application of the concepts are not as beneficial as when fashion companies are applied to the concepts.

THE MARKETING CONCEPT

The marketing concept remains the same regardless of the product. The marketing concept addresses the four *P*s—price, product, promotion, and place. This concept assists the marketing team in organizing, arranging, and delivering products and services. These actions focus on two objectives: satisfying consumers' wants and needs and fulfilling the organization's primary goal.

This text was written for the purpose of presenting the marketing concept to textile and clothing, retail-management, and fashion merchandising students. Stories of fashion designers, manufacturers, and retailers are applied to marketing concepts throughout the text. For example, Ralph Lauren's marketing concept focuses on understanding how to satisfy the wants and needs of the classic fashion domestic and international target market. The nature of these fashion-oriented products, influences how we implement the marketing concepts. One wouldn't approach a marketing campaign for Piggly Wiggly supermarkets the same way one might approach a campaign for Victoria's Secret. Product placement, timing, location, pricing, and message are influenced by the nature of the product.

Fashion is a billion-dollar industry. It crosses over product categories, lifestyles, generations, income brackets, and continents. Products that are considered fashionable by one target market may be considered passé by another target market. One common characteristic that binds people who enjoy fashion is that they all have an opinion regarding what constitutes fashion.

I've been teaching retailing and fashion merchandising students since 1989. A required course in the curriculum is Principles of Marketing. Throughout each glorious year, students have requested a marketing text that emphasizes fashion examples as opposed to nonfashion products. The purpose of *Fashion Marketing: Theory, Principles, and Practice* is to provide retailing and fashion merchandising students with a marketing course that focuses on the fashion industry.

The Market Planning Process

The marketing concept is a process. That is, the marketing team prepares the marketing campaign in stages. Some stages are completed simultaneously while other stages are considered later in the decision-making process. I have designed a Market Planning Process table to assist students in learning how to compartmentalize marketing decision-making efforts. Many students in textile and clothing, retail management, and fashion merchandising have told me that they are visual learners. I, too, am a visual learner. The Market Planning Process table provides students with: (1) a list of activities that the marketer accomplishes at each stage, (2) the associated topics discussed in the chapter, and (3) a pictorial diagram showing the flow of information and/or activities. At the conclusion of the chapter, if the student is unaware of information on the Market Planning Process table, he or she should reread some or all of that chapter.

Organization around the Market Planning Process

The text is divided into 12 chapters. With the exception of Chapter One, "Introduction to Fashion Marketing," each chapter focuses on one aspect of the marketing concept. At the conclusion of the text, the student will have thoroughly learned the marketing concept.

The first two chapters focus on introducing and describing the impact of the fashion industry. Throughout Chapter One, "Introduction to Fashion Marketing," the reader will learn about fashion marketing efforts as they relate to the market, the basics of marketing (i.e., product, price, promotion, place), a company's mission statement, and a company's strategic plan. The marketing concept and SWOT analysis are also examined in relation to the dynamic nature of the fashion industry. Chapter Two, "The Impact of Fashion," addresses the market planning process. *Inspiration* is Step One of the market planning process. Sources of inspiration are also addressed in this chapter.

Chapters Three, Four, and Five focus on fashion marketing efforts. Chapter Three, "Product, Price, Distribution, and Placement," focuses on traditional marketing efforts. The target market, geographic distribution, the proportion of products carried, and product placement are examined in relation to marketing efforts. Chapter Three corresponds to Step Two on the Market Planning Process table.

Perhaps at no other time in history have different social classes crossed so many boundaries through the adoption of fashion. Theories that influence the fashion industry and consumers' behaviors are presented. In Chapter Four, "Public Relations, Promotion, and Advertising," specific marketing campaign techniques are addressed. This section of the Market Planning Process corresponds to Step Three.

Similarly, the rich and famous are a making significant impact on all target markets' purchasing behaviors. Fashion marketers have taken notice and taken action. The influence of Hollywood, celebrities, television shows, and the overall media is aggressively used in the marketing of all types of fashion products. Step Four of the Market Planning Process is analyzed in Chapter Five, "Fashion and the Entertainment Industry."

Where merchandise is purchased, the quantity of merchandise purchased, and the number of competitors selling the same fashions all influence how a retailer decides to market its garments (Step Five of the Market Planning Process). Chapter Six, "The Buying Season: Marketing Fashions to Retailers," provides students with information regarding different buying sources, methods of gaining valuable information, and the impact buying sources have on their marketing efforts.

Having a clearly defined target market is perhaps one of the most important decisions a retailer can make. When a retailer states, *everyone is my target market,* I usually think that the retailer: (1) doesn't have a clear idea of the target market, (2) doesn't have effective marketing results, and/or (3) is offering inconsistent merchandise. When a retailer doesn't have a clear and well-defined target market, the company is literally giving sales and profits to its competitor. Chapter Seven, "Targeting the Fashion Consumer," discusses the importance of and methods for identifying and marketing to a specific target market (Step Six of the Market Planning Process).

The nature of retailing has evolved dramatically with the improvement of technology.

Brick-and-mortar stores, direct marketing, and Internet retailers offer consumers a variety of ways to view, analyze, and purchase fashions. These cross-channel shopping options lead manufacturers and retailers to select a variety of different methods of communicating marketing messages to the consumer. Throughout Chapter Eight, "Cross-Channel Shopping," the impact of multiple channels on marketing efforts is examined (Step Seven of the Market Planning Process).

Branding designers' names, images, and fashions has become an important component of the fashion marketing concept. Branding is used as an effective tool to help consumers readily recognize specific fashions and become loyal purchasing consumers. Ralph Lauren, Donna Karan, and Chanel have built international fashion empires through effective branding. Chapter Nine, "Image and Branding," illustrates the concepts, tools, and outcomes used throughout the fashion industry (Step Eight of the Market Planning Process).

While branding has helped build consumer loyalty, designers and manufacturers have further expanded their fashion empires by crossing product boundaries. Fashion style has bolted out of the closet and exploded throughout the entire home, yard, and consumer's lifestyle. Designers and manufacturers either lend their names to licenses or develop fashion products for an entire lifestyle. The results lend themselves to marketing multiple product categories simultaneously, as well as to increasing the number of target markets obtained. Chapter Ten, "Crossing Product Boundaries," addresses this subject (Step Nine of the Market Planning Process).

Two trends continue to grow in the fashion industries: counterfeit merchandise is flooding the marketplace, and fashions are marketed globally at an increasingly rapid pace. China is a primary source of counterfeit high-end merchandise. These products harm sales of genuine products, as well as companies' images and reputations. Chapter Eleven, "Counterfeiting, Legislation, and Ethics," addresses the ramifications of counterfeit merchandise on fashion marketing (Step Ten of the Market Planning Process).

The final chapter, Chapter Twelve, "Marketing Fashions Globally," focuses on the international marketing efforts of the fashion industry. The advanced use of technology has allowed fashion designers, manufacturers, and retailers to expand their marketing efforts globally (Step Eleven of the Market Planning Process).

Designers, manufacturers, and retailers may have fabulous products to offer their target markets. If the products aren't successfully marketed to the consumers, the products may forever sit on shelves, in warehouses, or in distribution centers. Successful marketing efforts can mean the difference between regional, national, and international product recognition.

ACKNOWLEDGMENTS

This book would not be possible without the encouragement and support of many people. The Fairchild Books team is more like a family than colleagues. From the conversation regarding fashion marketing as a topic to the final revision, each member of the Fairchild team demonstrated an enormous amount of creativity, patience, enthusiasm, and guidance. I am forever grateful to them for bringing me into the world of textbook writing. Executive Editor Olga Kontzias, Assistant Acquisitions Editor Amanda Breccia, Editorial Development Director Jennifer Crane, Senior Development Editor Joseph Miranda, Development Editor Robert Phelps, Creative Director Carolyn Eckert, Production Editor Jessica Rozler, and Production Director Ginger Hillman enriched my world. Thank you very much!

The development reviewers provided valuable information and guided the direction of the text. Many thanks are given to Elizabeth Hinckley of the Fashion Institute of Design and Merchandising; Fr. Joanne Leoni of Johnson & Wales University, Florida; Jacquee

Leahy of the Art Institute of California, San Diego; and Dianne Erpenbach of Columbia College, Chicago.

Across the country, different individuals provided interviews for the textbook. Their primary purpose in participating in the text was for the higher education of students. Each person gave interesting fashion marketing stories. Appreciation is given to: Freddie Barnes of Barnes Jewelers; Linda Carlson, curator of the Avenir Museum of Design and Merchandising; George and Marty Carson of Marty Rae's of Lexington; Shirley Ellsworth of Lambspun; Brandi Gayle, executive team leader at Target; Patricia "Missy" Hollifield of Biltmore Estate; Jackie Howie of Kicks Exceptional Shoes; Sonya Ingram and Karen Hiter of HandPicked; Annabelle LaRoque of LaRoque; and Arden Korn of Little Lambs & Ivy II.

The faculty and staff of the Department of Retailing at the University of South Carolina-Columbia provided continual support and encouragement for this textbook. They include: Barney Allman, Dan Berry, Sallie Boggs, Jason Carpenter, Richard Clodfelter, Reenea Harrison, Karen Lear, Jiyeon Kim, Jung-Hwan Kim, Michael Moody, and Susan Reeves. I am truly fortunate to work with such a fabulous team.

Dianne Bousquette, Bill Bousquette, Janine Mayville, Vicki Smith, Michele Sullivan, and Dianne Witten are all a constant source of encouragement. I am truly fortunate to have such a diverse and strong group of friends. This book was a wonderful joyride. Thank you for joining me on the ride.

Introduction

TO FASHION MARKETING

"I love to take things that are everyday and comforting and make them into the most luxurious things in the world." —Marc Jacobs

chapter objectives

After reading this chapter, you should be able to:

+ Comprehend the purpose of marketing.
+ Comprehend the fashion-marketing concept.
+ Analyze a company mission statement.
+ Evaluate a strategic plan.

Marc Jacobs's philosophy demonstrates the core theory of fashion marketing. Much of fashion is not original. What makes fashion original, long-lasting, important, or memorable is the combination of fabrics, accessories, and, ultimately, marketing efforts. As you progress through this text, you will be asked to answer questions. Although many of the questions have specific answers, others do not have one single correct answer. Answers to some questions are based on your perceptions and opinions; as in fashion, opinions vary based on an individual's background, perceptions, and preferences.

Designers, marketers, and retailers gain valuable insight by discussing ideas and opinions with others. You are encouraged to talk with your classmates, instructors, and friends about your opinions on the questions posed throughout this text. Like Marc Jacobs, we all have our own ways of taking the everyday and making it unique. Sharing these ideas, we begin to appreciate others' perceptions, their wants and needs, and how they envision their fulfillment. Developing this awareness is the very basis of marketing.

POINT OF VIEW

Marketing can be viewed from the manufacturer's (e.g., Ralph Lauren) or the retailer's (e.g., Neiman Marcus) point of view. Regardless of the point of view, the marketing efforts are similar. The purpose of marketing is to successfully exchange products and/or services between the vendor (the manufacturer and/or retailer) and the customer. Throughout this text, examples will be provided from both fashion manufacturers and retailers. The purpose of using examples from both channels is to provide the reader with a comprehensive explanation, an understanding, and examples of the marketing process.

Marketing activities influence companies of all sizes. In fact, many large international companies began as micro-entrepreneurial organizations. Ralph Lauren, perhaps one of the best-known marketers in the world, started his organization in his kitchen. Ralph and his wife, Ricky, manufactured men's ties and developed the marketing plan from their

figure 1.1 Ralph Lauren's all-American fashions come through in this advertisement. The focus is on an overall marketing of the image and brand instead of a particular product.

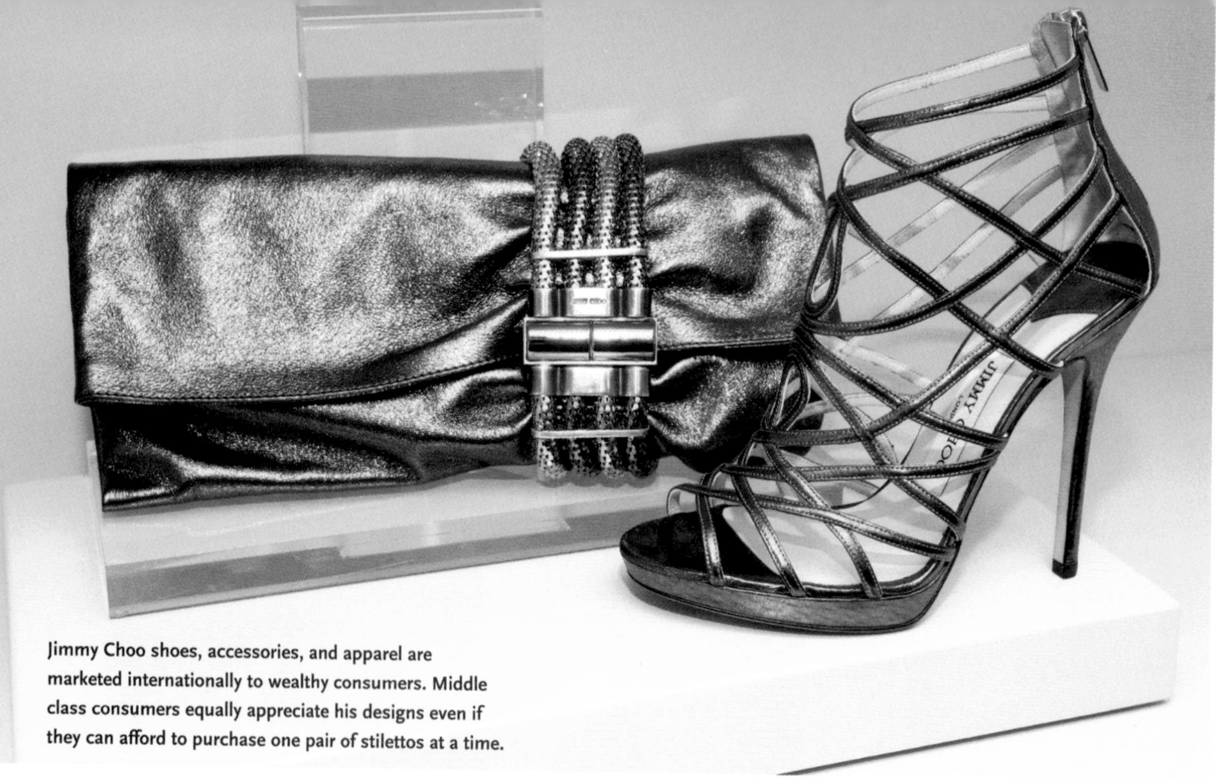

Jimmy Choo shoes, accessories, and apparel are marketed internationally to wealthy consumers. Middle class consumers equally appreciate his designs even if they can afford to purchase one pair of stilettos at a time.

BOX 1.1 Jimmy Choo

For some individuals in the fashion industry, it takes a lifetime to successfully market products and brands. Jimmy Choo's success came quickly and has not stopped. Choo's entry into the shoe industry in 1986 began in East London. During 1988, *Vogue* magazine devoted eight pages to his shoes. This marketing exposure rocketed him to international fashion iconic status. Industry awards rapidly followed Choo. His company, J. Choo Limited, offers couture fashions and handbags to complement the shoes the world so loves. Stakeholders of J. Choo Limited include royalty (e.g., the late Princess Diana); celebrities; consumers; advertisers; and the shoe, apparel, and handbag industries (www.indobase.com).

home (Gross, 2003). All companies, large and small, require marketing efforts. Throughout this text, a wide variety of examples will be provided. In each chapter, examples of high-fashion companies and small entrepreneurial companies will be presented. The dichotomous company examples will provide the reader with an understanding of how marketing is applied, regardless of the size of the company.

MARKET

Companies identify the market to which they want to sell their products and services. The **market** is defined as "a set of actual and potential buyers of a product." Furthermore, "these buyers share a particular need or want that can be satisfied through exchanges and relationships" (Kotler & Armstrong, 2001, p. 12). The correct identification of the market is essential for a company to succeed. All company efforts revolve around the attempt to satisfy needs and wants of the market. If the market is not correctly identified, the company's efforts will fall short of their goal.

Isaac Mizrahi's designs for Target brought glamour, fun, fashion, and savings for the fast-fashion consumer. In 2009, he made a significant change in his career by moving to Liz Claiborne, Inc. to become creative director. Mizrahi has an extraordinary talent for: (a) understanding the market, (b) identifying products it will purchase, and (c) marketing

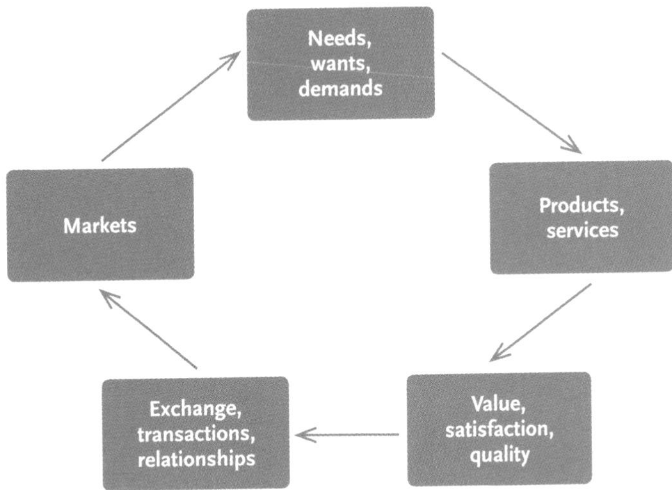

figure 1.2 The Core Marketing Concepts are circular and repetitive in nature. Marketers must address each of the concepts (Kotler & Armstrong 2001, p. 6).

the lines. According to chief executive officer of Liz Claiborne William L. McComb, "We knew it would take somebody who was not just an extraordinary designer, but somebody who could create an amazing amount of intrigue and buzz and give people this reason to say, 'Oh my God, I need to take another look' " (Iredale, 2009, p. 7).

The company gives the market signals in written, verbal, and visual methods. **Signals** may include new product offerings, press releases, changes in leadership, or the enhancement of store interiors (Table 1.1).

Signals may communicate positive or negative attributes regarding a company.

MARKETING

Marketing is defined as "managing markets to bring about exchanges and relationships for the purpose of creating value and satisfying needs and wants" (Kotler & Armstrong, 2001, p. 13). Notice that marketing is *not defined* as advertising, promotion, selling, or public relations. Marketing consists of comprehensive activities that bring products and services to the market. All divisions within a company are involved in the marketing effort. Marketing, at its core, is to define the company's territory. It is important to answer the following question first: *Who are we, and what do we offer?* All divisions and departments within the company must be clear on the answer to work together.

In order for marketing to be effective, marketing must be clear in the customers' mind. This means that the market must clearly understand the signals regarding:

- Product
- Price
- Placement
- Communication

figure 1.3 Isaac Mizrahi's designs brought high-fashion appeal to the Target discounter. It also brought Mizrahi loyal consumers nationwide. This marketing effort was a win–win for the designer and the retailer.

What do the following signals indicate to you?

- Macy's offers 20 percent off all merchandise at least twice a month.
- Saks Fifth Avenue is placing a heavier emphasis on lifestyle components (Palmieri, 2009).
- Red and blue open-toe star heels by Marc Jacobs or navy and white striped shorts from J. Crew (Magsaysay, 2009).
- More than 500 women showed up for the marketing extravaganza of the Liz Claiborne brand designed by Mizrahi (Beckett, 2009).
- Serena Williams, tennis superstar, is designing and selling her accessory line on the Home Shopping Network (Tell, 2009).
- Metal fabrics, such as gold and silver, were heavily featured on the designer runway fashion shows during spring 2009.
- Baccarat jewelry is considered a luxury status symbol.

TABLE 1.1
Marketing Signals

SIGNAL	IMPLICATIONS
Fabrizio Freda is named president and chief executive officer of the Estée Lauder Companies Inc. (Born & Prior, 2009b)	Possible changes in: • Executives • Product lines • Marketing strategies • Product placement
H&M will feature designer Matthew Williamson's designs for a limited time. (Edelson, 2009)	• H&M may continue to offer designer-name garments for less. • Other companies may follow these actions.
Advertising luxury brands is becoming more difficult with tighter advertising budgets. (Wicks, 2009)	Possible changes include: • The frequency of promotional efforts • Brands promoted • Markets targeted • Celebrity endorsements
Calvin Klein introduces a new jean that enhances the body.	Possible expansion in: • Sales • Profits • Market share

Throughout the marketing process, the company assesses how resources will be allocated. A clear brand strategy is critical. **Brand strategy** is defined as "the plan employed to create, introduce, and promote a particular brand. Strategies involved include picking a name, selecting an image to project, [or] position the product in the marketplace" (Ostrow & Smith, 1988, p.28).

MISSION STATEMENT

All companies, large or small, apparel or accessories, should have a formal **mission statement**. A mission statement is a written statement of the company's purposes—its reason for being in business and its overarching mission or goal. Although this may seem like a simple task, writing a mission statement can be difficult. The mission statement should encompass the aspects of the market, not the product (Kotler & Armstrong, 2001). Mission statements are long term while products may change from year to year. All company activities are driven by the mission statement. If an activity is contrary to the company's mission statement, the company has two possible courses of action: (1) to abandon the activity or (2) to change the mission statement.

Two examples are provided below regarding company mission statements. The companies are diverse in nature; however, you will understand that their mission statements make clear the companies' actions, including their marketing efforts.

Manolo Blahnik's mission statement reads as follows:

> Manolo Blahnik creates shoes not based on peoples' opinions but based on his instincts. He creates the designs independently, sketching and making the prototype. Quality fabrics such as silks and

figure 1.4
Manolo Blahnik shoes typically have a high heel and are designed to make women feel sexy.

satin are trademark. The cost of the shoes are the result of quality fabrics, superior craftsmanship, and style. Each "Manolo" is truly designed by Manolo Blahnik (Design Museum, 2009; Watson, 1999/2000).

Whereas Manolo Blahnik designs and markets luxury shoes, Target is nationally known for its marketing efforts to the mass market. The company's mission statement is designed to remind the employees and consumers that Target is ready to assist in fulfilling their fashion needs.

Target's mission statement reads as follows:

> To make Target the preferred shopping destination for our guests by delivering outstanding value, continuous innovation, and exceptional guest experience by consistently fulfilling our "Expect More. Pay Less." brand promise (Target, 2009).

Target includes its company slogan in its mission statement. "Expect More. Pay Less." is a reminder to all divisions of the company that Target has an obligation to its customers. The obligation is to provide more than its customers expect. In order to provide more, Target employees must be conscious of their efforts at all levels. Merchandising, promotions, sales, operations, security, and distribution all impact the company's ability to fulfill this mission statement (Table 1.2).

THE STRATEGIC PLAN

A **strategic plan** is a series of goals and objectives identified by the company. The attributes of the strategic plan need to be very important to the target market; otherwise the plan won't be successful. The competition is considered in the formation of the plan; in doing so, the company is able to distinguish itself from its competitors, to lure the competitors' customers to patronize its business, and to ultimately understand its competitors' strategies.

Strategic plans are typically developed along one- or five-year time lines. Throughout the planning process, the company's mission statement must continually be considered. The goals and objectives must never contradict the company's reason for existence. Every division within the company participates in the strategic planning process. The goals and objectives developed for each division help guide the efforts throughout the year.

To be effective, goals and objectives must be measurable, realistic, and time specific. Goals should be developed for the fashion marketing department effort. Attributes included in a fashion marketer's strategy will be closely linked to its corporate mission statement. The fashion companies that excel in consistently communicating their strategy emphasize three or fewer attributes. Examples of attributes include low price, excellent customer service, and craftsmanship.

Fashion marketing is a formula. Retailers need the right product. Consumers must have access to the right product. Even if retailers

TABLE 1.2
Slogans in Company Mission Statements

COMPANY	SLOGANS IN MISSION STATEMENTS	WEB SITE URL
Coach	Accessible luxury lifestyle collections	http://www.coach.com
Fashion Bug	Pure comfort. Great fit. Exceptional value.	http://www.fashionbug.com
Fossil	Fusing the best of the past with the best of today	http://www.fossil.com
Gap	To make it easy for you to express your personal style throughout your life	http://www.gap.com
Kohl's	To be the leading family-focused, value-oriented, specialty department store offering quality exclusive and national brand merchandise to the customer in an environment that is convenient, friendly, and exciting	http://www.kohls.com
Jones New York	Innovative, consumer-focused, and efficient play in the apparel industry	http://www.jny.com
Kate Spade	Elegance, simplicity, and enduring quality	http://www.katespade.com
The Limited	An iconic fashion retailer that offers high-quality private-label apparel designed to help the modern woman succeed	http://www.thelimited.com
GUESS by Marciano	Pure glamour in everyday fashion	http://www.marciano.com
Swarovski	Radiance, joy, and sparkling abundance	http://www.swarovski.com
Target	To make Target the preferred shopping destination for our guests by delivering outstanding value, continuous innovation, and exceptional guest experience by consistently fulfilling our "Expect More. Pay Less." brand promise.	http://www.target.com
Tiffany & Co.	To protect the beauty of nature and the creativity of human nature	http://www.tiffany.com
Vera Wang	Celebrates the romance, sensuality, and spirit of modern young women.	http://www.verawang.com

do have the right product in the right location, they are not guaranteed sales. Part of the fashion marketing formula consists of "courting the customer" (Kotler & Armstrong, 2001). Successful fashion marketers interact with consumers on a continual basis before, during, and after the purchasing process. The interaction may include advertisements, direct marketing, e-mail communication, Internet coupons, and in-store personal discussions. Each positive interaction further promotes the customer's propensity to patronize the retailers through various channels (e.g., in-store, catalog, Internet). Tips for building strong relationships with existing or prospective customers include:

figure 1.5 Newsletters are an important marketing piece for informing customers of upcoming new merchandise, designer merchandise carried, sales, and store events.

- Emphasizing benefits that will encourage customers to contact your company (e.g., customers receive 20 percent off products ordered within the next five days).
- Sending your customers beneficial information related to but not necessarily geared directly toward selling merchandise (e.g., fashion marketers may send customers a newsletter on recent fashion trends).
- Building a strong relationship with your customer.

MARKETING CONCEPT

The **marketing concept** is defined as "a marketing management orientation in which the satisfaction of the customer's wants and needs is regarded as the primary goal of the organization, although these wants and needs may not as yet be apparent to (and, thus, not expressed by) the consumer." In essence, the marketing concept recognizes "the importance of the consumer in the buying process" (Ostrow & Smith, 1988, p. 146). The marketing concept examines, evaluates, and focuses on ways to satisfy the consumer's needs and wants. These needs and wants may be satisfied through tangible products, intangible services, or a combination of products and services. A **SWOT** analysis of the marketing concept enables the company to realistically examine its success at delivering the products and services to its market. A SWOT analysis stands for the analysis of Strengths, Weaknesses, Opportunities, and Threats facing an organization. SWOT analysis will be discussed later in this chapter.

NEEDS, WANTS, AND DEMANDS

Marketers must continually examine the needs, wants, and demands of the target market. **Needs** are defined as absolute requirements needed to be met for the target market to purchase. The needs may be physical (e.g., garment fit, warmth from the cold) or psychological (e.g., the feeling of being secure by purchasing an extra pair of gloves).

When was the last time you said or heard statements similar to those below?

- "I have to purchase that bebe dress."
- "I need that Dolce & Gabbana purse."
- "I must try on those shoes. I don't care what they cost."
- "I'll charge the Louis Vuitton purse. It's an investment."

If you have overheard or experienced shopping situations when someone "had to" purchase a fashion product regardless of circumstances, that person was demonstrating his or her wants. **Wants** are defined as consumers' preferences. These preferences distinguish which products and services they will purchase.

BOX 1.2 Galliano's SWOT Analysis

In 1996, John Galliano, at the age of 36, became the head designer for the house of Christian Dior. With success at such a young age, some could say that Galliano has no weaknesses or threats. Galliano would be the first to admit that he struggled to obtain his position and works diligently to keep the house of Dior at the forefront of luxury fashion. Galliano's strengths include his talent, his promise to his vendors, his commitment to deadlines, and his passion for excellence. These business strengths, combined with his creative genius, have provided Galliano with the competitive advantage needed to be the head of a fashion house. His primary weakness prior to joining the house of Dior was obtaining financial backing. Dior provided Galliano with that much-needed backing, and as a result Galliano gained creative support and extensive resources for marketing his creations.

As Galliano continues to create fashions for Dior, the threats include changes in the economy (e.g., consumers' capacity for spending less on luxury items), increased competition, and the need for fresh designs. The threats, however, are minimal considering the strengths and opportunities facing this creative designer (Watson, 2001).

John Galliano makes a statement with his outlandish personal fashion style. He brandishes his creativity, energy, and marketing abilities to bring Dior fashion to the highest levels.

Demands are defined as specifications that consumers require in a company. Demands may include level of product quality, services offered, diversity of channels (e.g., in-store, catalog, Internet), or reputation. (See Figure 1.1.) Consumers' demand for **fast fashion** has changed the fashion marketing process significantly. Fast fashion is defined as the process of moving fashion quickly through retail stores. Fast fashion allows designers, manufacturers, and retailers to present a wider variety of fashions to consumers during the fashion cycle. The fashions tend to be targeted toward the mass market.

Giorgio Armani stated that "fast fashion is a young and dynamic segment of the market which I find particularly stimulating" (Zargani, 2008). Armani Exchange stores select fashions that offer continually fresh impressions to their consumers.

Products and Services

Companies continually examine the products and services offered. **Products** are tangible objects that satisfy consumers' needs and wants. **Services** include activities and benefits that enhance the shopping experience (Kotler & Armstrong, 2001). Services are typically intangible. Where products can be copied, services often serve as a point of competition. The intangibility of services acts as a marketing method for attracting consumers away from the competition, encouraging loyal consumers to remain, and enticing purchasing behaviors.

The following quote demonstrates how Gap Inc. examines its products and services in relation to the market's needs and wants:

> While the previous seasons have been devoted to white shirts, Patrick Robinson, Gap Inc.'s executive vice president of design, decided 2009 was time for change. [He] felt that after two years of doing white shirts, it was time to stay current and stay cool but also stay Gap and keep surprising the customer. Khaki was a curveball of sorts for the designers, as well. That was a big thing for us because khaki usually connotes preppy American sportswear and we are not preppy. Nothing about our brand is preppy (Iredale, 2009b, p. 6).

Value, Satisfaction, and Quality

Value, satisfaction, and quality are three very important words for every company and all consumers.

Think about it. How many times have you heard a company say, *We purposely make crappy products, we don't care about satisfying the consumer, and our products are low-quality?* Even if the statement is true, companies won't admit these facts. Take the three words one step further. Think about the last time you purchased:

- A product even though you knew it would fall apart while using it the first time
- A product even though you were dissatisfied with the quality
- A product even though it wasn't exactly what you wanted
- A service even though you knew it was overpriced
- A service even though you knew the service provider wasn't qualified

Marketers attempt to satisfy consumers' desire for value, bring them satisfaction, and offer quality products and services. When the value, satisfaction, or quality falls short of the consumer's desires (which, in turn, may or may not be realistic), companies' profits suffer.

Each company determines the level of value, satisfaction, and quality that is to be provided to the consumer. For example, Five Below stores, located in New York and New Jersey, sell teen fashions, accessories, and novelty items for $5 or less (Bowers, 2009). The consumers (i.e., teens) perceive the value as a price savings. They are satisfied that (a) they are able to purchase more for their money and (b) the entire store is targeted to their needs. The quality of the novelty items, such as posters and mugs, are equivalent to those sold in discount stores. The products aren't necessarily cohesive. The main theme of the store's marketing effort is price (i.e., everything for $5 or less). Compare the value, satisfaction, and quality of the products

figure 1.6
A picture is worth a thousand words. In the case of marketing, a picture can be worth a thousand dollars. Gap changed the color palette of their fashions from white to khaki. Using photos to demonstrate new apparel combinations, the marketing efforts encouraged consumers to purchase new outfits.

figure 1.7
Michael Kors's lifestyle marketing emphasizes a "pulled-together" look for every event. The designer matches the fashions to event, thereby creating cohesion with the consumer's lifestyle.

at Five Below with that of Michael Kors's lifestyle concept. **Lifestyle concept** is defined as an approach that presents products in a group setting based on a set of behaviors, activities, interests, opinions, or attitudes. Michael Kors's lifestyle concept brings together pants, tops, jackets, bags, and shoes based on a way of living (e.g., urban, rural) (*Women's Wear Daily*, 2009).

RELATIONSHIP MARKETING

The marketing of products and services is often not enough for a company to be successful. In order to generate long-term customer loyalty, relationship marketing must be undertaken. **Relationship marketing** exists when companies build long-term relationships with their stakeholders. **Stakeholders** include individuals or groups that conduct business with the company. Stakeholders may include employees, manufacturers, distributors, advertising companies, shareholders, retailers, and consumers. Regardless of the business interactions between the company and each group, the goal of relationship marketing is to continually build and maintain strong, loyal, and mutually beneficial working relationships (Kotler & Armstrong, 2001).

Companies are wise to never take relationships for granted. While some constituencies may complain, others may simply leave. Relationship marketing is strengthened by continually asking questions and reexamining the strength of the relationship between constituencies. Examples of questions to ask of employees include:

- What type of working environment is important?
- What benefits are important to your employees?
- Are salary requirements, perks, or benefits more important to employees?

Potential questions to ask manufactures may include:

- Can the manufacturer produce merchandise within the necessary timeframes?
- Are the manufacturer's requirements (e.g., timeframe) realistic?
- Is there an incentive for providing merchandise in advance of the deadline?
- Does the manufacturer have easy access to the decision maker (e.g., cell phone)?
- Are calls returned on a timely basis?

Think about the following constituencies. Each group is very important to the fashion marketing industry. Which questions should be regularly asked regarding the following constituencies? Should a company automatically satisfy each group with its requests? How do you know which requests should or can be satisfied?

- Distributors
- Advertising companies
- Shareholders
- Retailers
- Consumers

figure 1.8
Luggage was the first product made by Gucci. Still considered a classic, the styles manufactured and marketed by the company are chic, sophisticated, and desired by a wide target market.

SWOT ANALYSIS

All areas of a company are examined in relation to SWOT analysis. For example, products and services offered, financial well-being, effectiveness of marketing efforts, domestic sales, and international sales are all examined. Each area is also examined in relation to the company's competitors.

The Gucci Group was started in 1921 by a luggage maker named Guccio Gucci. By 1989, the company had built an international reputation for luxury, quality, craftsmanship, and excellence. The company's SWOT analysis changed the projection of the company forever (Table 1.3). The company's product offerings expanded beyond luggage to include men's shoes, leather bags, and leather backpacks. While the products and services offered by Gucci continued to be successful, "it was hard to create an image with a handbag and a pair of shoes. . . . Gucci needed to have ready-to-wear for the image" (Forden, 2001, p. 170).

Tom Ford was hired as the creative director for Gucci. Prior to Ford's arrival at Gucci, sales had been declining. Retailers were increasing the amount of Yves Saint Laurent, and carrying fewer Gucci products. It was Ford's responsibility to turn Gucci's fashion weaknesses into strengths. Instead of the classic brown or navy traditionally used by Gucci, Ford created fashion-forward styles. "Gucci was not a fashion house until Tom made it into a fashion house, and nobody realized he would do that" (Forden, 2001, p. 254). (See Table 1.3.)

TABLE 1.3
SWOT Analysis of Gucci

Strengths	• Loyal customer base • Internationally known • Long-term marketing expertise • Quality products • Branded products
Weaknesses	• Need to stay fresh • Need to communicate with the customer • Stay financially strong • Develop new product without repetition • Obtain positive marketing exposure (e.g. people who are wearing Gucci)
Opportunities	• Expand into other products (e.g., perfume) • Expand into other global markets • Licensing
Threats	• Increased competition • Luxury markets have limited market size • Luxury market influenced by the economy

figure 1.9
As the head designer for Gucci, Tom Ford's creative spirit helped the company go from conservative to hip. The resulting designs and marketing efforts have made Gucci products heavily sought after by celebrities and the general population alike.

SUMMARY

Marketing efforts consist of comprehensive activities that bring products and services to the market. All divisions within the company are involved in the marketing efforts. Marketing, at its core, is to define the company's territory. It is important to answer the questions, *Who are we, and what do we offer?* All divisions and departments within a company must (a) be clear on the answer and (b) work together. Effective marketing efforts result in consumers understanding signals regarding the (a) products, (b) price, (c) placement, and (d) communication.

A strategic plan assists the company throughout its marketing efforts. Strategic plans are typically developed in one- or five-year time lines. Throughout the planning process, the company's mission statement must continually be considered. The goals and objectives must never contradict the company's reason for existence. Every division within the company participates in the strategic planning process. The goals and objectives developed for each division help guide the efforts throughout the year.

All areas of a company are examined in relation to its SWOT analysis. For example, products and services offered, financial well-being, effectiveness of marketing efforts, domestic sales, and international sales are all examined. Each area is also examined in relation to the company's competitors.

REFERENCES

Beckett, W. (2009, March 30). Mizrahi wows crowds at Claiborne launch. *Women's Wear Daily*, p. 1.

Born, P. & Prior, M. (2009, March 26). Changing of the guard: Estee Lauder Cos. taps Fabrizio Freda as CEO. *Women's Wear Daily*, p. 1.

Bowers, K. (2009, March 19). Five Below: A bargain-hungry teen's dream. *Women's Wear Daily*, p. 11.

Design Museum (2009). Manolo Blahnik. Retrieved June 15, 2009 from www.designmuseum.org/design/manolo-blahnik.

Edelson, S. (2009a, March 11). Sticking to the plan: Despite loss, J. Crew sees room to grow. *Women's Wear Daily*, p. 1, 14.

Edelson, S. (2009b, March 26). Williamson gets colorful for H&M. *Women's Wear Daily*, p. 3.

Forden, S. G. (2001). *The house of Gucci: A sensational story of murder, madness, glamour, and greed.* New York: HarperPerennial.

Gross, M. (2003). *Genuine authentic: The real life of Ralph Lauren.* New York: HarperCollins.

Indobase. (n.d.) Jimmy Choo. Retrieved on July 8, 2009 from www.indobase.com/fashion/fashion-designers/jimmy-choo.html.

Iredale, J. (2009a, January 20). Isaac targets Liz. *Women's Wear Daily*, p. 1, 6–7.

Iredale, J. (2009b, May 20). Gap, CFDA finalists team up on Khaki campaign. *Women's Wear Daily*, p. 6.

Kors light. (2009, March 20). "Kors light," *Women's Wear Daily*, p. 4.

Kotler, P. & Armstrong, G. (2001). *Principles of marketing* (9th ed). Upper Saddle River, NJ: Prentice Hall.

Magsaysay, M. (2009, June 28). Fashion: Long may they wave. *Los Angeles Times*, p. 3.

Ostrow, R. & Smith, S. R. (1988). *The dictionary of marketing.* New York: Fairchild Books.

Palmieri, J. E. (2009, March 27). Corneliani refreshes shop at Saks. *Women's Wear Daily*, p. 15.

Tell, C. (2009, March 24). Serena Williams in deal with HSN. *Women's Wear Daily*, p. 3.

Target. (2009). Mission Statement. Retrieved on July 8, 2009 from http://sites.target.com/site/en/company/page.jsp?contentId=WCMP04-031699).

Watson, L. (1999/2000). *Twentieth century fashion: 100 years of style by decade and designer* (Vol. 3). Philadelphia: Chelsea House.

Wicks, A. (2009, March 26). Brands turn to target marketing. *Women's Wear Daily*, p. 6.

Zargani, L. (2008, December 22). Giorgio Armani increases stake in A/X. *Women's Wear Daily*, p. 3.

KEY TERMS

Define or briefly explain the following terms:

Brand strategy ______

Demands ______

Fast fashion ______

Lifestyle concept ______

Market ______

Marketing ______

Marketing concept ______

Mission statement ______

Needs ______

Products ______

Relationship marketing ______

Services ______

Signals ______

Stakeholders ______

Strategic plan ______

SWOT analysis ______

Wants ______

TABLE 2.1

THE Market Planning PROCESS

step 1 CHAPTER 2 | **Be inspired; become passionate regarding a product/service; be driven to succeed and committed to working toward a goal.**

step 2 CHAPTER 3 | Intrinsic attributes of the products and services are marketed in terms of value, satisfaction, and quality. Building upon the mission statement, in this step you will make decisions regarding the pricing, communication, value, satisfaction, and quality associated with the purchase or the products and/or services.

step 3 CHAPTER 4 | Identify a comprehensive list of products and services offered by the company.

step 4 CHAPTER 5 | Examine the products and services component of the core marketing concept related to the trickle-down theory, media and celebrities, and the belongingness theory.

step 5 CHAPTER 6 | Examine the buying season in relation to the marketing process.

step 6 CHAPTER 7 | Examine marketing methods of targeting the consumer.

step 7 CHAPTER 8 | Examine the methods of exchange and relationships with the consumers. This includes making decisions to sell products and services through brick-and-mortar retail operations, direct marketing, and the Internet.

step 8 CHAPTER 9 | Examine the image and brands of the company in relation to marketing efforts.

step 9 CHAPTER 10 | Conduct a market analysis of how companies are able to successfully cross product boundaries.

step 10 CHAPTER 11 | Examine trends in the fashion industry regarding a) counterfeit merchandise and b) the impact of such merchandise on the industry's sales, profits, product design, consumers' attitudes.

step 11 CHAPTER 12 | Conduct a market analysis of fashions in the global environment in order to determine impact to the company's existing marketing efforts.

THE Impact of Fashion

"The future belongs to those who believe in the beauty of their dreams."
—Eleanor Roosevelt

chapter objectives
After reading this chapter, you should be able to understand Step One of the Market Planning Process. This includes being able to:

+ Examine the influence materials have on fashion.
+ Analyze sources of fashion inspiration from society.
+ Examine sources of fashion inspiration from culture and history.
+ Analyze the fashion industry in relation to competition.
+ Discriminate between the benefits of employing a mass-market and market-segmentation efforts.

Eleanor Roosevelt, wife of the thirty-second president of the United States, stated those words during the 1940s. The statement is applicable to today, more than six decades later. When examining the fashion industry, most of the designers, manufacturers, and retailers who started their own businesses will state that they began the business based on a dream. For example, Gilbert Adrian (known as *Adrian*) was a famous costume designer for the theater during the 1930s and 1940s. Bill Blass was driven to design beautiful women's fashions. He also understood, however, the importance of promoting his name and having a financially successful company. His combined talents of design and marketing allowed him to be one of the first designers to successfully market his name as a product. Dolce & Gabbana believe their fashion line can include sexy lines and suits; women are multidimensional, so their fashions are multidimensional as well (Watson, 1999/2000).

figure 2.1 Dolce & Gabbana are internationally known for impacting fashion. The design team introduces sexy lines, multi-dimensional features, and transforms what was a traditional suit. Rihanna wore this Dolce & Gabbana tuxedo suit to an awards show.

MARKET PLANNING STEPS

There are eleven steps in a market plan. They must be completed in consecutive order; each step should be given careful attention. (Refer to Table 2.1.) Failure to correctly assess each step could mean financial ruin for the company. Step One consists of being inspired. Prior to developing and marketing a product or

figure 2.2
The red carpet has come to have an important impact on fashion. Designs such as this Halston dress are copied, redesigned, and manufactured for the mass market. Consumers will typically think, "I have a dress similar to one designed by Halston and worn on the red carpet."

A market analysis of trends in the fashion industry regarding counterfeit products is conducted in Step Ten. The final step, Step Eleven, examines the market analysis of fashions in the global environment.

MARKET PLANNING STEP ONE: INSPIRATION

This chapter focuses on Step One of the Market Planning Process: Inspiration. Inspiration can come from a variety of sources. It is deeply personal. Halston was inspired by fashion in general but was *driven* by the prospect of famous people wearing his clothing. More than anything else, he wanted his fashions to be associated with celebrities and well-known (i.e., extremely wealthy) consumers. Halston said, "You're only as good as the people you dress" (Watson, 1999/2000).

The fashion industry is glamorous, fun, exciting, and lavish. It is also extremely fast-paced. To succeed, designers, retailers, and service, designers, manufacturers, and retailers must be driven to succeed. During Step Two, intrinsic attributes of the products and services are marketed in terms of value, satisfaction, and quality. Step Three consists of identifying a comprehensive list of products and services offered by the company. The products and services of the core marketing concept are examined in Step Four. During Step Five, the buying season's impact on marketing efforts is examined. Throughout Step Six, the methods of targeting the consumers are examined. Step Seven addresses methods of exchange and relationships with consumers. This includes making decisions on methods in which to sell products and services. During Step Eight, the image and branding process is examined in relation to the marketing efforts. Step Nine addresses the market analysis of how companies successfully cross channel product boundaries.

figure 2.3
Magazine articles have become a popular method of learning how to adopt fashions or avoid being a fashion mistake.

figure 2.4
Motorcycles aren't only for bad boys. This marketing effort clearly demonstrates that mixing leather and lace (once a fashion-forbidden rule) is now acceptable.

marketers must have a deep dedication to the industry and not be easily distracted by problems. They must always watch the competition, but not worry or obsess about criticism (Gallagher, 2008). The fashion industry is fluid. A popular trend this month or year can be out-of-date the next. It is important to carefully observe where the marketplace is going. Slight changes in the marketplace may result in significant financial changes to a company. Competition among fashion marketers is increasing due to technology. It is becoming easier to reach consumers via the Internet. Consumers are becoming more selective and savvy regarding their purchases, and are able to purchase via multiple channels (e.g., store, Internet). Watching the marketplace on the surface is not sufficient. The observation of design, elements, colors, hem lengths, materials, and accessories is paramount. To be successful in business, particularly the fashion business, marketers must observe, analyze, and understand why trends are occurring. The environment influences fashions. The symbiotic and powerful relationship of fashion to environment cannot be denied. Whether people enjoy high fashions from Paris and Italy, country fashions inspired by Nashville, or a leather-and-lace outfit suitable for a long-distance Harley Davidson ride, fashion impacts their lives, their way of living, and their method of spending disposable income.

Fashion designers, manufacturers, marketers, and retailers must recognize and understand the variables that influence consumers' wants, desires, and, above all, purchasing behaviors. National and international forces that influence the fashion industry include: (a) the economic well-being of a country, (b) international ties between the United States and other countries, (c) weather's impact on the growth of natural fibers, (d) technology, and (e) societal differences (Gwinn, 2009).

INSPIRATION FROM MATERIALS: TECHNOLOGICAL IMPACT

Technology plays an important role in the fashion industry. Research has resulted in new fibers and fabrics. Gabrielle "Coco" Chanel was one of the first designers to use knit fabrics as a source of inspiration. Chanel used jersey fabrics for suits during an era when jersey was only used for undergarments. According to a 1917 interview by *Vogue* magazine:

> This designer made jersey what it is today —we hope she's satisfied. . . . It's almost as much [a] part of our live[s] as blue serge is. . . . Modernity and comfort come naturally to Chanel. This was the key reason why the classic Chanel suit—collarless, simply cut, trimmed with braid and a discreet chain sewn into the hem —has transcended every single movement of the twentieth century (Watson, 1999/2000a, p. 30).

figure 2.5
The Queen of Classic, "Coco" Chanel mixed jersey fabrics and wool. Jersey fabrics were typically only used in undergarments. This design change continues to impact fashion more than 80 years later.

Technology is also being used to learn about fashion, as well as to provide personal opinions about fashion. Blogs, **YouTube**, television shows, radio talk shows, and the Internet all focus on designers, fashions, and the fashion industry. Prior to the Internet, consumers were displaced from the fashion industry. Now, consumers are invited into the fashion scene. They may interact, provide comments, and stay informed of the industry's advancements.

Because of technology, we live in a world of instant gratification. By the end of the twentieth century and into the first years of the new millennium, consumers were able to instantly change the television by remote control, call a friend with a cell phone, purchase an outfit from another country on the Internet, watch an international fashion show on YouTube, bid on designer shoes through eBay, and the list goes on and on. The influence of technology on fashion marketing will be addressed in-depth in Chapter Four, "Public Relations, Promotions, and Advertising."

Aspects of the retail and technology environments have significantly changed customers' expectations as they relate to marketing efforts. Customers are smarter and more sophisticated and demand more information regarding the products and services being offered. Now more than ever, consumers are inundated with print, audio, and electronic sources of information. To be truly effective, fashion marketers must communicate with consumers in clear, repeated, and integrated methods. Customers expect an invitation and a reward for visiting and purchasing products from a company. Examples of rewards include discounts, loyalty programs, and rebates.

INSPIRATION FROM SOCIETY

During the 1950s and 1960s, fashion designers and the fashionable looked to Paris for inspiration and outfits. Paris reigned as the capital of the fashion empire. To be fashionable meant that your clothes were custom made. Garments were fitted to your personal measurements and fabrics were selected specifically for their design. A garment could take weeks or months to create (Agins, 1999). Only 40 to 50 years

figure 2.6
The classic Chanel jacket in jersey and wool is copied by high fashion and ready-to-wear manufacturers. The collarless jacket can be seen on fashions for all age ranges.

figure 2.7
YouTube has opened up the runway experience to the entire world. Once available only to the privileged few, anyone who has access to the Internet can view new fashions previewed on the catwalk.

later are customers able to be fashionable by purchasing ready-to-wear, or *prêt-â-porter*, apparel. Italy, Hong Kong, China, and, of course, the United States began making ready-to-wear fashions that fit the consumers' needs and desires. Fashions are now available to the consumer throughout the world. Whether shopping in a brick-and-mortar store, looking at a catalog, or surfing the Internet, the availability and options for internationally made fashions are at an all-time high.

According to Colleen Sherin, fashion market director of Saks Fifth Avenue,

> The key message in Paris was one of polished Parisian chic with a powerful edge: the idea of sculpted tailoring and a return to investment dressing in terms of beautiful fabrications, double-faced cashmere and flannel, leathers, and furs. Paris redefined the idea of a suit—a skirt suit, a pantsuit, or taking the jacket as a separate item (*Women's Wear Daily*, 2009, p. 4).

figure 2.8
Consumer rewards are used as a marketing technique to instill customer loyalty.

or 12 percent of all women's wear sold at retail, and represented the top price range at most department stores. By comparison, top-tier designer lines accounted for about $1 billion in retail sales and were only available at select locations (Agins, 1999, p. 38).

figure 2.9
The proper fit of garments makes all the difference between a garment can be marketed as "fashionable apparel" and one that can be marketed simply as "clothing."

Fashion Differentiation in Society

Today a designer's inspiration and creativity expresses itself more than ever in marketing than in the actual clothes. In a sense, fashion has returned to its roots: selling an image. Image is the form and marketing is the function (Agins, 1999). Image must be considered throughout all aspects of marketing and the fashion process. Style, design, price, location within the store, marketing channel, who wears the products, and how the products are promoted all influence a company's image. Consumers, in turn, view the image and decide whether the products fit *their* desired image. If the product complements or enhances the consumer's desired image, there is a likelihood of product adoption. Fashion that has a contrary image may be rejected. Branding and

The mystic draw of Parisian fashions is being overtaken as customers are willing to forgo custom-made fashions for quality ready-to-wear. **Bridge fashions** appeared on the fashion market during the late 1980s. Bridge fashions feature a designer label with a 30-percent lower price tag than the original line (Agins, 1999). Bridge fashion merchandise is made at a lower quality and sports fewer design features than the couture line. **Couture fashions** are custom-made designs and are hand made with master craftsmanship. Still, bridge fashions clearly represent the brand and image of a designer label.

Bridge merchandise extends the brand by serving a secondary target market. Because this secondary target market is different from the primary target market of designers' higher-end fashions, the fashion marketing campaign must also be distinctively different for the two brands.

In 1996, bridge brands such as Donna Karan's DKNY, Anne Klein II, and Ellen Tracy accounted for about $4.7 billion,

figure 2.10
Calvin Klein's products became a household name as a result of his marketing tight fitting jeans. He sold an image of young, hip, and sexy.

figure 2.11
Fashions historically were used to indicate a person's status. The fashions worn by this late sixteenth century woman indicate that she is of noble blood.

image is addressed in-depth in Chapter Nine, "Image and Branding."

Throughout the centuries, clothing has been used as a method of differentiating a person's station in life. Prior to the French Revolution in 1789, the amount and type of fabric used in fashions revealed a person's status. In the United States, wealthy women wore different fashions throughout the day. The style, quality, and color of garments worn revealed much about the person and his or her sense of fashion.

Fashion choices may reveal consumers' social and economic backgrounds. Fashions always play an important role in differentiating and communicating a person's image, values, and beliefs. A significant impact of fashion and its marketing efforts is that fashions have become the great equalizer among consumers. Fashion designers, manufacturers, retailers, and magazine editors influence fashions. Hem lengths rise and fall; pant widths narrow and widen; heels of shoes become higher, lower, bulkier, and thinner, and are made of different materials. Changes in fashions directly influence consumers' spending behavioral patterns. During the roaring 1920s, women's dresses became shorter. The flapper style represents an era of the "free" woman (Figure 2.13). Betsey Johnson's inspiration was the liberation of women and "flower power." Her clear vinyl dress that featured motifs applied by the consumer revealed more than just skin; it showed that Betsey Johnson thought designing fashions could be extended to consumers' inspiration (Watson, 1999/2000). The 1960s hippie style featured women without bras, tie-dyed T-shirts, and hip-hugger jeans. The first decade of the twenty-first century saw a wide variety of fashions. Entertainers and celebrities such as P. Diddy and Jennifer Lopez created fashions. Ralph Lauren and Tommy Hilfiger featured all-American designs. Couture and designer fashions by Versace, Chanel, and Dolce & Gabbana were snapped up by the rich and famous.

Prior to the 1980s, fashion was divided into categories: (a) "good clothes" that people wore to work or to a party, and (b) "play clothes," or clothes that people wore around the house. "Fashionable" meant more expensive. Cost was always equated with quality. After 1980, fashion wasn't dictated by price or style. Consumers became more relaxed in their dress. Jeans were worn for most occasions.

figure 2.12
Women's hemlines change throughout the decades. The changes in the style require marketing efforts to convince consumers of the fashion changes.

Mixing expensive clothing with inexpensive items became fashionable (Agins, 1999). Vera Wang's philosophy of placing fashions together is: "Luxe is always more luxe when thrown against something that isn't" (Zimbalist, 2007). The popularity of discount retailers significantly influenced how consumers dressed. Target and Walmart offered fashionable merchandise for less. They also changed their marketing efforts to be more fashion forward. No longer did their marketing focus solely on staple products. (A **staple** product is an item that is used frequently and is fashion insensitive.)

Consumers soon realized that dressing for less was possible, profitable, and easy. Fashion continues to evolve; it can no longer be defined by a style or a group of persons who can offer the merchandise. Fashion has evolved into the province of all socioeconomic and psychographic backgrounds (Agins, 1999). **Socioeconomic** characteristics include attributes regarding the consumer's social (e.g., age, education, marital status) and economic (e.g., income) status. **Psychographic** background focuses on the consumer's interests, behaviors, and attitudes (Ostrow & Smith, 1988). The understanding of consumers and consumer markets is addressed in Chapter Five, "Fashion and the Entertainment Industry."

Historically, designers created and made fashions that they believed were important. Consumers accepted the fashions based on the designer's name. Today consumers drive much of the fashion industry. When a product or brand is considered irrelevant, too expensive, or not appropriate, sales will falter.

According to Michael Kors, "designing simple is the hardest thing in the world" (Watson, 1999/2000, p. 36). Designers', manufacturers', and retailers' inspirations have resulted in the advent of marketing niches. One of the most profitable niches is the ready-to-wear market. The fashion industry traditionally focused on women's apparel and accessories and, to some extent, menswear. Inspiration has created men's, women's, and children's sportswear industries. The marketing of menswear has become increasingly more important and effective. Men's casual and businesswear became increasingly more important as international designers expanded their marketing efforts. Michael Kors, internationally known for his womenswear, also created and marketed menswear. Teens and children are not to be forgotten. These two groups are important markets in the fashion industry. They represent the all-important brand-loyal building stage of the fashion industry. It is during the early years of the consumer that the fashion industry attempts to tap into loyal purchasing behaviors.

figure 2.13
The shorter flapper-style dresses of the 1920s revealed body parts never before seen in public. This "new, young, and free" woman wore fashions that made her feel alive.

Fashion crosses over into all aspects of consumers' lifestyles. No longer are fashion-forward consumers willing to sacrifice function over fun. Products must have it all —function, style, design, quality, and personality. **Hard lines**, once considered strictly functional products, now incorporate and are marketed using the element of fashion. Examples of hard lines that are now being marketed with a focus on fashion elements (e.g., color, design) include home furnishings, cell phones, luggage, cars, and school supplies.

Products once considered boring (e.g., vacuum cleaners, kitchen trash cans) are offered in a variety of colors, shapes, and sizes to coordinate with the home's decor. Kitchen appliances purchased in candy-apple red, canary yellow, bird's-egg blue, jet black, or stainless steel reveal the consumer's fashion sense. Boring, predictable products have been replaced. Fashionable products throughout the spectrum of the consumer's lifestyle are available. Fashion marketers throughout the industry will assist consumers in becoming aware of the many product, brand, and style choices that are available. The significance of the fashion industry, and marketers in particular, crossing product boundaries is addressed in Chapter Eight, "Cross-Channel Shopping."

As previously mentioned, fashions were once used as a method of segregating the wealthy from the poor. Now, fashions are marketed and adopted to a wide variety of cultures and socioeconomic segments. For example, a consumer can purchase one of many fashion magazines for a reasonably low price. She can read about products, learn or recognize which garments are by which designer, and learn how to copy the look for less. Consumers who don't care if they have a genuine product can purchase knockoffs of designer brands. A **knockoff** brand can look remarkably similar to the genuine product, and this further strengthens the similarities between markets.

The increasing number of styles being adopted by consumers represents the diversity of the marketplace. **Styles**, or characteristics in apparel and accessories, offer consumers a way to associate themselves with a brand, a designer, or a way of life. Examples of styles include classic, contemporary, casual, hip-hop, grunge, and athletic.

Most consumers can tell the difference between a classic style and a hip-hop style. Furthermore, it is probably safe to say that a consumer who prefers classic styles won't be in the hip-hop target market. This makes it easy for fashion marketers in each segment to clearly identify their customer base. However, the fashion industry is growing at such a rapid rate that the industry is (and must) differentiate in order to survive and thrive. Take classic fashion styles, for example. Think about all the different companies that offer polo-style shirts. What is the customer really saying when he or she says, I want to purchase a polo shirt? As a fashion marketer of polo shirts, your job is to make sure he or she wants to purchase your brand—and only your brand. To accomplish this very important task you, as a fashion marketer, must differentiate.

The entire fashion industry is in the process of differentiating. Why? Two reasons: (1) There

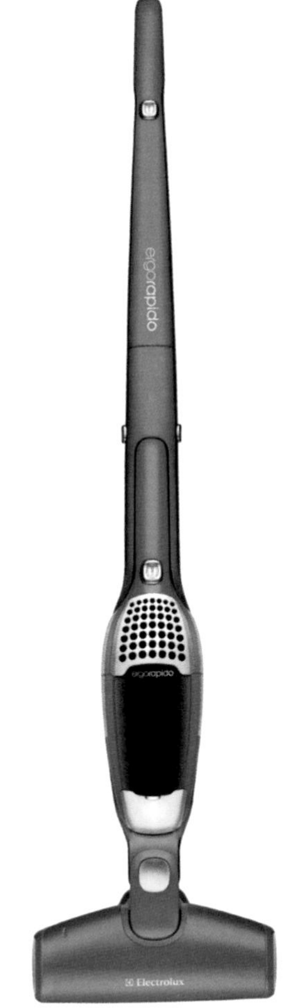

figure 2.14
Fashion is not just for clothing and accessories. Fashion crosses over to the home. Purchasing domestic products, such as a vacuum cleaner in your favorite color, stimulates sales and brightens up the home.

figure 2.15
Branding using a logo is extremely successful in marketing. Ralph Lauren's polo player logo is used on marketing, products, and store signage. Consumers associate the logo with quality.

aren't that many truly unique products in the marketplace (once a unique product arrives in the marketplace, someone copies it and it is no longer unique) and (2) The number of fashion competitors across the globe continues to increase at a phenomenal pace. If you don't differentiate, your products, your brand, and your company will soon be lost in the clutter.

Ralph Lauren's Polo brand polo shirt is perhaps one of the best examples of fashion differentiation. Similar to other company brands, Polo Ralph Lauren has a logo. The well-known polo player on a horse has long been discreetly displayed on the brand's polo shirt. This form of differentiation told anyone in close proximity that the wearer purchased a polo shirt of quality. The fashion tycoon then made a fashion marketing move to further differentiate the Polo brand. The logo was increased in size; the logo was enlarged to approximately one-fourth the size of the shirt. The logo clearly stated, *I am wearing a Ralph Lauren shirt and I am proud.* **Was the change in logo size needed to be recognized?** Not necessarily, but it did differentiate the brand. That is, the greater a product or brand is differentiated, the easier the company makes it for consumers to make a decision. Fashion differentiation helps promote consumer decisions and brand loyalty. Ralph Lauren's differentiation effort further solidified the company's global dominance in the fashion industry.

Fashion differentiation also occurs when a product is modified for a new use. Crocs were originally designed as gardening shoes (http://www.crocs.com). The rubberized shoes fit loosely and promote comfort over fashion. Despite the enormous success of stilettos, strappy sandals, and athletic shoes, Crocs took the fashion world by storm. Men, women,

figure 2.16
Crocs changed the way consumers wore shoes. Originally designed for use in the garden, the comfort of Crocs resulted in an expanded target market. Crocs are now marketed in a wide variety of colors for men, women, and children.

figure 2.17 Macy's is a national sponsor of the American Heart Association for the Go Red for Women movement. On February 6, Macy's Wear Red Day Sale, consumers who wear red receive 20 percent off their purchases.

girls, boys, and babies wear crocs in a wide variety of colors. Often, a consumer purchases a pair of Crocs and then purchases additional shoes in multiple colors. Sales in excess of $360 million demonstrate the popularity of these clunky shoes (Wellington, 2007).

SOCIAL MARKETING

The fashion industry is fast paced, often glamorous, and extremely competitive. The fashion marketing industry focuses on selling more fashions and accessories than the prior year, enhancing the image of the brands, building customer loyalty, and helping society. **Social marketing** has become an integrated component of many fashion companies' mission statements. Social marketing efforts provide the fashion company with the opportunity to give back to society in a responsible manner, which has the added benefit of generating goodwill in consumer markets.

In an effort to help alleviate AIDS in Africa, Bono and Bobby Shriver developed a global product marketing campaign called (Product) RED. Participating companies designate 50 percent of their proceeds from RED products to the Global Fund. Gap Inc. made a significant social marketing effort toward this effort (Laird, 2007). Sotheby's, the auction house known worldwide for its high-quality art, sculpture, and jewelry, also participated in Bono's campaign to end AIDS with its (RED) Auction (Lee, 2008).

Red seems to be a popular color both in fashion and in attracting attention to a social issue. Heart disease in women has long been a problem. Since 1998, heart disease has killed women more than any other disease (*Drug Week*, 2009). In response to the dramatic impact of the disease, fashion marketers are using their talents to raise money for research. The Go Red campaign is designed to provide recognition to women's propensity to heart disease and generate funds for research. Macy's is a principle sponsor of the Go Red campaign, raising more than $800,000 in 2009. Since 2004, more than $19 million has been raised to fight heart disease (Moin, 2009). Bono's, Oprah's, and Macy's influence in bringing awareness to the dangers of heart disease cannot be overstated. The interaction between fashion and the entertainment industry is further examined in Chapter Five, "Fashion and the Entertainment Industry."

POLITICAL IMPACT

Fashion marketing efforts have long been involved in promoting politics. It doesn't matter if the consumer is Republican, Democrat, independent, or somewhere in between —politics means big business for the fashion industry.

Every Fourth of July, fashion marketers capitalize on red, white, and blue images and the remembrance of America's Independence Day. Belts, hats, handbags, totes, T-shirts, apparel, shoes, and flags of all shapes, sizes, and styles are promoted and sold during this annual event. In 2008, history was made when Barack Obama was elected the first African-American U.S. president. His likeness and name were placed on T-shirts, hats, totes, plates, umbrellas, drinking glasses, and every possible product that would sell. Independent companies that sold trinkets made fashion designs. Big-name designers also honored President Obama. Diane Von Furstenberg created tote bags. Zac Posen, Narciso Rodriguez,

figure 2.18
Apparel in fabric that represents the U.S. flag communicates the consumer's patriotic feelings toward the country.

figure 2.19
The image of Barack Obama, the first African American U.S. president, was marketed on a wide array of products.

figure 2.20
Benetton's marketing efforts consistently focus on an acceptance of diverse cultures working together.

Juicy Couture, and Donna Karan designed T-shirts. Alexander Wang designed a scarf. These famous designers created unique items to help pay for the inauguration and to promote a message of change. Other vendors marketed their fashions, realizing the enormous potential for sales. Regardless of the reason, the impact of politics on the fashion industry cannot be denied (Crane, 2006).

INSPIRATION FROM CULTURE AND HISTORY

As areas throughout the United States (e.g., New York, California, Atlanta) continue to play a more important role in the fashion industry, the world continues to shrink. Fashion is no longer considered to be headquartered in one country—France, for example. Designers get their fashion inspiration from around the world; all different aspects of the environment influence their designs and products. The color red may represent aspects of the Orient while the color blue may symbolize the Atlantic Ocean. World travel influences fashion designs. Consumers' exposure to the world influences their desires for exotic fashions. There is a reciprocal relationship between fashion and culture. That is, fashion is influenced by culture, and culture is influenced by fashion. Fashion designers, retailers, and marketers weave aspects of culture into their products, store environments, and marketing campaigns. The interjection of one's culture provides a sense of understanding and belonging. Benetton's marketing efforts, for example, have emphasized global connectedness. Mary McFadden has worked in many different cultures. These life experiences influence her designs; her fashions often have simple lines with exotic prints. According to McFadden, "[I'm] more into fabric than fashion" (Watson, 1999/2000, p. 49).

Some fashions are influenced by a variety of arts and history. The eclectic interest of a designer may bring a constant evolution of color, design, and surprise to a fashion line. Take, for example, Mitsuhiro Matsuda, whose

> [i]nfluences are diverse; from pre-Raphaelite paintings to the Arts and Crafts movement. His clothes contain lush embroidery, medieval construction and subliminal references to jazz. . . . [H]is collections have a medieval touch which appeals to Renaissance women (Watson, 1999/2000b, p. 53).

figure 2.21
Victoria Beckham is famous for her fashion style and sleek elegance.

Fashion helps define us. Consumers use apparel, accessories, and home furnishings as a form of personal expression. Fashion can't be categorized based on use; apparel is fashionable or it isn't fashionable. Brand names, designer labels, and bridge merchandise bring consumers entirely new options in fashions. Over the centuries, culture has influenced the adoption of fashions. During the twentieth century, fashion had a significant impact on the culture of youth. More casual fashions encouraged a more casual lifestyle. Nike's logo, "Just do it," has inspired men, women, and children of all ages to go outside and start walking, running, biking, and becoming more active. Serena and Venus Williams's tennis prowess and passion for fashion have shown the world that women can be, at once, extreme athletes and fashion forward. Victoria Beckham, aka "Posh Spice," is photographed by paparazzi primarily for her fashions every time she is seen in public. When Naomi Campbell completed her final day of community service as part of her sentence for throwing a cell phone, she was photographed wearing an evening gown by paparazzi.

Regardless of whether it is internationally known or regional, culture may significantly influence designers', manufacturers', and retailers' role in fashion and fashion marketing. Fashions can be created from the minds and imagination of talented industry personnel. Fashions often evolve and are recreated from previous decades. The arts have proven a rich source of creative energy for fashion designers. Colors, shapes, images, and themes may be used as a source of inspiration in fashion. Designers look at paintings, architecture, nature, and sculpture in order to find a new fashion design characteristic. It is no secret where Christian Lacroix obtained his inspiration for his beautiful creations. At the inception of

figure 2.22
Community service can't get Naomi Campbell down. On her last day, she marketed herself by walking outside in a high fashion gown as if it was a red carpet event.

his fashion career, he studied art history and museum studies in Paris. His couture fashions featured colors from nature and inspiration from the arts (Watson, 1999/2000). Lacroix relies heavily on luxurious fabrics similar to the fabrics featured in paintings. His designs are meant to create glamour, drama, and a sense of regal living. When you look at paintings or dresses from earlier centuries, you can witness a time when fabric was not limited by "need." Fabric flowed. Lacroix's inspiration from such paintings flowed over into his own designs (Paris Fashion Week, 2009).

For an assignment, you are encouraged to go to the local art museum, view a historic costume book, or access the Internet.

View paintings from past centuries, and then ask yourself:

- Do the paintings inspire your fashion sense? If so, how?
- What similarities do you see among the works of art and today's fashions (e.g., colors, styles)?

We have been shown the influence of the arts and history on famous designers. The arts and history have also been an inspiration on local designers and retailers. For example, Shirley Ellsworth is the owner of Lambspun of Colorado. The independently owned store features natural fibers that Shirley dyes for her knitting store. Her Lambspun brand of yarns has become extremely popular among knitters because of its unique blend of colors. The colors are not available anywhere else on the market. When asked how she decides on a color for a particular batch of yarn, Shirley replied, "I look to the masterpieces. I look at works of art. I look at their palettes for inspiration. Their colors provide me direction" (Ellsworth, 2009). The natural yarns Shirley dyes include bamboo, cashmere, cotton, silk, hemp, linen, wool, and angora (Ellsworth, 2009).

A museum houses **artifacts**, or objects of importance. The museum curator is typically responsible for deciding which artifacts belong in the museum. According to Linda Carlson, curator of the Avenir Museum, "A museum with fashion is for everyone. Unless you live in a cave, fashion impacts all of us" (Carlson, 2009). Nationally and internationally, museums are the guardians of history, including the history of fashion. Think about the last time you watched the red carpet show for the Oscars. The majority of the fashions, if not 100 percent of them, were inspired from designs from the past. Designers and fashion marketers receive much of their inspiration from the past. Museums preserve the rich history of the past so that we as individuals may learn, grow, and build for the future.

The fashion industry has a rich history of benefiting from museums. One of the most famous museums in the world is the Metropolitan Museum of Art in New York (informally called the Met). This museum houses works of art ranging from paintings, sculpture, literature, coins, textiles, and fashion. The Met features different exhibits regarding fashion. Don't think that museums only exhibit fashions from the previous decade or century. During 2009, the Met exhibited "Superheroes: Fashion and Fantasy," which addressed the impact fashion has made on the imagination, dreams, and image of superheroes.

> Fashion not only shares the superhero's metaphoric malleability, but actually embraces and responds to the particular metaphors that the superhero represents, notably that of the power of transformation. Fashion celebrates metamorphosis, providing unlimited opportunities to remake and reshape the flesh and the self. Through fashion and the superhero, we gain the freedom to fantasize, to escape the banal, the ordinary, and the quotidian. The fashionable body and the superhero body are sites upon which we can

Linda Carlson, curator of the Avenir Museum of Design and Merchandising, Colorado State University.

BOX 2.1 Curating the Fashion Museum

Regardless of size and scope, all fashion museums are important. They all tell a story about the history of the fashion artifacts. As the curator of the Avenir Museum of Design and Merchandising, Linda Carlson oversees more than 12,000 garments. She is responsible for the care of the collection as well as for the exploration of the significance of the fashions displayed and archived in this museum. Some of the artifacts or objects in the museum are typical, meaning they were used in everyday life. Other artifacts are atypical, meaning a person did not normally use the objects in everyday life. During Ms. Carlson's 20 years as curator, she has added more than 6,000 artifacts to the museum (Carlson, 2009).

Not just any artifact is added to a museum; the curator tries to make appropriate selections. For Ms. Carlson, the most important consideration when reviewing artifacts comes in recognizing the importance of the artifact from the eyes of the donor. Each fashion item donated is the family member's treasure; this treasure needs to be recognized and honored (Carlson, 2009).

> project our fantasies, offering a virtuosic transcendence beyond the moribund and utilitarian. (The Metropolitan Museum of Art, 2009).

Examine the superhero characters in Figure 2.23. As you look at the different body types, answer the following questions:

- What fashion industries (e.g., menswear) were inspired by a superhero body type (e.g., the Graphic Body; the Patriotic Body, the Postmodern Body)?
- Can you identify specific fashion designers who were inspired by a superhero body type?
- What superhero body type inspires you the most? Why?

figure 2.23
Fashions designed after superheroes give us strength, resilience, sensuality, and a sense of power.

THE FASHION INDUSTRY AND COMPETITION

The standard **channel of distribution** consists of designers, manufacturers, wholesalers, retailers, and ultimate consumers. It is "the route along which goods and services travel from producer/manufacturer through marketing intermediaries" (Ostrow & Smith, 1988, p. 44). The **designer** is responsible for creating the fashions. The **manufacturer**, nationally or globally, produces fashions. The **wholesalers** are the middlemen who collect merchandise in large bundles. Merchandise is then broken down into smaller quantities and sold to the retailer. The **retailer** sells merchandise to the ultimate **consumer**. The consumer is the end user. (See Figure 2.24.)

In a successful fashion company, the marketing efforts do not support the organization. The organization supports the marketing (Godin, 2008). Without carefully crafted, integrated, and implemented marketing efforts, the company's mission statement and goals will likely not be realized. Marketing drives the success of the company's efforts.

Think about the answers to the following questions:

- What makes Ralph Lauren's products so infinitely better than Lacoste? Are the polo shirts really that different in quality? Inexpensive fashions sold at Kmart once made it the number-one discounter in the United

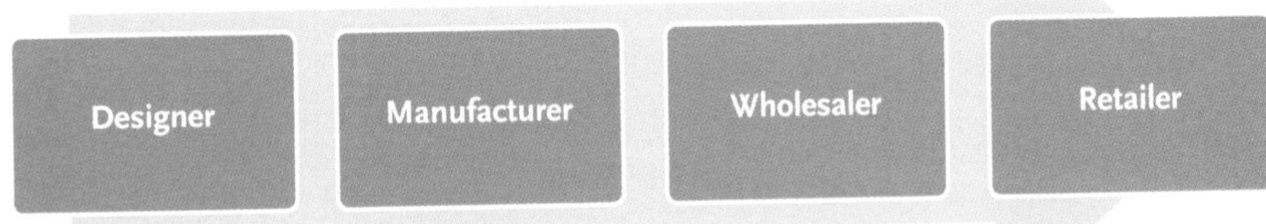

figure 2.24
Channel of distribution

States. In the twenty-first century, the retailer has had significant financial difficulties. What happened to make consumers change their shopping patterns?

- Sean Combs doesn't know how to design or sew, yet his clothing line, Sean John, is enormously successful. What makes his fashions so readily accepted by his target market?

figure 2.25
High-end children's apparel is marketed at grandparents. They have a large discretionary income and are willing to purchase more expensive fashions.

The products and services of a company support the marketing organization. Yes, this sounds backwards. However, in the fashion industry, marketing literally "makes or breaks" the company. The effectiveness of the marketing organization also helps decide how fast and far the company can go into the future. It isn't enough to make an excellent product. It also isn't enough to make a product that consumers want. Marketers have to express the message of the fashions. In short, marketers have to make their message heard. In today's environment, this can be difficult. The message has to be (a) believable, (b) clear and understandable, (c) memorable, and (d) related to the needs and wants of the consumers.

The children's market has been a large influence on the fashion scene. Designers, retailers, and fashion marketers are focusing a greater amount of attention on this group. Grandparents, dual-income families, and parents having children later in life provide consumers with additional funds to spend on children's clothing and accessories. Arden Korn, president and owner of Little Lambs & Ivy, states that her children's clothing store is definitely dictated by the needs of her target market, yet the company will never abandon its mission statement. Little Lambs & Ivy's primary target market consists of "grandmothers who have waited for what may seem an eternal time for grandchildren." These grandmothers are "willing and able to spend time and money on quality clothing for their grandchildren." The secondary target market consists of the "professional mother, typically one who is well educated . . . [and] wants to clothe her children in high-end apparel" (A. Korn, personal interview, March 3, 2009). Throughout the buying and marketing efforts of Little Lambs & Ivy, the company's mission and theme continually guide its efforts: "The store celebrates innocence and childhood."

Fashion Marketing

Fashion marketers play an integral role in the success of the designer, merchandiser, and retailer. They help communicate the desired message through the retailer and to the target market. Try to think of fashion marketers as a hybrid of pit bull and angel. The pit bull aspect of the marketer comes through in fierce protection of the brand. Marketers continually promote fashions to the best of their abilities, never letting down their guard. The angel side of the marketers emerges in the presentation of a positive image of the company. Fashion marketers continually teach, enhance, and improve the target market's life through its adoption of the brand.

When Isaac Mizrahi started out in the fashion industry, he was his own best fashion marketer. Before the days of Facebook, Twitter, and Web sites, Mizrahi was on the selling floor, marketing his fashions. Customers adored Mizrahi for his personality. In 1988, the fashion director of Bloomingdale's recognized the talent Mizrahi had for reaching customers. The company put him "up front and personal" with the target market (Agins, 1999).

Fashion marketing is essential because no matter how wonderful the runway shows, the fashion reviews, the accolades, or the designer's personality, if the fashions don't sell at the retail level, the designer will not continue to have financial backing. And the fashion industry and all those entities involved require financial backing. Isaac Mizrahi received wonderful reviews from *Women's Wear Daily*. However, Chanel dropped the designer in 1998 because he wasn't making a profit (Agins, 1999). But about ten years later, Isaac Mizrahi's design talents and his acceptance of the importance of fashion marketing brought him once again to the forefront of the fashion industry. His designs began to sell again as he once again became his own best marketing agent.

Competition: Evolving Organizations

Fashion companies are required to evolve in order to survive, grow, and be profitable in the long term. Throughout this evolution, the type of merchandise carried and services offered may also evolve. A company may carry merchandise considered to be fads, while other merchandise is considered classic. A fashion company may choose to market a fad for a variety of reasons. **Fad merchandise** is typically very popular for a short amount of time. If the profit margin is high on the product, or the demand for the product is high, marketing of the fad can be very profitable. However, the marketer must be very careful to avoid marketing the fad merchandise for an extended period of time; this will result in wasted resources (i.e., time, money, effort) and it may also create a negative image, making the company look stale.

The majority of fashion companies market lines of classic merchandise. **Classic merchandise** is timeless, remaining popular through the years. While a fashion company may market a composition of classic and fad merchandise, the industry itself requires the company to evolve. Entering the second decade of the twenty-first century, competition within the fashion marketing industry is at an all-time high. Domestic and global companies actively market to the consumer in an attempt to instill loyal purchasing behavior. Consumers have a wider variety of options for purchasing products (e.g., bricks-and-mortar, Internet). Repeated marketing efforts blur the promotional cycle (e.g., Valentine's Day promotion, St. Patrick's Day promotion). Fashion marketing companies that either do not evolve fast enough or fail in their marketing efforts become extinct.

SPIN-OFF INDUSTRIES

The fashion industry has helped stimulate the birth of new businesses while reinvigorating existing ones. The toy industry has long been known for offering a wide range of dolls, cuddly stuffed animals, and model trains and trucks. A target market age range for a stuffed-animal toy store would have normally been between newborn and 14 years old—that is, until fashion entered the scene.

Fashion has positively impacted the stuffed-animal world. In addition to stimulating the sales of stuffed animals for children of all ages, a new twist on the "life" of stuffed animals was born. Two companies have successfully marketed an entire line of fashions items to all age ranges. Build-A-Bear Workshop and Teddy Mountain offer a wide variety of stuffed animals and various fashion items for the animals. Consumers can select from a wide variety of outfits including casual wear, evening wear, swimsuits, and thematic wear (e.g., sailor suits). Dressing the stuffed animals indirectly

teaches young children, and girls in particular, a sense of fashion at an early age. (See Figure 2.26.)

Fashion has also influenced the traveling consumer's idea of individuality. Until relatively recently, suitcases were only offered in a few standard and very drab colors. Consumers were able to select from matte gray, black, off-white, pale blue, and olive green. The suitcases all looked about the same. During this time in luggage sales, it was considered exciting when Samsonite offered their standard line in matte red. However, the extent of the options for luggage ended there.

As the twentieth century came to a close, luggage began to be offered in a wider variety of colors. Plums, burgundies, beautiful reds, and tans were offered. The arrival of the twenty-first century saw the fashion luggage arena burst into full bloom. Luggage that fits everyone's personality, fashion sense, and interest is now offered. Patterns, colors, shapes, and textures grace once-drab luggage. As travelers hurry through the airport or train station, they now demonstrate their sense of fashion and style via their luggage.

Economic Influence

The fashion marketing industry is a multi-billion-dollar business impacting numerous constituencies. In the United States alone, $172 billion in apparel revenues were generated during 2006. The fashion industry's impact to the economy is multifaceted. Over 4.64 million people in the United States work in the industry. These jobs include 470,000 in textile production, 573,000 in apparel production, and 3.6 million in retail sales (The Fashion Industry, 2006). Over 100,000 people throughout New York City (NYC) are employed in the fashion business. This employment figure makes the industry a powerful employment generator for the state of New York. It also makes New York City an important central location for the fashion industry. Because of the significant number of employees in the fashion industry in NYC, the city is considered the fashion capital of the United States. The volume of fashion production in this dense city represents 18 percent of women's outerwear (i.e., coats, suits, and sportswear) and 28 percent of dresses (The Fashion Industry, 2006).

figure 2.26
If you think your closet is too small, what about the closet for a stuffed animal? Marketing fashions for stuffed animals is big business. Examples of fashions for stuffed animals are available in lifestyle (e.g., sailor suits), evening wear, night gowns, and leisure apparel.

STATUS OF THE ECONOMY

The status of the economy directly impacts fashions design, as well as how fashion marketers promote those designs. In a stable and healthy economy, fashion designers are able to use a lot of fabric, full features, and excessive adornment. During World War II, the scarcity of fabric resulted in women wearing shorter dresses with a narrower silhouette. At the end of the war, in 1947, Christian Dior created "the new look." This look featured an hourglass figure with a cinched waist and an

figure 2.27
Long gone is the boring standard luggage option of black. Luggage is often selected based on the consumer's personality.

figure 2.28
Dior's "The New Look" in 1947 resulted in a fuller and longer skirt and cinched waist. Dior created the look to instill a more feminine look after the war efforts.

extenuated full skirt flared by using a petticoat underneath. The skirt skimmed the woman's lower leg, close to her ankle. More than 60 years later, fashions have again been influenced by a weakened economy (*Women's Wear Daily*, 2009, January 23). Dior stated that "the prime need of fashion [is] to please and attract. . . . [U]niformity is the mother of boredom" (Watson, 1999/2000a, p. 44).

The global economy during 2008 and well into 2009 continued to weaken. Banks, the automobile industry, and insurance organizations experienced massive employee layoffs. During 2008, homeowners across the country faced foreclosures as they struggled to pay their mortgages (Fulmer, 2009). These significant changes influence purchasing power in the fashion industry. National retailers such as Pier 1 Imports, Linens 'n Things, and Steve & Barry's declared bankruptcy.

Designers and fashion marketers adapt to the changing consumer mood. When consumers are feeling nervous and pressed financially, the fashions reflect these attitudes. As a result of consumers' anxieties from financial burdens, the 2009 runway shows in Paris revealed a more subdued line of fashions (Figure 2.29). Designs were more structured with less fabric, and subdued colors were featured without making the fashions look drab (*Women's Wear Daily*, 2009, January 23).

Bankruptcy

When the economy weakens, consumers often lose their jobs, worry about paying bills, and purchase fashions that are less expensive. Instead of purchasing the $300 suit, they may buy the $150 suit. Fashion marketers of lower-priced fashions typically have a more attentive market during difficult economic times. Consumers want to learn how they can obtain quality fashions at a lower-than-anticipated price. Fashion marketers of expensive

figure 2.29
The 2009 Paris runway featured subdued colors.

garments may find themselves struggling to sell products that once easily sold through a loyal consumer base.

When companies find themselves unable to successfully market their fashions, they may ultimately need to file for **Chapter 11 bankruptcy**. Chapter 11 declares the company bankrupt. For example, in 2009, Hartmarx Corporation, a company that had been in existence since 1872, filed for Chapter 11. Three-fourths of the company is devoted to men's apparel; one-fourth is devoted to women's apparel. The company owes $70 million of trade debt. The company stated that the reason for the debt is the decline in sales of moderately tailored apparel (Young & Thomas, 2009). Other fashion companies that filed Chapter 11 during this time include Goody's and Gottschalks (Young, 2009). The influence of legislation, ethics, and counterfeit merchandise is addressed in Chapter Eleven, "Counterfeiting, Legislation, and Ethics."

Changing Marketing Efforts

The stability of the economy influences the composition of fashion marketing efforts. As consumers become more cautious about spending money on luxury fashion items, they seek similar benefits from alternative fashion products. Everyday pricing—the act of pricing merchandise using a low markdown—becomes increasingly popular during difficult economic times. The low markdown results in offering consumers merchandise at a perceived value but not necessarily a deeply discounted price. The everyday pricing strategy is constructed to (a) avoid having frequent sales and (b) instill loyal customer purchasing behavior based on the knowledge that your company consistently has everyday pricing. Marketing efforts during tough economic times should focus on the quality of the brand. This emphasis assures the consumer that despite the lower price, the company stands behind its product (Seckler, 2009 January 14).

For example, instead of purchasing a designer brand of perfume at full price, consumers may either wait until the product is on sale or ask for the item as a gift. The purchasing of everyday "necessities" such as cosmetics may be influenced by creative fashion marketing efforts. Consumers who were once loyal to a cosmetic brand may try lower-priced products offered by a different company. Companies such as Revlon, Max Factor, and L'Oréal entice consumers through discounted prices; wide varieties of lipstick, eye shadow, and nail polish shades; and extensive print advertising. The widespread availability of fashion products at discount retailers and drugstores also helps increase merchandise turnover during a slow economy.

SUMMARY

Inspiration for fashion comes from many sources; textiles, technology, society, culture, arts, and history all play an influential role in the designing and marketing of fashions. Fashions often evolve and are re-created from previous decades. The arts have proven a rich source of creative energy for fashion designers. Colors, shapes, images, and themes may be used as a source of inspiration in fashion. Designers and fashion marketers obtain inspiration from famous painters, sculpture, architecture, and previous fashions, which are often exhibited in museums.

Understanding the inspiration of fashion is important. It is equally important, however, to understand how economic factors influence fashion. Throughout history, fashion and the fashion industry have played an important role with consumers and the economy. In the United States alone, $172 billion in apparel revenues were generated during 2006. Fashion's impact on the economy is multifaceted. Fashion marketers play an integral role of the success of the designer, merchandise, and retailer. Fashion marketers help communicate the desired message through the retailer to the target market. No matter how wonderful the runway show, the fashion review, the accolades, or the designer's personality, if the fashions don't sell at the retailer, the designer will not continue to receive financial backing; thus, fashion marketing forms the bond that holds the entire business together.

REFERENCES

Agins, T. (1999). *The end of fashion: The mass marketing of the clothing business.* New York: William Morrow.

Carlson, L. (2009, March 10). Personal interview with curator of Avenir Museum of Design and Merchandising.

Crane, Diana and Bovone, Laura (2006, November). Approaches to material culture: The sociology of fashion and clothing. *Poetics*, 34: 319–333.

Drug Week. (2009). The national coalition for women with heart disease. Women heart patients from your viewing community go heart to head with docs at Mayo Clinic and come out educating. p. 1965.

Ellsworth, S. (2009, March 10). Personal interview with owner of Lambspun.

Fulmer, M. (2009). Foreclosure rates across the U.S. msn.com. Retrieved on June 3, 2009 from www.real-estate.msn.com/article.aspx?cp-documentid=13107798.

Godin, S. (2008). *Meatball sundae: Is your marketing out of sync?* New York: Penguin.

Kotler, P., & Armstrong, G. (2001). *Principles of marketing* (9th ed.). New York: Prentice Hall.

Laird, T. (2007, July 9). GAP: Product RED. *Advertising Age*, p. 34.

Lee, D. (2008, February 11). David Lee's pick of the week: It's a beautiful day, so hats off to Bono. *The Scotsman*, p. 52.

Metropolitan Museum of Art, The (2009). Super Heroes: Fashion and Fantasy. Retrieved June 17, 2009 from http://www.metmuseum.org/special/superheroes/index.asp.

Moin, D. (2009, March 5). Macy's raises $800K for "Go Red." *Women's Wear Daily, 47,* p. 19.

Ostrow, R., & Smith, S. R. (1988). *The Dictionary of Marketing.* New York, NY: Fairchild Publishers.

Paris Commune, The (2009, January 23). *Women's Wear Daily,* p. 6–7.

RTTNews Global Financial Newswire (2009) Retrieved from http://www.rttnews.com/articlenewsview.aspx.

Seckler, V. (2009, January 14). Consumers driving harder bargains for price. *Women's Wear Daily*, p. 10.

Thatcher, Andrea Kiliany Thatcher (2008, October 3). Paris Fashion Week Spring 2008: Christian Lacroix. Retrieved April 22, 2010 from http://www.shinystyle.tv/2008/10/paris_fashion_week_spring_2009_4.html.

Watson, L. (1999/2000a). *Twentieth century fashion: 100 years of style by decade and designer* (Vol. 3). Philadelphia: Chelsea House.

Watson, L. (1999/2000). *Twentieth century fashion: 100 years of style by decade and designer* (Vol. 4). Philadelphia: Chelsea House.

Wellington, E. (2007, July 5). Fashion attack: Crocs are taking a big bite out of the shoe market, as their legions of the fans choose clunky comfort over style. *The Philadelphia Inquirer*, p. E01.

Women's Wear Daily staff (2009, March 16). In 'solid' Paris season, stores reduce budgets, demand lower prices. *Women's Wear Daily*, p. 1, 4–5.

Young, V. M. (2009, January 15). A tightening squeeze: Goody's, Gottschalks in Chapter 11 filings. *Women's Wear Daily*, p. 1, 14.

Young, V. M. & Thomas, B. (2009, January 26). A fraying Hartmarx: Famed U.S. suit marker files for Chapter 11. *Women's Wear Daily*, p. 1–2.

Zimbalist, K. (2007). Magical thinkers: They've orchestrated America's current luxury boom, lifting the consumer even higher. Meet Neiman Marcus' leading ladies. *Time Style & Design*, p. 90–92.

KEY TERMS

Define or briefly explain the following terms:

Artifact ______________________________

Bridge fashions ______________________________

Channel of distribution ______________________________

Chapter 11 bankruptcy ______________________________

Classic merchandise ______________________________

Consumer ______________________________

Couture fashions ______________________________

Designer ______________________________

Fad merchandise ______________________________

Hard lines ______________________________

Knockoff ______________________________

Manufacturer ______________________________

Psychographic ______________________________

Retailer ______________________________

Social Marketing ______________________________

Socioeconomic ______________________________

Staple ______________________________

Style ______________________________

Wholesalers ______________________________

YouTube ______________________________

CLASS OR TEAM DISCUSSION QUESTIONS

1 | Discuss how the fashion industry influences the financial well-being of the economy. Give specific examples of different segments of the economy (e.g., designers, manufacturers).

____

____

2 | Discuss how bridge merchandise has influenced the fashion industry. How have designers needed to adapt? What influence does bridge merchandise have on consumers' purchasing and ability to participate in fashion?

3 | Select an example of a fashion product other than the polo shirt. Analyze the role fashion differentiation has played in communicating the product's image, benefits, and attributes. Do you think the fashion marketers have been successful in their efforts? Explain.

4 | Explain the following statement: "Consumers drive the fashion industry."

INTERNET ACTIVITIES

1 | Select a product of your choice. Go on the Internet and find ten variations of the item. Look for different styles, patterns, colors, sizes, and shapes. Examine how fashion has influenced and impacted this product.

2 | Access the Internet to find five examples of fashions that are considered iconic. Discuss the reason why the styles influenced other fashions, people's behavior, or ways designers create fashions.

STUDY QUESTIONS

1 | What is the economic impact of the fashion industry?

2 | Why does New York City have so much influence on the fashion industry?

3 | What is the purpose of a curator?

4 | What is niche marketing?

5 | How does fashion influence niche marketing?

6 | Are all companies required to evolve? Why or why not?

7 | What are some examples of ways companies evolve?

8 | Does fashion influence consumers' behavior? Explain?

9 | What are the examples of spin-off industries that are influenced by the fashion industry?

10 | What is an artifact?

11 | What is bridge merchandise?

12 | How has bridge merchandise influenced the fashion industry?

13 | How have museums influenced consumers' understanding of fashion?

MULTIPLE-CHOICE QUESTIONS

1 | _____ extends the brand by serving a secondary target market.

- **a.** Ready to wear
- **b.** Bridge merchandise
- **c.** Fashion differentiation

2 | During the 1950s and 1960s, which city was considered the capital of the fashion empire?

- **a.** New York
- **b.** Milan
- **c.** Paris
- **d.** Venice
- **e.** London

3 | Isaac Mizrahi's first job as a designer at a high-profile couture house was with _____.

- **a.** Dior
- **b.** Chanel
- **c.** Dolce & Gabbana
- **d.** Versace

4 | In order for fashion marketers' efforts to be successful, the message must be _____.

- **a.** believable
- **b.** understandable
- **c.** memorable
- **d.** related to the needs and wants of the target market

5 | How many U.S. residents work in the fashion industry?

- **a.** In excess of 4.6 million
- **b.** Between 3.8 and 4 million
- **c.** Between 3.5 and 3.7 million
- **d.** 3.5 million

TRUE-OR-FALSE QUESTIONS

1 | _____ Everyone is impacted by fashion.

2 | _____ The societal influence of fashion is far more important than the cultural influence of fashion.

3 | _____ A mission statement directs the actions of a company.

TABLE 3.1

THE Market Planning PROCESS

step 1 CHAPTER 2 | Be inspired; become passionate regarding a product/service; be driven to succeed and committed to working toward a goal.

step 2 CHAPTER 3 | **Intrinsic attributes of the products and services are marketed in terms of value, satisfaction, and quality. Building upon the mission statement, in this step you will make decisions regarding the pricing, communication, value, satisfaction, and quality associated with the purchase or the products and/or services.**

step 3 CHAPTER 4 | Identify a comprehensive list of products and services offered by the company.

step 4 CHAPTER 5 | Examine the products and services component of the core marketing concept related to the trickle-down theory, media and celebrities, and the belongingness theory.

step 5 CHAPTER 6 | Examine the buying season in relation to the marketing process.

step 6 CHAPTER 7 | Examine marketing methods of targeting the consumer.

step 7 CHAPTER 8 | Examine the methods of exchange and relationships with the consumers. This includes making decisions to sell products and services through brick-and-mortar retail operations, direct marketing, and the Internet.

step 8 CHAPTER 9 | Examine the image and brands of the company in relation to marketing efforts.

step 9 CHAPTER 10 | Conduct a market analysis of how companies are able to successfully cross product boundaries.

step 10 CHAPTER 11 | Examine trends in the fashion industry regarding a) counterfeit merchandise and b) the impact of such merchandise on the industry's sales, profits, product design, consumers' attitudes.

step 11 CHAPTER 12 | Conduct a market analysis of fashions in the global environment in order to determine impact to the company's existing marketing efforts.

3

Product, Price, Distribution, AND Placement

"Genius is 1 percent inspiration and 99 percent perspiration."
—Thomas A. Edison

chapter objectives

After reading this chapter, you should be able to understand Step Two of the Market Planning Process. This includes being able to:

+ Identify differences among product lines.

+ Differentiate characteristics of pricing strategies.

+ Evaluate strengths and limitations of distribution decisions.

+ Analyze differences among product placement decisions.

Some may think Ralph Lauren, Gucci, Versace, Chanel, or Dolce & Gabbana are genius fashion marketers. These companies have international product distribution and excellent acceptance by their target markets. They are excellent fashion marketers because of their attention to detail and their commitment to a marketing concept. They don't take shortcuts or skimp on products, quality, or service toward their target markets. One percent of a marketing message may be the result of genius. Ninety-nine percent of the outcome is the result of perspiration.

Fashion permeates our lives. Consumers who enjoy fashion read about it, watch trends on television and in the movies, and tear out pages from magazines as a reminder of what to wear and, more importantly, what to avoid. Fashion, regardless of the quality or style, will not be widely accepted by the target market without a successful marketing strategy. At times, even bad fashion can be sold if the marketing efforts are good. Four components of the Marketing Concept that will be addressed in this chapter relate to how consumers identify with (a) the marketing of fashions (i.e., products), (b) the pricing of fashions, (c) access to fashions (i.e., location), and (d) the ease of finding products within a store (i.e., product placement). Promotion and advertisement of fashions, an important component of the Marketing Concept, are addressed in Chapter Four.

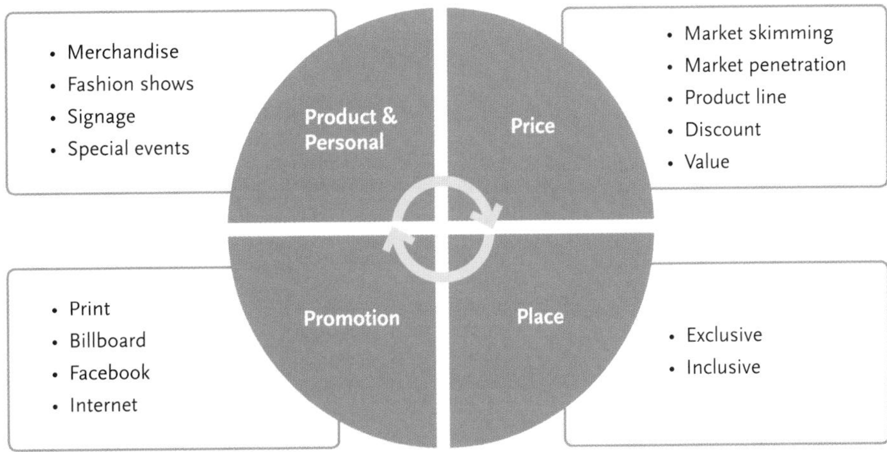

figure 3.1 The Products and Services component of the Core Marketing Concept consists of the implementation of the product, price, distribution, and product placement associated with the marketing efforts. Step 2 of the Market Plan is conducted to assist in endeavor.

figure 3.2
This Prada billboard emphasizes image and fashions. Consumers can clearly recognize the brand from a distance.

PRODUCT

Fashion marketers rarely market just one product. One product alone can rarely, if ever, be successfully marketed for the company. Multiple products are needed to stimulate interest in the products and company. The more products a fashion marketer offers, the greater the probability the target market will purchase multiple items, increase repeat sales, and generate loyal consumer behavior. The product line has a strong presence for the company's image and brand. Image and brand are addressed in depth throughout Chapter Nine. Prior to discussing image and brand, it is important to have a clear understanding of how a product line evolves and influences marketing efforts.

Companies make a strategic plan regarding their product strategy. The majority of fashion companies offer 70 percent new or updated products each season. The remaining 30 percent of the product offerings consist of **classic product lines**. A classic product line is a product line that is offered consistently over a period of time. Styles within the product line remain constant over time.

Updated styles are typically marketed at least six months prior to the season the consumers will wear the products. The styles are featured in print advertisements and billboards shortly prior to, or immediately upon, their arrival in the stores. Classic product lines are an important component to the fashion marketer's product strategy. Classic lines remain popular over an extended time frame—sometimes years, sometimes decades (Jarnow & Dickerson, 1997). Classic styles are marketed by mixing them with updated fashions. The fashion marketer's goal is often to encourage the target market to realize that the new styles can be added or used to enhance pieces purchased from prior seasons. The emphasis can then be on building a wardrobe, rather than simply purchasing products.

figure 3.3
Gap marketed striped fashions during the holidays. The recognizable striped knit sweaters, hats, and scarves were used in television and print advertisements. They became as recognizable as part of Gap as the logo itself.

Gap, Burberry, Ralph Lauren, and Coach have all marketed classic styles with an emphasis on being fashion forward. During the early 2000s, fashion marketers at Gap focused heavily on featuring items that were striped. Striped cardigans, sweaters, and scarves were featured in print and television advertisements. The products were classic, but the striped designs added a contemporary flair. Burberry, known for its plaid, is also well known for its classic trench coat and accessories. The formerly staid company has become fashionable by marketing its plaid fashions in pink, red, gray, and pale blue, as well as the traditional camel.

Gabrielle "Coco" Chanel, internationally known as "Coco," designed fashions that were ahead of their time. The classic Chanel suit combined comfort, chic sophistication, and modern design, and continues to be sold internationally more than 50 years later. The Chanel suit also continues to be copied by mass-market designers. According to Coco, "I have always been copied by others. If a fashion isn't taken up and worn by everyone, it's not a fashion but an eccentricity, a fancy dress" (Watson, 1999/2000a, p. 30).

figure 3.4
The Burberry trench coat is popular with a wide variety of demographic groups. The classic style offers quality, craftsmanship, and long-term fashion appeal.

The Chanel suit's characteristics are: (a) a simple cut, (b) a collarless design, and (c) braid trim around the edges of jacket. The Chanel shoes are two toned.

As you look at the fashions being marketed in magazines, store windows, or on television, do you see any variations of the Chanel design?

- Do you see any sweater, shirts, or jackets that are collarless?
- Do any of the fashions use braid around the edges?
- Can you find shoes that are two toned?
- Are the two-toned shoes ballerina flats, medium heels, or high heels? What is the implication?
- How would you classify the products that you identified (e.g., classic, fad)?
- How would you market these fashions?
- Prior to reading this chapter, would you have thought the products evolved from the Chanel suit?
- Can you identify other designers' products that have evolved into current products?

Logo

A **logo** is defined as "generally one or more letters worked into some distinctive typographic or calligraphic design" (Ostrow and Smith, 1988, p. 138). A logo is particularly important to a product line. A company's logo is traditionally used uniformly throughout the company. That is, one logo is used on the same brand. It provides (a) visual representation of a company, (b) brand awareness, (c) marketing presence, and (d) potential enhancement of the product's status or value. Logos also help the company fight against counterfeiters. Logos act as verification of the actual merchandise. Counterfeit merchandise will be address in depth in Chapter Eleven, "Counterfeiting, Legislation, and Ethics."

Logos play an important role in the marketing process. Logos are typically displayed prominently on the product as well as throughout the promotion and advertising of the product, which is addressed in Chapter Four. Perhaps the ultimate marketer of classic fashions is Ralph Lauren. In 2008, he enlarged the polo logo on selected garments. The logo is embroidered in gold thread and covers approximately one-fourth the size of the front of the garment. The classic garment's statement is "loud and clear."

As you think about different product lines, visualize their logos.

- How many logos can you identify?
- Of the logos you identified, which are designer/luxury products and which are products for the mass market?
- Which attributes do you recognize in designer/luxury fashion logos?
- Which attributes do you recognize in fashions produced for the mass consumer market?

Hangtag

A **hangtag** is an information tag generated by the manufacturer and attached to the product. Technically the hangtag is not a part of the product. It is, however, an important component of the marketing process of the product. Information that is always included on the hangtag includes (a) the company's name, (b) its brand, (c) product information (e.g., size), and (d) the logo. This identification information provides consumers with further loyalty-generating reminders of the company. Hangtags are typically small and easy to store for consumers to remember product information.

What are your initial thoughts regarding the importance of a hangtag? Let's say that in the December shipment, Benetton sweaters were delivered without hangtags. You are the marketing director for the sweaters.

- Could you be 100 percent confident that the sales persons would know how to effectively sell the sweaters?
- Would consumers be willing to take additional time to search through the labels?
- Can you identify other negative repercussions from the missing hangtags?

Packaging

Like hangtags, **packaging** is technically not a part of the product. It is, however, a very important component of the product. Packaging is a subtle yet highly effective method of fashion marketing. Packaging includes bags, boxes, gift wrap, tissue paper, and any other form of material used to hold the target market's purchases. The image of the packaging provides the purchasers with the statement, *We care about you after you have left our store.* Consumers respond to the visual sensation of a product as well as to the touch and scent of a product. The only thing better than receiving new fashions is the anticipation of opening the packages. Fashion marketers understand the importance of packaging. Packaging is an extension of the product. It adds value to the product. The packaging also adds widespread

figure 3.5
Although not technically considered part of the product, hangtags are an important marketing piece. The brand name and logo on the hangtag reinforce the name recognition on the consumer's purchasing pattern.

figure 3.6
Product packaging is an important component of marketing efforts. Color, style, and design influence consumers' perceptions of the merchandise value. The Tiffany Blue Box is symbolic of sophistication and style.

recognition of the corporate brand to others. Packaging can be simple or complex. The most important aspect of packaging for fashion marketing is that the packaging be consistent regardless of the product. Examples of successful fashion marketing through packaging include the bird's-egg-blue box of Tiffany & Co. and Bloomingdale's "big brown bag." The Bloomingdale's brown paper bags are completely void of the Bloomingdale's name, yet consumers nationwide are familiar with them.

When developing a shopping bag as part of a fashion marketing effort, it is important to keep in mind the company's logo and dominant color, font, and name. A shopping bag can be a long-term reminder of an enjoyable fashion purchase, shopping experience, or consumer service. The shopping bag embodies the memories of a company; it does not sell a product. Once a design is decided upon, consumer recognition of the shopping bag is important; the bag acts as a fashion marketing device. Unlike other fashion marketing efforts, the shopping bag should remain relatively constant over time.

PRICE

The price of fashions begins with the cost set by the designer. The designer's costs related to the design, creation, and production of the fashions are identified. The price that fashions are ultimately set at are historically dictated not by the designer but by the retailer's designation. For example, a **discount store** typically operates on a low profit margin (hence the name *discount store*). Discounters offer merchandise at low, competitive prices. **Department stores** are categorized based on the type of merchandise sold. They offer a wide variety of soft lines (i.e., apparel for the entire family) and hard lines (e.g., home furnishings). A department store features semiannual storewide sales. Continuity in pricing strategy provides security to retailers and consumers. Retailers are able to predict at a relatively good rate of assurance when their competitors will promote

TABLE 3.2
Summary of Fashion Marketing Efforts

MARKETING CONCEPT	ATTRIBUTE
Product	• Brands • Lines
Pricing	• Discount • Market skimming • Market penetration • Product line • Discount • Psychological • Promotional • Membership • Value based
Distribution	• Exclusive • Inclusive
Product Placement	• Destination • High traffic • Impulse

sales and how much of a price reduction consumers will be offered. As the new millennium approached, fashion retailers catering to various target markets were faced with increased competition from e-retailers, catalog retailers, and stronger marketing efforts by brick-and-mortar retailers. Retail formats are discussed in depth throughout Chapter Eight, "Cross-Channel Shopping."

Target Corporation looks more like a value department store, but it is classified as a discount retailer. Once identified as a competitor of Walmart, Target has evolved into a retailer that offers fashion products for less than department stores. Effective November 26, 2007, Target changed its pricing strategy to include "limited-time-only" pricing on 20 selected items. The timing of the strategy was specifically designed to draw customer traffic into stores after Thanksgiving, encouraging holiday purchasing efforts (O'Donnell, 2007).

TABLE 3.3
Pricing Strategies

STRATEGY	LINE OF ATTACK
Market skimming	Set prices high; generate a larger-than-average gross margin.
Market penetration	Set initial price low; entice consumers to shop.
Product line pricing	Price-point each quality level within a merchandise line.
Discount pricing	Set a low price to stimulate customer traffic.
Psychological pricing	Price merchandise as the basis of making customers "feel more favorable" toward the merchandise.
Promotional pricing	Design prices to encourage customers to purchase a newly introduced product.
Membership pricing	Have customers sign up for a retailer's membership.
Value-based pricing	Pricing strategy whereby the customer perceives the value of the product to be worth the price.

Market-Skimming Pricing

A company doesn't always price its products to maximize market share. Some products are meant to be unique, special, and highly prized by the target market. Products may also be identified as high profit-margin items. Under these circumstances, the fashion marketer will employ a market-skimming pricing strategy. A **market-skimming pricing** strategy exists when a high price is set, generating a larger-than-average gross margin. The company sells fewer of the products but earns a higher-than-normal profit on each unit sold. This strategy is used only if the product's quality and image can support the market-skimming pricing. Harrods in London is considered to be the most expensive store in the world: Judith Leiber handbags sell in the $90,000 range and a Chanel handbag can be purchased for $260,000 (yes, the zeros are in the correct spot). If this is a bit out of your range, Dolce & Gabbana (D&G) fashion marketers offer cotton and linen dresses ranging in price from $495 to $645. While it is true that cotton and linen are not expensive fabrics, the extremely high-quality styling and craftsmanship are characteristics of D&G. In addition, the quality of cotton and linen used by D&G is excellent. A higher pricing strategy is adopted because the high image the company wishes to portray. The D&G dresses are also sold at Saks Fifth Avenue for the fashion-forward female.

figure 3.7 Symbolic words are often used in advertisements and fliers to stimulate consumer purchasing. Encouraging phrases such as "deep discounts" and "final days" provide consumers with a sense of urgency to spend.

Market-Penetration Pricing

Companies that want to capture a deep portion of the target market often choose a **market-penetration pricing** strategy. Market-penetration pricing occurs when the product's initial price is set low, thereby enticing consumers to purchase. The greater the number of consumers purchasing the product, the likelier the company penetrates the market. High merchandise turnover provides the company with increased profits. As the profits increase, the company is able to continue passing savings on to the consumer. Market-penetration pricing works best when the target is sensitive to price. As is the case in all pricing scenarios, costs (e.g., production, distribution, and marketing) must be covered when considering the markup. Competition is also a consideration when using market-penetration pricing. Some companies use a "meet or beat the competition" strategy at this stage.

Designer Shoe Warehouse (DSW) uses market-penetration pricing. DSW sells men's, women's, and children's shoes at a fraction of the retail cost. Brands carried include Prada, Reebok, Miu Miu, Stuart Weitzman, Frye, and Coach, just to name a few. Prices range from $30 to $300. DSW is able to use market-penetration pricing because not all styles and sizes are available (Designer Shoe Warehouse, 2009).

Product-Line Pricing

Fashion marketers frequently promote entire product lines. A **merchandise line** consists of a group of products that are similar in style and design; they coordinate with each other and are by the same designer and/or manufacturer. Merchandise lines may be developed at varying quality levels (e.g., good, excellent, luxurious). **Product-line pricing** is used to price-point each quality level within a merchandise line. To be effective, significant price differences should exist between each price point. The price points should also be relatively the same distance apart. The difference between price points allows consumers to make comparisons with ease. Levi's fashion marketing team aggressively uses product-line pricing. For each style, jeans are marketed at a price point. The product-line pricing provides the target market with an easy method of selecting jeans based on style, design, and price.

Discount Pricing

Consumers respond positively to symbolic words (e.g., *save, value, deep discount*). Fashion marketers frequently use discount pricing to stimulate customer traffic, encourage the purchase of multiple products, instill brand-loyal purchasing behavior, and spread positive word-of-mouth promotion. Two types of discount-pricing strategies are popular in the fashion industry: quantity discount and seasonal discount.

QUANTITY DISCOUNT

A **quantity discount** is provided when merchandise is purchased in bundles or multiple units. Payless ShoeSource builds its entire mission statement around quantity discounts. The company's slogan "Buy One, Half Off Everything" has made the company a favorite among shoe-loving consumers. Victoria's Secret frequently uses quantity pricing as a marketing strategy. The company offered $15 off each $100 order, $30 off each $150 order, and $75 off each $270 order. Other companies that effectively use quantity discounts include Hanes and Just My Size. The bundling of socks, undershirts, underpants, and bras also encourages consumers to purchase in bulk.

SEASONAL DISCOUNT

A **seasonal discount** is used to sell merchandise that is out of season. Crew-neck sweaters from last season may be discounted by 5 percent because the color is from the prior season. Jeans from two years ago may be discounted by 20 percent because the stitching is not vuiewd to be as desirable by this year's target market. The discount offered by seasonal pricing eliminates old merchandise. Bloomingdale's online channel markets its seasonal pricing merchandise under the clearance icon. Merchandise ranging from $75 to $4,995 is marketed through this link. Seasonal pricing discounts as large as 49 percent have been given in an attempt to move merchandise (Bloomingdale's, 2009).

A popular seasonal sale is a **calendar sale**. A calendar sale is a promotional method whereby during a particular month, a sale is offered every day. Each day, something different is on sale. For example, on Friday, October 4, everything pink in the store is on sale. The computerized register assists with keeping up with the point of sale (POS). The marketing of fashions using a calendar sale helps build anticipation in the target market's minds.

figure 3.8 This Victoria's Secret advertisement allows consumers to receive $15 off any $100 order. This marketing is designed to stimulate consumer spending. Consumers who would not traditionally cross the $100 purchase price may add another item in order to receive $15 off the order. This marketing technique encourages larger spending patterns and store loyalty.

Psychological Pricing

One of the first lessons a merchandiser learns about pricing is to cover the **cost of goods sold (COGS)**. The company will soon go out of business if the price is set below COGS. Once COGS is taken into consideration, the amount associated with discount pricing strategies can be identified. While the fashion industry is serious business, many of the products themselves can also be considered emotional. **Psychological pricing** occurs when pricing is used as the basis to make consumers "feel more favorable" about the product. High pricing is often used to denote quality, luxury, and/or superior craftsmanship.

Louis Vuitton (LV) fashion and leather goods are marketed using psychological pricing. No one can deny the superb quality and craftsmanship of Louis Vuitton products. When a consumer purchases something from 1 of the 60 LV brands, they are making a lifetime investment. Psychologically, purchasers of LV products are saying, *The product is worth the price and I am worth the product* (Louis Vuitton, 2009).

Promotional Pricing

Whenever a new product is introduced, marketers encourage existing customers of the brand to adopt the product. The marketing campaign may also be designed to entice customers' away from the competition's brand if a similar product is currently on the market. **Promotional pricing** is used during this strategy. Promotional pricing is a method whereby the product is introduced at a lower-than-normal price. The product's price is raised after the promotional time line ends.

figure 3.9 Special events within a store are designed as a marketing effort. The event builds product excitement, reminds consumers about the store, and encourages purchasing behavior.

Membership Pricing

A **membership pricing** strategy is a selling strategy whereby consumers sign up for a retailer's membership. Upon membership entrance, the consumer is eligible for discounts. Membership may cost an annual fee or may be free. Membership pricing instills loyal shopping patterns (Nunes & Johnson, 2004).

Consumers are typically required to give the retailers their name, mailing address, phone number, and e-mail address. The target market's information is used as a database. Promotional information and surveys are gathered using consumers in the database. The retailer will send out promotional brochures, e-mail sale information, and update consumers on special events.

The consumer database (e.g., name, address) built by a retailer provides valuable information regarding the retailer's target market. The retailer is able to better understand the geographic location of the target market, its spending patterns (i.e., frequent purchasers vs. infrequent purchasers), preferred brands, price points purchased, and which days the store is patronized. Fashion companies that use a form of membership pricing include: DSW, Saks Fifth Avenue (SAKSFIRST), J.C. Penney (JCP Rewards), and Kohl's (Box 3.1).

Value-Based Pricing

Value-based pricing is a form of pricing strategy whereby the consumer perceives the value of the product to be worth the price (Nunes & Johnson, 2004). Value-based pricing may result in prices in excess of 100 percent of the wholesale cost of the merchandise or in lower-than-average pricing. For some products, this pricing strategy is not sufficient. Customers are looking for value. This pricing strategy is often used on clearance and luxury items.

SAKSFIRST The ultimate Saks experience

SAKSFIRST MEMBERSHIP
GETTING STARTED
REWARDS
MEMBERSHIP LEVELS ▸
PARTNER BENEFITS ▸
THE LITTLE BLACK CARD ▸
SAKS STORE CARD
COMPARE CARDS

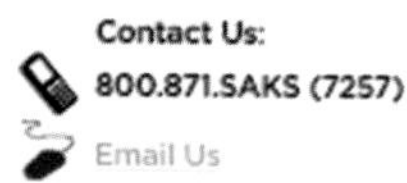

Contact Us:
800.871.SAKS (7257)
Email Us

FAQs
TERMS & CONDITIONS

SAKSFIRST

Members get showered with SAKSFIRST points — points that add up to a rich SAKSFIRST Gift Card to splurge with at Saks.

With the little black card, get SAKSFIRST points with every purchase, inside and outside of Saks, starting with your very first purchase.

With the Saks Store Card, SAKSFIRST members receive SAKSFIRST points for purchases inside of Saks.

		Points	Rewards
First Saks purchase	Diamond bracelet $5,000	10,000	$100
Second Saks purchase	Suit & Handbag $5,000	20,000	$200
Third Saks purchase	Dress & Shoes $5,000	30,000	$300
Fourth Saks Purchase during Triple Points Event	Watch for Him $5,000	90,000	$900
First purchase outside Saks	Gala Tickets $2,000	2,000	$20
Total SAKSFIRST Gift Card Value:			$1,520

▸ Learn more

EXISTING MEMBER LOGIN

VIEW SAKSFIRST POINTS:

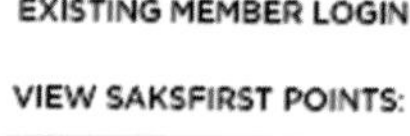

SAKSFIRST ACCOUNT

PAY BILLS AND MANAGE SAKS CREDIT:

MASTERCARD CARD ACCOUNT

SAKS STORE CARD ACCOUNT

GET THE LITTLE BLACK CARD

▸ Upgrade your existing Saks Store Card

SAKSFIRST membership pricing strategy provides exclusivity, privileges, and additional services for consumers who frequently purchase merchandise at Saks Fifth Avenue.

BOX 3.1 Saks Fifth Avenue Membership Pricing

Fashion marketers at Saks Fifth Avenue understand that their target market appreciates the latest fashions and superior quality. While the merchandise offered by the retailer is at an above-average price point, it doesn't mean that the target market is averse to saving money. SAKSFIRST is a membership pricing strategy designed to provide exclusivity, privileges, and additional services for people who frequently purchase Saks merchandise. The greater the dollar amount of money spent at Saks during the year, the greater the number of points generated toward a store gift card. The fashion marketers also understand that their target market is segmented into different levels based on spending levels. SAKSFIRST memberships are segmented in a similar manner: SAKSFIRST Premier for persons who spend $1,000–$4,999 annually; SAKSFIRST Elite for those who spend $5,000–$9,999 at Saks annually; SAKSFIRST Platinum for members who spend $10,000–$24,999 annually; and SAKSFIRST Diamond for members who spend $25,000 or more annually at the fashion company.

The reasoning behind value-based pricing is based on the exclusivity of the product, the designer's name, and/or the quality and craftsmanship of the product. Value-based pricing may also be implemented on items that have a limited geographic distribution. The exclusivity, difficulty in acquiring the merchandise, and perception of the product's uniqueness add to the perception of value (Nunes & Johnson, 2004). When value-based pricing is used on clearance items, consumers are able to purchase fashions at deep discount prices because a limited quantity and/or selection of merchandise is available. Value-based pricing may be used by higher-quality manufacturers to liquidate small quantities of merchandise.

A direct contradiction to value-based pricing is embodied in eBay. eBay is the world's largest online retailer (eBay Investor Relations Report, 2010). The online company offers consumers a Web portal to buy and sell merchandise at or below retail selling price. Merchandise may be new or used. The Web portal is open 24 hours a day, 7 days a week, 365 days per year. Each second, $1,900 worth of merchandise is traded through eBay. Value pricing is set based on the buyer and seller. A consumer may bid $100 on a Chanel handbag that may be value-priced at $2,500 retail. The difference between the retailer's value-pricing strategy and e-Bay's is that the merchandising on eBay is being traded by either consumers or vendors. Merchandise being traded by vendors is typically sold at cost or higher.

As you review the various pricing strategies:

- Does price influence your perception of the quality of the product? Explain.
- Is one pricing strategy superior to another? Explain.
- Log on to the Internet. Identify specific product lines and discuss the pricing strategies used.

figure 3.10
Holidays are an important time for marketers to promote fashions and accessories. Key words to stimulate sales include *sale, percent off, value,* and *special.*

DISTRIBUTION

Marketing fashions in the correct location is critical. Fashion marketing must reach the target market. Prior to online retailing, retailers were required to carefully assess where the largest primary target market was geographically located. Online retailing and catalog operations now allow retailers to market their fashions nationally and internationally. Fashion marketers are able to greatly expand their reach to target markets and are only restricted by their distribution limitations.

When retailers are located primarily in one geographic location but market fashions nationally or internationally using catalogs or a Web site, there are several considerations. One consideration is culture. The city, state, and/or nation's culture must be considered when marketing fashions. Cultural and societal beliefs and values, as well as slogans, should be considered when developing a marketing message. A particular location can enhance a company's message if its marketing effort is decentralized or localized to a specific area. Avoiding messages and statements is often useful when considering the social and political nature of a city, state, or country. Fashion marketing efforts rarely involve political statements. One exception is celebrating national holidays: Fashion marketers often use national holidays as an excuse to offer the target market a discount (e.g., a 10 percent discount off all casual wear July 1 through July 5 in honor of Independence Day).

When a retailer carries multiple levels of brands (i.e., store brand, national brand, designer brand), the fashion marketer must identify a strategy regarding (a) how to promote each brand and (b) how much emphasis to place on each brand. The ultimate decision regarding this fashion strategy will be based on the company's desired image. The desired image is not necessarily the same as the actual image. **Desired image** is defined as the image the store is trying to portray to consumers, employees, and stakeholders. The **actual image** is defined as the image that is perceived by consumers, employees, and stakeholders. Image is addressed in depth throughout Chapter Nine, "Image and Branding."

When marketing its jewelry, HandPicked continually thinks about its mission statement. The location of HandPicked stores is just as important to satisfying the company's mission as are the other marketing components. The company's mission and storefront are featured on its flyer. The company wants its female target market to clearly understand why it is in business. Physical brick-and-mortar operations are selected strategically, with specific sites servicing specific target markets. Company offices expand into other regions. HandPicked is determined to maintain a consistent image and measure of quality regardless of the number of its store locations.

figure 3.11
Many women have a love affair with shoes. Some women think they need "just one more pair of black shoes." The marketing efforts of the designers in the shoe industry continue to be strong because of consumers who have a passion for fashionable shoes.

figure 3.12
Jimmy Choo made history when he designed shoes for H&M. Consumers lined up outside the retailer for hours before the store opened to be first in line for Jimmy Choo shoes at H&M prices.

Exclusivity

A designer's, manufacturer's, or retailer's image can be influenced by the level of exclusivity of its products. **Exclusivity** refers to the limited distribution of a product. The product may be distributed to one retailer or one location of a retailer.

Fashion marketers often use exclusivity during the introduction of a product line as an attempt to enhance the allure and excitement of the product. Exclusive distribution is typically reserved for fashion capitals like New York and Los Angeles. The exclusive distribution of the fashion merchandise is extensively promoted. Once the merchandise is accepted by the consumers in a particular market, the fashion marketer has two options. One option is to promote the exclusivity of the product and keep selling it in only those markets. Consumers who desire the merchandise must obtain the merchandise from the selected stores. This fashion marketing strategy enhances the brand's image as selective, special, and valuable in both intrinsic and extrinsic value. **Intrinsic value** is value as perceived by the consumer. Each consumer may view the value of a product differently. **Extrinsic value** is the value of the product as viewed by others. An example of intrinsic value is the thinking of a consumer who purchases her fifth pair of black high-heeled shoes because "they make her feel pretty." Technically, the other four pairs of black shoes are acceptable. The fifth pair, however, makes her happy. The intrinsic value of the shoes is worth spending $350. An example of extrinsic value in this case might be the compliments her friends give her on the new shoes.

A retailer and its fashion marketer may decide to offer the product through exclusive distribution. **Exclusive distribution** occurs when a brand is offered through only one retailer. The retailer typically features the name of the brand. Exclusive distribution generates a strong and loyal target-market following. In addition, the merchandise brands complement one another.

Temporary limited exclusive distribution is a fashion marketing strategy that is often used to create excitement for a new brand. Temporary limited exclusive distribution exists when a product is offered at one retailer for a limited time. Exclusive distribution is marketed heavily, featuring the name of the retailer, the brand, and the product's qualities. Marketing efforts emphasize the fact that consumers are able to obtain the product only at the particular retailer. The objectives of a temporary limited exclusive distribution are to increase customer traffic in the retail store, encourage high merchandise turnover of the brand being marketed, and ultimately

instill a sense of customer loyalty to both the retailer and the brand. Jimmy Choo shoes being sold at a select number of H&M stores is an example of temporary limited exclusive distribution. After a limited time, the line will be extended internationally. According to Joshua Schulman, Jimmy Choo's chief executive officer,

> The H&M collection is meant to be a fun, accessible flash for a moment in time. . . . [W]e know there is a different customer who dreams of wearing Jimmy Choo and this is a fantastic opportunity for her to enter our brand for a limited time only. . . . The H&M collection will of course have a different finish from the Jimmy Choo-branded footwear, but it will be more accessible and allow us to reach a broader audience" (Berton, 2009, p. 3).

Exclusivity provides the customer with a perception of individuality. Consumers who desire a fashion garment or accessory that is unique, high quality, and well suited to their personality are willing to purchase an exclusive product (albeit an often-expensive product).

A fashion marketer may also decide to offer exclusivity during a limited time and then offer widespread distribution at a later time. Initial promotion of the product's exclusivity builds anticipation and excitement for the product and additional recognition for the brand. This fashion marketing strategy is typically only implemented when the product is designed to be carried by the company long term.

Online fashion marketers frequently use exclusivity to promote their products. Online and home-shopping networks (e.g., QVC, Home Shopping Network) will often provide merchandise that is either not available in stores or not readily available in a consumer's location. When consumers access some retail Web sites, they will see a meter. The meter displays the number of remaining fashion products available. The number is designed to be an incentive to encourage purchasing behavior and to be a reminder that once the consumer purchases the item, he or she has purchased one of the few items left (Rosenthal, 2006). Online shopping will be addressed in more detail throughout Chapter Eight, "Cross-Channel Shopping."

Because a product is limited in distribution, consumers who have access to the product typically pay a high price for it and often make a significant effort to acquire it. This effort and pricing increase the perceived image. Exclusive fashion products are typically of a high quality. Consumers may keep exclusive garments for years, even decades. For example, a custom-made jacket in the style of the Chanel jacket from 1960 can still be worn and considered highly fashionable in the twenty-first century. Gucci shoes and apparel continue to be timeless. Ferragamo's classic shoe designs continue

figure 3.13
Isaac Mizrahi, Mossimo, and Alexander McQueen made shopping for fashions at Target hip, fashionable, fun and affordable. The outfit pictured here is from Alexander McQueen's line.

to be marketed and sell well to the company's loyal customers; whereas the more fashion-forward Ferragamo designs are targeted to a younger, hipper target market.

Fashion designers and manufacturers typically use exclusivity as a strategy to take advantage of small retailers and boutiques. Instead of producing large quantities of a design, small orders (e.g., 100–500 units) are produced. Fashion marketers can then make a more frequent number of design changes and introduce those changes to the consumer sooner and on a more intimate level. Fashion marketers provide boutiques and small retailers with additional product knowledge, selling techniques, and information to offer to their customers (Hamilton & DeQuine, 2006).

Fashion retailers use exclusivity to build customer traffic into their specific stores. For example, Target offers exclusive brands by designers at popular prices. Designer brands the company has offered in the past include Isaac Mizrahi, Mossimo, and Alexander McQueen. Nordstrom, Neiman Marcus, Saks Fifth Avenue, and J. C. Penney have all been successful in developing exclusivity through the use of store brands.

Massclusivity

Exclusivity was originally designed as a fashion marketing strategy for expensive products (e.g., perfume, designer clothing). The potential of mass-market sales changed this strategy. The mass market, like the upper-class market, appreciates limited-edition fashion items.

To satisfy the mass market's need for exclusive products and stimulate their purchasing behavior, fashion marketers have designed a strategy called **massclusivity**. Massclusivity refers to a strategy whereby retailers offer limited-edition merchandise to a mass market. The strategy is designed to stimulate consumer enthusiasm toward the limited-edition item(s) and promote merchandise turnover (Boorstin, 2005). An increasing number of mass-fashion retailers are offering limited-edition products in order to create excitement. High-fashion designers Karl Lagerfeld and Stella McCartney

figure 3.14
Karl Lagerfeld is known for his expensive fashions and intricate designs. In 2009, he designed and marketed fashions for the hip consumer at H&M.

both created limited-edition lines for H&M. In both cases, the merchandise sold out in a matter of hours (Boorstin, 2005).

PRODUCT PLACEMENT

The placement of products within a store influences consumers' ultimate purchasing behaviors. Store layout plays an integral part of consumers' shopping ease, enjoyment, and ultimate purchasing behavior. Product placement can serve as the ultimate, most influential, yet subtle, marketing effort.

Fashions that are in high demand are often placed in the back of the the store, department, or area. This placement requires consumers to walk throughout the area, thereby maximizing the breadth and depth of products offered by the retailer. This strategy is called **destination placement**.

Another type of product placement is called **impulse placement**. The items sold by impulse placement are typically located within the immediate vicinity of the cash register. Characteristics of these products include a low price and a high profit margin. While impulse products are rarely the focus of marketing campaigns, they greatly enhance the number of products each consumer purchases.

Think about the last time you purchased a fashion item (e.g., dress, purse), or, better yet, go to your favorite fashion store.

- What are the primary products that you would like to purchase at this store? Which products are located near the cash register?
- Which products near the cash register did you pick up and look at, perhaps without even thinking about the price?
- Did you purchase any of the products near the cash register?
- What was the additional cost of the products near the cash register?

SUMMARY

The success of a company's marketing efforts often means the difference between an average year and an excellent year for the company. Each campaign must be thought of individually, based on the marketing team's goals and objectives. Most marketing efforts are designed to sell a product or service. Regardless of how many industry awards a commercial wins or the number of consumers who enjoy watching a commercial, if the marketing effort doesn't stimulate sales, the marketing campaign is not effective.

The product is typically the first component considered in the marketing mix. Hangtags, logos, and packaging all play a role in the overall marketing efforts of the product and its line.

Pricing strategies vary significantly. The designer's costs related to the design, creation, and production of the fashions are identified. The price fashions are ultimately set at are historically dictated not by the designer but by the retailer's designation (e.g., department, discount). Eight pricing strategies have been discussed: (1) market skimming, (2) market penetration, (3) product line, (4) discount, (5) psychological, (6) promotional, (7) membership, and (8) value based.

Fashions are marketed locally, nationally, and/or internationally. The method of distribution ultimately chosen depends on a company's desired exclusivity or mass appeal. The choice of where to place products within retail operations is based on the classification of the product (i.e., destination, impulse).

REFERENCES

Berton, E. (2009, June 18). Choo hooks up with H&M. *Women's Wear Daily*, p. 3.

Bloomingdale's (2009). Company Web site. Retrieved June 25, 2009 from www1.bloomingdales.com/catalog/index.ognc?.

Boorstin, J. (2005, August 22). What's in fashion this fall? *Scarcity*, 152(4). Retrieved June 18, 2009 from http://wf2dnvr4.webfeat.org/BP39K171.

Cass, J. (2008, December 10). The design process of creating a creative billboard campaign. Retrieved December 23, 2008 from http://justcreativedesign.com/2008.

Designer Shoe Warehouse (2009). Company Web site. Retrieved June 25, 2009. from http://dsw.com/dsw_shoes/catalog/index.jsp).

Dolce and Gabbana (2008). Company Web site. Retrieved December 23, 2008 from http://www.dolcegabbana.it/eBay (2008).

eBay Investor Relations Report (2010). Ebay Inc. reports strong first quarter 2010 results. Retrieved April 21, 2010 from http://files.shareholder.com/downloads/ebay/898242620x0x367980/ee7d0407-3a51-4ec3-8e22-bea8d8049da0/Q12010EarningsReleaseFINAL.pdf.

Jarnow, J. & Dickerson, K. G. (1997). *Inside the fashion business*. Upper Saddle River, NJ: Prentice Hall.

Hamilton, A. & DeQuine (2006, March 5). Freaking for sneakers. *Time*, p. 2.

Korn, Arden (2009, March 3). Personal interview with owner of Little Lambs and Ivy.

Kotler, P. & Armstrong, G. (2001). *Principles of marketing*. Upper Saddle River, NJ: Prentice Hall.

Louis Vuitton (2009). Company Web site. Retrieved June 25, 2009 from www.lvmh.com.

Nordstrom (2009). Company Web site. Retrieved January 30, 2009 from www.nordstrom.com.

Nunes, P. & Johnson, B. (2004). *Mass affluence: Seven new rules of marketing to today's consumer.* Boston: Harvard Business School Press.

O'Donnell, J. (2007, November 9). Target plans alternative to cutting prices. *USA Today*, p. 1B.

Ostrow, R., & Smith, S. R. (1988). *The dictionary of marketing*. New York: Fairchild Books.

Rosenthal, J. (2006, June). Hold the fistfights. *Fast Company*, 106. Retrieved June 18, 2008 from http://wf2dnvr4.webfeat.org/BP39K198.

Watson, L. (1999/2000a). *Twentieth century fashion: 100 years of style by decade & designer.* Philadelphia, PA: Chelsea House Publishers.

KEY TERMS

Define or briefly explain the following terms:

Actual image ______________________________

Calendar sale ______________________________

Classic product line ______________________________

Cost of goods sold ______________________________

Department store ______________________________

Desired image ______________________________

Destination placement ______________________________

Discount store ______________________________

Exclusive distribution ______________________________

Exclusivity ______________________________

Extrinsic value ______________________________

Hangtag ______________________________

Impulse placement ______________________________

Intrinsic value ______________________________

Logo ______________________________

Market-penetration pricing ______________________________

Market-skimming pricing ______________________________

Massclusivity ______________________________

Mass marketing ______________________________

Membership pricing ______________________________

Merchandise line ______________________________

Packaging ______________________________

Product-line pricing ______________________________

Promotional pricing ______________________________

Psychological pricing ______________________________

Quantity discount ______________________________

Seasonal discount ______________________________

Stakeholder ______________________________

Staple ______________________________

Style ______________________________

Temporary limited exclusive distribution ______________________________

Value-based pricing ______________________________

CLASS OR TEAM DISCUSSION QUESTIONS

1 | There are an increasing number of young fashion designers successfully designing and marketing products nationally and internationally. Provide your opinion regarding the products, pricing, and distribution strategies one of the successful designers/marketers has used. Examples of young designers who have marketed their fashions successfully include Stella McCartney, Dolce & Gabbana, and Jimmy Choo.

____

____

2 | Assess the various pricing strategies. Match up the various pricing strategies with specific brand-name and/or designer companies.

____

____

3 | Is there a fashion designer who you believe is making mistakes regarding his or her marketing efforts in relation to his or her product line, pricing, or distribution? Explain.

____

____

4 | As a fashion marketer, discuss the advantages of temporary limited exclusive distribution. When would this distribution strategy be a disadvantage?

____

____

INTERNET ACTIVITIES

1 | Using the Internet as a resource, examine three different companies in their distribution of products. Where are the products sold? How do the companies communicate in written format to consumers in different regions, nationally and internationally? Evaluate the methods whereby companies communicate visually and orally (e.g., pictures, sound).

2 | Select a company and fashion product category. Access the Internet. Collect data on the company's Internet marketing efforts in relation to pricing, distribution, and placement. Placement can be assessed online in terms of the visibility of items on the Internet site.

STUDY QUESTIONS

1 | What are the purposes of a logo?

2 | What are the purposes of a hangtag?

3 | How is a product's packaging an extension of the product?

4 | What does exclusivity mean in relation to distribution?

5 | What is extrinsic value?

6 | What is value-based pricing?

7 | Give examples of membership pricing. Is this a good fashion marketing technique? Explain.

8 | Describe market skimming as a pricing strategy.

9 | How can packaging be integrated into fashion marketing efforts?

10 | What is the difference between intrinsic and extrinsic values?

11 | What role do intrinsic and extrinsic values play in the marketing of fashions?

12 | What is an example of market-penetration pricing?

13 | Discuss an example of temporary limited exclusive distribution.

14 | Discuss the concept of integrated fashion marketing. Provide an example in your discussion.

MULTIPLE-CHOICE QUESTIONS

1 | What percent of new or updated products are featured each year by fashion companies?

a. 30
b. 50
c. 70
d. 100

2 | Which of the following statements is accurate about packaging?

a. Packaging can add widespread recognition of a corporate brand.
b. Packaging is a subtle yet effective method of fashion marketing.
c. Packaging can make a statement that says, *We care about you after you have left our store.*
d. All of the above are accurate statements regarding packaging.

3 | _____ occurs when pricing is used as the basis to make consumers "feel more favorable" about a product.

a. Value-based pricing
b. Discount pricing
c. Membership pricing
d. Psychological pricing

4 | Information included on a hangtag includes _____.

a. The company's name, logo, and company history
b. The company's name, brand, logo, and product information
c. Information about the fashion designer
d. Information about the retailer

5 | _____ is a form of pricing strategy whereby the consumer perceives the value of the product to be worth the price.

a. Discount pricing
b. Value-based pricing
c. Promotional pricing
d. Psychological pricing

TRUE-OR-FALSE QUESTIONS

1 | _____ The Chanel suit has been copied repeatedly by mass merchandisers over the past 50 years.

2 | _____ Market-penetration pricing occurs when the product's initial price is set low.

3 | _____ H&M uses temporary limited exclusive distribution as part of its marketing concept.

TABLE 4.1

THE Market Planning PROCESS

step 1	CHAPTER 2	Be inspired; become passionate regarding a product/service; be driven to succeed and committed to working toward a goal.
step 2	CHAPTER 3	Intrinsic attributes of the products and services are marketed in terms of value, satisfaction, and quality. Building upon the mission statement, in this step you will make decisions regarding the pricing, communication, value, satisfaction, and quality associated with the purchase or the products and/or services.
step 3	**CHAPTER 4**	**Identify a comprehensive list of products and services offered by the company.**
step 4	CHAPTER 5	Examine the products and services component of the core marketing concept related to the trickle-down theory, media and celebrities, and the belongingness theory.
step 5	CHAPTER 6	Examine the buying season in relation to the marketing process.
step 6	CHAPTER 7	Examine marketing methods of targeting the consumer.
step 7	CHAPTER 8	Examine the methods of exchange and relationships with the consumers. This includes making decisions to sell products and services through brick-and-mortar retail operations, direct marketing, and the Internet.
step 8	CHAPTER 9	Examine the image and brands of the company in relation to marketing efforts.
step 9	CHAPTER 10	Conduct a market analysis of how companies are able to successfully cross product boundaries.
step 10	CHAPTER 11	Examine trends in the fashion industry regarding a) counterfeit merchandise and b) the impact of such merchandise on the industry's sales, profits, product design, consumers' attitudes.
step 11	CHAPTER 12	Conduct a market analysis of fashions in the global environment in order to determine impact to the company's existing marketing efforts.

4

Public Relations, Promotion, AND Advertising

"As a fashion designer, I was always aware that I was not an artist, because I was creating something that was made to be sold, used, and ultimately discarded." —Tom Ford

chapter objectives

After reading this chapter, you should be able to understand Step Three of the Market Planning Process. This includes being able to:

+ Comprehend the differences between and similarities among public relations, promotions, and advertising.
+ Examine public relations efforts associated with fashion marketing.
+ Assess methods of promoting fashions.
+ Distinguish among the various methods of advertising.
+ Evaluate integrated marketing efforts.

Tom Ford's statement brings about an all-important concept regarding fashion: The widespread success of fashion is dependent upon successful marketing efforts and consumers' adoption of the fashions. Fashions are marketed on a continual basis because fashions change, and so do consumers' desires.

Fashion permeates our lives. Fashions, regardless of the quality or style, will not be widely accepted by a target market without a successful marketing strategy. At times, even bad fashions can be sold if the accompanying marketing efforts are good. The target market, as well as all consumers (e.g., persons who may or may not be interested in the fashions), need: (a) information about the fashions, (b) a desire for the fashions, (c) access to the fashions, and (d) a perceived value in the fashions. In today's

FASHION POLICE

Out in Las Vegas.

Pink
KEMBLE: This is more Rainbow Brite than Pink.
BRICKLEY: Somewhere, a preschooler is missing her first-day-of-school outfit.
WETANSON: Ironically, she's wearing every color except for pink.

AnnaLynne McCord
CANNON: *90210-ho!*
WOLF: I can't comment on her clothes if she's not wearing any.
FEINSTEIN: Borat wants his bathing suit back.
ROSE: At least she had the modesty to cover up.

Jessica Alba
WOLF: Escaped from the Beverly Hills Penitentiary.
FEINSTEIN: She has an accessory for every season – but this is ugly all year round.
ROSE: I liked her better when she was Invisible Girl.

Kimora Lee Simmons
CANNON: Just spotted: Kimora Lee Simmons looking totally ridiculous.
BRICKLEY: Me Tarzan, you lame!
KEMBLE: Someone hurry up and stuff that cat back in the bag!

Sharon Stone
BRICKLEY: My *Basic Instinct*: gag reflex.
LO: She actually needs to cover up the cover-up.
ROSE: Throw this look overboard!
WETANSON: At least she has bottoms on this time.

CITIZEN'S ARREST
Your best comments from Usmagazine.com

Lindsay Lohan
TOMMY BOY: Lindsay's so broke, she can't afford pants.
JESSE: Getting ready for her cage fight with Samantha Ronson.
BRADSHAW: Winter on top, summer on the bottom!
ANONYMOUS: That dress is like a Rorschach test — if they had an inkblot that looked like bad decisions.

Rank these style offenders at Usmagazine.com

126 | SEPTEMBER 21, 2009

Us | 127

figure 4.1 Consumers learn what not to wear from promotional articles in magazines. An article about fashion "crimes" is provided to help consumers avoid making similar mistakes.

society of overstimulation, consumers require creative forms of communication in order to successfully retrieve information. Examples of methods of marketing (e.g., communicating) fashions include: fashion shows, billboards, television, print, radio, Internet, and direct marketing. In some cases, good fashions may never be successful in the marketplace.

The failure of good products can be the result of poor marketing efforts. In addition to product, distribution, price, and placement, effective marketing consists of efforts in public relations, promotion, and advertising.

figure 4.2
An excellent advertisement presents the designer's fashions, reminds consumers about the designer's name, and stands out from the other fashion marketing efforts. This Guess marketing advertisement accomplishes all three goals.

PUBLIC RELATIONS

Public relations consists of "activities aimed at enhancing the public image of an organization, individual, or [the] public. . . . Public relations includes the dissemination of information intended to generate good will on behalf of the organization and to identify its activities with the public interest" (Ostrow & Smith, 1988, p. 199). The public relations component of the marketing mix continues to be an important and valuable tool for fashion companies. Public relations provides stakeholders with current information regarding the company's product lines, marketing efforts, and interaction and assistance to the community through good works.

Large fashion organizations typically have a public relations organization that is a separate entity from the marketing organization. The members of this division are responsible solely for developing positive information about the company's activities to

figure 4.3
Effective fashion marketing efforts are often the result of an integrated approach. Combining product with an extremely popular movie franchise, True Religion Brand Jeans maximizes its exposure using the Internet.

its stakeholders. Small fashion organizations may incorporate the public relations responsibilities into the duties of the owner or lead manager. Regardless of the size of the organization, public relations should be an integral part of the marketing concept of every fashion organization.

Methods of communicating with stakeholders vary. Print literature, press releases, and stockholders' meetings are three common forms of communication. In today's technological era, perhaps the most used method of public relations is the Internet. Fashion companies include a link on their Web sites to press releases, fashion shows, new product lines, customer service, and blogs. Blogs will be discussed later in this chapter.

There may be multiple goals to public relations efforts, including

- Building positive, strong, and ever-increasing brand awareness (Branding is addressed in depth in Chapter Nine.)
- Communicating with stakeholders
- Instilling stakeholder confidence in the company
- Promoting a social cause
- Recruiting the best employee talent worldwide. As employees throughout the industry read the press releases, they will obtain a better understanding of the company's culture.

For example, Gucci has developed a line to assist UNICEF and schools in Africa. Twenty-five percent of the retail price of merchandise sold under "Gucci for UNICEF" was donated to the cause. The public relations efforts are located on Gucci's Web site link, "Gucci news" (Gucci, 2009).

figure 4.4
Gucci's line of Tattoo Heart Collection benefits UNICEF. Actress Monet Mazur attended the New York launch of the collection to benefit UNICEF.

figure 4.5
Sean Combs is the creative director, designer, marketer and model behind the Sean John line. The billboard in Times Square needs very little wording. The brand Sean John and the name of the fragrance I Am King says it all.

consumers additional products that complement the original purchase.

Publicity consists of "unpaid, nonpersonal public notice in the print or electronic media . . . which may stimulate the sales of a product or service, or enhance the reputation of a person" (Ostrow & Smith, 1988, p. 198). The public relations department assists with publicity. That is, this department informs newspapers of special events, activities, and donations made by the company. Newspapers may or may not publish articles on the company. It is important, however, for the public relations department to try to spread as much positive publicity as possible.

- What methods should a public relations department use to garner positive publicity?
- Is it possible for a company to have negative publicity? Explain.

PROMOTION AND PUBLICITY

Promotion is "short-term non-recurrent efforts to increase buying response on the part of the consumers or to intensify sales efforts by the firm's sales force" (Ostrow & Smith, 1988, p. 216). Cosmetics companies frequently use promotional efforts to stimulate sales. A gift with purchase is designed to encourage new customers to try the products as well as encouraging loyal customers to add to their collection of perfumes, makeup brushes, and cosmetics.

A promotional theme may revolve around a holiday, new store opening, new product line, or an event at the retail operation. Regardless of the theme, the promotion typically offers consumers an incentive to purchase products in the store (as opposed to online). Internet sales will be discussed in Chapter Seven. Promotional sales (as opposed to Internet sales) should focus heavily on sales assistance. That is, sales associates should be trained to offer

ADVERTISING

Despite the extensive use of the Internet, print media continues to be popular with consumers. The Sunday paper remains the most read edition of the week in part because of the inserts and advertisements. Eighty-four percent of consumers read newspapers on Sunday, whereas eighty-seven percent of consumers read them daily (Newspaper Association of America, 2008). Other types of print media include billboards, postcards, flyers, and newsletters.

Newspaper Copy

Four guidelines exist when developing print media.

INCLUDE A HEADLINE

First, include a headline. A headline tells the consumers where to focus their attention and what to expect from a retailer (e.g., Dillard's 66-percent-off Labor Day Sale).

David Lauren, son of Ralph and Ricky Lauren, has strong views on the importance of marketing. Even in difficult economic times, David Lauren believes that companies must continue to market their fashions. This continual effort demonstrates to consumers that the company is fiscally strong.

BOX 4.1 Ralph Lauren's View on Advertising

Ralph Lauren—as in the company, not the person—is known globally for continually leading the fashion industry in evolving fashions, record consumer acceptance of product lines as demonstrated through sales and profits, and wildly successful marketing efforts. The avenues to market fashions are changing rapidly with the advent, acceptance, and adoption of new technology. The Internet, YouTube, Twitter, and social marketing sites are enormously popular among consumers and the fashion industry alike. David Lauren, Polo Ralph Lauren's senior vice president of advertising, marketing, and corporate communication (and, yes, Ralph and Ricky Lauren's son), emphasizes the importance of all forms of advertising. Lauren states that one form of promotion or advertising is not sufficient to successfully communicate a company's brand. During strong and weak economic times, companies should continue to advertise. According to Lauren:

> Print is more important than ever, because as people pull out, as people get scared, you have to look strong. People get behind a leader. They get behind something they feel is powerful and says something. And if you don't say anything, then you are obsolete. Our goal is to constantly have a strong message that reinvents itself and feels fresh. . . . [W]e show them hope and get them excited (Karimzadeh, 2008, p. 14).

BOX 4.2 Guidelines for Developing a Fashion Print Advertisement

- Include a heading.
- Focus on the benefits offered.
- Include original, witty, and accurate copy.
- Invite the target market into the store to purchase specific items.

FOCUS ON BENEFITS

Second, focus on the benefits offered by a retailer (e.g., Dillard's is open late and early on Labor Day). The majority of retailers offer mass-produced products. As such, competing retailers offer comparable, if not identical, products. Focusing on benefits will provide consumers incentives for shopping at your store as opposed to your competitors.

MAKE YOUR PRINT COPY ORIGINAL

Third, print copy should be original, witty, and accurate. Print media (which is expensive) are often wasted because the copy is boring. Worse, the information is wrong. Incorrect information can lead to long-term ill will on the part of the consumer.

CLOSE THE DEAL

Fourth and finally, all print media should close the deal by inviting the consumer into the store to purchase specific items (Quinn, 2007). Many times sales are not made because the consumer is not asked to purchase the product. The same is true with print media. The advertisement must specifically ask the consumer to come in and purchase the product.

The amount and frequency that consumers read newspapers is rapidly changing. Fashion marketers are well aware of the social impact newspapers have on the environment, economy, and consumers. Marketers must be fiscally responsible to their company; they must also act as good stewards to society. Companies have increasingly more sophisticated databases about their customers. Store credit cards and loyalty programs provide fashion marketers with the necessary information to send marketing information to customers electronically. An increasing number of fashion marketers are decreasing the amount of paper used on advertisements while electronic marketing efforts are increasing at a significant rate. Macy's believes its marketing efforts are better directed by using its customer mailing lists and electronic media (Macy's, 2009). The company is being more responsive to the values of the community and to the environment simultaneously.

Billboards

Billboard advertising is a marketing tool used in extremely high-traffic areas. Airports, sports venues, train stations, major streets (e.g., Times Square), and underground subway stations provide large open spaces for fashion marketers to promote merchandise. Similar to radio advertising, billboards provide marketers with widespread target distribution at a low cost (Williams, 2003). The average billboard is 12 by 24 feet and can cost between a few to several hundred dollars, plus the cost of printing, for 30-day advertising (Williams, 2003).

Billboards located within a city or town (as opposed to located on an interstate highway) are often placed in close proximity to an intersection. This location maximizes the reading exposure when drivers and pedestrians are stopped at the traffic light. New York City's Times Square, London's Tube, and the Metro in Paris all feature fashion products on billboards. Repeated exposure to the fashions and/or retailer as consumers travel daily through the tube, metro, or train to work act as a reminder to purchase a brand or patronize a store.

figure 4.6
Top: Galleries Lafayette is the largest department store in Paris, France. The billboard is more than five stores high. In addition to promoting fashions, the marketing piece guides tourists toward the fashionable department store.
Bottom: The store window in Paris, France, gives consumer testimonials regarding the fabulous fashions offered by the boutique.

figure 4.7
Consumers can see a lot of fashion ideas walking in Times Square. Billboards fill the sky. A frequent fashion marketing effort is by Calvin Klein Underwear. Where else but in the fashion capital of the United States can you see a five story man in his Calvins?

TABLE 4.2
Summary of Fashion Marketing Efforts

MARKETING CONCEPT	ATTRIBUTE
Public relations	• Designed to communicate with the company stakeholders • Operates from a different department than promotion or advertising
Promotion	• Designed to promote product and/or store awareness. Marketing efforts may include special events or activities.
Advertising	• Includes print, television, radio, in-store, and social marketing. • Most companies have some form of integrated marketing effort.

Although billboard advertising is shown to be highly accepted by consumers, to be effective the message must be very dissimilar than that provided by other mediums (e.g., television, radio, newspaper) (Cass, 2008). Consumers may view a billboard for anywhere from a few seconds while driving in a car to a few minutes while standing on a sidewalk. Their ability to comprehend part of the billboard's entire message depends on the effectiveness of the marketer's development of the advertising message.

Effective billboards are those that either teach consumers about a brand or encourage consumers to purchase a product or service immediately. Effective billboards have eight components:

1 Perhaps most importantly, the product being marketed must be clearly identifiable. Words should not be needed to tell the consumer what is being sold.
2 Because the billboard is being viewed from a distance, the copy should be brief.
3 The font should be legible. There are many different font types and sizes to select. This doesn't mean they are all legible from a distance. Nor are all font types and sizes congruent with the image of the product (Cass, 2008).
4 Visual-element considerations should include the amount of the billboard that the visual covers, color versus black-and-white images, and the number of images included in the advertisement. The decision to include a visual image isn't typically difficult when developing a billboard marketing effort. The difficult decision is obtaining the "right" visual image that will either promote the brand or sell the product. There are a lot of billboard images that are inferior (i.e., forgettable). Only a minority of billboard visual images are truly unforgettable (Figure 4.7).
5 Layout takes into consideration the visual placement of the product and the text. The layout has to flow visually, making the product and text cohesive.
6 When possible, the text should be creative, humorous, innovative, or memorable.
7 The billboard's background should be simple, thereby focusing on the product.
8 When marketing fashions on a billboard, keep it simple. A cluttered billboard may provide the consumer with a lot of information, but it doesn't mean the consumer can or will read it all. The most effective billboards have few words, a lot of white space, and visual images that clearly define the brand and/or product offerings (Cass, 2008).

Postcards

Postcards remain a popular method of fashion marketing. A **postcard** is typically a 4 ¼-by-6-inch card that allows full advertising on one side and partial advertising on the other side. Postcards can be printed in color or black-and-white, and on a shiny or matte finish. Because postcards are typically mailed in large quantities, they can be sent using a bulk rate.

There are multiple advantages for using postcards as part of a fashion marketing campaign. One benefit of a postcard is the quality of the paper. Unlike traditional paper, postcard paper stock is stiff. It can withstand mailing without being bent and damaged. The cost of mailing the postcard is also significantly lower than the cost of mailing a catalog. A postcard can also successfully take advantage of full-color advertising.

With increased methods for marketing fashions through the use of technology (e.g., e-mail, social-networking Web sites), an integrated use of fashion marketing efforts may be used with postcards, thereby saving marketing money. Prior to the aforementioned innovations in technology, a fashion marketer may have sent out two sets of postcards: one postcard was sent out as an early-bird announcement regarding the sale and then a follow-up postcard went out regarding the actual sale. This two-stage fashion marketing effort further helped the target market remember details about the sale.

Arden Korn, owner of Little Lambs & Ivy, a traditional children's specialty store offering high-quality merchandise, frequently sends out a postcard to announce a sale. She then sends out a reminder of the sale using e-mail. The postcard acts as a formal fashion marketing effort. The e-mail acts as a more personal fashion marketing effort. Regardless, Korn states that it is important to provide the target market with a reminder of the sale. Customers should never be expected to remember the dates or details of the sale.

Flyers

Flyers are not a widely used method of fashion marketing. Flyers use paper, text, and images to promote fashions. Because the fashion marketing message is printed on paper, the copy can easily be damaged by natural elements such as rain or wind. Flyers can be mailed in an envelope for the price of postage plus the cost of the envelope. The flyer can also be e-mailed as an attachment.

Flyers typically are not used by large fashion organizations. They can be very successful for small or independent fashion retailers and fashion marketers. Independent retailers have a particularly good understanding of their communities. The owners often live in the community and interact with other retailers. Likewise, they carefully analyze the fashion marketing efforts of their competition (Korn, 2009). This information can be used to develop and implement an effective flyer.

Similar to other fashion marketing efforts, only one theme, or message, should be included on the flyer. Multiple themes or messages will confuse the target market. For example, informing the target market with a flyer about a 15-percent-off sale on dresses uses only one theme. It is easy to remember.

Depending on the size of the community, flyers can be distributed in addition to being mailed to the target market. Concentrated locations are ideal areas for posting flyers. Needless to say, obtaining permission to post a flyer is essential. Posting a flyer without permission is unethical and not worth ruining the company's image.

Selecting the location for posting flyers depends on the fashions being marketed. From January through the first week of March, the dressmaker LaRoque in South Carolina is busy custom-making dresses for the Carolina Cup. Horse racing is very popular in the South. At the Carolina Cup, ladies and gentlemen dress to impress. LaRoque fashions ensure that no two ladies show up in the same dress.

Many students from the University of South Carolina attend the Carolina Cup. LaRoque flyers promoting the custom-made dresses adorn various locations of the campus and community. During other seasons, Annabelle LaRoque, owner of LaRoque, makes the flyers unique so that ladies will read the text. She "understands that there are many flyers and

Freddie Barnes, owner of Barnes Jewelers, carefully monitors the success of each marketing effort. Radio has proven to be the best method of marketing for this retailer of fine jewelry.

BOX 4.3 Radio Spot Success Story

Freddie Barnes has been in the fine jewelry business for more than 27 years. He and his wife, Janet, own and operate Barnes Jewelers in Lexington, South Carolina. Fine jewelry includes gold, platinum, diamonds, gemstones, and fine timepieces. Three attributes have made Barnes Jewelry successful: (1) their merchandise meets the needs of their target market, (2) the company offers excellent customer service, and (3) their marketing efforts—particularly their radio spots—are effective in increasing customer traffic. According to Freddie Barnes,

> The success of our radio advertisement is based on the copy and the reach. We have a playful marketing message focused toward the men. Our company understands that men are the purchasers of fine jewelry. As such, we focus the message toward the men, not the women who will ultimately be receiving the jewelry as a gift. The results of the advertisements include increased customer traffic and sales. It is an excellent method of promotion of this type of retailer.

Barnes Jewelers's advertisements are heard on sports talk stations and oldies music stations. The sports talk stations capture the younger male target market; the oldies music station attempts to capture the more mature male and female target market. Men typically purchase the more expensive fashion pieces; women typically purchase smaller items for gifts or as trinkets for themselves. Either way, radio has been a highly effective medium for reaching their target market (Barnes, 2009).

that the fashion marketing needs to get the customer's attention" (LaRoque, 2009).

Newsletters

The newsletter can be an important tool in the overall marketing of a company and brand. A newsletter should contain three attributes: (1) the company's name, (2) a consistent image, and (3) new information. Newsletters can be delivered in print or electronically and are typically published quarterly. Information about a company in a publication that comes out four times annually is less likely to be redundant (Bly, 1993).

Newsletters can be internal, external, or both. An **internal newsletter** is published solely for the company's employees. News about new brands, products, hires, and events may be included in this newsletter. An internal newsletter helps promote internal communication and a sense of commitment and loyalty.

An **external newsletter** is published for the benefit of stakeholders. An external newsletter is distributed to persons outside the company. Current customers, persons who shop but who have not yet purchased merchandise from the store, and stockholders are considered stakeholders.

ELECTRONIC MARKETING

Traditional electronic marketing includes radio, television, and Internet marketing.

Radio Advertising

Radio is a powerful form of marketing. Americans in excess of 228 million listen to the radio weekly. They listen in the car, at work, and at home. If they can't get a signal on the radio, they can often get access to the radio station through live streaming on the Internet. In short, Americans enjoy listening to the radio (Gordon, 2007).

Fashion marketers' use of radio advertising has changed as a result of the changing technology being adopted by consumers. Traditionally, radio advertising was considered a successful marketing tool because it offered a high reach with the ability to target specific audiences at a relatively low cost (Moriarty, Wells & Mitchell, 2008). **Reach** is "the number of readers or viewers who are exposed to a medium" (Ostrow & Smith, 1988, p. 204) (Table 4.3).

Radio advertisements can be adapted to the needs of the marketer. Spots are typically sold in 15-, 30-, and 60-second time slots. Needless to say, 15 seconds is not much time to get a message across effectively. Regardless of the radio spot, the advertisement is typically more about generating excitement about the company, brand, an event, or a specific product rather than increasing general sales. Effective radio advertisements result when consumers remember the slogan, jingle, or marketing message. These all need to be simple, specific, and identifiable with the fashion marketer's company. When consumers listen to the radio, they are probably doing other tasks

TABLE 4.3
Radio-Format Listening by Age

AGE GROUP	MUSIC FORMAT
Teens 12–17	Primarily Christian, Urban, Alternative
Adults 18–24	Christian, Alternative, Urban
Adults 25–34	Alternative, Rock, Christian, some Urban, Adult Contemporary
Adults 35–44	Rock, primarily Adult Contemporary
Adults 35–44	Oldies, Adult Contemporary
Adults 55–64	Classical, New Adult Contemporary
Adults 65+	Adult Standards, Classical, News Talk

(Katz Media Group, 2008)

TABLE 4.4

Questions to Ask Prior to Advertising on a Radio Station

QUESTION	REASON FOR THE QUESTION
What is the percentage of male versus female listeners?	The percentage of listeners of each gender should match or exceed your target market.
What is the average household income of your listener?	The average household income should mimic your target market.
Where does your average listener live? What city? What specific area within the city?	Geographic sizes of cities can vary (e.g., New York City vs. Manhattan, Kansas). As a marketer, you should know the population of the city that the radio reaches.
What is the range of your listening station?	The range of a listening audience may go into multiple cities. If a company has a Web site, sells online, or offers mail services, a marketer should clearly understand the geographic listening regions.
Does your station stream live on the Internet?	Stations that stream their programs live provide additional methods for listeners to hear the fashion marketing message.
Do you have any companies similar to mine that advertise on your radio?	If your competitor advertises with the radio station, try to find out the CPP of the advertisement. If the companies advertising offer products or services that are completely at odds with your own, determine if the listeners could be viable consumers of your product.
What is the cost of advertising?	The cost of advertising will influence the CPP.
Does the cost of advertising vary based on the time of day or specific programming, such as a sports event?	Always know the pricing options. This will assist you during the negotiation stage.
What is the CPP per hour from previous advertisers?	Use this information when determining which radio station to patronize.

and are unable to write down facts about the advertisement.

The choice of radio stations on which to advertise is largely dependent on the age and gender of the target market. Age is a strong predictor of the type of music a person prefers. For example, baby boomers and the elderly may prefer oldies and classical over hip-hop or rap. Men tend to listen to sports talk radio. If the majority of your fashion marketing efforts are targeted at men, then consider advertising on a sports talk radio station. For example, the target market for Barnes Jewelers (Box 4.3) is men and women. Men make the majority of high-end purchases. A fashion marketing radio advertisement was developed for the jewelry store specifically targeted for men. Barnes Jewelers advertises on a sports talk station to reach the male target market. To reach the female target market, the jewelry company advertises on an oldies station. The radio advertisements have brought in new customers as well as positive feedback from loyal customers.

Think about the average number of drivers in your town: 6,000, 30,000, 100,000, or more. The majority of drivers either listen to the radio or play CDs. Those drivers that listen to the radio will undoubtedly encounter commercials. A few of the fashion retailers known to advertise via the radio include Macy's, Belk, and Target.

Ask yourself:

- Can you remember a radio commercial from a fashion retailer? If so, what was the message?
- What do you perceive as the benefits of advertising via the radio in your community? Why?
- What do you perceive as the limitations of advertising via the radio in your community? Why?
- Which fashion products do you perceive as most successfully advertised via the radio in your community? Why?
- Which fashion products would probably have limited success if advertised via the radio in your community? Why?

Internet radio, radio stations that stream live through the Internet, are increasing in popularity (Ahmadi, 2009). Perhaps one of the most popular locations for listening to Internet radio is the workplace. Consumers access radio stations through their workstation PC or Mac computer. This provides them with up to eight hours of radio-listening time. It also provides fashion marketers with extended opportunities for reaching consumers during the workday hours.

The low cost of radio advertising—on average $100 per spot compared to $2,000 and higher per spot for Internet or television ads (Direct Radio, 2008)—makes this type of advertising an excellent medium for small fashion marketers. Small and independently owned businesses often act as their own fashion marketers, and they are able to develop affordable fashion marketing campaigns for Internet radio (Gordon, 2007).

The **targetability** of using the radio is also an important benefit for fashion marketers, regardless of their budget and company size. Targetability is defined as the ability to reach the right customer at the right time for the right cost (Moriarty, Wells & Mitchell, 2008). Successful fashion marketers continually examine the composition of their target market (refer to Chapter Five, "Fashion and the Entertainment Industry," for additional information on target markets). Target markets have similarities in their demographics and psychographics (i.e., hobbies, interests). Radio stations base their music selections on listeners' demographics and psychographics. Examples of types of radio stations include: easy listening, oldies, country, jazz, classical, hip-hop, sports, and news and commentary. A fashion marketer can easily identify the type of radio that matches its fashions by the music played (Moriarty, Wells & Mitchell, 2008).

Research on listeners reveals that different age groups both have specific interests and overlapping musical interests. Teens as well as adults aged 18–34 listen to urban music stations. Adults aged 35–44 are the primary listeners of oldies stations. The listener's gender, geographic location, and listening location are also considered when deciding to market through radio (Moriarty, Wells & Mitchell, 2008).

FOUR PRINCIPAL CONSIDERATIONS FOR RADIO MARKETING

Just because radio is less expensive than other forms of advertising doesn't mean fashion marketers shouldn't be equally careful of their strategy. Low-cost does not mean low care when developing a marketing plan. There are four principal considerations when marketing fashions through the radio. These include: (1) correctly targeting your audience, (2) selecting the correct radio advertising package, (3) sponsorships, and (4) entertainment.

1. Correctly Targeting Your Audience. With any marketing campaign, it is essential to strategically target your audience. This means that as a fashion marketer, you must understand your target market. You must also understand the target market of the radio station you are considering advertising on. Your target market may be in the same age category, but if it isn't in the same geographic region, the radio advertisement will not be effective. Likewise, the majority of the listeners should be the same gender as the consumers you are targeting (Gordon, 2007).

2. Selecting the Correct Radio Advertising Package. Fashion marketers advertising on the radio emphasize reach, frequency, and cost per thousand (CPT). **Frequency** is the "number of times an audience is exposed to a message." CPT is the "expense involved in reaching one thousand potential customers with a specific advertisement" (Ostrow & Smith, 1988, p. 62). The radio station will tell the fashion market the frequency—that is, the number of times listeners will hear the advertisement. The cost per point is a tool used to determine the financial effectiveness of the advertisement. As the cost per point decreases, the financial effectiveness of the advertisement increases. Needless to say, if a fashion marketer decides to utilize radio advertisements, it is financially prudent to have the message played multiple times. Otherwise, the cost per point will be high (Gordon, 2007).

3. Sponsorships. Fashion marketers promote a company, a brand, or a specific product. The promotion of a company or brand is by far more important than that of a specific product. Consumers will purchase a product once or perhaps twice, but they may become life-long patrons of a company or brand (refer to Chapter Nine, "Image and Branding," for information on branding).

Most radio stations are diverse. They typically offer music, traffic information, and sports. Each of these divisions offers the opportunity for sponsorship (Gordon, 2007). Sponsorships can be effectively tied in with a fashion marketer's products. For example, a swimsuit retailer sponsoring a sports report would generate a lot of interest by listeners.

4. Entertainment. To be effective, listeners must remember the purpose of the advertisement. The listener must understand what exactly to purchase and where to purchase it, as well as feel good about the company. Thoughts and emotions must occur in 30 seconds or less without the aid of visual stimuli. In short, radio demands that the advertising be entertaining. Facts and figures about new fashions aren't enough. Fashion marketers can't visually show listeners how the newest Wonderbra provides miracles by lifting and separating. Using sounds, words, and/or music, fashion marketers must creatively entertain the listeners, drawing them into their companies, their brands, and their products (Gordon, 2007).

Television Advertising

Television is believed to be the most effective marketing tool. It offers a wide geographic distribution as well as audio, visuals, and movement to demonstrate the marketing message (The lowdown on television, 2008). During 2008, $69.8 billion was spent on television

Men's Wearhouse has maintained a consistent marketing message throughout the years. Their success is based on knowing the target market and the product, and on implementing the marketing accordingly.

BOX 4.4 Men's Wearhouse

Men's Wearhouse, a nationwide men's clothier, offers stylish casual wear, suits, and tuxedos. The company's focus on quality clothing, quality individualized service, fit, and attention to detail has served it well. Its fashion marketing efforts, however, have brought the company to the attention of men and women who may have previously ignored the retailer. In nationwide and cable advertising, a baritone voice emanates from the television. The spokesman for the company discusses the products. He looks directly into the camera and states, "You're gonna like the way you look. I guarantee it." His demeanor is assured, confident but not arrogant, and believable. The marketing efforts on the company's Web site take a different approach. A variety of styles, products, and brands are listed. The information also reminds the consumer of the company's commitment to offering value and top-quality customer service and to helping people become self-actualized. In a time of high nationwide unemployment, the Web site features tips for interviewing, including appropriate clothing options. The choices are placed in bullet points for easy reading. That is, Men's Wearhouse's marketing efforts are multidimensional in nature. Some efforts focus on the garments while others educate consumers (Men's Wearhouse, 2009).

advertising. This accounts for 25 percent of the $284.8 billion in total advertising sales (Kean, 2008).

There are two distinct purposes of marketing when using television. You may think that the number-one purpose is to make money. You would be incorrect. Of course, the majority of marketing efforts are to generate sales and profits. Let us not forget, sales are not the same as profits. **Sales** are the amount of money generated from goods or services sold. **Profits** are the amount of money available after the cost of goods and services sold. The emphasis is on the word *cost*. How much did it *cost* us to sell the merchandise? We need to include factors such as sales associates, marketing personnel, and overhead in order to determine the profit.

Television is used to market a company's brand or image, or to promote an immediate response from the viewer (Keane, 2008). Brand advertising is used for long-term marketing effectiveness. The marketing messages are designed to instill loyal customer attitudes toward the brand as opposed to toward a particular style. The advertising and its messages are typically heartfelt, combined with music, and easily recognizable (Keane, 2008).

Television advertising that uses an **immediate-response marketing message** is designed to encourage viewers to purchase the product immediately (Keane, 2008).

Infomercials use this type of marketing message (Hetsroni & Asya, 2002). The message is designed to stimulate sales of the product. Immediate-response marketing does not necessarily emphasize the product's brand. The primary goal is to sell a predetermined quantity of the merchandise.

The audio, visual, and reach capabilities of television make it an extremely beneficial tool for fashion marketing efforts. Fashions, accessories, beauty, and home furnishings can be featured in a natural setting. Multiple products can be featured together, thereby encouraging the purchase of complete outfits. Macy's, Sears, Target, and J. C. Penney are examples of companies that use television to successfully market their fashions.

Recent technological advances in television make advertising through television challenging. **TiVo** has become a popular technology adopted by TV viewers. TiVo allows TV viewers to record a television show and watch it at a later date. The viewer is then able to skip the commercials. The digital video recorder (DVR) is a similar form of technology. The manufacturer is different; the outcome is the same: television viewers are able to avoid commercials (Jaffe, 2005).

AUDIO VS. VIDEO

Television provides fashion marketers with audio and visual communication to promote their merchandise. It is important to know, however, which is more important in order to successfully market specific fashion products. Fashion consumers are really after the final look of the garment and accessories. This may mean that the video portion of the television commercial is the most important aspect of the marketing effort. However, fashion-oriented consumers are also attuned to music, fashion instructions, runway show dialogue, and entertainment. Some consumers may perceive the audio portion of the advertisement as the most important part of the television advertisement.

In actuality, both audio and video are equally important components of any fashion marketing effort (Duncan, 2008). An effective television advertisement is one in which the viewer can completely understand the concept when the audio or video is turned off. That is, if the sound of the television is turned off and the viewer continues to watch, enjoy, and participate in the commercial (i.e., want to purchase the product advertised), the commercial is successful. Likewise, a television marketing effort is successful when a viewer is in another room (i.e., not seeing the video) and still understands and is interested in the advertisement (Duncan, 2008).

As a professional in the fashion marketing industry, what actions would you take to effectively promote your fashions given the following facts?

- Much of the marketing mix is being conducted using technology. When would flyers be effective in promoting fashion products? When would flyers not be effective? Explain.
- Many consumers skip commercials by using technology (e.g., TiVo). Does this mean that fashion marketers should avoid television altogether? If not, what percentage of the marketing effort should be allocated to television?

Internet Advertising

Fashion marketers promote their merchandise wherever they can reach a viewing audience. In December 2008, 413,183,671 people throughout the Americas accessed the Internet (Internet World Stats, 2009). With significant numbers of consumers accessing Web sites, the Internet has become an important marketing medium for fashion merchandisers. Some marketers are replacing their use of radio and print advertising with Internet advertising. This is based on declining newspaper sales and increasing satellite subscriptions that are void of commercials (Holahan, 2006).

Internet advertising is beneficial to fashion marketers in a wide bracket of target markets. Young girls, tweens, teens, and adults use the Internet for e-mail, research, and specifically to find products and services (e.g., via Google or Yahoo!). The consumer/computer user views fashion advertisements that are in color, are interactive, have sound, and may prompt immediate purchase through a series of questions. As the consumer clicks onto the fashion-advertising icon, the marketer is able to measure the number of consumers accessing the site. Some advertisements also prompt consumers to enroll in a store membership. This electronic membership results in the store sending promotional information via e-mail. The fashion marketer is able to automatically send personalized promotions to the consumer electronically. The cost of electronic promotions includes a Webmaster and a person/persons to continually update the database. The cost of sending out the e-mails however, is far less expensive than print or radio advertising (Holahan, 2007).

Consumer confidence regarding spending through the Internet continues to grow. During the 1990s, consumers were concerned about purchasing products over the Internet. Their primary concern was Internet fraud and having their credit card number stolen. Fashion marketers needed to find methods of making it safe for consumers to purchase their products via the Internet. By the early twenty-first century, consumer confidence in purchasing online has grown significantly. The amount of online sales worldwide is estimated to be between seven and ten percent (Urwin, 2008). It is estimated that by 2011, consumers will spend more than $73 billion on products purchased via the Internet (Smith, 2007).

SOCIAL MARKETING

Social marketing is a relatively new form of marketing. The various social marketing media allow consumers to interact with the company. Consumers provide feedback about products, marketing efforts, and the company in general. Social marketing allows consumers to feel more connected to the company.

Mobile Advertising

Mobile advertising is among the newest forms of marketing products. Mobile advertising is accomplished by advertising through a personal digital assistant (PDA), Blackberry, or other handheld wireless device. Mobile advertising may consist solely of text; a combination of text and visuals; or a combination of text, visuals, and sound. The level of sophistication of a mobile advertisement depends on the fashion marketer's campaign. Regardless of the level of sophistication, messages regarding the newest fashions, special offers, and brands offered can be sent any time of day or night. Unlike print, radio, catalog, and Internet advertising, a greater percentage of consumers is more likely to read mobile advertisements, simply because they have continual access to their mobile devices (Smith, 2007).

Mobile advertising is minor in comparison to advertising done on the Internet. The amount of money spent on mobile advertising worldwide in 2006 was $871 million; Internet advertising in the same year amounted to $24 billion. Approximately $416 million was spent on mobile advertising worldwide; this figure is expected to climb to $1.5 billion by 2013

(Guynn & Sarno, 2010). Despite this relatively small amount, mobile advertising is effective and is expected to increase in adoption by marketers.

Mobile advertising is more expensive (up to ten times more) to implement than Internet advertising. Mobile carriers are able to charge higher prices because of the services they provide. It would be a mistake to confuse mobile advertising with Internet advertising. Unlike Internet advertising, which is geared to the general public, mobile advertising is more specific and personal. Mobile advertising enables the fashion marketer to personalize messages specifically to the mobile user. In addition, mobile users typically take their device with them everywhere—24/7. This constant connection with the mobile device, paired with the ability to personalize messages, enhances the fashion marketer's effectiveness in communicating with the audience. During 2006, marketers spent $1.5 billion in mobile advertising. Forecasters predict that by 2011, the frequency and amount of mobile marketing efforts will increase to $14.1 billion in mobile advertising dollars (Smith, 2007).

A fashion marketer's advertising budget depends in part on the company's financial well-being. When a company's profits decrease, so does its ability to spend money on marketing efforts. During 2008, fashion marketers nationwide struggled as consumers rejected products. Consumers were worried about job security; many were laid off from their jobs. As the national economy grew increasingly unstable, consumer spending patterns changed dramatically. As a result, fashion marketers' advertising budgets decreased significantly.

Consumers aged 18–24 are known to be extremely active mobile users. This age group is believed to be an excellent market to target using mobile advertising. This form of advertising is twice as effective among this age group as younger consumers (Perez, 2008). Neiman Marcus, Bloomingdale's, Nordstrom, Tommy Bahama, Belk, Ralph Lauren, Just My Size, Aerosoles, and Hancock Fabrics are examples of companies using mobile marketing to reach their target market. The fashion marketers send e-mail messages to consumers. Full-color marketing campaigns are attached to the e-mail.

Large and small fashion retailers alike use mobile advertising. Nordstrom sends its customers text messages regarding "what's hot" and "what's new." The fashion marketing tool keeps customers up-to-date on Nordstrom's fashions, builds store traffic, and generates loyalty to brands. HandPicked sends out e-mail messages twice monthly. This type of e-mail communication has been effective with its target market (Hiter, 2009).

Little Lambs & Ivy sends out mobile-marketing messages prior to its print promotions. The duplication of marketing efforts reinforces the message and company name (Korn, 2009).

Mobile advertising provides fashion retailers with immediate access to its consumers. Short messages provide consumers with reminders of the retailer, brands, logo, or upcoming sales.

Ask yourself:

- Which characteristics comprise the most successful mobile advertising?
- Are there specific fashion products and/or services that should not be marketed through mobile advertising? Why or why not?
- Does mobile marketing replace the need for other forms of advertising (e.g., print)? Why or why not?

Facebook

Facebook is an international social marketing technique originally adopted by teens to get to know one another. Using the Internet, Facebook provides a venue for sharing photos, information, news, and sales; it allows marketers to have an interactive Web presence with

figure 4.8 Consumers are very connected to their mobile devices. With this connection, fashion marketers are sending communications to consumers regarding "what's hot," the latest trends, and upcoming sales.

their existing clientele, as well as to encourage prospective customers to try their products. Consumers are encouraged to become "fans," post messages, and encourage their friends to become a friend of the fashion site. Nordstrom, Versace Couture, Chanel, and Saks Fifth Avenue use Facebook as a fashion marketing tool. It is an inexpensive, targeted, and highly effective method for reaching their primary target market.

Annabelle LaRoque's private brand, LaRoque, has become extremely successful since its inception in 2005. In 2008, more than 1,000 custom-made designs were sold. What is so amazing about this figure is that the LaRoque brand is marketed solely by flyers, Facebook, and word of mouth. LaRoque says that Facebook has become the best marketing effort for her fashion house. Every design is featured on Facebook. The company receives at least five new orders through this medium every week. LaRoque and her customers e-mail each other, talk about fashions, and discuss new fabrics, styles, and designs—all through Facebook. Customers tell her when they are on their way to her store. Facebook "is amazing for my business," she says. "I change my profile picture every day. My picture is always one of my garments. I always tell people what I am doing at the store. Facebook provides a social relationship with my customers."

One of LaRoque's Facebook marketing efforts is the Rainy Day Sale. Any day it rains, the store has a 15-percent-off sale. Customers will log on to Facebook and e-mail Annabelle; they give her the weather forecast and a reminder that they will be in the store the next day. This marketing promotion instills loyal customer behavior and encourages the target market to continually look on Facebook for new ideas and additional contact with the owner, thereby instilling a sense of friendship.

Fashion marketers must always evaluate the success rate of any advertising strategy. As advertising dollars decrease, it is even more important to verify that every advertising strategy reaches its intended audience and that they retain the information. **Retention** is "a form of competitive advertising calculated to keep a product, service, industry, or viewpoint in the public eye" (Ostrow & Smith, 1988, p. 207). Research on mobile advertising reveals that 40 percent of viewers recall mobile advertising. This recall level is very important in product advertising and encouraging purchase behavior (Ankeny, 2008).

YouTube

YouTube is a social marketing medium whereby videos, television commercials, and

TABLE 4.5

Facebook Marketing Efforts Based on Active Use in February 2009

COMPANY	PURPOSE	MONTHLY ACTIVE USERS AND/OR FANS
Anna Sui	Fashions	11,655
Burberry	Fashions	415,181
Burberry Gifts	Send Burberry Gifts	34,289
Chanel	Fashions	262,551
Donna Karan	Fashions	1,516
Hugo Boss	Fashions	114,365
Marc Jacobs	Fashions	115,082
Nordstrom	Fashions	284
Oscar de la Renta	Fashions	8,083
Saks Fifth Avenue	Fashions	1,643
Versace Couture	Fashions	74,110

photos are posted on the Internet. Average YouTube viewers are 44 percent female and 56 percent male, between the ages of 12 to 17. The popularity of YouTube is widespread. Each month, more than 2.5 billion videos are watched (Woog, 2009). Its viewing frequency makes YouTube an excellent tool for the fashion marketing industry, and yet, despite the enormous number of consumers looking on YouTube on a daily basis, it would be a mistake to use this tool as your primary fashion marketing effort. An *integrated* fashion marketing effort remains vital to promote merchandise. Integrated efforts include a variety of marketing efforts that repeatedly demonstrate the fashion's benefits to consumers.

YouTube began as a social marketing tool among the younger target market. This marketing media is now used by a wide range of fashion companies. Companies are able to reach their stakeholders by posting television advertisements and fashion shows. Designers use YouTube to continually build brand loyalty, market awareness, and product knowledge.

Access the Internet and go to http://www.youtube.com. Select a fashion designer of your choice (e.g., Chanel, Versace, Dolce & Gabbana).

- Describe the specific type of message the company includes on YouTube (e.g., advertising, fashion show).
- What messages are conveyed on YouTube (e.g., product, brand, geographic location)?
- Assess the effectiveness of the company's use of YouTube. Explain.

Infomercials

Americans watch an average of four hours of television per day (Herr, 2007). Their obsession with television makes infomercials a very tempting method of advertising. An **infomercial** is a 30- to 60-minute programmed commercial. The commercial can be live or taped. During the entire time of the infomercial, the host discusses the price, attributes, benefits, and success stories associated with the product (Hetsroni & Asya, 2002).

Have you ever wondered why marketers use infomercials? Who would watch infomercials? More importantly, with all the various methods of purchasing products, who would sit through an infomercial and actually purchase products through infomercials?

A lot of consumers actually do purchase merchandise through infomercials. Direct sales in excess of $1.7 billion are attributed to infomercials (Malonis, Gale Group, & Malonis, 1999).There are many variables to take into consideration with this form of marketing. First, infomercials often use inexpensive sets and props. While the cost may be low to a marketing budget, the overall viewing impression may also be less than impressive. Second, infomercials are aired during non-primetime television spots. As such, the marketing costs for disseminating the information are lower than that of a traditional television advertisement. Third, the number of cable stations continues to increase. As this number increases, the opportunity to market fashions to a more expansive target audience increases exponentially. Fourth and finally, once taped, the infomercial can be showed indefinitely as long as the content is relevant and the marketing message improves sales. The taped infomercial may have a long shelf life with careful planning of the actor's wardrobe and dialogue.

Infomercials are perhaps one of the earliest forms of social marketing. Infomercials initially became popular because of three reasons: (a) the celebrity promoting the product was friendly, personable, approachable, and well-known; (b) the product was reliable; and (c) the infomercial brought the promoter, typically a celebrity, into the home. For example, George Foreman was a giant in the boxing industry. On television, he came across as a wonderful man with a terrific smile. Men could admire him for his boxing prowess. Women could relate to his approachability. George Foreman is the reason the "George Foreman grill" continues to sell millions nationwide. Once consumers purchased the George Foreman grill, the product worked. Positive word-of-mouth promotion further helped sell the product.

Infomercials continue to be popular because of consumers' connection with television. Whether they actively watch the show or simply listen to the show while working around the house, consumers watch and purchase merchandise through infomercials. They build a loyal connection with the celebrity promoters and brands.

MARKETING REQUIREMENTS FOR INFOMERCIALS

A marketer's first goal is to grab the viewer's attention. Some viewers purposefully seek out infomercials for products that interest them; others simply happen upon them. The television remote control can be both the marketer's worst enemy and best friend. When randomly switching from one channel to another, the viewer may land on an infomercial, and if it's interesting, the viewer is hooked. Of course with another rapid click of the button, the station can be changed and the viewer is no longer watching the infomercial. Therefore, the infomercial's second goal is to be entertaining, attention-grabbing, exciting, and enticing for the consumer to watch, so that he or she waits for the next important piece of information (Brown, 2007). Always remember, no matter how funny, memorable, or outrageous the marketing effort, the outcome is not successful unless consumers purchase the product. As such, the infomercial is only successful if the second goal is achieved. The first one works toward reaching the second.

METHODS FOR ACHIEVING INFOMERCIAL MARKETING GOALS

Consumers respond positively to **testimonials**. A testimonial is a statement from a consumer regarding the qualities, benefits, and attributes of using the product and/or service. Testimonials provide the viewer with a perception of the possibilities of what the product and/or service can do for the consumer.

Testimonials are designed to bring honesty, ethics, security, and other consumers into the home of prospective consumers. Testimonials are scripted and delivered by consumers who have used the product and service. The topic of the testimonial may range from the quality of the customer service on the Internet, the consumer's satisfaction with the products and/or delivery, or the money-back guarantee (Hill, 2007). Because the testimonial is from a consumer, the information lends greater credibility than if the words were from a company executive.

Celebrities are often used to stimulate sales of infomercials. The celebrities often give a testimonial or interview audience members regarding their personal use of the product (Brown, 2007). Celebrities add glamour, prestige, and validity to the use of the product. Football great Dan Marino helped promote Nutrisystem. Singer and actor Jessica Simpson gave testimonials for Proactiv (Brown, 2007).

Throughout an infomercial, viewers are shown multiple demonstrations and applications of a product. The viewer may also see the product compared to that of other brands. The comparison is made to demonstrate the superior attributes of the brand being featured; particularly if the brand name is not well known. The results of the product's comparison are designed to give the viewer a feeling of security and a feeling of desire for the brand (Hetsroni & Asya, 2002).

The pricing strategy of the infomercial's products is very important. Regardless of the ultimate cost to the consumer, the perceived cost must seem like a very good value. **Ultimate cost** is the total amount the consumer pays for the item. The **perceived cost** is the amount the consumer perceives that he or she pays for the product. Items featured on an infomercial that are priced above $50 are often sold in a monthly payment plan. For example, a viewer is offered a product for two payments of $29.99; the perceived cost is much lower than the ultimate cost of one payment of $60.00. The perceived cost is more favorable because the viewer can spread the payments across two months (Brown, 2007). In order to enhance the perceived cost, the pricing is stated as being offered only to those viewers of the infomercial (Hetsroni & Asya, 2002). The implication is that purchasing the product at a retail store would result in paying a higher price. Infomercials' marketing efforts also encourage the viewer to act immediately. Throughout the infomercial, the announcer will encourage the viewer to *Call now!* These words will be repeated over and over again. Repetition is the basis for encouraging the viewer to purchase the product immediately. This encouragement is unlike any other form of marketing effort (Brown, 2007).

Finally, some infomercials have a method of **continuity of patronage**. Continuity of patronage exists when the product is disposable, and the consumer is automatically replenished with a new product on a monthly basis. The consumer is automatically billed via a credit or debit card. Continuity of patronage promotes automatic monthly sales and continued consumer loyalty (Brown, 2007). Examples of products that are disposable include makeup, skin-care products, and health-care products.

Blogs

Blogs have become a popular method of communicating with others, both nationally and internationally. Using the Internet as a medium, a blog is a column written about a subject matter. The subject can be anything. More than 80 million active blogs are posted on the Internet worldwide. Successful blogs—meaning blogs that people read, respond to, and learn from—are those that have the reader in mind. A blog is an excellent tool when the goal is to communicate with a regional, national, or international audience. Successful bloggers remember that the information posted is rarely, if at all, about the writer. The important information posted on the blog should positively impact the reader (Godin, 2009).

Marketing companies can successfully use blogs to build and maintain a connection with their target market. Through daily, weekly, and monthly blogs, the target market can immediately feel a sense of loyalty to the company. Discussions through the blog provide insight into the company's actions and decisions (Flynn, 2006).

Blogs are interactive. This means that while the company blogs about their activities, consumers can post any type of information on the blog. Company oversight of the blog is essential. Regardless of who posts information on the blog, the company is responsible for the oversight and upkeep of its Web site.

BOX 4.5 Questions to Answer Before Starting a Company Blog

1 Which division within the company is responsible for the blog?
2 Who will have primary responsibility for the blog?
3 What is the main objective of having a company blog?
4 What are the policies regarding information being posted on the blog?
5 Are the policies in writing and distributed to employees?
6 Who will educate employees on posting messages to the blog?
7 Do the blog policies ensure that confidential company information is maintained (i.e.., not posted on the blog)?
8 Does the company have a method of allowing its target market to contribute to the blog?
9 Does the blog provide the company's target market with guidelines for posting information?
10 How will the company monitor daily customer additions to the blog?

(Flynn, 2006)

Information that is contrary to the company's image should be avoided (Flynn, 2006; Godin, 2009).

Blogs are becoming increasingly popular in the fashion industry. They act as another aspect of fashion marketing efforts. Companies also use blogs as a medium for company newsletters. This social marketing tool allows consumers to interact with the fashion marketer. Consumers are able to feel part of the company, fashion team, and fashion industry. Fashion questions can be asked and answered. Information regarding the newest products and upcoming sales and promotions can be provided to the consumers. This one-on-one communication inspires a sense of loyalty with both brand and company (Box 4.5).

The Little Lambs & Ivy blog was developed primarily as a newsletter. New products, brands carried, and promotional events are discussed on the blog. The inexpensive method of promoting the store's fashions also allows the store's owner to keep in touch with the loyal customer base in Tennessee, where the store's first location was opened. Fellow bloggers help to measure the effectiveness of the fashion marketing efforts in general and the blog in particular (Korn, 2009).

PERSONAL MARKETING

Personal marketing is the best opportunity to feature the products marketed by the fashion marketer. Consumers are more likely to purchase an item once they have held the item. It is far more difficult to turn away from a purchase after you see yourself wearing it, using it, or, better yet, experiencing the sensation of using the item at an event.

Can you honestly say that you have never —and I mean absolutely never—made an unplanned fashion purchase?

In the fashion marketing industry, the retailer must never be ignored, discounted, or forgotten. Successful fashion marketing efforts through print, television, radio, the Internet, and so forth may encourage consumers to purchase products through any one of the four channels of distribution: catalogs, Internet, phone, and in-store purchases. However, when consumers elect to shop at the traditional brick-and-mortar store, retailers' fashion marketing outcomes may still influence the consumer's final purchase decisions.

In-Store Signage

Fashion marketing efforts of retailers include visual merchandising, store signage, window displays, and the presentation of fashions on the selling floor. As fashion marketers plan their strategy for each campaign, it is important to think about the retailers.

figure 4.9
In-store signage continues to be an important fashion marketing tool. Signage drives consumer traffic throughout the store, informs consumers, and stimulates multiple product purchases.

Questions to consider include:

- What type of signage used in the store is similar to the fashion marketing efforts used in magazines?
- Will different geographic locations feature different marketing efforts based on the demographic and psychographic composition of the target market?

Special Events

Fashions can successfully be marketed through the use of special events. Perhaps the most popular event used in the fashion industry is a fashion show. Fashion shows highlight merchandise and accessories for the upcoming season and teach consumers methods for mixing and matching merchandise. Some fashion shows provide attendees with a discount on all merchandise purchased directly after the show. This form of marketing effort stimulates immediate sales, while consumers remember the fashions and are still excited about the day's event.

Special events that occur throughout the year are particularly timely and appropriate for fashion marketing efforts. Consumers have historically made larger purchases on fashions during holiday seasons (e.g., Thanksgiving, Christmas, Easter). It is during various holiday seasons that fashion marketers "pull out all the stops" at offering consumers special events. Macy's Thanksgiving Day Parade has a worldwide television-viewing audience. Throughout the entire parade, Macy's logo and front door are clearly displayed. Thousand of New Yorkers line up along the streets for a view of the parade. The day after Thanksgiving marks the beginning of the presence of Santa in most retail stores. Parents bring their children into malls and stores to visit Santa. While in the store, fashion marketers have prearranged different venues for consumers to experience "the magic of the season." Valentine's Day, Easter, St. Patrick's Day, Independence Day, Halloween, and indeed any local holiday can be integrated into fashion marketing efforts.

figure 4.10
The Macy's Thanksgiving Day parade is watched by millions nationwide. This event provides Macy's with a unique opportunity for branding, reinforcing its logo, and spreading an image of goodwill.

Integrated Marketing Efforts

The majority of fashion marketing efforts are integrated. Integrated fashion marketing efforts occur when two or more forms of marketing media are used during a campaign. Integrated fashion marketing efforts tend to be more successful than one-dimensional marketing campaigns. Although the demographics and psychographics of a target market are similar, not all consumers may be attainable by the same marketing methods. In addition, many consumers may require repeated and additional stimuli in order to be encouraged to purchase fashions based on a specific marketing campaign. Stimuli frequently used in fashion marketing include price savings, a wide selection of colors offered, delivery options (if sold through the mail or Internet), fashion statements the products make, and a limited time during which the offer is available.

Think about the number of friends you may have who have said, *I am an impulse shopper*. **Impulse shopping**, or shopping without forethought, may be good for fashion marketers, as long as the consumer is purchasing the products featured in the marketing campaign. However, it is far better for the fashion marketing campaign to stimulate consumers to purposely purchase the featured products. It is better yet if they purchase the products and tell their friends and relatives about the fabulous fashions, encouraging them to also purchase the featured products. Companies that use integrated fashion marketing efforts include Macy's, Nordstrom, Bloomingdale's, Saks Fifth Avenue, Ferragamo, Sears, J. C. Penney, Kohl's, Payless, and bebe.

REVIEWING MARKETING EFFORTS

Consumers can be overstimulated by information. They surf the Internet while watching television, read fashion magazines while riding the bus or train to work, and look at billboards as they speed along the highway. Fashion marketers compete for the consumer's attention. Marketers must constantly evaluate the success

figure 4.11
If it's free, it's for me! Marketing efforts that offer a free item with purchase are very popular and successful in the fashion and accessory industry. The free item typically has the brand name and/or logo displayed. Each time the consumer uses the free gift, she will remember that she didn't pay for the item.

of their marketing efforts. If the marketing plan is not resulting in the desired sales goals, the company must identify (a) where the plan fell short, (b) what changes need to be made, and (c) how fast changes to the fashion marketing plan can successfully be implemented (Rao, 2007).

Fashion marketers are all too aware of the 4 *P*s (price, place, product, and promotion). The majority follow the rules to the best of their abilities. Some marketers are better than others at this. There are ways to entice consumers to pay attention to your fashion marketing program *and* purchase products from one or more of your channels.

The saying, *If it's free, it's for me,* is true for most consumers. Free samples are proven traffic generators for in-store and Internet retailers. Free samples encourage consumers to pick products up, look at other products, view the company as generous, and generally get the consumers in a shopping frame of mind (Hill, 2007).

Similar to offering a free sample, offering a "bonus with purchase" is a successful marketing tactic. Offering a bonus with a purchase is a financially wise strategy because consumers are typically required to purchase a product in excess of $25. This purchase is designed to encourage the first-time buyer to try the brand or encourage repeat purchasers to make a purchase (Hill, 2007).

Money-back guarantees are used on expensive items or products marketed through the Internet and television. The retailer typically places the guarantee on products that have a high markup. The guarantee provides the consumer with a feeling of security (i.e., *If I don't like the product, I can return it without losing any money*) (Hill, 2007).

Finally, consumers should be surveyed. Ask consumers what they liked, disliked, what they want from a retailer, and what is important. Consumers place a high value on being asked their opinion. More importantly, however, act upon the results of the survey (Hill, 2007). If the results of your consumer survey reveal that your company should improve your online marketing efforts, changes should be made.

SUMMARY

The success of a marketing effort often means the difference between an average year and an excellent year for a fashion company. Each campaign must be thought of individually based on the marketing team's goals and objectives. Some marketing efforts are designed to give back to the community. The majority of marketing efforts are designed to sell a product or service. Regardless of how many industry awards a commercial wins or the number of consumers who enjoy watching a commercial, if the marketing effort doesn't stimulate sales, the marketing campaign was not effective.

Print marketing efforts continue to be widely used in the fashion industry. Regional fashion marketers may use radio and the Internet to reach the target market. Social marketing is becoming an increasingly more popular and effective method of interacting with the target market. Facebook, mobile marketing, and YouTube provide marketers with the opportunity to obtain daily responses from marketing efforts.

REFERENCES

Ahmadi, S. (2009, June). An overview of next-generation mobile WiMAX technology, *IEEE Communications*, 47(6), 84–98.

Ankeny, J. (2008, November 7). Mobile advertising answers questions about its future. *Fierce Mobile Content*. Retrieved December 23, 2008 from http://fiercemobilecontent.com/story.

Bly, R. W. (1993). *Targeted public relations*. New York: Henry Holt.

Brown, A. (2007, November 1). 7 Marketing lessons we can learn from TV infomercials. Retrieved December 22, 2008 from www.articlealley.com/article_234494_12.html.

Cass, J. (2008, December 10). *The design process of creating a creative billboard campaign*. Retrieved December 23, 2008 from http://justcreativedesign.com/2008.

Duncan, A. (2008). Television advertising: Sights, sounds & sales. *Strategic Media*. Retrieved December 22, 2008 from www.strategicmediainc.com/radio-advertising.php.

Flynn, N. (2006). *Blog rules*. New York: AMACOM.

Godin, S. (2008). *Meatball sundae: Is your marketing out of sync?* New York: Penguin.

Gordon, A. (2008). Marketing your products through TV. *Ezine Articles*. Retrieved December 23, 2008 from http://ezinearticles.com/?Marketing-Your-Products-Through-TV.

Gordon, K. T. (2007, April 13). 4 keys to radio advertising. *Entrepreneur.com*. Retrieved December 23, 2008 from http://www.entrepreneur.com/article.

Guynn, Jessica and David Sarno (2010, April 9). Apple leaps into mobil ad market: Racing with Google, the firm aims to reach users of its popular portable devices. *Los Angeles Times*, p. B1.

Herr, N. (2007). Television & health. Retrieved February 17, 2009 from www.csun/science/health/docs.

Hetsroni, A. & Asya, I. (2002). A comparison of values in infomercials and commercials. *Corporate Communications: An International Journal*, 7(1), 34–45.

Hill, K. (2007). 10 high powered ways to magnify your profits. Retrieved August 28, 2007 from *www.emailmarketing.inc*.

Holahan, C. (2006, December 7). Advertising goes off the radio. *Business Week*. Retrieved December 23, 2008 from http://www.businessweek.com/technology/content/dec2006.

Infomercials (2008). *Encyclopedia of business*. Retrieved December 22, 2008 from www.enotes.com/biz-encyclopedia/infomercials.

Internet World Stats (2009) Internet penetration rate in the Americas. Retrieved March 23, 2009 from www.internetworldstats.com/stats2.htm.

Jaffe, J. (2005). *Life after the 30-second spot*. Hoboken, NJ: John Wiley and Sons.

Karimzadeh, M. (2008, December 9). WWD Media Summit: Follow the leader. *Women's Wear Daily*, p. 14.

Katz Media Group (2010). Focus on Radio Seminar: Understanding Radio Formats. Retrieved April 22, 2010 from www.katz-media.com/uploadedfiles/OUR.../KRG/.../FORMATS.ppt.

Keane, M. (2008, November 18). Television advertising to shrink 4.6 percent in 2009. *Wired Blog Network*. Retrieved December 22, 2008 from http:blog.wried.com/business/2008/11/television-adve.html.

Korn, Arden (2009, March 3). Personal interview with owner of Little Lambs and Ivy.

LaRoque, Annabelle (2009, March 15). Personal interview with owner of LaRoque.

Malonis, J.A., Gale Group, and Malonis, J. (1999). *The encyclopedia of business.* Florence, KY: Cengage Gale.

Men's Wearhouse Company Web site (2010). Retrieved April 21, 2010 from http://www.menswearhouse.com/webapp/wcs/stores/servlet/Menswear_-1_10601_10051_10051_10051_Menswear.html.

Moriarty, S., Wells, W. D., & Mitchell, N. (2008). *Advertising: Principles & practice.* Upper Saddle River, NJ: Prentice Hall.

Newspaper Association of America (2008). 2008 NAA Readership Reports. Retrieved November 30, 2009 from http://www.naa.org/trendsandnumbers/leadership.aspx.

Nunes, P. & Johnson, B. (2004). *Mass affluence: Seven new rules of marketing to today's consumer.* Boston: Harvard Business School Press.

Ostrow, R., & Smith, S. R. (1988). *The Dictionary of Marketing.* New York, NY: Fairchild Publishers.

Perez, S. (2008, June 27). Mobile advertising has potential. *Read Write Web.* Retrieved December 22, 2008 from www.readwriteweb.com/ archives/mobile_advertising_has_potential.

Quinn, P. (2007). Some copy tips from an old hand. *Emailmarketing.inc.* Retrieved August 28, 2007 from http://www.emailmarketing.inc.

Rao, V. P. (2007). Why insight and flexibility is more important than perseverance in marketing. *Emailmarketing-inc.* Retrieved August 28, 2007 from http://www.emailmarketing.inc.

Smith, B. (2007, August 15). Mobile advertising reaches for the sky. *Wireless Week.* Retrieved December 22, 2008. www.wirelessweek.com/Mobile-Advertising.aspx.

The lowdown on television advertising. (2008). *Businesstown.com.* Retrieved December 22, 2008 from http://www.businesstown.com/advertising/television.asp.

Williams, R. H. (2003, August 4). Outdoor ads that get results. *Entreprenuer.com.* Retrieved December 22, 2008 from http://wwwentrepreneur.com/article.

Woog, A. (2009). *YouTube.* Chicago: Norwood House.

KEY TERMS

Define or briefly explain the following terms:

Billboard advertising __________

Blog __________

Calendar sale __________

Continuity of patronage __________

External newsletter __________

Facebook __________

Flyer __________

Frequency __________

Immediate-response marketing message __________

Impulse shopping __________

Infomercials __________

Internal newsletter __________

Internet radio __________

Mobile advertising __________

Perceived Cost __________

Postcard __________

Profit __________

Public relations __________

Reach __________

Retention __________

Sale __________

Targetability __________

Testimonial __________

TiVo __________

Ultimate cost __________

YouTube __________

CLASS OR TEAM DISCUSSION QUESTIONS

1 | Discuss the concept of an integrated marketing effort. When would a fashion retailer use an integrated marketing effort? Give an example. Is there any time when a company would choose not to use an integrated marketing effort? Why or why not?

2 | Discuss the benefits and limitations of a public relations department.

3 | Discuss the strengths and limitations of marketing fashions through infomercials. Develop a list of products and brands that succeed at this type of marketing effort. What type of fashion products and/or brands would be diminished through infomercial marketing efforts?

INTERNET ACTIVITIES

1 | Using the Internet as a resource, find fashion marketing efforts that demonstrate mass marketing techniques. Critically evaluate the strengths and limitations of the fashion marketer's efforts.

2 | Select a company and fashion product category. Access the Internet. Collect data on the company's Internet advertising efforts over the past year. Compare (a) the product categories marketed, (b) the image presented, (c) the copy (i.e., the writing), and (d) sales and profits generated (if the company is public). If the company is public, a good source of information is its weekly marketing press releases. Press releases are listed on the company's Web site.

STUDY QUESTIONS

1 | What type of information is disseminated through public relations? In what format is the information disseminated?

2 | Why are testimonials successful in fashion marketing campaigns?

3 | What types of sponsorships are most successful when marketing fashions?

4 | Which aspects must be taken into consideration when advertising fashions and accessories over the radio?

5 | When would a fashion marketer consider using YouTube? List the benefits and the limitations to using this form of social marketing.

6 | With the rapid adoption of technology and the decline of newspaper sales, are there specific times when a fashion marketer would use—or avoid—print advertisements? Explain.

7 | Discuss the strengths and limitations of the following fashion marketing strategies: flyers, post-cards, billboards, and newspapers.

______

______

8 | What is the difference between public relations and promotion?

______

______

9 | Provide examples of public relations.

______

______

10 | Discuss the concept of integrated fashion marketing. Provide an example in your discussion.

______

______

MULTIPLE-CHOICE QUESTIONS

1 | If a fashion marketing plan does not result in the targeted sales goal, the company/marketer should identify ______.

- **a.** Where the marketing plan fell short
- **b.** What changes need to be made
- **c.** How quickly changes to the fashion marketing plan can be successfully implemented
- **d.** All of the above (*a*, *b*, and *c*)

2 | Situation comedies, soap operas, game shows, and news shows attempt to depict everyday consumers, thus ______ brands are avoided.

- **a.** Fashionable
- **b.** Low end
- **c.** Affordable
- **d.** Expensive designer

3 | It is thought that viewers begin following fashions during their _____ years.

- **a.** Childhood
- **b.** Adolescent
- **c.** Adult
- **d.** Elderly

4 | Effective billboards have _____ components.

- **a.** Ten
- **b.** Nine
- **c.** Eight
- **d.** Seven
- **e.** Six

5 | _____ is a statement from a consumer regarding the qualities, benefits, and attributes of using a product.

- **a.** An immediate-response marketing message
- **b.** A sponsorship
- **c.** An infomercial
- **d.** A testimonial

TRUE-OR-FALSE QUESTIONS

1 | _____ Continuity of patronage exists when the product is disposable and the consumer is automatically replenished with a new product on a monthly basis.

2 | _____ Marketing fashion through mobile devices is as popular as marketing through the Internet.

3 | _____ Infomercials use an immediate-response marketing message.

TABLE 5.1

THE Market Planning PROCESS

step 1	CHAPTER 2 | Be inspired; become passionate regarding a product/service; be driven to succeed and committed to working toward a goal.
step 2	CHAPTER 3 | Intrinsic attributes of the products and services are marketed in terms of value, satisfaction, and quality. Building upon the mission statement, in this step you will make decisions regarding the pricing, communication, value, satisfaction, and quality associated with the purchase or the products and/or services.
step 3	CHAPTER 4 | Identify a comprehensive list of products and services offered by the company.
step 4	CHAPTER 5 | **Examine the products and services component of the core marketing concept related to the trickle-down theory, media and celebrities, and the belongingness theory.**
step 5	CHAPTER 6 | Examine the buying season in relation to the marketing process.
step 6	CHAPTER 7 | Examine marketing methods of targeting the consumer.
step 7	CHAPTER 8 | Examine the methods of exchange and relationships with the consumers. This includes making decisions to sell products and services through brick-and-mortar retail operations, direct marketing, and the Internet.
step 8	CHAPTER 9 | Examine the image and brands of the company in relation to marketing efforts.
step 9	CHAPTER 10 | Conduct a market analysis of how companies are able to successfully cross product boundaries.
step 10	CHAPTER 11 | Examine trends in the fashion industry regarding a) counterfeit merchandise and b) the impact of such merchandise on the industry's sales, profits, product design, consumers' attitudes.
step 11	CHAPTER 12 | Conduct a market analysis of fashions in the global environment in order to determine impact to the company's existing marketing efforts.

5

Fashion AND THE Entertainment Industry

chapter objectives

After reading this chapter, you should be able to understand Step Four of the Market Planning Process. This includes being able to:

+ Apply the trickle-down theory as it relates to fashion marketing.

+ Apply the trickle-down theory to an entertainer's brand.

+ Compare methods of fashion marketing efforts that use entertainers and celebrities.

+ Analyze the importance of entertainers and celebrities for obtaining fashion exposure.

+ Conduct a SWOT analysis of entertainment-industry personnel in marketing campaigns.

+ Evaluate the influence television has on fashion marketing.

+ Explain how the belongingness theory applies to fashion marketing.

"Luck is a matter of preparation meeting opportunity."
—Oprah Winfrey

Oprah Winfrey's statement regarding luck and opportunity can be applied to fashion marketing and the entertainment industry. Successful marketing campaigns don't "just happen." They are the result of careful planning, analysis of marketing concepts, and follow through. Although it may seem exciting to work with the entertainment industry, these marketing efforts consist of the same concepts and require a lot of planning and preparation.

Since the glamorous days of the 1940s, when movie stars would wear designer gowns to nightclubs, fashion has been an important part of the entertainment industry. The statement "to see and be seen" is epitomized by the actions of celebrities, want-to-be celebrities, actors, musicians, newscasters, authors, and television personalities being seen wearing brand-name merchandise and accessories. Award shows such as the Oscars, the Grammys, and the People's Choice Awards are watched primarily for the red carpet. The television audience is carefully looking for the good, the bad, and the downright tragic; fashions, accessories, and hair are closely analyzed by everyone in the fashion industry, as well as everyone who enjoys fashion. People talk for days about what each celebrity wore, how they wore it, and which stylist was the most influential.

The merchandise and accessories become as much a part of the personality and success of a celebrity as does his or her creative work. Likewise, it is equally important and profitable for the designers, manufacturers, and retailers to have the exposure of entertainers wearing their fashions and accessories.

figure 5.1 The designer's name and brand get international exposure at red carpet events. Weeks after the event, consumers are still viewing the fashions on television and in magazines.

THE TRICKLE-DOWN THEORY

Consumers who adopt fashion based on the fashion marketing efforts of the entertainment industry are representative of the **trickle-down theory**. The trickle-down theory is in play when fashions that are worn by the upper class (e.g., wealthy people, celebrities) first are adopted by the middle class and then lower classes. This theory suggests that those with wealth, status, and appearance set the fashion trend. By the time the fashion begins to trickle down, the fashion is considered either stable (e.g., becoming a classic) or old (e.g., on the way out). Diamonds, gold chains, "bling," fur, and designer brands are examples of fashion products worn by entertainers. Fashion-conscious consumers examine the size and amount of jewelry worn as well as the type, style, and combination of apparel displayed on television, magazines, and Internet sites.

Entertainers' comments also influence consumers' actions. While on the red carpet at the 2008 Oscars, Sean Combs stated that men needed to start dressing better and that they would always dress smart in Sean John apparel. His fashion marketing message was received by millions of viewers around the world. During the 2009 SAG (Screen Actors Guild) red carpet, Holly Hunter talked about selecting her gown based on the color. She stated that she loved the color (on television, it looked fuchsia) and that it was very comfortable. Holly Hunter's fashion marketing efforts included promoting the designer, the color, and comfort. Women who like Holly Hunter may consciously or unconsciously look for a dress similar to the dress she wore that day.

Think about your experiences with watching celebrities:

- Have you ever watched a red-carpet event and thought, *I would look good in that dress, or I should buy something in that particular shade of blue?*

figure 5.2
Holly Hunter selected this gown for the 2009 SAG awards because she liked the color.

- Have you ever read fashion magazines and thought, *I need to update my wardrobe to look more like [insert your favorite model or celebrity here]?*
- Have you ever watched a movie and wondered if you could wear a particular fashion style?

Celebrities' opinions and use of fashions help market and influence consumers' adoption of fashions.

Celebrity Lines

Entertainers play an important role in the marketing of fashions beyond just wearing or promoting fashion. Some entertainers have become invested in the marketing of their own fashion lines. Cheryl Tiegs was one of the first celebrities to lend her name to a line. Tiegs was a popular model who was featured on the cover of *Sports Illustrated* magazine frequently throughout the 1970s and early 1980s. She became internationally known for her photos in tiny bikinis. Tiegs initially lent her name to a variety of products, including wigs.

Since then, numerous entertainers, athletes, and celebrities have developed and are marketing their own lines of fashions. The level of involvement each person has in the development of the efforts varies. Celebrities don't actively design the fashions in the traditional sense. They may, but not necessarily, have approval of fashion and marketing efforts.

For example, in 1985, Jaclyn Smith, of *Charlie's Angels* television-show fame, placed her name on clothing and home furnishings and started selling them through Kmart. The clothing and home furnishings sponsored by Jaclyn met a predetermined quality level. The quality and Kmart's name alone were not responsible for the longevity, sales, and profitability of the Jaclyn Smith brand. During the 1980s, women wanted to look like Jaclyn—some women perhaps even wanted to *be* her—and men wanted to date her. Over the past 20 years, Jaclyn Smith has carefully guarded her image and brand. She maintains her positive marketing efforts using the personality and fashion image from her *Charlie's Angels* era. More than twenty years later, Jaclyn Smith continues to market her extremely successful brand of apparel and home furnishings through Kmart; more than 40 million pieces having been sold by the "blue light" discounter (Gibson, 1994, December 13).

The twenty-first century has seen the most significant growth of celebrities marketing fashions based on their fame. Jessica Simpson had a rocky start in the music and reality show businesses. She turned her fashion sense into a multimillion-dollar business. Within only a few years, Jessica Simpson placed her name on footwear, handbags, wigs, hair extensions, and swimwear. In each case, she carefully branded the products with her name prominently in the customer's view (Gibson, n.d.).

Jennifer Lopez (also known as J.Lo), the multitalented recording artist and actress, also decided that her career would not be complete without marketing multiple fashion lines. J.Lo's company, named Sweetface, carries junior sizes, plus sizes, girls' sizes, and accessories.

The fashion marketing efforts clearly make the entertainers a significant amount of money and provides continual name recognition to the target market. These fashion marketers have also revolutionized how and what consumers purchase. Rapper Jay-Z, with partner Damon Dash, formed Rocawear in 1994. The company features urban sportswear that was never before marketed on a wide-scale basis. The company has expanded into **licensing**. Jay-Z and Damon Dash have licenses with Kids Headquarters (kids), Signature (juniors), Gina Group (socks), M. London (handbags

figure 5.3
For more than 20 years, Jaclyn Smith has teamed up with Kmart. The former Angel lends a fashionable image to the apparel line at a moderate price.

figure 5.4
Jessica Simpson's shoe collection is known for its high heels, sexy attitude, and moderate pricing. Her fashions sell well in department stores, such as Macy's, throughout the country.

and belts), Endurance (big & tall), Nas Industries (headwear), Lucas Design (jewelry), Age Group (intimates), Topline (ladies' shoes), The Vestal Group (watches), and Colors in Optics (sunglasses) (Vesilind, 2009).

In 2009, the country singer Taylor Swift had a very successful year. Her album *Fearless* won Album of the Year at the Academy of Country Music Awards; she had a part on the hit television show *CSI*; and she launched her own fashion line with L.e.i. (lifestyle, energy, intelligence), a jeans manufacturer for the teen market. The company focuses its product designs on "fashion with attitude . . . [and] style

TABLE 5.2
Celebrity Lines

CELEBRITY	LABELS	ITEMS
Jessica Simpson	Jessica Simpson	Footwear, swimwear, handbags, wigs
Milla Jovovich	Jovovich-Hawk	Dresses from vintage fabrics
Jennifer Lopez	Sweetface	Juniors, plus sizes, girls, perfumes, accessories
Pamela Anderson	Pamela Anderson	Accessories
Elizabeth Hurley	Elizabeth Hurley Beach	Beachwear
Reba McEntire	Reba	Women's
Elle Macpherson	Elle Macpherson Intimates	Lingerie
Jaclyn Smith	Jaclyn Smith	Women's, watches, shoes, handbags, sunglasses, perfume, home furnishings
Sean "P. Diddy" Combs	Sean John	Men's
Snoop Dogg	Snoop Dogg Clothing	Men's
Curtis "50 Cent" Jackson	The G-Unit Clothing Company	Men's
Jay-Z and Damon Dash	Rocawear	Men's
Mary Kate and Ashley Olsen	Olsenloye, The Row, Elizabeth and James	Tweens' clothing, limited edition, furniture
Pharrell Williams	Billionaire Boys Club, Ice Cream	Menswear, limited edition, shoes
Eminem	Shady Ltd.	Hoodies, tees, denim, jackets
Nelly	Vokal, Apple Bottoms	Men's and Women's

with a little sass." The comfortable, affordable sundresses will be sold at Walmart. Taylor will price her dresses at $14. She recognizes that fashion doesn't have to be expensive. The multitalented singer likes the fact that Walmart is open twenty-four hours a day. The store hours offer the flexibility of being able to shop any time (Kaplan, 2009).

Spokespersons

Entertainers are often employed as spokespersons for fashion products. Not having their own brand, being a spokesperson simply means they endorse the brand. This type of marketing effort focuses around the celebrity stating that he or she wears the fashions or uses the products. The spokespersons are typically individuals who are instantly recognized around the world. Their fans consider their lifestyle glamorous, exciting, fun, exotic, or unattainable because of their stardom. Fans follow the entertainers' lives: where they shop, what they drink, even what type of coffee they buy at Starbucks.

Because successful entertainers have such a huge fan base and are recognizable throughout the globe, they are excellent spokespersons for marketing campaigns. They lend credence to the message. Often times, very few words are included in a celebrity-endorsed print advertisement. The products are predominantly featured next to the entertainer's face. The company may include a clause in the fashion marketing contract that the entertainer (a) be seen in public a certain number of times wearing the product, (b) publically state his or her commitment to the product, or (c) wear the product to prominent events such as runway shows.

Sports figures, models, and actors have been spokespersons for fashions and accessories. The celebrity must clearly represent the values and attributes of the brand. Charlize Theron is the spokesperson for Dior. Throughout her contract with Dior, she represents the company's products in print and television. You can view some of her advertisements on YouTube. As the Dior spokesperson, she exclusively wears Dior gowns on the red carpet. This exclusivity further solidifies her commitment to the Dior brand. Viewers connect Charlize with Dior and vice versa (Table 5.3).

Special Appearances

Special appearances of entertainers—on the red carpet, in music videos, or on television talk shows (e.g., Oprah, David Letterman)—offer fashion marketers the opportunity to showcase their products to a large audience. Products are frequently loaned to celebrities for special appearances. In return, the celebrities predominately show the merchandise and accessories. Positive response to a garment and/or accessory can bring widespread consumer acceptance and purchasing behavior, increased loyalty toward a particular designer, and inspire merchandise knockoffs.

figure 5.5 John Galliano and Charlize Theron pose for photographers on the red carpet. Theron is the face of Dior.

TABLE 5.3

Celebrity Endorsements and/or Sponsorships

COMPANY	CELEBRITY
Cover Girl	Drew Barrymore
Cover Girl	Rihanna
Dior	Charlize Theron
Emporio Armani Diamonds	Beyoncé Knowles
L'Oréal	Andie MacDowell
Macy's	Clinton Kelly
Neutrogena	Jennifer Garner
Nike	Tiger Woods
Pantene Pro-V Nature Fusion	Padma Lakshmi (actress, writer, and host of Bravo's *Top Chef*)
Revlon	Elle Macpherson
Tod's	Gwyneth Paltrow
L'Oréal Vive Pro	Linda Evangelista
Tide TOTALCARE	Tim Gunn

Knockoffs

Fashion marketing efforts using entertainers provide a secondary market for designers, manufacturers, retailers, and consumers. Expensive, high-quality products worn by entertainers are frequently (and immediately) copied for the mass market. The designs are simplified, using fewer seams and less expensive fabric. The copied designs are then offered to the mass market through retailers like J. C. Penney, Sears, Nordstrom, or Dillard's. Consumers can feel like they have a part of the celebrity status without paying the big-ticket price tag. Knockoffs are addressed in more detail in Chapter Eleven, "Counterfeiting, Legislation, and Ethics."

Print Exposure

Magazines are an important business to the marketing of fashions. They show the fashions in a controlled environment. The fashions are often beautifully and carefully poised on a celebrity or high-fashion model. The photographer has taken careful steps in making sure all the right hair, makeup, and lighting effects present the fashions in the most pleasant setting. All the time, money, and effort of print marketing exposure is worthwhile—especially in terms of circulation. Circulation is the number of copies sold each month (Table 5.4). Also remember that with each copy sold, the magazine is probably read by at least two other people. **Can you honestly say you haven't shared a fashion magazine (and your opinions) with friends at least once in your life?** If you haven't, perhaps it is because you hold the fashion magazines close to your heart and your closet (for guidance). Print fashion marketing efforts are very powerful tools. They provide visual and tangible opportunities for consumers to evaluate, compare, and even obsess about product offerings.

figure 5.6
Consumers may try to live vicariously through the entertainment industry. This consumer is a Victoria Beckham look-alike. She is wearing a dress worn by Victoria Beckham and her hair is styled in a similar fashion.

figure 5.7 Magazines are used extensively by the industry to market fashions. The glamour of the entertainment industry lends added allure for consumers.

During 2008, more than 23 million consumers had an annual subscription to a fashion magazine. More than 5.7 million purchased a fashion magazine at the newsstand (Smith, 2009, February 6). While articles are important, enlightening, and very helpful, these 28.7 consumers were devouring something ever more important on a monthly basis. They were finding out about the most up-to-date fashions, learning which celebrities were wearing specific designers' brands, learning how to look more fashionable—or like a celebrity—for less, and noting which celebrities attended which parties wearing what fashions. In short, 28.7 million consumers gained access (legally) into other people's lives through the pages of these fashion publications; at the same time, they learned how to improve their own sense of fashion. An important part of the focus on entertainment and celebrity in the fashion industry is aimed at providing us with a sense of connection to that world of glamour.

Dooney & Bourke's fashion marketing efforts are an example of how print exposure is used to promote fashions to a large target market. The company's leather handbags, watches, and iPod cases are easily recognizable by their bright pastel colors and designs. The company markets their products as "affordable luxury," fashions that are used by celebrities but available for the mass market. Fashion marketing print efforts for Dooney & Bourke have effectively been conducted in *Vogue*, *Teen Vogue*, *Elle*, *Vanity Fair*, *Lucky*, *InStyle*, and *W* magazines. Magazines' extensive readership and readers' interest in fashion make the advertising effort a financially wise marketing move for the company.

Supermodels

Runway shows are a source of entertainment for the fashion industry. The invention of the supermodel helped build anticipation for the fashions. Fashion lovers would wonder which model would be wearing which garment (Agins, 1999). While supermodels are photographed for their fashions on the runway,

TABLE 5.4

Fashion Magazine Circulation (2008)

MAGAZINE	NEWSSTAND SALES	TOTAL PAID CIRCULATION
Allure	228,667	1,062,778
Cosmopolitan	1,753,700	9,915,867
Elle	332,167	1,072,729
Essence	233,265	1,089,495
Glamour	685,633	2,262,242
Harper's Bazaar	167,300	722,058
InStyle	753,358	1,780,681
Lucky	237,750	1,167,020
Marie Claire	289,700	971,348
Town & Country	44,400	461,571
Vanity Fair	376,500	1,153,517
Vogue	385,500	1,301,575
W	34,974	457,996
Esquire	112,900	721,133
GQ	211,700	931,694
Men's Vogue	53,600	307,501
Total fashion magazine sales	5,733,981	23,116,963

(*Women's Wear Daily*, 2008)

they are equally sought after off the runway. Paparazzi actively seek out supermodels, anxiously waiting for a photo of them crossing a street, holding hands with a close friend, or hailing a cab. Every aspect of their daily lives is photographed and written about in magazines. Supermodels have the power to increase sales of the fashions they are wearing simply by their status. Fashionistas and "want-to-be" models follow the trends set by the supermodels. The saying "a picture is worth a thousand words" could be translated into *A picture of a supermodel wearing a designer's garment is worth a million dollars in free publicity.*

Royalty

When one uses the term *royalty*, different images may come to mind. You may think of the Queen of England. Perhaps you think of Princess Diana. You may even think of Jacqueline Kennedy Onassis. When discussing fashion, the term *royalty* may be placed in a variety of contexts. The word is indicative of a person of royal blood. The person is special, extremely high profile, and typically well bred. The royal person does not necessarily have a sense of fashion. Fashion is not based on income, education, or status. Fashion and having a sense of fashion are based on knowing which garments to put together. More importantly, fashion exists when the individual knows how to wear the garments with confidence.

The importance to a company's fashion marketing efforts of a popular and positive royal person wearing their fashions and/or accessories in public cannot be understated. The impact is particularly important to the company if the royal person wears the item repeatedly. The repeated behavior acts as a subliminal message saying, *I am loyal to this product and company.*

In 1995, Princess Diana carried a Lady Dior quilted handbag. Being seen with the handbag, compliments of the paparazzi, Princess Diana generated excessive free and positive promotion for the Lady Dior accessory. By 1997, over 100,000 handbags were sold, each bag retailing at $1,200 (Agins, 1999). Dior's fashion marketing team was able to focus the majority of their efforts on other fashion products. The free promotion of the Lady Dior handbag made the accessory a staple product in many households.

figure 5.8
Princess Diana inadvertently helped sell millions of the Lady Dior handbag. Once Diana was seen wearing the handbag, consumers flocked to the neared Dior retailer for the accessory.

figure 5.9
Drew Barrymore wore Dior haute couture and Lorrain Schwartz accessories to the Golden Globes. She was featured on international television and in fashion magazines for weeks afterward.

MOVIES

Ever since men and women were featured in movies, fashions played an integral part of the plot. Fashions and accessories helped shape actors' on-screen personalities and images and promoted merchandise to the viewing audience (Garron, 2008). In *The Devil Wears Prada*, Meryl Streep and Anne Hathaway wore designs by Prada, Chanel, and Dolce & Gabbana. Worldwide, women watched as dozens of fashions passed before them throughout the movie. Sales of the DVD proved equally successful. Women learned more about the specific styles and this further enhanced the fashion marketing efforts. Examples of other movies that have successfully promoted fashion include *Pretty Woman, 27 Dresses, Sweet Home Alabama, Sex and the City, Clueless*, and *The Women* (original and remake).

Movies are particularly important to the fashion industry because consumers (a) watch the DVD version of the movie multiple times, (b) compare opinions with friends regarding the fashions, and (c) are able to examine the movie and fashions in each scene.

For example, in *The Devil Wears Prada*:

- Can you name the brand of boots Anne Hathaway wore during her initial makeover by Stanley Tucci?
- What was the color of the belt used with the ballerina skirt and jacket during the scene when Anne Hathaway said "all the belts were the same color"?

The point is that consumers worldwide watched *The Devil Wears Prada* in the movie theater for the plot. They purchased the DVD to view the fashions at their leisure.

AWARD SHOWS

Designers, celebrities, fashion marketers, stylists, and fashion-lovers worldwide anxiously await the arrival of spring. The award season brings glamour, high fashion, diamonds, and the latest in hair and makeup. Watching the celebrities walk the red carpet has become a more popular event than the actual award show. Fashions are analyzed from every vantage point. Each strand of hair is evaluated regarding its ability to enhance the gems. The size, quality, and brand of diamonds, emeralds, and rubies are discussed in relation to the wearer's eyes, hair color, and stature. In other words, the red carpet offers the world an opportunity to be a fashion stylist. Days later, men and women continue talking about the fashion triumphs and tragedies. Fashion designers' and jewelers' names are continually repeated during these conversations. The fashion marketing value of the successful designs is invaluable. The men and women are featured in *Women's Wear Daily* and on such television channels as the Style Network and E!. During the Golden Globe Awards, Drew Barrymore was photographed and featured in Dior Haute Couture and Lorraine Schwartz jewelry (Figure 5.9). Kate Winslet, who ultimately won an Oscar, wore Yves Saint Laurent. Olivia Wilde wore Reem Acra and Van Cleef & Arpels, and Marisa Tomei wore Oscar de la

Renta and Neil Lane and Sevan Bicakci jewelry (*Women's Wear Daily*, 2009, January 13). The Golden Globes is a positive event. The fashions are associated with beautiful, successful, and positive women. This method of marketing the brand is very successful, and the international integrated marketing efforts provide the brand with extended exposure.

Throughout the awards shows, designers are adapting the couture designs for the mass market. Lines are simplified, the amount of fabric is minimized, and less expensive fabrics are identified. Fashions are designed, manufactured, and marketed based on the similarities they have to those worn by celebrities.

TELEVISION

Consumers enjoy their television. They enjoy their television so much, that according to A.C. Nielsen, in 2008 to 2009, 114.5 million American households possessed televisions. Despite a financially troubled economy, this figure was up 1.5 percent from 2007 to 2008. In a survey of consumers' television habits, the following was found: (a) 99 percent of the group had at least one television; (b) 66 percent of the sample had three or more televisions; (c) on average, participants watched 6 hours and 47 minutes of television a day; and (d) 66 percent of the participants watched television while eating dinner. In 2008 to 2009, over 285 million people watched television (Herr, 2008).

It's no wonder then that television is considered an excellent medium for commercials and an excellent opportunity to showcase fashions. Television offers sight, sound, action, and the occasion to incorporate celebrities. Television is used to entertain, to soothe people when they are sad, to serve as a companion when they are lonely, and to provide them a bridge to other parts of the world.

Television shows are made to look effortless and real. When the viewer watches a television show, it should be believable. The producer carefully selects stylists that can craft each actor's character. The clothing worn and the combination of accessories are carefully selected; together, they help portray the character's personality. The fashions and accessories help bring images into viewers' homes.

Television producers strive for high viewership. One method of reaching high viewership is through the effective use of fashion. This strategy builds strong brand awareness for the show. For example, *Gossip Girl* on the CW network is watched primarily by female teens. In addition to enjoying the storyline, the audience is invested in the fashions worn by the actors on the show. They are highly sought after in retail and online stores. Teens regularly write to the show asking about the fashions and where they can purchase specific garments worn by their favorite actors. This fashion correspondence serves multiple purposes. First, it helps the show's writers know which portions of the show are particularly popular with the audience. Second, the actors are promoting the fashions, directly or indirectly. Third, the actors have an excellent talking point when they appear as guests on talk shows (e.g., *This jacket is a popular request by my fans*) (Kinon, 2007; 2008).

figure 5.10
The television series *Gossip Girl* has a following for the script and the fashions. Viewers write into the show asking where to find specific fashions worn by the cast.

As you examine you own personal fashion experiences, think about the following:

- How many hours of television do you watch per day?
- What is your favorite show and character?
- Do your fashions look similar to anyone on your favorite show?
- If so, did you purposely purchase items you saw on the show?
- Do your friends also dress in a similar manner?
- How do you think other shows influence your fashion purchasing behavior?

Fashion Marketing and Television

Television is an excellent medium for marketing fashions. Television offers sight, sound, and action. With the invention of HDTV, the colors of apparel and accessories are brought into the viewer's home with clarity and brilliance. With the advent of cable and the home theater, residents throughout the world are watching TV at an increasingly higher rate (Herr, 2008). Fashion marketers clearly understand the influence television viewers and successful shows have on the acceptance of their products. The more a television show is accepted and the more people watch and talk about a show, the greater the probability fashion-conscious consumers will evaluate the clothing and products used on the show.

The impact of television on consumers' purchasing is so significant that it is predicted that in the near future marketers will pay production costs. Fashion products used on television include apparel, accessories, and home furnishings. If a fashion marketer's products are used in a television show, the products are typically shown throughout the entire show and/or series. This provides the fashion marketer multiple opportunities to build loyalty to the brand and promote the specific product (Atkinson, 2008).

Marketing fashions as they are intertwined throughout a television show is often more successful than a series of 30- or 60-second commercials. While television commercials can be effective, commercials, with a few exceptions such as the Super Bowl, are not the reason people watch television. When watching a television series that lasts 30 to 60 minutes and is repeated every week, consumers get hooked. They may watch the show for the story line, the characters, or the fashions. Marketing branded fashions as they are intertwined throughout a television show is expected to be an extremely effective marketing strategy (Atkinson, 2008) (Box 5.1).

Entertainment as Fashion Marketing Tool

Situation comedies, soap operas, game shows, news shows, and teen shows typically attempt to depict the personality of "everyday" consumers. Fashionable brands are worn; however, expensive designer brands are typically avoided. Television is an excellent marketing

figure 5.11
Hannah Montana can sing, dance, and market fashions. Tweens seem to want anything that she is seen wearing or anything that sports her name.

tool for fashion brands. Typically, a relatively unknown designer markets the fashion brands worn on television shows. The success of a show or the popularity of a character may result in the fashion being adopted nationally or internationally.

Viewers begin following fashions during their early adolescent years. As they age, their interest in fashion continues to be satisfied through different television shows. Marketing the fashions through a television show is subtle; that is, the actors don't state outright, *Purchase my clothing*. The popularity of the characters the actors play markets the fashions.

Fashion marketing begins with young children's fashions. If the marketers can capture the interest in consumers at a young age, they have a stronger opportunity of obtaining a loyal following. *The Suite Life of Zack and Cody*, *Hannah Montana*, MTV, and *Entertainment Tonight* all have two things in common: entertaining television viewers and serving as a fashion marketing tool. Fashions worn on the shows are widely sought-after, adopted, and modified by loyal viewers. Each show is targeted toward a different market segment (Tables 5.5a and b).

SOAP OPERAS

Daytime and evening soap opera shows have long dressed their actors in high fashions. During the 1980s, viewers from around the world

Jennifer Aniston's haircut and fashion style is copied by millions of women worldwide.

BOX 5.1. Jennifer Aniston and the "Rachel Cut"

Jennifer Aniston made international headlines throughout her years on the sitcom *Friends*. As millions of viewers faithfully watched the show, women followed Jennifer Aniston's fashion sense. Women wanted to look like Jennifer; men wanted to date her. When Jennifer's character, Rachel, wore a style, the trend was soon adopted by millions of women. Her haircut set off an international craze for the "Rachel cut." If women couldn't look like Aniston, at least they could adopt her haircut.

Whether on camera or off, Aniston's fashions, accessories, and haircut were closely emulated throughout the ten seasons of *Friends*. Since the beginning of the show in 1994, Jennifer Aniston continues to influence positive marketing of fashions each time she is seen on television, in movies, and in print. She has since grown her hair long, but women and men still enjoy following her every move. From her red-carpet moments to walking out of Starbucks, paparazzi photos of Aniston continue to get high praise and lots of publicity.

Tommy Hilfiger's casual, all-American designs are created for easy but fashionable living.

BOX 5.2 Tommy Hilfiger: Multimedia Marketing

Tommy Hilfiger is known globally for his casual designs and a marketing campaign focused on a relaxed and easy lifestyle. His success over the years can be attributed to understanding fashion, design, fit, and, above all, the needs and wants of his particular target market. Music, the music industry, entertainment, and interaction with persons in the industry (virtual or live) are important needs and wants of the Tommy Hilfiger target market. Realizing this need, Hilfiger created Tommy TV. Tommy TV consists of musical performances that can be watched via the Internet. Viewers can try to win a spot to participate in the taping of the segment. Sessions are held around the world (e.g., Madrid, Berlin, Rome, New York). Viewers can also join the My Tommy TV fan base. While listening to music videos, viewers may also access the other portions of the Tommy Hilfiger Web site. The music will continue to play as you scroll through an online podcast of the most recent fashion show or view the catalog of fashions available for purchase. You can also learn about Tommy Hilfiger's charity efforts with Race to Erase Multiple Sclerosis.

watched the television show *Dallas* partly for the plot and partly for the fashions worn by the characters. Throughout the decades, faithful followers of daytime soap opera viewers tune in daily to watch their shows. Shows such as *All My Children, General Hospital, One Life to Live*, and *The Bold and the Beautiful* are popular for their plots and beautiful actors. The marketing of the fashions, however, continue to keep young and old television viewers tuning in on a daily basis. The fashions play an integral role in the marketing of the show, the actors, and the plot. In turn, the fashions worn on the shows stimulate sales in stores, in catalogs, and on the Internet.

REALITY SHOWS

The twenty-first century is known for its reality-show craze. Viewers are offered more versions of "reality" than ever before in the history of television. The fashion marketing industry has become an important part of the

TABLES 5.5A AND B

Examples of Media's Influence on Fashion and the Target Market

A. Movies

MOVIE	TARGET MARKET
High School Musical 3: Senior Year	Teens
Mamma Mia!	California teens and adults
The Devil Wears Prada	Fashion-lovers everywhere; women aged 16–70
Picture Perfect	Fashion-lovers everywhere; women aged 16–70
Working Girl	Fashion-lovers everywhere; women aged 16–70
Annie Hall (broadcast)	Women aged 30 and up
Ready to Wear (broadcast)	Women aged 16–50

B. Television Shows

TELEVISION SHOW	TARGET MARKET
Gossip Girl	Women aged 16–25
90210	Women aged 16–25
Ugly Betty	Fashion-lovers everywhere; women aged 16–70
Sex and the City	Women aged 18 and up
Say Yes to the Dress	Young brides
Dallas	Women over 35

reality show industry. Everyday consumers are videotaped making decisions regarding their fashion decisions. The shows *Say Yes to the Dress* and *Platinum Weddings* both have high ratings. Viewers get an inside look at the various designer wedding gowns, jewelry, veils, and accessories that make a wedding magical.

Another reality show that influences the fashion industry is called *What Not to Wear.* The show, hosted by Stacy London and Clinton Kelly, teaches women from everyday walks of life how to empower themselves using fashion. Friends or family nominate participants for the show. In other words, participants don't necessarily know they need help with their fashion style. The hosts teach the participant about body image, body proportion, and using clothing to present themselves well in different settings (e.g., work, play). This show demonstrates the importance of shopping with a judicious frame of mind. The lessons of the

figure 5.12
Michael Kors, Heidi Klum, and Nina Garcia of *Project Runway* bring high fashion into the homes of every consumer. They teach contestants that one of the major skills required to be in the fashion industry is to understand your consumer.

figure 5.13
Sean "P. Diddy" Combs in Sean John apparel.

show teach participants to: (a) try on apparel; (b) purchase only clothing that fits; and (c) buy fewer, but perhaps more expensive, items to make the cost and effort worthwhile. These lessons promote the fashion marketing industry nationally.

Reality shows have significantly influenced how everyday people get involved in the fashion industry and how television viewers interact with fashion marketers. Shows like *Project Runway*, *What Not to Wear*, and *Shear Genius* have revolutionized the fashion marketing industry. *Project Runway* provides a platform for designers to create and show their designs on national television. Through weekly intense competitions, designers are challenged to build upon their skills, creativity, and marketing savvy. Fashion knowledge and expertise is not enough to win the competition. The designers market the fashions using a model, accessories, hairstyle, makeup, and the runway. All fashions created on the reality show are marketed through blogs, photos, videos, and the *Project Runway* Web site.

The judges on *Project Runway* incorporate a significant fashion marketing focus to the popular show. Heidi Klum, a top Victoria's Secret model (Figure 5.12), acts as the principal commentator and guides the panel of experts. The rest of the panel consists of designer Michael Kors and fashion editor Nina Garcia. Kors is famous for his menswear designs. Garcia is the executive editor of *Elle* magazine. Tim Gunn, chief creative officer at Liz Claiborne, Inc., works with the designers on a weekly basis. The four industry experts bring together the various fashion marketing components (e.g., design, product, print, runway, and product) and provide input, expertise, and candid advice to the contestants and the viewing audience. The show aggressively markets to people in the fashion business, to those who aspire to be in fashion marketing, and to those who are simply "**armchair fashionistas**." An armchair fashionista is a person who is not in the fashion business, but thoroughly enjoys watching and critiquing fashion.

As of January 2008, the reality show has completed five seasons. The show's success is so great that sewing patterns are marketed after the *Project Runway* designs.

BOOKS

Books are also used as a method to market the fashion industry. Books can be classified into two categories: nonfiction and fiction. Nonfiction books contain information that is factual. Nonfiction genres include biographies, autobiographies, business, and self-improvement. Books that are classified as fiction contain information that most often comes from the author's imagination. These books are intended to be read for pleasure and/or enlightenment.

Fashion in Biographies and Autobiographies

A story written about a designer is a biography. A life story written by the same fashion designer that the book is about would be called an autobiography. Regardless of who writes the story, consumers worldwide are eager to learn about the rise, struggles, glamour, and, sometimes, fall of fashion designers. Most readers of biographies and autobiographies of people in the fashion industry do so for one

Mr. Blackwell was the first to design plus-size fashions and use African-American models. He opened the doors for many fashion firsts.

BOX 5.3 Beyond the "Worst-Dressed List" with Mr. Blackwell

Today's younger generation is familiar with Mr. Blackwell's "Worst-Dressed List." For those under 40, you may not realize that Mr. Blackwell is a very famous, talented, and indeed innovative designer. According to Linda Carlson, curator of the Avenir Museum of Design and Merchandising and longtime friend of Mr. Blackwell, he provided inspiration to other designers. The black silk velvet evening dress is one of Mr. Blackwell's many creations. According to Carlson,

> some of Mr. Blackwell's truly remarkable talents were that he was the first designer to create really beautiful dresses for the plus-size woman. He worked with African-American and Asian models at a time in history when other designers did not think of crossing this boundary. He used television to show his designs when others only used runway shows.

Many may remember him for his famous and highly marketed "Worst-Dressed List," but there is so much more to this designer.

In 1997, he visited Colorado State University to teach design students. He encouraged, mentored, and nurtured the students. He pushed boundaries, realizing that in order to make it in the fashion industry a person needs more than talent. They need contacts, luck, inspiration, and skill. Mr. Blackwell gave back what he received. Although he passed away in 2008, he will be remembered for his beautiful designs, his history of breaking boundaries in the industry, and his contributions to society and the industry as a whole.

of two reasons: to see into the lives of the rich, famous, and fabulous; or, as people interested in fashion, to learn from and about the subjects of these books. Anyone interested in the fashion industry should know the background of fashion designers, fashion marketers, and fashion retailers. The most comprehensive way of learning about the lives of these individuals is through reading biographies and autobiographies.

A designer in his own right, Mr. Blackwell was perhaps best known for his "worst-dressed list." Each year, fashion enthusiasts ran to the fashion columns and Web sites to learn who made his list. The attraction wasn't so much to find out who was dressed badly, but to see how Mr. Blackwell phrased his critiques. Mr. Blackwell marketed himself and his sense of fashion. I met Mr. Blackwell in 1996 during his visit to Colorado State University. I knew how he became a fashion critic and a marketer, but I didn't realize the charisma of his personality.

Seven faculty members were present at my initial meeting with Mr. Blackwell. He was personable, funny, and definitely charming. His posture was so straight that I constantly found myself wishing I had listened to my grandmother and practiced sitting up straight as a child. When Mr. Blackwell talked, he spoke eloquently and passionately about the industry. He quoted so many facts as if they were yesterday's lunch receipt. He cared about women and the fashions that adorned them. My defenses were eliminated. I was enamored with the man. He inspired me.

Mr. Blackwell spoke about how women should dress well. He didn't mean they need to dress expensively, but that they should dress to enhance their physical features. As I looked across the table, I noticed that he was dressed in dark trousers, a cashmere turtleneck, and a black leather jacket. He looked like a movie star and acted like—royalty or a true gentleman. That evening a black tie event was held for Mr. Blackwell. He spent time with every person—as much time as the individual wanted. The saying, "work the room," means that an individual should meet everyone; it is an obligation. Mr. Blackwell did not "work the room." He didn't seem obligated. He came to Colorado State University to help the students and community. He allowed the community to take photos, mingled with the crowed throughout the entire night, and helped make the event a success. In his autobiography, *From Rags to Bitches*, Mr. Blackwell talks about changes in the fashion industry. Mr. Blackwell may have been a designer, but he was the ultimate fashion marketer (Box 5.3).

When you see a Gucci product or logo, what is the first thing you think? Characteristics of the product may include: (a) quality, (b) price, (c) luxury, (d) symbolism, (e) durability, (f) style, or (g) glamour. **But do you know how or when the Gucci Group started? Do you know the background of the company?** If not, you aren't ready to be in the fashion business.

Fashion marketers need to know everything—yes, everything—about the various companies in the industry. Mr. Richard Blackwell chose to write his autobiography. Not every designer and/or fashion marketer chooses to place his or her life in the open for all to read. Autobiographies give us a glimpse into the company and the lives of the leading players—namely, their families. The House of Gucci, though shining brightly today, has gone through some difficulties. Its products needed to evolve, as did its company structure. If you are interested in learning about murder, glamour, and greed, read *The House of Gucci*. More importantly, by reading this book, you will learn the importance of evolving to a company. The House of Gucci demonstrated how to effectively turn a company around to dominate the fashion industry. A list of recommended titles is provided at the end of this chapter.

Fashion in Fiction

Fiction books are typically made-up stories that may or may not reflect the real world. Fiction includes both literary and purely pleasurable mysteries, love stories, dramas, fantasies, thrillers, and many books that merge these genres. The world of fashion is big business in the fiction book industry. *The Devil Wears Prada*; *Knit One, Kill Two*; *Lipstick Jungle*; and the Harry Bosch novels are examples of fiction books featuring fashion. In each case, the fashion industry is featured, promoted, and indeed placed in front of the reading market. In the case of *The Devil Wears Prada*, fashion-watchers worldwide read the book and then watched the movie in

Maggie Sefton writes mysteries that are interwoven with a yarn theme.

BOX 5.4 Spinning a Good Yarn

When Maggie Sefton, author of history books for more than thirty years, entered the Lambspun yarn shop for the first time in May 2003, she didn't know the world of knitting existed. It took her a long time to browse through the store. The yarns, knitted fashions, and particularly the people amazed her. Maggie soon learned how to knit and came back to the store every Tuesday. By September 2003, Maggie's characters in her first mystery, *Knit One, Kill Two,* were being developed. The author always followed the characters; she simply started to write.

Five years and six books later, Maggie has a large following of readers, mystery awards, and national bestselling books. The series of books have a common thread—or yarn. The connection among the five books is in fact the theme of yarn. The Sefton mystery books include *Knit One, Kill Two, Needled to Death, Deadly Yarn, A Killer Stitch, Dyer Consequences,* and *Fleece Navidad.* The author lives in gratitude for the reader's responses to her books. Maggie Sefton states that the series came out of sheer joy. The joy of knitting fashions, being with friends at the yarn shop, and writing keep Maggie writing mystery novels.

delight. Consumers watched the movie multiple times—once for the plot and the second time to examine the high fashion. Each time that a work of fiction featuring the fashion industry is successful, the designers, fabrics, textiles, and industry are positively promoted. A list of recommended titles is provided at the end of this chapter.

BELONGINGNESS THEORY

There has to be a logical reason that entertainers, other celebrities, and rising celebrities have so much power in the fashion industry. Many of the celebrities promoting brands and fashions are thin, beautiful, and rich. These attributes alone don't make them the object of everyday consumers' obsessions. For example, Ellen DeGeneres promotes a brand of makeup.

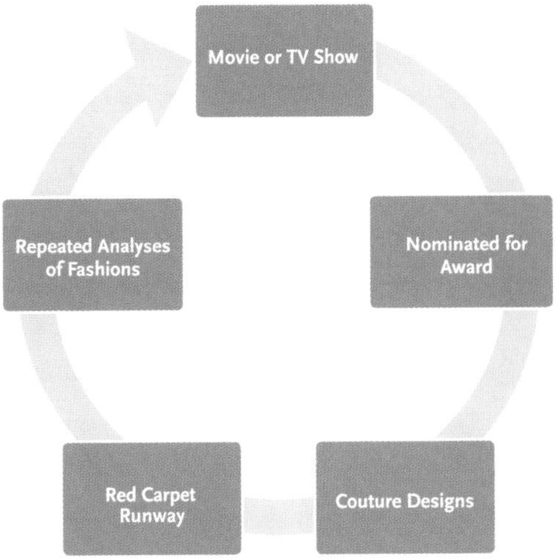

figure 5.14
Represented by the belongingness theory, consumers often feel a need to have a connection to the entertainment industry, celebrities, and persons who are famous simply because they are rich. Stimuli through the media further promote consumers' desire for the connection with this group who are the height of the fashion industry.

Movie or TV Show

Nominated for Award

Couture Designs

Red Carpet Runway

Repeated Analyses of Fashions

No one would say that her selection of shoes or vests is necessarily a fashion statement. **Why was she chosen as the spokesperson? Was it simply because she has a successful talk show?**

The **belongingness theory** states that people need social acceptance. We, as a society, need to feel as if we belong—to our community, to our society, to a world that is bigger than ourselves (Halpern, 2007). Consumers who follow entertainers' and celebrities' fashions have a sense of belonging through a parasocial relationship. That is, when consumers adopt similar or identical fashions worn and/or promoted by celebrities, they feel like part of the celebrity's life. The fashions offer the target market a feeling of connection to a different, perhaps bigger, life.

Fashion magazines depict the belongingness theory when they provide photos of celebrities using fashion products and then provide information where consumers can purchase the product either at full-price or for less. A popular segment in magazines shows consumers how to get the celebrity look for less. On one side of the page, photos are provided with a celebrity wearing designer products. On the other side, similar fashion products are provided for a fraction of the cost. This type of fashion article promotes the parasocial relationship with celebrities and their fashions.

figure 5.15
Fashion magazines teach consumers how to obtain a celebrity look for less.

SUMMARY

The twenty-first century has seen the most significant growth of celebrities marketing fashions based on their fame. The fashion marketing efforts by entertainers clearly makes entertainers a significant amount of money and provides continual name recognition to the target market. Fashion marketers have also revolutionized how and what consumers purchase. Athletes, models, and actors have been spokespersons for fashions and accessories. The celebrity must clearly represent the values and attributes of the brand.

Movies, award shows, and television shows promote fashion brands. Fashion marketing products used on television include apparel, accessories, and home furnishings. If a fashion marketer's products are used in a television show, the products are typically shown throughout the entire show and/or series. This provides the fashion marketer multiple opportunities to build loyalty to the brand and promote the specific product.

We, as a society, need to feel as if we belong —to our community, to our society, to a world that is bigger than ourselves. Consumers who follow entertainers' and celebrities' fashions gain a sense of belonging through a parasocial relationship. The belongingness theory states that people need social acceptance. When consumers adopt similar or identical fashions worn and/or promoted by celebrities, they feel part of the celebrity's life. The fashions offer the target market a feeling of connection to a different, perhaps bigger, life.

REFERENCES

Agins, T. (1999). *The end of fashion: The mass marketing of the clothing business.* New York: William Morrow.

Atkinson, C. (2008, April 14). Testing the boundaries of branded entertainment, *Advertising Age.* Retrieved December 22, 2008 from www.lexisnexis.com/us/lnacademic/results/docview/docview.do?.

Garment Industry Development Corporation (2007). GIDC services & NY apparel industry. Retrieved July 3, 2007 from http://www.gidc.org/ enter.html.

Garron, B. (2008, November 24). TV review: Starz inside fashion in film, *THReviews.* Retrieved December 22, 2008 from http://login.vnuemedia.com/hr/tv-reviews/.

Gibson, Valerie. (1994, December 13). Ex-angel enjoys divine success. *The Toronto Sun*, p. 67.

Golden retrievers. (2009, January 13). *Women's Wear Daily*, p. 4.

Halpern, J. (2007). *Fame junkies.* Boston: Houghton Mifflin.

Herr, N. (2008). Television & health. Retrieved from March 12, 2009 from www.csun.edu/science/health.

Hilfiger, T. (2009). Retrieved on June 26, 2009 from http://tommytv.com.

Kaplan, J. (2009, January 29). L.E.I. Swift decision: Taps singer for ads. *Women's Wear Daily*, p. 3.

Kinon, C. (2007, September 20). 'Gossip Girl' for sale: If you love the show, you'll love buying the clothes. *Daily News*, p. 81.

Kinon, C. (2008, April 23). 'Gossip' fans are dishing about the 'girl's' clothes. *Daily News.* Retrieved December 3, 2008 from www.lexisnexis.com/us/lnacademic/results/docview.

Sefton, M. (2009, February 15). Personal interview.

Smith, S.D. (2009, February 9). A tough second half for newsstand sales. *Women's Wear Daily.* Accessed November 30, 3009 from http://www.wwd.com/media-news/a-tough-second-half-for-newsstand-sales-1968635//.

Vesilind, Emili. (2009, May 31). Stars of the street: It seems that every major hip-hop artist is turning a buck in the rag trade these days. *Los Angeles Times*, p. P4.

Nonfiction Books Related to the Fashion Industry

Agins, T. (2000). *End of fashion: How marketing changed the clothing business forever.* New York: HarperCollins.

Ascoli, P. M. (2006). *Julius Rosenwald: The man who built Sears, Roebuck and advanced the cause of black education in the American south.* Bloomington: Indiana University Press.

Barmash, E., Klapper, M., Rutberg, S., & Parker, S. (2005). In *Fashion retailing and a bygone era: Inside Women's Wear Daily.* Fredrick, MD: Beard Books.

Blackwell, R. (1995). *Mr. Blackwell: From rags to bitches.* Los Angeles: General Publishing Group.

Calasibetta, C., Tortora, P. G., & Abling, B. (2002). *The Fairchild dictionary of fashion.* New York: Fairchild Books.

Charles-Roux, E. (2005). *Chanel and her world: Friends, fashion, and fame.* New York: Vendome.

Forden, S. G. (2001). *The House of Gucci: A sensational story of murder, madness, glamour, and greed.* New York: Perennial.

Gehlhar, M. & Von Furstenberg, D. (2008). *The fashion designer survival guide: Start and run your own fashion business.* New York: Kaplan.

Gross, M. (2004). *Genuine authentic: The real life of Ralph Lauren.* New York: HarperCollins.

Lauder, E. (1985). *Estee Lauder: An intimate memoir.* New York: Random House.

Madsen, A. (1991). *Chanel: A woman of her own.* Austin, TX: Holt McDougal.

McCarthy, P. D. & Spector, R. (1996). *Nordstrom way: The inside story of America's #1 customer service company.* New York: John Wiley & Sons.

McCarthy, P. D. & Spector, R. (2005). *The Nordstrom way to customer service excellence: A handbook for implementing great service in your organization.* New York: John Wiley & Sons.

McDermott, C. (2000). *Versace.* New York: Carlton Books.

Olsen, M. K. & Olsen, A. (2008). *Influence.* New York: Penguin.

Rodriguez, N. & Berne, B. (2008). *Narciso Rodriguez.* New York: Rizzoli.

Sischy, I. (2006). *Donna Karan.* New York: Assouline.

Sozzani, F. (2005). *Dolce & Gabbana.* Jackson, TN: Perseus Distribution Services.

Spade, K., Peltason, R. A., Leach, J., & Johnson, V. (2004). *Style.* New York: Simon & Schuster.

Tippins, S. & Young, R. G. (1992). *Donna Karan: Designing an American dream.* Ada, OK: Garrett.

Vosovic, D., Turek, M., & Gunn, T. (2008). *Fashion inside out: Daniel V's guide to how style happens from inspiration to runway and beyond.* New York: Watson-Guptill.

Weatherly, M. (2008). *Business leaders: Ralph Lauren.* Morgan Reynolds

Wintour, A., Mower, S., & Martinez, R. (2007). *Stylist: The interpreters of fashion.* London: Random House.

Yohannan, K. & Koda, H. (2009). *Valentina: American couture and the cult of celebrity.* New York: Rizzoli.

Fiction Books Related to the Fashion Industry

Alderson, M. (2005). *Handbags and gladrags.* New York: Penguin.

Allingham, M. (2009). *The fashion in shrouds.* New York: Felony & Mayhem.

Brown, S. (1993) *French silk.* New York: Grand Central.

Bushnell, C. (2007). *Lipstick jungle.* New York: Hyperion.

Harbison, B. & Harbison, E. M. (2008). *Secrets of a shoe addict.* New York: St. Martin's Press.

Sefton, M. (2005). *Knit one, kill two.* New York: Penguin.

Sefton, M. (2005). *Needled to death.* New York: Penguin.

Sefton, M. (2006). *Deadly yarn.* New York: Penguin.

Sefton, M. (2008). *Dyer consequences: A knitting mystery.* New York: Penguin.

Sefton, M. (2008). *Fleece Navidad.* New York: Penguin.

Sefton, M. (2008). *A killer stitch: A knitting mystery.* New York: Penguin.

Weisberger, L. *The devil wears Prada* (1st ed.). New York: Doubleday, 2003.

Weisberger, L. *Chasing Harry Winston.* New York: Simon & Schuster, 2008.

Yampolsky, K. (2008). *Falling out of fashion.* New York: Kensington.

KEY TERMS

Define or briefly explain the following terms:

Armchair fashionista ______________________________

Belongingness theory ______________________________

Licensing ______________________________

Trickle-down theory ______________________________

CLASS OR TEAM DISCUSSION QUESTIONS

1 | As a fashion marketer, when do you decide to use entertainers and/or celebrities to endorse your products? How can you, as a marketer, verify that the entertainer's actions will not harm the company?

____

____

2 | Can a company be overexposed in terms of celebrity endorsements? Explain.

____

____

3 | If marketing a newly formed fashion company, which marketing strategy would you implement to encourage celebrities to publicly use and endorse your products? List the guidelines you would enforce when using a celebrity to endorse your fashion products.

____

____

INTERNET ACTIVITIES

1 | Using the Internet as a resource, find examples of celebrities' use of fashion products that have (a) harmed and (b) helped fashion marketing efforts. Explain the potential long- and short-term implications of celebrities being associated with the fashion products.

____

____

2 | Use the Internet and YouTube as resources for the following assignment. Examine the strategic marketing efforts of (a) a celebrity's fashion line, (b) an entertainer's fashion line, and (c) a name-brand fashion line. What are the similarities and differences in the marketing mix?

---

3 | Provide specific examples and time lines of fashion marketing strategies that demonstrate the trickle-down theory. Use the Internet to obtain data to support your answer. Examples of data may include: (a) the year a fashion design was introduced, (b) a visual of the fashion, (c) a visual of a person wearing the fashion, and/or (d) a time line of the fashion.

STUDY QUESTIONS

1 | Define trickle-down theory. Give examples of fashions that explain trickle-down theory.

---

2 | Define licensing. How does the practice impact fashion marketing?

---

3 | Which entertainers have been successful in presenting a fashion brand?

---

4 | What does it entail to be a spokesperson for a brand?

---

5 | What are the benefits of having a celebrity lend his or her name to a brand?

6 | How have movies influenced the fashion industry?

7 | How has television influenced the fashion industry?

8 | Discuss the interaction between branding fashions and television.

9 | What is the difference between a biography and an autobiography?

10 | Why would a fashion marketer use an RBO?

11 | How do supermodels influence the fashion industry?

12 | What is belongingness theory? How does the theory interact with the fashion industry?

MULTIPLE-CHOICE QUESTIONS

1 | Fashion marketing using the entertainment industry as a venue begins with the _____.

a. Children's market
b. Teenage target market
c. Adult target market

2 | Fashion marketers use entertainers and celebrities as spokespersons for fashions because _____.

a. Consumers often want to emulate famous people.
b. Entertainers and celebrities will wear the clothing for free.
c. Entertainers and celebrities are typically thin and will look good in the fashions.
d. Entertainers and celebrities like expensive fashions.

3 | Using a spokesperson in a fashion marketing campaign may require _____.

a. Having the spokesperson be shown in public a predetermined number of times wearing the product
b. Having the spokesperson publicly state his/her commitment to the product
c. Having the spokesperson wear the product to prominent events
d. All of the above are reasonable expectations for a spokesperson.

4 | _____ influence the fashion industry and its marketing efforts.

a. Situation comedies
b. Television shows
c. Soap operas
d. Reality shows, television shows, and soap operas

5 | One of the most successful entertainers in the fashion marketing industry is _____.

a. Jessica Simpson for Walmart
b. Jaclyn Smith for Kmart
c. Jennifer Lopez for Target

TRUE-OR-FALSE QUESTIONS

1 | _____ Technology has positively influenced the marketing efforts between the fashion and entertainment industries.

2 | _____ All fashions worn by entertainers are created and marketed by well-known fashion designers.

3 | _____ The entertainment industry plays a minor role in the marketing of fashions.

TABLE 6.1

THE Market Planning PROCESS

step 1	CHAPTER 2	Be inspired; become passionate regarding a product/service; be driven to succeed and committed to working toward a goal.
step 2	CHAPTER 3	Intrinsic attributes of the products and services are marketed in terms of value, satisfaction, and quality. Building upon the mission statement, in this step you will make decisions regarding the pricing, communication, value, satisfaction, and quality associated with the purchase or the products and/or services.
step 3	CHAPTER 4	Identify a comprehensive list of products and services offered by the company.
step 4	CHAPTER 5	Examine the products and services component of the core marketing concept related to the trickle-down theory, media and celebrities, and the belongingness theory.
step 5	CHAPTER 6	**Examine the buying season in relation to the marketing process.**
step 6	CHAPTER 7	Examine marketing methods of targeting the consumer.
step 7	CHAPTER 8	Examine the methods of exchange and relationships with the consumers. This includes making decisions to sell products and services through brick-and-mortar retail operations, direct marketing, and the Internet.
step 8	CHAPTER 9	Examine the image and brands of the company in relation to marketing efforts.
step 9	CHAPTER 10	Conduct a market analysis of how companies are able to successfully cross product boundaries.
step 10	CHAPTER 11	Examine trends in the fashion industry regarding a) counterfeit merchandise and b) the impact of such merchandise on the industry's sales, profits, product design, consumers' attitudes.
step 11	CHAPTER 12	Conduct a market analysis of fashions in the global environment in order to determine impact to the company's existing marketing efforts.

THE Buying Season
MARKETING FASHIONS TO RETAILERS

"Don't be afraid to take time to learn. It's good to work for other people. I worked for others for 20 years. They paid me to learn."
—Vera Wang

chapter objectives

After reading this chapter, you should be able to understand Step Five of the Market Planning Process. This includes being able to:

+ Distinguish between centralized and decentralized buying practices.
+ Apply centralized buying characteristics to marketing efforts.
+ Apply centralized buying characteristics to decentralized buying practices.
+ Explain attributes of international fashion weeks.
+ Document fashion councils.
+ Explain the purpose of fashion councils.
+ Assess the beneficial components of fashion marts and councils as they impact fashion marketers' efforts.

Vera Wang is perhaps the most famous bridal designer in the world. Her designer skills, creativity, and marketing abilities are not the result of being a fashion prodigy. Her success is the result of hard work, long hours, and a belief in herself. Step Five in the Market Planning Process addresses the products-and-services component of the Core Marketing Component. Vera Wang consistently focuses her wide array of products and services around the bridal industry. Beginning with the bride's fairy-tale dress, Vera Wang's products extend to bridesmaids' dresses, china, flatware, stationery, etc. Vera Wang's products and services satisfy an increasingly more demanding target market.

Fashion marketing efforts tell a story about the products. To be successful, fashion marketers must carefully choose the language (i.e., media such as print, radio, television) that tells this story. Fashion marketing efforts can be expensive and will impact the company's long-term financial success positively or negatively; therefore, fashion marketers must carefully select the information they deliver to their target markets in order to create successful marketing strategies.

The selection of merchandise carried in a store influences the fashion marketing message. For example, a national marketing campaign requires its products to be carried at all or at least a majority of retailers nationwide. Merchandise offered regionally may influence the marketing message, medium, and certainly the products featured throughout the campaign. Prior to February 2008, Macy's employed a centralized buying

figure 6.1 Vera Wang began her fashion design career in the ice skating industry. When she crossed over into the bridal industry, her success rocketed to the top. The industry and her target market recognized her talent and skill.

figure 6.2
The MAGIC trade show in Las Vegas provides an excellent opportunity for buyers and marketers to meet with vendors, learn about upcoming fashion trends, attend seminars, and attend fashion shows.

practice. Merchandise buying decisions for every branch location throughout the nation were made at the company's buying headquarters in New York City. Poor sales and profits were cited for changes in the company's buying practices. In February 2008, Macy's announced that the company would decentralize some of its merchandise-purchasing activities. Merchandise would be selected based on the needs and wants of customers at the various Macy's branch locations throughout the nation. The change in merchandising practices had significant implications for the Macy's fashion marketing team. Decisions needed to be made regarding products to be promoted nationwide; media used to promote products nationwide; whether or not regional products should be promoted, given the additional cost incurred with individualized marketing campaigns; if regional marketing campaigns were to take place, which products should be featured in each regional campaign; and, finally, given regional differences in the market, what changes in the promotional campaign should be made.

In order to effectively respond to national and regional promotional campaigns, marketers must have a comprehensive understanding of the merchandising processes and must convey this understanding through carefully crafted strategies.

TRADE SHOWS

Marketing concepts remain the same regardless of the size of the campaign. Enormous differences can be made both financially and in terms of exposure when dealing with a large company. The start of a marketing campaign is not the time to be naïve. Everything matters. Attention to detail can help a company make or break a marketing campaign. Losing money, even a small amount of money, is a big deal. Marketing campaigns are designed to generate sales, profits, customer traffic, and long-term customer loyalty. There are many requirements a buying office and a marketing office complete. One recommended (although not required) assignment is to know your competition.

Trade shows are sponsored by organizations in the fashion industry. A trade show is an event where meetings, conferences, and seminars are held regarding the industry. During predetermined annual dates, manufacturers from around the world display merchandise. The event typically runs three days. During this time, retail buyers are able to place merchandise orders for their stores, attend information seminars and fashion shows, and meet with colleagues from around the world. The U.S. fashion trade show is called MAGIC. The event is held in Las Vegas. Products represented include menswear, women's wear, children's wear, and accessories. International trade shows are hosted in Spain, China, Japan, Australia, Turkey, Berlin, London, Paris, and Italy, just to name some of the major players.

So what does a trade show have to do with marketing fashions? It all depends on how you look at the target market and the competition. Trade shows provide companies with time to interact with other people in the industry. In addition to purchasing merchandise for the upcoming season and learning about new sourcing opportunities, attending trade shows provides us with information. Information can be priceless, particularly if it is something you didn't know the day before.

For large organizations, trade shows help the buyers focus, maintain product awareness in relation to the target market niches, and infuse new merchandise with merchandise from last season. According to Julie Gilhart, senior vice president and fashion director of Barneys New York, the company "is looking at everything with a precise and strategic fashion consciousness. We are making it easier for our customer by editing even more than usual." According to Jeffrey Kalinsky, executive vice president and designer of merchandising of Nordstrom:

> Our vendor matrix out of Paris will remain the same as last season. The only difference is our buy will be tighter, focusing on pieces we loved the most for our stores. . . . [T]he fall collection of Givenchy was so precise, and the energy around what Riccardo Tisci is doing for the house is another formula for success. Haider Ackermann's palette, materials, and shapes created one of the strongest shows of the season. For me, Yves Saint Laurent was just short of perfection (WWD Staff, 2009, p. 5).

The designs purchased by Nordstrom will play an important role in marketing messages to the consumer.

What happens if you are a small retailer, perhaps one who cannot attend the international trade shows? Your fashion marketing team may consist of your sales associates and your sister. Granted, your sister is a very talented part-time graphic artist. Talking with other participants at the trade show may provide you with ideas of fashions similar companies have successfully marketed. Your talented sister may learn an easier, less expensive, and more effective way of developing flyers, in-store signage, and print materials during a free trade show seminar. Meanwhile, you learn about a new Webmaster who provides discounts in setting up a home page for Internet marketing and sales. In other words, networking works! Trade shows are excellent resources for networking, generating marketing ideas, and finding out what other companies are doing. Even if your company has a big marketing team, it won't be isolated—and neither should a small marketing team.

Go to the MAGIC marketplace through the Internet: http://www.magiconline.com/magic/v42/index.cvn#wwd. Log on to MAGIC Facebook.

How can MAGIC Facebook help with understanding:

- Targeting a market niche?
- Product placement to capture a greater share of the target market?
- How to obtain new products?
- Pricing methods?

APPAREL MARTS

Apparel marts play an important role in building excitement within a fashion marketing campaign. The services they offer can enhance the perceived value of the fashion merchandise.

The United States hosts four major apparel marts in distinct geographic districts: Dallas, Atlanta, Chicago, and Los Angeles. Smaller apparel marts (e.g., the Denver Merchandise Mart) are located throughout the United States. Manufacturers and merchandise buyers for retailers attend the various marts to sell and buy products. These locations are used in addition to the garment district in New York City (Guérin, 2005).

The Dallas Market Center is the largest mart in the country. Buyers from more than eighty-four countries and every state in the nation attend this mart annually (Guérin, 2005). Although not as large as the Dallas Market Center, The AmericasMart Atlanta is significant in its own right. The AmericasMart is the largest wholesale-buying mart. Unlike the Dallas Market Center, patrons of the AmericasMart are mainly regional stores. The geographic target market of the AmericasMart is the Southeastern and Midwestern states (Guérin, 2005). Similar to the Dallas Market Center and the AmericasMart Atlanta, the Chicago Apparel Center provides wholesalers and retailers with a complete line of services. These services are designed to better promote and sell merchandise. Chicago's Apparel Center sponsors fashion companies across product boundaries, showcasing apparel fashions and accessories, gifts, home furnishings, home accessories, and commercial furnishings (Guérin, 2005). The fourth major mart is the California Mart, which is held in Los Angeles. This mart specializes in fashion, textiles, gifts, and the home market. This mart is large, with more than 1,000 showrooms and approximately 10,000 product lines. The California Mart is active with five fashion markets, four home and gift markets, and two textile markets annually.

The decision to patronize one or more apparel marts is primarily dependent on the product categories a retailer carries. Patricia "Missy" Hollifield of the Biltmore Estate completes the merchandising-buying process for all eleven stores at the AmericasMart Atlanta (Hollifield, 2009). Arden Korn, president of Little Lambs and Ivy, attends buying seasons in New York, Dallas, and Atlanta. Arden attends the New York market because "I meet the principals of the company," he says. "When I have a promotion, I am able to call the owner and get help. I attend the regional shows [Dallas and Atlanta] to meet the competitors. I learn what they are doing, what merchandise they are carrying, and how they are promoting their merchandise. Most of all, I learn from their mistakes. Competitors I have met at the market have become my friends. I stay close to them and learn from them."

Mart Fashion Marketing

The U.S. apparel marts play an important role in marketing fashions. The four major U.S. apparel marts offer a variety of marketing services that promote the mart, companies, brands, and products. The services are designed to build excitement for the product, provide information regarding how to increase store sales, and show upcoming trends. Services include press releases regarding events, conferences, trade shows, seminars, informational brochures, and fashion shows.

Print fashion marketing efforts conducted by marts is significantly different from print fashion marketing efforts for consumers. Both efforts are, however, equally important. Information provided in mart print marketing is designed to promote a large number of styles. The marketing efforts include detailed information about SKUs (stockkeeping units), which detail everything about the product —e.g., manufacturer, color, size, year), wholesale price, color selection, and size offerings. The marketing campaign may also include a suggested retail price. Similar to fashion marketing efforts toward the ultimate consumer, the company's image, merchandise quality, and contact information are emphasized.

All major and many of the minor apparel marts sponsor fashion shows. These shows feature merchandise sold by the various manufacturers at the mart. The preshow cocktail party, music, and fashion show build excitement within the buying process. This form of marketing is similar to the marketing efforts designers use to kick off their new fashions.

BUSINESS RESOURCES

External business resources provide valuable insight throughout the decision-making process. Information regarding trends, the competition, and global issues help the merchandiser and marketer make decisions. Two resources in particular assist the fashion industry: resident buying offices and trade publications.

Biltmore Estate is the largest privately owned home in the United States. Patricia "Missy" Hollifield keeps busy buying for the 12 retail stores located on the estate.

BOX 6.1 Buying for the Biltmore

As the director of merchandising of the Biltmore Estate, Patricia "Missy" Hollifield is responsible for the oversight, implementation, and effectiveness of 4 centralized buyers, 11 stores, and the ultimate purchasing acceptance of the target market. Throughout the buying process, whether attending the Atlanta mart or visiting with vendors on the Biltmore Estate, Hollifield and her team always consider: (a) if the merchandise fits with the company's image, (b) how the merchandise will be promoted, and (c) whether the target market will adopt the products.

Hollifield and her team negotiate discounts with orders and freight in order to pass on the savings to the target market. The success of the buying team's negotiation efforts is not, however, based on the size of their orders; it's based on the relationships they have built with the vendors. Successful buying efforts revolve around building long-term relationships with vendors. The Biltmore Estate brings large vendors to the estate on a regular basis. The vendors visit the gift shops in order to better understand the target market, theme promotional efforts, and retailing efforts. Vendors' participation of activities on the Biltmore Estate offers them a better vision regarding how to best serve their merchandising needs (Hollinsfield).

Resident Buying Offices

A **resident buying office (RBO)** is a formal fashion intelligence source. An RBO is defined as "a purchasing agent located in a national or international market center whose representatives shop the market daily in order to provide its clients or member stores with information and to select and buy merchandise for them" (Ostrow & Smith, 1988, p. 208). Designers, manufacturers, and retailers of all sizes may hire a resident buying office. The RBO is hired to consult and provide valuable (and time-consuming) information regarding consumer trends. Based on the trends, designers, manufacturers, and/or retailers are better equipped to make short- and long-term strategic decisions that impact their target market. The RBO may be hired for a limited number of services or an extensive number of services, depending upon the needs of the client. Typical services of an RBO include:

- Reading and interpreting fashion articles (as opposed to simply viewing the photos).
- Maintaining an extensive knowledge of all companies in the industry as well as companies that may be newly forming.
- Obtaining up-to-date information about the competition and interpreting how changes in the companies may impact the target market's purchasing behaviors
- Reading trade magazines (e.g., *Women's Wear Daily*) on a daily basis and interpreting how the day's events impact the client and its target market.
- Critically evaluating differences among designers as opposed to simply reviewing what he or she likes about each designer.
- Assessing trends in target market's acceptance of brands.

There are few resident buying offices, however. The existing offices are large and typically located in the heart of the U.S. fashion capital —New York City. Persons working for an RBO are experts in the global, holistic fashion industry. That is, it is an RBO's responsibility to know everything that is happening throughout the fashion industry. RBOs are "information hounds." They don't design, manufacture, or sell merchandise. RBOs, do however, know every fact about every designer, manufacturer, and retailer in the industry. Sir Francis Bacon said "knowledge is power." Resident buying offices have the power to make designers, manufacturers, and retailers powerful.

People are often the wisest when they know when to ask for help. Leaders succeed when they delegate. RBOs assist leaders (e.g., executives of companies) who delegate. Additional businesses that are designed to assist the fashion marketing industry are documented in Table 6.2.

Ask yourself:

- As the president of a large fashion-forward organization, what type of services would you purchase from a resident buying office?
- Would the president of a medium-sized fashion company purchase the same type of services as would the president of a large company? How would the information be verified for accuracy?

Trade Publications

Trade publications are important resources for merchandise buyers and fashion merchandisers. Trade publications provide valuable

TABLE 6.2

Business Assistance in New York City

RESOURCE	WEB SITE
NYC Department of Small Business Services	http://www.ci.nyc.ny.us
NYC Economic Development Corporation	http://www.nycedc.com
NY Loves Small Biz	http://www.nylovessmallbiz.com & www.nylovesbiz.com
NYS Small Business Development Center	http://www.nyssbdc.org
IRS site for Small Businesses	www.irs.gov/smallbiz
U.S. Commercial Service	www.export.gov
U.S. Department of Commerce	www.commerce.gov
U.S. Small Business Administration (SBA)	www.sba.gov
Alliance for Downtown NY	www.downtownny.com
Women's Venture Fund	www.womensventurefund.org

(Garment Industry Development Corporation, 2009)

figure 6.3 *Women's Wear Daily* is considered the most influential trade publication in the fashion industry. Industry experts read the publication to keep abreast of the changes in the fast-paced industry.

information regarding the overall status of the industry. Marketing efforts, business ventures, designers' efforts, and special events are addressed in trade publications. *Women's Wear Daily* and *Daily News Record* are examples of trade publications that chronicle the industry's efforts. Merchandisers and fashion marketers must continually examine the company's product offerings, as well as the industry itself, in order to fully understand the market. Reading trade publications is one method of accomplishing this goal.

As future professionials in the fashion industry, it is essential to continually gather industry information. Information should be gathered and verified.

Obtain recent issues of *Women's Wear Daily* or the *Daily News Record*. Using these publications, consider the following:

- Make a list of the range of topics the trade publications offer its readers. How would this type of information help you as a student?
- How can you as a student use the information in *Women's Wear Daily* or the *Daily News Record* as a competitive advantage? Hint: Can you use the information to obtain a better job? Does the information provide you with tips regarding your own business? If so, how?
- In your opinion, what is the most valuable marketing tool provided by reading *Women's Wear Daily* or the *Daily News Record?*

INTERNATIONAL FASHION WEEKS

U.S. apparel marts sponsor buying seasons *based on* product category. International fashions are marketed annually during predetermined weeks. Retailers throughout the world travel to Paris, London, Italy, Montreal, Hong Kong, and Madrid for fashions. Spring/Summer collections are shown in October; Fall/Winter Collections are shown in March (Guérin, 2005).

Paris

Paris has long been thought of as the capital of the fashion world. This moniker was given the city because of the number of custom design houses originating from Paris. Chanel, Dior, Giorgio Armani, John Galliano for Christian Dior, and Alexi Mabille all feature their designs on the runway during Paris Fashion Week (*Women's Wear Daily*, 2009, January 27). The hype, glamour, parties, and opportunities to mingle with the designers and models are all important components of fashion marketing efforts.

The two significant Parisian fashion organizations are the Fédération Française de la Couture and the Chambre Syndicale du Prêt-à-Porter. The **Fédération Française de la Couture** is the association that supports the promotion of French couturier designers. The **Chambre Syndicale de Prêt-à-Porter** is a comparable association in support of French Prêt-à-Porter designers (Guérin, 2005). Their marketing efforts bring national and international recognition to the designers, their fashions, and the country.

London

The British are well known for their ready-to-wear fashions. John Richmond, Charles James, Beatrix Ong, Stella McCartney, John Galliano, and Betty Jackson are some of the many English-born designers. With more than 50 fashion shows (e.g., runways) presented during London's Fashion Week, the fashion marketing efforts for this single week is enormous. The **British Fashion Council (BFC)** provides assistance for this effort. The BFC's purpose is to promote and stimulate the British fashion industry. The organization is the major fashion marketer for the entire country. It promotes, markets, and implements all components of the fashion week (Guérin, 2005).

Milan

Italian designers are well-known for craftsmanship, elegance in design, and creativity. Similar to London, Italy has a fashion marketing organization to help promote and stimulate their fashion industry. The **National Chamber of Fashion** is specifically charged with increasing the number of fashions exported annually (Guérin, 2005). Its fashion marketing efforts positively influence designers' and manufacturers' sales, the taxes generated, and the international reputation of the country as a fashion leader.

Ready-to-wear fashion in Italy is called **moda pronta**. Moda pronta is widespread in women's wear, menswear, and children's wear. The National Chamber of Fashion assertively promotes moda pronta to international markets. The export of moda pronta fashions is important to the Italian economy as well as to the overall stimulation of the Italian fashion industry.

Hong Kong

Prior to the 1970s, Americans rejected fashions made in Hong Kong due to improper sizing and poor quality. Since then, designers and manufacturers have refined the sizing and improved the quality. Indeed, the standards have improved to such a level that most Americans cannot tell if a fashion was made in Hong Kong or in the United States. To help market Hong Kong fashions, the country sponsors the **Hong Kong Trade Development Council** (Guérin, 2005). The council provides national and international buyers with information about designers from Hong Kong and Asia. Similar to other fashion councils and apparel marts, the council sponsors fashion shows, and provides product information and purchasing information to ease the international process.

figure 6.4
Store signage that emphasizes discounted prices is designed to stimulate store traffic and increase merchandise turnover.

IMPACT OF THE ECONOMY

The nature of the economy influences where merchandise is purchased, how far and frequently merchandisers are willing to attend apparel marts, and the marketing promotions of the fashions. There is a direct relationship between the health of the economy and the amount of merchandise purchased internationally. When the economy worsens, merchandise sales weaken. Retailer buyers are often forced to cancel international orders. Existing merchandise that is not selling at a brisk pace is featured during the next company marketing campaign. The marketing campaign will typically focus around price. Examples of messages featured in the marketing campaign may include "price savings," "20 percent off," "deep-discount prices," or "buy one, get one free sales" (Goth, 2009).

As the health of the national and international economies strengthens, international merchandising orders increase. Fashion marketing efforts move away from focusing on price and emphasize brand characteristics. Characteristics may include quality, craftsmanship, image, or value (Goth, 2009).

TYPES OF BUYING ORGANIZATIONS

There are two forms of retail buying practices: centralized and decentralized. One form isn't necessarily better than the other. The best method for a retailer is dependent upon the characteristics of the organization and the composition of its target market.

Centralized Buying Office

A **centralized buying office** (also known as a **central merchandising plan**) exists when the buying for the entire company is conducted from headquarters (Clodfelter, 2008). This type of buying has become increasingly popular among large retailers. Examples of companies that use a centralized buying office include Sears, J. C. Penney, Gap Inc., Lane Bryant, Old Navy, and Biltmore Estate (Clodfelter, 2009).

The advantages of a centralized buying office far outweigh the disadvantages. Buyers are located in one building. As such, communication among buying divisions and management is enhanced. On-site meetings can take place without added expense. The clarification of buying and marketing efforts can be handled face-to-face. Relationships can be built, thereby fostering better understanding of how each division operates as a group. Each of these aspects can assist the productivity of the buying office.

Because merchandisers and fashion marketers are located at company headquarters, both divisions are able to interact with each other on a regular basis. The success of the fashions acquired by the buying team is largely dependent on the company's marketing efforts. The fashion marketing team needs to have a comprehensive understanding of which products are featured at each branch location, then coordinate products, brands, brand identification, and future trends that will be featured by the company. The more product information the fashion marketers have, the better they can promote individual products, brands, and the company. A clear, comprehensive understanding of the buying process will benefit the fashion marketing efforts of a company.

A centralized buying office may be responsible for purchasing fashions for one, five, or twenty stores. Regardless of the location, the merchandise must be promoted to the target market. Fashion marketers have the challenge of making sure that the marketing efforts provide a consistent company image throughout the entire store, within each region, and across the country and globally.

As with any strategy, some disadvantages exist with centralized buying. Centralized buying offices may limit the ability to serve individual needs of stores throughout the country. Similarly, the fashion marketing team must be diligent to clearly understand the target market in each region. Remember the merchandising and marketing statement, "One size fits all." Not all merchandising or fashion marketing actions work the same way. One size does not fit all. Or stated another way, merchandise purchased from one perspective isn't always accepted by the entire target market.

Centralized buying may result in losing touch with the target market. Subtle regional merchandise preferences, marketing messages that influence purchasing behaviors, and cultural nuances can sabotage the advantages of a centralized buying office. Companies must carefully examine the existing locations of their fashion stores as well as the needs of their target market to fully understand if a centralized office will work for the organization.

Decentralized Buying Office

A **decentralized buying office** (also known as a **departmentalized merchandising plan)** exists when the company uses different buying offices based on geographic region, merchandise category, and/or divisions (Clodfelter, 2008). Decentralized buying offices can provide valuable information to fashion marketers, particularly if a national marketing firm is used. There are numerous advantages for using decentralized buying offices. This type of structure enables the merchandisers to have an excellent understanding of the target market's needs and wants. Buyers are able to examine the social and cultural differences among consumers that geographical locations may influence in their fashion needs. Decentralized buyers are less likely to rely on stereotypes when making purchasing decisions.

As with any organization, when offices are spread out across the country, effective communication becomes more difficult. Despite the fact that the twenty-first century is equipped with excellent communication technology, multiple buying offices across multiple states and/or nations can result in delayed or disrupted communication. It is essential for all buying offices to maintain the organization's buying guidelines and procedures. As the number of buying offices increases, the possibility for errors increases.

Decentralized buying offices often provide the retailers and consumers with fashions specifically targeted to the regional and cultural needs. While the adaptation of buying can enhance consumer acceptance of merchandise, it can also negatively influence marketing efforts.

Fashion marketing efforts feature specific products. Multiple marketing efforts are typically undertaken during each campaign. Decentralized buying may also require decentralized fashion marketing efforts. This decentralized fashion marketing effort has the same advantages and limitations as do decentralized buying offices. Expenses and communication difficulties need to be weighed against the possible advantage of specifically marketing to a smaller geographic market. For example, Macy's has an initiative called "My Macy's." A portion of its decision making is decentralized to accommodate different needs among the stores. The company has stores in forty-five states, the District of Columbia, Guam, and Puerto Rico, and it operates http://www.macys.com.

MISSION STATEMENT'S IMPACT ON BUYING

Regardless of the type of buying—centralized or decentralized—buyers must continually remember the company's mission statement. The mission statement, company's vision, and goals will guide the buying process, fashions purchased, and, ultimately, the marketing methods used. According to Missy Hollifield, director of merchandise at the Biltmore Estate, the traits the company focuses on are genuine quality, authenticity, integrity, and loyalty. Eleven stores are located on the Biltmore Estate. The four buyers continually ask themselves the following questions:

- Is the product genuine and authentic to the image of the Biltmore Estate?

- Does the product contain the integrity that the company name demands?
- If we carry this product, will our target market remain loyal (Hollifield, 2009)?

Buyers also use fashion intelligence to track trends (Hume, 2007). **Fashion intelligence**, or the ability to identify or track trends, is an important part of merchandise buying and fashion marketing. People with fashion intelligence look to the past, examine the present, and predict how future trends will be shaped. Fashion intelligence involves an understanding of national and global fashion marketing patterns related to products. For example, fashion intelligence of lace may encompass its use in lingerie, coats, jeans, accessories, shoes, couture wear, and merchandise sold at discount retailers. Fashion intelligence involves understanding how the fabric, color, size, or texture will impact the market's acceptance of a product.

As a student in the fashion industry, you must continually think about the Core Marketing Concepts. Throughout this chapter, the target market is being considered. Log on to YouTube and analyze different designers' and/or manufacturers' fashion shows.

Analyze the fashion shows by answering the following questions:

- Which specific target market would purchase the merchandise line that is presented?
- What message is being communicated?
- How should the fashions be placed throughout a store?
- Does the product offering have specific requirements regarding an advertising campaign?
- Would the product line be accepted nationwide and/or internationally? If not, explain.
- Which of the product's attributes should be emphasized in the marketing campaign?

MAJOR FASHION PRICE ZONES

Throughout the buying and marketing of fashions, the designer, retailer, and marketer continually must keep in mind the following considerations: (1) the company's mission, (2) the characteristics of the brands carried, and (3) the needs and wants of the target market. These three considerations play an important role in the selection of merchandise during the buying season. The designs, styles, quantities, and brands of merchandise purchased influence the marketing efforts. The full marketing efforts do not need to satisfy an entire market. However, the merchandise does need to fit into the major fashion price zone.

Six major fashion price zones exist. The zones include: (1) designer signature, (2) bridge, (3) contemporary, (4) better, (5) moderate, and (6) budget (Table 6.3).

The **designer signature fashion price zone** is the highest price zone (Stone, 2007). This zone is reserved for high fashions that are created from quality fabrics, styling, designs, and craftsmanship. Examples of merchandise that

TABLE 6.3
Major Fashion Price Zones

PRICE ZONE	EXAMPLES
Designer signature	Dior Stella McCartney
Bridge	Donna Karan DKNY Ellen Tracy
Contemporary	bebe Karen Kane
Better	Liz Claiborne Jones New York
Moderate	Gap The Limited
Budget	Walmart store brand Mary-Kate and Ashley Olsen

figure 6.5
The continuous line of Gucci high-fashion garments and accessories on the runway simultaneously remind consumers of the availability of extensive fabrics, colors, and textures.

falls into the designer signature fashion price zone include Dior, Oscar de la Renta, YSL, Stella McCartney, Ralph Lauren, Gucci, Ferragamo, and Versace.

The second major fashion price zone is **bridge pricing** (Stone, 2007). Bridge pricing represents a bridge between designer and better-priced merchandise. Fashions in designer labels may offer a bridge label, extending the bridge label to a secondary market. The bridge label is offered at bridge pricing. This means that the price is lower than the designer signature price zone, but the fashion, style, and design continue to be higher than average. Bridge fashions are manufactured using fewer styling features than the designer merchandise. Lesser-quality fabrics would also be used. For example, instead of using silk, a blended fabric might be used on a bridge fashion.

The bridge pricing zone is an excellent marketing tool for fashion designers. The pricing zone extends the designer's name, promotes their fashions into a wider target market, and generates sales and profits. Designers using the bridge pricing zone include Donna Karan DKNY and Ellen Tracy.

The third pricing zone, the **contemporary price zone**, is targeted at quality, yet affordable, fashions (Stone, 2007). This price zone allows for marketing to a large target market. Comparable to the name, the contemporary pricing zone is popular among designers who are new to the industry and those with innovative fashions.

Better pricing, the fourth major fashion pricing zone, offers affordable and stylish fashions in national and store-brand names to the target market (Stone, 2007). The designs, styles, and quality of fabrics are good. Department stores and independent retailers regularly carry better-pricing-zone fashions. The fashions are also regularly featured in fashion marketing efforts because of brand-name recognition and popularity among the target market. Examples of fashions in the better pricing zone include Liz Claiborne, Jones New York, and Nautica.

The fifth fashion pricing zone, the **moderate fashion pricing zone**, is targeted to the mass market (Stone, 2007). The fashions are typically items the majority of the population wears. Marketing efforts for this fashion may emphasize value and a low price without sacrificing quality, a brand name, style, and design.

figure 6.6
Fashions are marketed in a group, also called a line. This technique serves two purposes: (a) marketers maximize the number of fashions featured in one advertisement, and (b) consumers are able to visualize several items that fit their personality.

Stein Mart markets to the fashionable yet price savvy consumer.

BOX 6.2 Stein Mart: Current Fashion at Discount Prices

Marketing fashions at Stein Mart is different than at traditional discount-oriented retailers. The majority of department and discount stores bring in merchandise at a predetermined price. The fashion marketing efforts then focus on selling the merchandise at the price for a predetermined number of weeks. After the weeks have passed, the merchandise is then marked down. Stein Mart buyers find department and specialty store fashions, shoes, home décor, and linens and offer them from anywhere between 20 and 60 percent below the competition. Stein Mart fashions consist of current and brand-name merchandise. Customer traffic is generated through coupons, advertisements, and flyers. To receive the full benefit of the low prices, customers must shop frequently because quantities of each style are limited. Consumers do not seem to mind the necessity of repeat visits to the store. The Stein Mart buying model has successfully turned customers into a loyal target market. Nationwide, Stein Mart has made a reputation of turning customers into purchasers. Customers are willing to make frequent trips to the retailer in order to find current fashions at deep discounted prices.

Examples of companies that use this pricing zone include Gap Inc., Macy's, Hanes, The Limited, and Levi Strauss & Co. (Box 6.2).

The sixth and final fashion pricing zone is called the **budget pricing zone**, the least expensive pricing zone. Merchandise in this zone is specifically targeted to the mass market. Merchandise offered in the budget pricing zone is not necessarily a staple or fashion insensitive. Walmart has successfully merchandised fashions for the entire family. While much of its apparel offerings are staples such as jeans, the children's lines are fashion-forward. The buyers and fashion marketers have been successful with the Mary-Kate and Ashley Olsen merchandise for many years. More recently, fashions by Miley Cyrus have stimulated additional interest in apparel and accessories (Petrecca, 2009).

BUYING SEASONS

Planning is the key element of success for designers, manufacturers, wholesalers, distributors, and retailers. As such, the fashion buying seasons occur on the same weeks year after year. Held on consecutive weeks, fashion buyers go to New York, London, Milan, and Paris during the months of February and March. During these packed eight weeks of travel, buyers examine the fashions for the next year (Guérin, 2005). While traveling to four cities and three countries in two months may sound exciting, the work is often exhausting. The preparation work in advance of the buying season includes monitoring trends, analyses of the target market's needs, changes in color forecasting, the number of units projected to sell in each category (e.g., tops vs. skirts), the number of SKUs that are required to fill the department's needs, **open-to-buy** (i.e., the amount of money the merchandiser has remaining in the budget during a particular season), the target market's preferred brands, and desired new styles to secure. Once the fashions are selected for the seasons, the buyers return to the shows in September and October for the spring buying season (Nurchai, 2002).

Fashion shows introduce the designer's new line. These events offer a combination of a party atmosphere with celebrities, fashion models on the runway, and new fashions. Not all fashion shows are designed to sell the fashions. Some of the fashion shows are designed to build hype and excitement for the designer. The amount of positive electronic and print coverage the fashion show and the fashion line receive is the desired fashion marketing outcome of the event (Guérin, 2005).

To New Yorkers, Bryant Park is known for its beautiful gardens, lush lawns, and serene gravel paths. The park has been an important part of the New York lifestyle since 1842. Located on Fifth Avenue, the New York Public Library rises above the park grounds. Bryant Park also has another dimension; to national and international fashion designers,

figure 6.7
Mary-Kate and Ashley Olsen market fashions to young children and teens. They are often seen at red carpet events.

figure 6.8
The Mercedes Benz Bryant Park fashion week in New York City is considered one of the biggest fashion show marketing efforts in the United States. This is a model from the Fall 2009 fashion week.

figure 6.9
Nina Garcia, Michael Kors, and Heidi Klum carefully examine each fashion as it passes them on the runway during the final competition on *Project Runway*. The judges are at Bryant Park, where the fashions are shown on the runway.

manufacturers, and marketers, it provides fashion designers with the locale for excellent fashion marketing efforts. Retailers, fashion editors, celebrities, and wealthy clients regularly attend Bryant Park for a first-hand view of next season's fashions. Openings, receptions, and parties are all part of the fashion marketing efforts designed to further promote the fashions and build designer and brand loyalty (Guérin, 2005).

The impact of marketing across product boundaries and the global recognition of Bryant Park are apparent by its sponsors. Mercedes-Benz is an internationally known manufacturer of luxury automobiles. Despite the fact that it doesn't sell apparel, it sponsors the "Mercedes-Benz Fashion Week" every February in Bryant Park. The company's global exposure on Bryant Park's Web site, and in the Fashion Week brochures, receptions, exhibits, and fashion shows gives a clear message that the Mercedes-Benz automobile is just another fashion extension to the luxury target's apparel.

Bryant Park has become the destination for other aspects of the fashion industry. The television reality show *Project Runway* was in its fifth season during 2008. International model and the show's host, Heidi Klum, international designer Michael Kors, and editor for *Elle* magazine, Nina Garcia, judged original fashion designs from sixteen contestants. Viewers throughout the United States watched as fashions unfolded. Designers blogged about their inspiration and desire to out-design contestants. The three finalists presented their fashions at Bryant Park via a fashion show. The winner of the competition won money, international exposure, and more. After five seasons, *Project Runway*'s popularity continues to increase. The show has also resulted in revealing just how much effort is required for fashions to be accepted by consumers.

Not all well-known U.S. fashions are marketed at Bryant Park. During 2009, the financial economy took a significant downturn worldwide. Consumers were spending less, resulting in financial problems at the retail level. Regardless of the amount of marketing, retailers had excess inventory. Spending lavishly was perceived negatively. Vera Wang's response to the macro environment was to show her 2009

figure 6.10
Vera Wang walks the runway after the show in her Mercer store in 2009. Wang decided to show her fashions in her store instead of Bryant Park.

TABLE 6.4
Examples of Fashion Behavioral Theories

FASHIONS INFLUENCED BY TRICKLE-DOWN THEORY	FASHIONS INFLUENCED BY TRICKLE-UP THEORY
Diamonds	Jeans
Designer handbags	Flip-flops
Tiffany charm bracelet	Scrunchies
Fur-trimmed jackets	Ball caps
Oversized sunglasses	T-shirts
	Tattoos

collection at her Mercer Street store instead of Bryant Park. According to Wang, "[t]he intimacy of a smaller show feels much more appropriate for these times" (Feitelberg, 2008, p. 3).

FASHION BEHAVIORAL THEORIES

Retail buyers look at trends when considering the fashions to select for their target market.

A **fashion behavioral theory** is a theory that helps explain the reason why consumers adopt or reject fashions. Two well-known fashion behavioral theories are the trickle-down and trickle-up theories. Both theories involve the examination of consumers' influence on fashion (Table 6.4).

Trickle-Down Theory

In 1953, Marilyn Monroe sang, danced, and stole hearts in a movie called *Gentlemen Prefer Blondes*. When she shimmied to "Diamonds Are a Girl's Best Friend," she made the song famous. Of course, some ladies may also think rubies, emeralds, and sapphires are also a girl's friend. Precious stones were once reserved only for the famous and definitely only for the wealthy.

The promotion, purchasing, and wearing of diamond earrings is an example of the trickle-down theory. This theory states that fashion trends are dictated by upper-income consumers. After widespread adoption at the top level, design modifications are made to the fashions. Ultimately, the fashions are offered in lower quality and price point, and marketing efforts are targeted to middle-income and lower-income consumers.

Prior to the 1970s, primarily upper-income consumers wore diamond earrings. They certainly were not worn every day and not with sweatpants or shorts. Diamond earrings were savored and worn for special occasions. After the 1980s, fashion marketing efforts, understanding consumer trends, retail buying practices, and the trickle-down theory significantly influenced who wore diamond earrings.

An increasing number of men are purchasing gems for themselves and not for girlfriends or spouses. Today, diamonds of every size and quality are popular among consumers of varying income brackets. Precious stones are also being placed into symbolic settings, representative of a hometown, university, or association.

figure 6.11
Marilyn Monroe dazzled the television audience nationwide when she sang and shimmied to the song "Diamonds Are a Girl's Best Friend."

Trickle-Up Theory

There was a time when fashions were always mimicked by the upper-income classes. Socialization changed and consumers started to enjoy blue jeans, country music, and relaxation. Fashion buyers quickly realized that fashions from different social classes could be adopted and marketed. Hence, the **trickle-up theory** was proposed.

The trickle-up theory shows how consumers at lower income levels influence fashion trends. Fashion trends have been influenced to a greater extent by trickle-up theory during the latter part of the twentieth century. The adoption of jeans is perhaps the most obvious example of trickle-up theory. Since Levi Strauss began manufacturing and marketing jeans in 1873, the products were considered a staple for the lower income. Today jeans are considered an important fashion statement in a wardrobe for all income levels.

SUMMARY

In order to effectively respond to national and regional promotional campaigns, marketers must have a comprehensive understanding of the merchandising processes. Trade shows, apparel marts, and international shows offer retailers and fashion marketers an opportunity to view upcoming merchandise, identify trends, and examine strategies used by the competition.

Business resources are used in an attempt to stay competitive in the global fashion industry. Resident buying organizations provide valuable information regarding trends; the information can then be used toward the enhancement of the fashion marketing campaigns. Trade publications provide up-to-date industry-wide information.

The method of centralized versus decentralized, buying offices influences the company's purchasing practices. This will, in turn, influence the fashion marketing campaign.

REFERENCES

Clodfelter, R. (2008). *Retail buying: From basics to fashion.* (3rd ed.) New York: Fairchild Books.

Feitelberg, R. (2008, December 17). Wang to scale back fashion show. *Women's Wear Daily*, p. 3.

Goth, S. (2009, March 3). Personal interview with merchandise manager, HandPicked, Columbia, South Carolina.

Guérin, P. *Creative fashion presentations* (2nd ed.). New York: Fairchild Books, 2005.

Hollifield, P. (2009, February 15). Personal interview.

Hume, M. (2007). A muse by any other name. *Time Style & Design*, p. 99.

In 'solid' Paris season, stores reduce budgets, demand lower prices (2009, March 16). *Women's Wear Daily*, 1, 4–5.

Master strokes. (2008, January 27). *Women's Wear Daily*, p. 4.

New York Business Assistance. Garment Industry Development Corporation. Retrieved April 21, 2010 from http://gidc.org/nycbizassistance.aspx.

Nurchai, S. A. (2002). Style piracy revisited. *Journal of Law & Policy, 10*, 489.

Ostrow, R. & Smith, S. R. (1988). *The dictionary of marketing.* New York: Fairchild Books.

Petrecca, L. (2009, January 31). Wal*Mart joins forces with Hannah Montana. *USA Today* online. Retrieved March 21, 2009 from http://www.usatoday.com/money/industries/retail/2008-01-29-hannah-montana-walmart_N.htm.

Stone, E. (2007). *In Fashion: Fun! Fame! Fortune*! New York: Fairchild Books.

KEY TERMS

Define or briefly explain the following terms:

Apparel marts ______________________________

Better pricing ______________________________

Bridge pricing ______________________________

British Fashion Council, The (BFC) ______________________________

Budget pricing zone ______________________________

Centralized buying office ______________________________

Central merchandising plan ______________________________

Chambre Syndicale du Prêt-à-Porter ______________________________

Contemporary price zone ______________________________

Decentralized buying office ______________________________

Departmentalized merchandising plan ______________________________

Designer signature fashion price zone ______________________________

Fashion behavioral theory ______________________________

Fashion intelligence ______________________________

Fédération Française de la Couture ______________________________

Hong Kong Trade Development Council ______________________________

Moda pronta ______________________________

Moderate fashion pricing zone ______________________________

National Chamber of Fashion ______________________________

Open-to-buy ______________________________

Resident buying office (RBO) ______________________________

Stock-keeping unit ______________________________

Trade publications ______________________________

Trade show ______________________________

Trickle-up theory ______________________________

CLASS OR TEAM DISCUSSION QUESTIONS

1 | Imagine you are a member of the marketing team for a fashion company, and provide examples of how you can help promote the company's fashions to the industry, retail buyers, and select consumers during Fashion Week. Give specific examples of marketing efforts. How are these marketing efforts different from the marketing mix presented to the ultimate consumer?

2 | Discuss the importance of marketing fashions at trade shows. Give specific examples of marketing efforts.

3 | Discuss the differences among the four major apparel marts located in the United States. As a member of a fashion marketing team for a medium-sized apparel manufacturing company, answer the following questions:

Which apparel mart would you show your merchandise in, and how often?

Which marketing strategy would you implement to make your fashions recognizable, memorable, and purchased by retailers?

INTERNET ACTIVITIES

1 | Using the Internet as a resource, access one of the fashion apparel marts. Document the events and activities of an upcoming market. As a member of a fashion marketing team, what types of information could you learn and use from the market to better prepare you for future marketing campaigns?

2 | Discuss the differences and similarities a fashion team must consider when preparing a marketing campaign for a centralized buying organization versus a decentralized buying organization. What

are the implications to the company's Web site? Provide support for your answer, using examples from companies that use each type of buying format.

STUDY QUESTIONS

1 | What is the purpose of a resident buying office?

2 | Who uses a resident buying office?

3 | Describe the purpose of a centralized buying office. Whom does it serve?

4 | What are the benefits and limitations of a centralized buying office?

5 | Describe the purpose of a decentralized buying office. Whom does it serve?

6 | What are the benefits of a decentralized buying office?

7 | What is the purpose of an apparel mart?

8 | Where are the major apparel marts located in the United States? What are the names of the marts?

9 | What are the services offered by the apparel marts?

10 | Where are the major international markets located?

11 | What are the names of the international fashion councils?

12 | What are the purposes of the international trade councils?

13 | What is a flagship store?

14 | What is Bryant Park?

15 | Why does Mercedes-Benz sponsor a fashion show?

____

____

MULTIPLE-CHOICE QUESTIONS

1 | _____ is a purchasing agent located in a national or international market center whose representatives shop the market daily in order to provide its clients or member stores with information.

- **a.** A trade association buying organization
- **b.** A decentralized buying organization
- **c.** A centralized buying organization
- **d.** A resident buying office

2 | _____ provides national and international buyers with information regarding designers from Hong Kong and Asia.

- **a.** The Asian Fashion Marketing Council
- **b.** The Asian Trade Development Council
- **c.** The Hong Kong Trade Development Council
- **d.** The Hong Kong Fashion Marketing Council

3 | What is the primary purpose of the National Chamber of Fashion? _____

- **a.** To develop fashion marketing programs in Paris
- **b.** To increase the number of fashion exported from the United Kingdom
- **c.** To increase the number of fashions imported into the United States
- **d.** To increase the number of fashions exported from Italy

4 | Buying seasons occur during _____.

- **a.** Different weeks each year
- **b.** The same weeks each year
- **c.** Weeks that vary each year and are dependent on the city
- **d.** Weeks that vary each year and are dependent on how the company markets fashion

5 | Centralized buying offices _____.

- **a.** May limit the individual needs of stores throughout the country
- **b.** Enable the merchandisers to have an excellent understanding of the target market's wants and needs.
- **c.** Are expensive to operate compared to other types of buying offices
- **d.** Allow for different needs among the stores

TRUE-OR-FALSE QUESTIONS

1 | _____ A centralized buying office is also known as a central merchandising plan.

2 | _____ A centralized buying office is always strategically better for the fashion marketing efforts of a company.

3 | _____ Fashion intelligence means understanding the fashion marketing mix.

TABLE 7.1

THE Market Planning PROCESS

step 1	CHAPTER 2 | Be inspired; become passionate regarding a product/service; be driven to succeed and committed to working toward a goal.
step 2	CHAPTER 3 | Intrinsic attributes of the products and services are marketed in terms of value, satisfaction, and quality. Building upon the mission statement, in this step you will make decisions regarding the pricing, communication, value, satisfaction, and quality associated with the purchase or the products and/or services.
step 3	CHAPTER 4 | Identify a comprehensive list of products and services offered by the company.
step 4	CHAPTER 5 | Examine the products and services component of the core marketing concept related to the trickle-down theory, media and celebrities, and the belongingness theory.
step 5	CHAPTER 6 | Examine the buying season in relation to the marketing process.
step 6	CHAPTER 7 | **Examine marketing methods of targeting the consumer.**
step 7	CHAPTER 8 | Examine the methods of exchange and relationships with the consumers. This includes making decisions to sell products and services through brick-and-mortar retail operations, direct marketing, and the Internet.
step 8	CHAPTER 9 | Examine the image and brands of the company in relation to marketing efforts.
step 9	CHAPTER 10 | Conduct a market analysis of how companies are able to successfully cross product boundaries.
step 10	CHAPTER 11 | Examine trends in the fashion industry regarding a) counterfeit merchandise and b) the impact of such merchandise on the industry's sales, profits, product design, consumers' attitudes.
step 11	CHAPTER 12 | Conduct a market analysis of fashions in the global environment in order to determine impact to the company's existing marketing efforts.

7

Targeting the Fashion Consumer

"I don't like people to feel completely described by the clothes they wear of mine. I want them to feel they're describing themselves."
—Isaac Mizrahi

chapter objectives

After reading this chapter, you should be able to understand Step Six of the Market Planning Process. This includes being able to:

+ Produce a fashion company's target market diagram including its primary, secondary, and tertiary levels.

+ Explain differences and similarities among generations.

+ Apply fashion marketing concepts to each generation.

+ Discriminate between the benefits of employing a mass market and market segmentation effort, and recommend questions to pose to consumers when surveying the target market.

Isaac Mizrahi has designed fashions for the luxury market, middle market and mass market. The above statement reveals his beliefs, goals, and aspirations regarding how each target market should view his designs. Regardless of the amount of design effort, construction, or cost, each consumer should shine in the fashions. The consumer should be the showcase as opposed to the fashions taking center stage. As the consummate professional designer who continues to succeed in the fashion marketing industry, Isaac Mizrahi understands how to design, produce, and market fashions to each individual target market.

Some may say that fashion is a universal language. Indeed, if you are enrolled in a course that uses this textbook, you are interested in fashion at some level. But look around your university.

Ask yourself:

- Do the students at your university wear identical fashions? Do students in the engineering major wear the same fashions as those studying fashion or history?
- Does everyone at your university spend the same amount of money on clothing?
- As you walk across campus, do you notice that some people carry designer handbags while other people carry their "stuff" in tote bags?
- How many people on your university campus wear clothing that is nationally branded versus store-branded?

figure 7.1 This Isaac Mizrahi off-the-shoulder floral dress is targeted toward a young, hip, and fun woman.

As you answer these questions, you are identifying fashion marketers' target markets. Try to remember that how or what a person wears isn't good or bad; it simply identifies them as part of a target market. A target market is part of a retailer's consumer group.

Careful selection of the target market is critical to the profitability and long-term success of any company. A target market that is excessively broad may have too few similarities to promote towards. A target market that is too narrow may result in such a small number of consumers that the company may be unable to realize a profit margin even when capturing a significant portion of the market share.

Successful fashion marketers continually examine the needs and desires of their target market. They must closely observe how the market learns about fashions, as well as the market's methods and frequency of shopping behaviors and brand loyalties. Never assuming a consumer's behavior, fashion marketers continually make inquiries in order to further refine the target marketing process. Examples of questions that a fashion marketer of a women's casual wear line may ask include:

- How often do you shop for casual apparel?
- On average, how much do you spend per shopping trip for casual apparel?
- How many items, on average, do you purchase during each shopping trip?
- What method of payment do you typically use when purchasing casual apparel?
- What are your three most frequently purchased casual apparel brands?
- What store do you purchase the majority of your casual wear?
- What hobbies do you enjoy?
- What activities do you enjoy?

The more marketers understand about the target market, the better they are able to develop and implement marketing strategies. Market segments are based on demographics and psychographics. Fashion marketers learn about the target market's psychographics through focus groups and survey interviews. The importance of understanding the company's target market is paramount. The fashion marketer's role in working with target marketing will be addressed in this chapter.

THE TARGET MARKET

Before we specifically discuss target markets, it is important to address how fashion has influenced target markets and market segmentation.

A **target market** consists of consumers on whom the company actively focuses its marketing efforts. Companies typically have a primary target market, a secondary target market, and a tertiary target market. A **primary target market** consists of the majority of the market that patronizes your store. Depending on the company, the primary target market may represent 60 to 70 percent of the market. Fashion marketing efforts focus on capturing this market. The marketing goal is to make this market purchase, preferably in multiple quantities and repeatedly. Notice that the words *consumers* or *shoppers* were not used. The term **consumer** means the person is a member of the marketplace; a consumer is not necessarily a member of a company's target market. A **shopper** refers to the person looking at merchandise. The term **shopping** reflects the activities of persons visiting and purchasing merchandise through a brick-and-mortar retailer, direct marketing retailer, or Internet retailer (American Heritage Dictionary, 1993).

The **secondary target market** consists of an additional 15 to 20 percent of the market. This portion of the market is not as important as the primary target market. However, additional sales and profits are generated through this target market. The third market segment is the **tertiary target market**. Few if any marketing efforts are focused on the tertiary target market. Consisting of 5 to 10 percent of the target market, this is the smallest segment of the market share. Marketing to this segment

figure 7.2
Juicy Couture fashions are heavily marketed to college-age students. Part of the marketing effort is placing their name in large font on their fashions.

has been made easier and inexpensive through the use of technology.

As you think about a target market, realize that the primary, secondary, and tertiary target market size captured by each company may vary. Influential variables include (1) the number of retailers, (2) the effectiveness of the company's marketing efforts, (3) the effectiveness of the competitor's marketing efforts, (4) the state of the economy (e.g., how much money consumers are spending), (5) the uniqueness of the product offerings, (6) the geographic distance between retailers, and (7) consumer loyalty.

For example, Juicy Couture manufactures, distributes, and markets casual fashions to college-aged females. The primary target market (60–70 percent) for Juicy Couture include females aged 16–24 (the demographic) who are fashion conscious and willing to spend slightly more money for comfortable yet stylish apparel (the psychographics). Celebrities who wear Juicy Couture include Jennifer Garner, Katherine Heigl, Jessica Alba, Fergie, Michelle Trachtenberg, and Britney Spears. The impact of celebrities' adoption of fashions is addressed in Chapter Five, "Fashion and the Entertainment Industry."

The secondary target market (15–20 percent) for Juicy Couture may consist of parents. Parents are a significant source of income for college-aged students. They are also a source of gift-giving. An example of a tertiary target market (5–10 percent) may consist of persons who would probably only give Juicy Couture upon request. Grandparents seem like a very probable tertiary target market.

Fashion marketers continually examine the composition of their market. They look at the number of consumers, their demographic and psychographic profiles, spending patterns, likes and dislikes, and financial resources. The more fashion marketers understand the consumer, the better able they are to communicate with them through the marketing process.

Fashion marketers' products rarely serve the needs of all consumers in the marketplace. All women do not prefer one style of Dooney & Bourke purses. Nor do all college men prefer one style of Abercrombie & Fitch shirts. Marketing success—that is, high sales and profits—requires fashion marketers to carefully understand the composition of their target market. Very few fashion marketers will say that the entire country or globe is their target market. It is important to remember that there is a difference between the target market and a consumer. The target market includes persons comprising the fashion marketer's demographic and psychographic profile. A consumer is a person in the geographic area (one who lives in the United States, for example),

figure 7.3
Kate Spade markets its products heavily in fashion magazines. The company uses magazines read primarily by its customers, featuring multiple products in each advertisement.

but who is not necessarily part of the company's target market.

It is more effective and profitable to target a smaller number of loyal consumers who regularly purchase your product merchandise. Marketers who choose not to target their efforts often spend time, money, and effort with little result. Consumers who are not interested in a company's marketing efforts carry a low probability of purchasing the product. Market segmentation takes careful consideration, effort, and planning. The results may mean the difference between minor success and global expansion.

Regardless of the company's ability to reach or exceed sales and/or profit goals, fashion marketers must continually strive to (1) communicate more effectively, (2) create excitement around the product offerings, and (3) build stronger consumer loyalty toward the company (Dunne & Lusch, 2005). Marketers must aggressively approach similar target-market customers of their competitors, increase the average dollar volume spent by existing customers, increase the average number of products purchased by customers per shopping trip, and, most of all, increase the purchasing loyalty to that company. As consumers and fashion marketers spend excessive amounts of dollars and effort on advertisements, store displays, vignettes, and window displays—no matter how wonderful they are—if consumers aren't buying the products, the fashion marketing efforts are wasted. They may be entertaining, but they will be a waste of time and money.

MARKET SEGMENTATION

Think about different fashion designers who also are master fashion marketers. Vera Wang, Ralph Lauren, Tom Ford, Isaac Mizrahi, Kate Spade, and Calvin Klein all reached fashion stardom because they were excellent designers who knew how to market their fashions. They targeted their products specifically to segments of the market. Each of the designers clearly understood the personality and behavior of the consumer who would appreciate, purchase, wear, talk about, and become loyal to their fashions. This action is called market segmentation.

The Four Levels of Market Segmentation

There are four levels of market segmentation: (1) mass marketing, (2) segment marketing, (3) niche marketing, and (4) micromarketing.

MASS MARKETING

Mass marketing exists when fashion products are targeted at all consumers. The marketing message goes out to a large audience. As such, the message is often diluted in order to be attractive to a wide variety of persons. Mass-marketing fashions may seem advantageous due to the relatively low cost in reaching such a large number of customers. This perceived benefit can be misleading. For marketing fashion in the United States, it is important to remember that consumers are very diverse in their demographics. The U.S. population consists of approximately 74 percent Caucasian, 12 percent African American or Black; one-eighth percent American Indian or Alaskan Native; one-tenth of one percent Native Hawaiian or other Pacific Islander; five percent some other race alone; and two percent two or more races (U.S. Census Bureau, 2005–2007). Think about each race. Persons who are native Hawaiians living in Maui, for example, may wear a Hawaiian print shirt every day. Persons who are native Alaskans may prefer fashions that are more representative of the mountains of their home state. It would be naïve and insensitive to believe that they would have identical fashion interests. Even if they have similar interests in a fashion product (e.g., shirt), they may have different preferences for the shirt's color, styling, or sizing.

The most common products that are mass-marketed are staple products. A **staple product** is an item that consumers need or use on a consistent basis. They consider these products essential in their wardrobe. The word *staple* may make you think that the products are boring. Indeed, some of the products *are* boring. For example, white cotton socks. I don't know any fashion maven who runs home from the store giddy with excitement after purchasing a pair of white cotton socks. (If you ever do become giddy with excitement from this purchase, I suggest you try to get on to the television show *What Not to Wear* with Stacy London and Clinton Kelly. London and Kelly can help you get some real fashion excitement into your life and your closet.)

Manufacturers of staple products realize that mass marketing often is very successful for their marketing strategy. After all, almost all customers need or want their staple product. Recently, in the past 15 years, these manufacturers have also added a fashion element to their merchandise offerings. Hanes is a well-known national brand of underwear and socks for men, women, and children. The company has added a fashion element to its staple products through the use of colors and patterns. Basketball great Michael Jordan; Cuba Gooding, Jr.; Matthew Perry; and handsome bad-boy actor Charlie Sheen promote Hanes products. Together, these superstars present a staple product and make it seem cool, fun, and fashionable by wearing the Hanes brand.

figure 7.4 Michael Jordan is a spokesperson for Hanes. His clean cut image, prowess on the basketball court, and smile make his personality appealing and marketable to a large target market.

Examples of mass marketing of Hanes staple products are available on YouTube. In times when consumers may miss a commercial or are unable to spend social time at a mall, YouTube offers consumers the opportunity to socialize with fashion marketers.

How would you answer the following questions?

- Which products do you consider staples?
- Are the staple products fashion-oriented? For example, a pair of black high heels?
  - Does your interest in fashion influence your classification of a staple product?

SEGMENT MARKETING

The second level of market segmentation is segment marketing. **Segment marketing** exists when fashion products are marketed specifically to individual consumer groups (i.e., segments). Consumer groups are based on demographic and psychographic characteristics. Demographics include statistics regarding the consumer (e.g., age, education, income). Psychographics consist of interests, hobbies, and lifestyle activities (e.g., sports, movies watched, music). This strategy enables the fashion marketer to incorporate messages that are important to the consumer group. The promotional messages are targeted to venues used most frequently by the group, thereby maximizing the marketing dollars spent (Kotler & Armstrong, 2001). Since 1990, Vera Wang has provided couture bridal and evening fashions. Her target marketing efforts included age, income, and psychographics. Her customers include women who were engaged, had discretionary income to spend on a custom-made wedding or evening dress, and believed in having a gown that expressed their sense of being. In 2008, Vera Wang designed and marketed fashions to a completely different target audience. She designed and marketed for women who wanted to express their sense

figure 7.5
Vera Wang couture fashions for the high-end target market are featured on the runway. These designs make a statement of quality, detail, and elegance.

figure 7.6
Simply Vera fashions are targeted to a budget-conscious fashion consumer and are sold at Kohl's.

of fashion. The primary difference was Wang was now offering fashions for consumers who could not afford custom-made fashions. Wang designed and marketed the line Simply Vera by Vera Wang. This line is offered exclusively by Kohl's. The two market segments are different in income and ability to acquire specific fashions. They also have differences in fashion needs. One group needs gowns and custom-made suits; the other group needs T-shirts and skirts. Both groups desire fashions; fashion transcends all segments.

figure 7.7
bebe promotes its fashions to the hip, style-conscious, and young target market.

As a fashion marketer, ask yourself:

- What are the demographics of university students?
- How do demographics influence your fashion marketing efforts?
- What are the psychographics of university students?
- How do psychographics influence your fashion marketing efforts?
- As a fashion marketer, would you use the same marketing messages for freshmen and seniors? Why or why not?
    - Which marketing techniques would you use to communicate with university students (e.g., print, radio)? Explain.

NICHE MARKETING

Niche marketing is the third level of marketing segmentation. Niche marketing occurs when subgroups are developed within segment marketing. A niche is defined with smaller parameters than a general market segment. For example, instead of segmenting a market solely by demographics (e.g., age and income), niche marketing may include psychographics (e.g., wants and/or needs) (Kotler & Armstrong, 2001). Consumers' purchase decisions regarding fashion are often based on psychographics. Once they have acknowledged that they are able to purchase a fashion item, either with cash or credit, consumers enter the realm of psychographics. Psychographics play an important role in the actual consumption of the product. As such, niche marketing is becoming ever more important in fashion marketing. Understanding why consumers purchase or reject fashions and the marketing efforts associated with them is vital to the success of fashion companies. bebe is an example of a niche market. The company markets their fashions to young, hip, and very thin women. The bebe brand uses niche marketing. Billboard, magazine, and direct mail are used to target the select niche market. This market is part of the boutique consumer. She is petite in stature, contemporary, edgy, hip, and fun-loving (bebe, 2009).

Think about some examples of niche marketing from your own experience:

- Identify the market niches on your university campus.
    - How would you market to the various niches?

MICROMARKETING

Micromarketing is the fourth and final level of market segmentation. Fashion marketers use a micromarketing strategy when they individualize a marketing program. This individualization may include a message that focuses on a geographic, regional, or population base (Kotler & Armstrong, 2001). Micromarketing enables the fashion marketer to emphasize an understanding of the culture as well as a commitment to the target market. For example, each October, Neiman Marcus distributes a Christmas catalog to its customers. Instead of marketing their regular merchandise, the catalog is marketed to a very small segment of the Neiman Marcus population. While all Neiman Marcus credit-card holders receive the annual Christmas catalog, the fashion marketers don't expect to sell products to the cardholders. The niche market consists of the top 1 percent—those who are excessively wealthy. In 2008, the catalog offered medieval and renaissance-era rings. Les Enluminures of Paris designed three styles. The designs and materials were of museum quality. The price tag of each ring matched the museum-quality rating, ranging from $25,000 to $45,000. If the company sold just one ring in each style, the fashion marketers would indeed have been successful.

As stated earlier in this chapter, fashion marketers typically identify their target market into a primary market, a secondary market, and a tertiary market. A target market is that particular subdivision, or segment, of a total potential market selected by a company as the target of its marketing efforts. The selection of a target market is usually based on some common characteristic possessed by the market segment (Ostrow & Smith, 1988, p. 238). These consumers are typically located in close proximity to the fashion retailer, have a close interest in the products carried, and are familiar with the retailer. The fashion marketer places the majority of his/her efforts toward enticing the primary target market.

The secondary target market consists of an additional 15 to 20 percent of the market. This market typically lives farther away from the store than the primary target market. With the adoption of online sales, the secondary target market has become an increasingly more important group to the fashion market. Fashion marketers' use of a Web site and an Internet channel to sell merchandise (refer to Chapter Eight, "Cross-Channel Shopping") makes it increasingly easier to capture part of the secondary target market.

The tertiary target market consists of the remaining 5 to 10 percent of the market. Fashion marketers typically do not actively promote this market. The tertiary target market consists of persons who come across the fashion retailer by accident, while visiting a friend, vacationing, or surfing the Internet.

Demographics and Psychographics

Market segmentation is "the subdivision of a population (frequently ultimate consumers) into smaller parts, or demand segments, having smaller characteristics" (Ostrow & Smith, 1988, pp. 144–145). Prior to the baby boom era, which officially began in 1957, marketers segmented consumers primarily on the basis of demographics. Demographics are "the vital statistics of a population, including the size of the group and the age, sex, birth and death rates, location, income, occupation, race, and education" (Ostrow & Smith, 1988, p. 70). Pre-baby boom era fashions were marketed through print and radio. Television was still a relatively new invention, so television advertisements were rudimentary and limited. Fashion market segments consisted of men, women, and children.

When the baby boom of 1957 occurred, fashion marketers realized the potential for immediate and future profits. Fashion marketing efforts for maternity, baby, children, and home products grew. Demographics were no longer the driving force behind segmenting markets; each market was simply too large to understand its needs. Market segmentation began and continued to evolve through the examination of consumers' psychographics.

Psychographics is "the result of a research procedure through which consumer behavior is explained, at least in part, by the study of such variables as personality, lifestyle, attitudes, and self-concept with a view of predicting consumer response to products, stores, and advertising" (Ostrow & Smith, 1988, p. 197). Psychographics influence the fashion-marketing message, promotional tools used, content of the messages, and shock factor.

SPEAKING TO THE MARKET SEGMENT

Technology has significantly influenced fashion marketers' ability to physically reach the market segment. Print advertisements in catalogs, magazines, and billboards can display the vivid colors of fashions. Internet, television, and cell phone capabilities provide fashion marketers with tools to present fashion shows, product demonstrations, and celebrity endorsements. The message of the fashion marketing effort, however, has to "speak" to the specific market segment—and to only this one market segment. Many marketers may think the message is, *Isn't this product wonderful?* The real marketing message is, *You must purchase this product.* The best fashion marketing messages encourage the market segment to purchase the product, not just enjoy the message.

When we discussed fashion marketing in the beginning of the text, you will remember that it required three chapters. Chapter Three covered product, price, distribution, and placement. Chapter Four covered public relations, promotion, and advertising. Chapter Five covered fashion and the entertainment industry. Each aspect of the marketing effort is important. Can you imagine what would happen if a company ignored pricing or public relations? Surely their marketing, sales, and profits would suffer.

The understanding of the target market's demographics and psychographics is similar to that of the marketing concepts. A fashion marketer uses all information to help make better-informed decisions and take appropriate actions. Demographics help marketers understand the general background of the target market. Psychographics, however, inform the marketer about the target market's overall lifestyle and habits. Placing both groups of information together, the marketer is empowered to communicate effectively and excite the consumer about his or her products.

CONSUMER SPENDING PATTERNS

Fashion marketers are continually monitoring the actions of their target market's purchasing

figure 7.8
Marketing fashions in the children's and maternity industries has become an important target market. Consumers are spending an increasing amount of money on maternity and children's fashions.

TABLE 7.2

Changes in United States Demographics

POPULATION	2008 (in millions)	2050 (in millions)
Hispanic residents	46.7	132.8
Black residents	41.1	65.7
Asians residing	15.1	40.6

(U.S. News & World Report, 2008)

behaviors. They analyze the styles, quantities, sizes, and frequency of purchases. In order to stay ahead of changing consumer trends, as well as understand the marketing efforts of the competition, it is wise for fashion marketers to understand the changing spending patterns of consumers. That is, fashion marketers must have a comprehensive understanding of who is making the purchasing decisions, how much influence each family member has on the purchase decision, and the manner of payment used for the majority of fashion products (Nunes & Johnson, 2004).

Ethnicity

The United States has often been referred to as a "melting pot." This phrase is based on the fact that so many people from different countries, cultures, societies, and backgrounds come to live in America. The number of Hispanics, Blacks, and Asians residing in the United States is estimated to grow at a significant rate through 2050 (Table 7.2). As the diversity within the United States expands, it provides an opportunity for fashion marketers to target their products to other groups. It is also an opportunity to develop new fashion products devoted solely for a specific ethnic market. For example, Sacha Cosmetics' products are designed and marketed specifically for women with yellow or dark skin tones. http://www.HispanicSurf.com is a fashion Web site marketing to Hispanic consumers. Information is presented in English and Spanish. Many of the fashions are imported from Puerto Rico, Mexico, and Cuba.

Generation

Generation is also an important factor in determining your market.

GENERATION Y

Generation Y, also referred to as *echo boomers*, is considered perhaps the most sought-after target market by fashion marketers (Kendall, 2009). Born between 1980 and the present, there are more than 60 million U.S. consumers in this segment. Thirty-one million are teenagers, and teenagers are primarily focused on fashion, shopping, and spending (often their parents') money. They shop as part of their socialization process (Spenceley, 2009).

For the most part, teens may hold a part-time job earning minimum wage working an average of 10 to 15 hours. After taxes, a teen may take home $75 a week (15 hours per week × $6.00 = $90.00 − $15 taxes = $75). After expenses, she may have $35 in **disposable income** per week (e.g., fashion magazines and a manicure). Disposable income is the amount

figure 7.9
Cross marketing to multiple target markets for the same company builds loyalty and stimulates product purchases. This photo features Gap products from its adult Gap retailer and its BabyGap retailer.

of money you have to spend after you pay all your bills. Anyone interested in fashion knows that $35 will not satisfy the needs of a teen who requires the $100 pair of jeans, $50 pair of Nike shoes, $60 top from bebe, or $50 in lingerie from Victoria's Secret.

The fashion marketing industry aggressively pursues that teen market. This market has reached in excess of $153 billion purchasing power. Teens' purchasing power doesn't come from their part-time jobs; it comes from their single- and dual-career parents' income. Gen Y's actions are documented and translated into the next teen fashion. Fashion marketers analyze the magazines teens read, products purchased and returned, colors worn, and items shared with friends. The fashion marketer's ultimate goal is to build teen loyalty into lifetime and family loyalty. For example, if teens begin to show loyal shopping behavior at Gap, they may continue shopping at the company well into their adult years. In addition, while at the store, the rest of the family may purchase products. Gap markets to tweens, consumers in their young teenage years. As tweens enter adulthood, Gap's marketing efforts are still attractive to the consumer; this attraction builds long-term company and brand loyalty. As the consumer has a family, marketing efforts from BabyGap and Gap Kids resonate.

Fashion marketers understand that in order to capture consumers during their older years, they need to start attracting them in their formative years. The preteen market has become a fashion marketing gold mine with such movie tie-in marketing efforts as Disney's *High School Musical*, *High School Musical* magazine, Hannah Montana, and *Bratz* magazine (Wignall, 2008). Although girls between the ages of 13 and 17 typically don't have full-time jobs, they spend like pros. The marketing departments at Kohl's, J. C. Penney, Macy's, Bloomingdale's, and Saks Fifth Avenue are consciously targeting these young consumers. Departments are being retrofitted to entice teens instead of their parents. Promotional materials are designed using teen images and slang. The short-term goal is to encourage these young consumers to begin shopping at the department store. The long-term goal is to make them lifelong consumers (O'Donnell & Kutz, 2008).

Teens shop differently than their parents did when they were young. Where parents were accustomed to paying cash during their youth, teens of today are all too familiar with the concept of credit. Fashion marketers use credit cards as a method for reaching their target market. The store's credit card is used to build loyalty. Fashion marketers guide the market's purchasing behavior by encouraging the purchase of specific products using the credit card.

As teens develop shopping patterns, they are building their adult consumer purchasing profile (O'Donnell & Kutz, 2008). This profile basically amount to their methods of finding merchandise (e.g., Internet use, number of hours walking through the malls, and number of catalogs and fashion magazines examined) in order to acquire the latest fashions to make them look hotter, slimmer, taller, sexier, or like the latest top model.

Fashion marketers strive to better understand teen shopping patterns (e.g., who they shop with, how long they shop, if they instant message their friends, and how often) to increase their **profit margin**. Profit margin is defined as the amount of profit a company makes for every dollar spent (Clodfelter, 2008).

As children mature into teens, they are less influenced by their parents' opinions and are increasingly influenced by their peers. During their preteen years, they may go to the mall in groups, being delivered by a parent of guardian. It is important to note that store, brand, and even style loyalty are often influenced by peer pressure for acceptance. As youths enter their teenage years, their reliance on their parents for fashion acceptance and rides to the mall decreases significantly. The acquisition of a driver's license enables teens to go to the mall more frequently and for longer periods of time than they may have experienced in the past.

Likewise, teens may now have increased access to a variety of retail locations.

The Internet has revolutionized the way consumers access information. With the click of a mouse, consumers find out the latest fashions across the globe, which retailers are selling a particular item, and if the retailer has the item in the desired size. A consumer who doesn't want to pay full price can log onto eBay and search through thousands of photos for designer products from Gucci handbags and Ferragamo shoes to Payless sneakers.

E-retailing captures 7–10 percent of all U.S. retail sales. Part of the stimulus for these sales is Generation Y. Sixty million Gen Y consumers have been actively spending. They are as comfortable using the Internet as they are shopping in a mall. As the largest consumer group, Gen Y is a formidable group for fashion marketers (Johnson, 2006).

While the mall offers opportunities for socialization, the Internet has revolutionized how Gen Y socializes. Internet sites like YouTube and MySpace allow Gen Y to share information about their daily lives. As they blog, they provide friends with an update of their recent purchases, brands and stores patronized, fashion magazines read, and items rejected. As literally thousands of like-consumers read the blog, fashion marketers offer free promotions about their merchandise and stores.

GENERATION X

Generation X was born between 1965 and 1979. These consumers are focused on their career and family. Their multidimensional lives include careers, having fun with the family, activities, events, and the community (Kendall, 2009). Fashion marketing efforts toward this generation emphasize various clothing needs. Generation X is not as well established in their careers as older consumers. Fashion marketing efforts often emphasize value and price without sacrificing quality. As Generation X families grow, home products are incorporated into fashion marketing efforts. Furniture and home accessories are considered an extension of consumers' sense of fashion.

Some experts in the fashion industry or those who simply enjoy fashion may use the statement *I love fashion*, or *I live for fashion*, or *I was born to shop*. In actuality, consumption (i.e., shopping) is a learned experience. Consumers learn which fabrics are better quality, the differences among brands, how to differentiate between the colors red and cranberry, and when you should pay $10 more for a dress that looks the same but fits differently. Shopping at brick-and-mortar stores allows consumers to analyze specific details of products prior to the purchase, evaluate customer service in all departments regardless of whether one makes a purchase, and view store layouts. The store is open for the customer's full inspection, and those in the Gen X market finds this a more comfortable way to shop than do those in the Gen Y market.

BABY BOOMERS

Baby boomers were born between the years 1946 and 1964. The consumer segment received the title because of the large number of babies born during these years. This was the first generation to earn a higher income and standard of living than their parents. With a higher income comes a taste for acquiring the finer things of life. High-quality fashions, designer brands, and merchandise purchased in multiple colors characterize their spending patterns. They are also willing to purchase additional fashions, expanding their closets to accommodate the newest style, version, color, and/or designer. With the ability to purchase high-quality fashions, baby boomers are opinionated.

Fashion marketers aggressively target this group with all types of products; baby boomers have high discretionary income and are willing to spend. Fashion marketing efforts integrate baby boomers' demographics and, more importantly, their psychographics. Integrated marketing and repeated marketing efforts are used to reach this group. Marketing efforts using technology are often more effective than print or radio forms of advertising.

GRAY MARKET

In the 1987 movie, *Fatal Attraction*, actress Glenn Close plays a psychotic woman having an affair with Michael Douglas. An unforgettable line is "I won't be ignored." Born prior to 1945, the gray market is repeating Close's line.

The **gray market** consists of consumers who are retired, typically have no credit card debt, have paid off the mortgage, and no longer have children living with them. In other words, the gray market doesn't have a lot of income, but they do have a lot of discretionary income. These individuals have also, for the majority of their lives, primarily shopped at brick-and-mortar retailers. Aging does not mean looking old or giving up fashion. It does mean, however, that this group may be more comfortable with the traditional form of shopping.

The gray market continues to read the newspaper and listen to the radio. As such, marketing efforts using flyers, newspaper advertisements, coupons, and radio can be effective for this market. Promotional efforts within the brick-and-mortar store and mall can also be effective. The gray market's tendency to patronize this channel can be maximized by the fashion marketing team.

By nature, people like to socialize. When fashions are introduced to the mix, socialization becomes even more important. Persons who are not confident about their sense of fashion may bring others to the store for advice. Fashion-conscious and self-assured shoppers may bring friends along to share in the experience or to demonstrate their sense of fashion. Either way, brick-and-mortar retailers offer consumers an avenue to satisfy fashion socialization goals.

GUIDELINES FOR FOCUSING ON A TARGET MARKET

Regardless of the size or classification of your target market (e.g., primary, secondary, or tertiary) rules must be followed when marketing fashions to the consumers. Note that the following are rules and not guidelines. As you read the rules, you may also think to yourself, *These rules are simple, basic, and obvious.* Unfortunately, multimillion-dollar fashion marketing efforts have been wasted because the rules were either forgotten or ignored. The problem with disregarding the rules is that the world is watching your fashion marketing efforts. Your success depends on them.

Focus on the Primary Target Market

Fashion marketing efforts—and all that they entail—should focus on the primary target market. This is because the primary target market represents the majority of the company's sales and profits. This group is the company's primary reason for doing business. The marketing messages, content, and products should be focused toward this group. The fashion marketer must know the television stations this group watches, the radio stations it patronizes, the newspapers and magazines it reads, the roads it travels, the places where it lives, and the ways it spends its money. The profile of the target market will influence how, when, and what the fashion marketer promotes.

Keep the Message Simple

The target market typically has anywhere between 30 to 60 seconds to look at (i.e., television, billboard) or hear (i.e., radio) an advertisement. This doesn't give the fashion marketer much time. The message must be simple, to the point, and recognizable. For example, if you, the fashion marketer, want the target market to purchase jackets, you must give the sale date and an encouraging statement to buy. Don't talk endlessly about the jackets, other products, or the company. The message must stay focused. Additional fashion marketing information can be provided with in-store signage, personal sales assistance, and flyers.

Repeat the Message Frequently

The target market has a lot of information thrown at it every day. Work, family, television, radio, and the Internet provide it with an abundance of information; some day's information overload occurs simply because too much is going on. Have you ever walked past a store and thought, *I don't remember that store being there*? This thought is a fashion marketer's nightmare.

The target market needs to be reminded of the message, and it needs to be reminded often. If you promote your fashions on television, it is better to have more frequent spots. In a magazine, multiple pages will help the reader remember your brand. Billboards throughout the community will remind people about the message and the product. In other words, once is not enough. Be a broken record. Repeat the message over, and over, and over. Successful fashion marketers make the target market remember the message. **Name a fashion advertisement that you remember.**

Communicate Your Company's Name

Name recognition is critical in the fashion industry. Even when a fashion designer or retailer becomes famous, the name is always visible. You may wonder why some companies need their names to be posted. After all, some logos have become so well recognized that most people throughout the world know the manufacturer. Chanel, Coach, Dooney & Bourke, Gucci, Ralph Lauren, Yves Saint Laurent, and Dolce & Gabbana all have extremely recognizable logos. **Despite the success of these companies, can you imagine the fashion marketers at any of them leaving the company's name off a marketing effort?** Absolutely not! Fashion marketing is to promote the fashions and the company.

Maintain a Consistent Corporate Image

Fashion marketers work hard to develop and maintain a particular image for the company. The image is developed through promotional efforts and packaging. Fashion marketers may use a wide variety of media to promote the company, including print, radio, television, YouTube, Twitter, direct marketing, and Web sites. In each medium, the products, message, and timing of each promotion may vary. The two attributes of promotional efforts that remain constant are the company's logo and name. Continuity of the company's logo and name provide the target market with a consistent understanding of the corporate image. For example, the font and style used by

figure 7.10
Logos permanently fixed to the products act as a marketing reminder to the target market. The logo also acts as a marketing piece to those who view the consumer wearing the fashion accessory.

figure 7.11
The JCPenney name in Times Square can be seen from down the street. The large marquee is used to attract the target market toward the retailer and away from the busy lights of the competition.

J. C. Penney, Rack Room, Ross, Belk, and Sears are used on all promotional materials. The consistency provides a sense of familiarity with the target market.

Don't Use the Same Message for Multiple Markets

By definition, each target market has different and very specific demographic and psychographic characteristics. For example, a bridal salon typically offers fashions for brides, bridesmaids, and the mother of the bride. The fashions may be grouped into different price points, ranging from moderate to custom-made gowns. The primary target market for the bridal salon is the moderate market ranging from $500 to $1,000. Messages used on marketing efforts may include: (a) quality, (b) many styles to choose from, (c) affordable yet elegant, and (d) layaway available. The previous messages would send the wrong message to the target market looking for a custom-made bridal dress; custom-made bridal dresses typically cost in excess of $1,500 and affordability is not a selling point.

As you think about marketing campaigns, whether on television, print, radio, or direct mail, try to answer the following questions:

- Which advertisement immediately comes to mind?
- Why is the advertisement memorable?
- Are you in the company's primary target market?
- What is the primary message (e.g., introduce a new product, sell an existing product)?
- How many times was the message repeated during the advertisement?
- How many times during the (a) day, (b) week, and (c) month did you view the advertisement?
- Did the frequency of the advertisement influence your preference for the advertisement?
    - How did the advertisement communicate the company's name and image? Were words and images used, or only images?

EVOLVING TARGET MARKET DESIRES

Target markets evolve over time. Consumers within a target market change interests and develop new hobbies, lifestyles, and interests. Their disposable income may dramatically increase as their professional careers prosper or diminish significantly if the economy weakens or if their careers falter. Shopping patterns may vary, depending on if the number and variety of persons living in a household change.

As the composition of target markets changes, the viability of retailers' profitability and gross margin also change. To be successful in the long term, fashion marketers must be skilled at adjusting to the changing status of the target market. The quicker and more responsive a fashion market is at responding to the environmental changes, the better the opportunities the retailer has for reaching the target market's fashion needs. For example, with a net income of $3.14 billion, Walmart is the world's largest retailer (*New York Times*, 2008, December 22). The retailer has traditionally focused on staple goods. With high consumer traffic, high daily volume sales, and loyal consumers, the international giant retailer is branching out. They are marketing to fashion-oriented consumers who also want value at a discounted price. The fashions are encouraging consumers to shop in the fashion aisles prior to walking down the grocery or staple aisles (Strauss, 2006). During the 2008 holiday season, Walmart was one of the few (if not the only) retailer realizing 10 percent profits during the third quarter (*New York Times*, 2008, December 22).

Companies can differentiate by adding product lines and brands. Brand names are typically a name similar to the higher-priced brands, but sold at bridge prices. Bridge pricing is a strategy whereby prices are set between moderate and high amounts. The products are typically sold at department stores. With the popularity of discount stores such as Kohl's and Target, some designers are also diversifying by adding a line of merchandise for these retailers. Isaac Mizrahi designed for Target, and Vera Wang offers apparel, accessories, and home furnishings called "Simply Vera by Vera Wang" for Kohl's. Formerly primarily targeting wealthy customers, both designers adopted a separate primary target market based on fashion retailers' clientele.

The success of having a couture primary target market and offering fashions to another, a discount target market is successful for Isaac Mizrahi and Vera Wang because both designers were extremely successful in the couture industry for many decades before adding an additional primary target market. In addition, the fashion retailers selected—Target and Kohl's—are well respected by consumers for their fashions. Notice that neither of the designers' products are offered at Walmart or Kmart. All four retailers are discounters. Walmart and Kmart, however, are known for basic products, not fashions. The primary target market of Target and Kohl's patronize the stores for the fashions.

Changing Household Size of a Target Market

Fashion marketers may continue to have a strong and loyal following for their products but also notice a decline in their overall **merchandise turnover** and profitability. Merchandise turnover is the number of times a particular merchandise category is sold (Clodfelter, 2009). Fashion marketers are confident that their target market is remaining loyal because they are tracking customers' purchases through store credit card purchases and frequent discount card purchases. There are several possible explanations for the decline in merchandise turnover and decreased sales. The explanations revolve around the changing composition of the demographics of a target market.

Consumers throughout the United States are growing older, more diverse (*U.S. News & World Report*, 2008), having fewer children, and spending more money on each child (Burke, 2007, April 9). Consumers within each target market may vary depending on the year, decade, and certainly the company. Fashion marketers must continually look at the changing demographics across the United States as well as those globally (See Chapter Twelve, "Marketing Fashions Globally," for more on global implications). As the target market's demographics change, so may its psychographics. For example, in 1970, it was unheard of to see newborns wearing Gucci loafers or toddler jeans selling for $200. Babies, toddlers, and tweens of the twenty-first-century luxury target market wear Gucci and Juicy Couture, just to name a few higher-end brands (Huguenin, 2009).

figure 7.12
Juicy Couture is marketing its fashions toward the young consumer. While the parent(s) or friends purchase the fashions, this technique is designed to build product loyalty among young consumers as they grow into their fashion decision-making years.

Target Markets Defined by the Originator

Target markets are to be taken seriously. When a company forgets who its target market is or what type of products or marketing efforts its target market responds to, its consumers readily respond by shopping at the competition. Marketing is not in charge; retailers are not in charge. The target market is always in charge. Pay attention to them; give them what they want, and they will reward you.

Most companies keep their same target market throughout the life of the company. For example, Mary-Kate and Ashley Olsen produce fashions for younger girls. Despite the fact that the Olsen twins are now in their twenties, they continue being very successful marketers of children's fashions.

Loyal Target Market

Loyal consumers are worth their weight in gold to any fashion marketer. It takes a lot of negative attention, marketing, or product placement to have a loyal consumer switch to another company and brand (Nunes & Johnson, 2004). As such, it is often prohibitively expensive and ineffective to market toward another company's loyal consumers. Fashion marketers focus their efforts on existing loyal customers of their own market and any untapped markets.

Reaching Your Luxury Target Market

Neiman Marcus, headquartered in Dallas, celebrated its 100th anniversary in 2007. Neiman Marcus has succeeded by providing "high luxury" to customers with households worth $5 million and more. CEO and president, Karen Katz, designed a customer-service program to this target market based on (a) income, and (b) an increased desire for luxury items by this target market. (Zimbalist, 2007).

Not willing to wait for consumers to enter the store, sales associates access a large database. Examples of items consumers receive sales calls about include a $150,000 Buccellati diamond-and-18-carat-yellow-gold cuff or the limited availability of a Chanel handbag (Zimbalist, 2007). Neiman Marcus has carefully kept pace with the psychographics of its target market. CEO Karen Katz states that she is "a 50-year-old woman who has the attitude of a 30-year-old woman and in many cases the body of a 35-year-old" (Zimbalist, 2007, p. 91).

IMPORTANCE OF TARGET FEEDBACK

Fashion retailing must continually obtain feedback from its target market. Companies try to assess consumers' perceptions and opinions regarding the level of customer service, quality of products, satisfaction with the products, the breadth and depth of products, cleanliness of the store, and safety. Methods of obtaining feedback are dependent on the amount of money the retailer is willing to spend on gathering data, the method of data collection (e.g., use of technology, survey, oral communication), and the length of time data are collected (e.g., continually, quarterly, annually).

Paper Survey

Fashion retailers used paper surveys before the Internet and e-mail. Paper consumer satisfaction surveys continue to be popular, particularly among direct retailers (i.e., catalogs, mailers) and in-store retailers. Similar to an electronic survey, paper surveys are short. The questions are typically designed to measure consumers' satisfaction toward the retailer. Because the survey is short, the question is typically an overall satisfaction question such as, *What is your overall opinion of the retailer?*, *Do you plan on shopping at this store again?*, and *Would you tell your friends about this experience?*

Paper surveys are specifically designed to benefit individual branch locations. The surveys are typically offered to consumers at the time of purchase. Unlike electronic surveys that can include up to 20 questions, paper surveys must be brief. Consumers are hesitant to wait long to complete a survey. Fashion marketers must identify the most important information they need from the consumers and ask only those questions. The majority of consumers will not complete and return the paper survey if they take the survey out of the store.

Paper surveys are beneficial to gather information about shoppers and the target market's feelings. When surveys are completed, after the target market has recent exposure to a marketing effort, the shopper may provide valuable information. For example, the fashion marketer may not have a clear understanding of why people purchase a brand. A paper survey can reveal feelings, beliefs, and desires. These attributes can then be incorporated into future marketing efforts.

Electronic Survey

The twentieth century is characterized by the development, implementation, and widespread use of the Internet. The twenty-first century and its business partners and consumers are "wired." Being *wired* means that businesses communicate regularly with consumers through electronic means. Likewise, consumers, regardless of their age, communicate with each other through the use of a wide variety of technology. Laptops, cell phones, Bluetooth devices, and PDAs are just a few of the electronic devices businesses and consumers use to send and receive information at regular intervals throughout the day. For many consumers, this method of communication is the preferred way to communicate over print or the phone.

Large fashion retailers often have the technological and financial capability to provide consumers with an electronic survey. The survey often lists as few as 5 questions or as many as 15 questions regarding purchasing behaviors. The surveys are often listed as pop-ups on the company's home page, sent to consumers who are on the company's e-mail list, or listed on other Web sites as pop-ups. **Pop-ups** are electronic advertisements that pop up on the computer site automatically while the user is logged on. Companies that use electronic surveys may entice the consumer's participation by a discount on the next purchase.

The benefit of an electronic survey is that data are collected immediately and can be analyzed rapidly, and top management can interpret the results and make appropriate changes to the company in a timely manner. Data can also be gathered rapidly throughout the nation in a rapid manner. Top executives can learn if a target market's needs are different based on location (e.g., Midwest, West), demographics, and/or psychographics.

Electronic surveys are often used to obtain information from customers. This form of gathering data has many advantages over phone or print surveys. Electronic surveys allow the fashion marketer to ask a relatively large number of questions (20 or more), and yet the survey is completed in a short amount of time. In addition, because the survey is sent via e-mail, it is relatively inexpensive to distribute. The cost of the survey is based solely on generating the e-mail distribution list and developing the survey. Customers have a higher likelihood of answering the survey because it is being given through technology. Finally, the data generated are formatted onto a spreadsheet and are ready for analysis.

Focus Groups

Unlike paper and electronic surveys, a focus group is conducted orally. The **focus group** consists of a group of consumers who are asked questions about the product and/or marketing effort. The use of focus groups is a successful method of obtaining in-depth feedback from the primary target market. Groups of five to six members of the primary target market are placed in a room. Marketers show the consumers different versions of their marketing efforts. After each marketing piece is shown to the focus group (e.g., print, television spot), a moderator asks the group a series of questions. Throughout the focus group session, the moderator asks specific questions about product details and obtains information regarding consumers' interactions with the fashions and how they use the fashions (e.g., formal use, informal use, mix and match). The moderator is careful not to influence the discussion by stating his/her opinions. The process is repeated multiple times using different focus groups.

The marketing team carefully analyzes the focus group's verbal responses and body language. Consumers' answers are recorded (videotaped or audiotaped) for analysis at a later time by the marketers. Fashion marketing decisions are based on focus groups' responses to the marketing efforts. The feedback may also provide insight into previously untapped fashion consumer desires that the marketer can fill. Focus groups provide valuable information to marketers because of the specific information not typically revealed by a survey. Perceived image, passion for a product, dislikes, likes, and beliefs can be revealed. The information can then be used in future marketing efforts.

Integrated Surveys

A fashion marketer does not need to select one form of survey. Indeed, a combination of surveys can provide a valuable source of information for the company. Using a combination of paper, electronic, focus group, and personal methods of data gathering is the most comprehensive method of understanding the target market. Various methods can then be used to obtain supporting data—for instance, to reassure the fashion marketer that the results were not based on one geographic region. In addition, a wider variety of questions may be posed. HandPicked, whose home office is located in South Carolina, uses an integrated marketing research effort in order to stay connected with the needs and wants of its customers. Their fashion marketing efforts change on an annual basis. The three primary marketing efforts used by the company include (1) in-store signage, (2) e-mail, and (3) direct marketing. Two monthly e-mail blasts are sent to the target market. In-house marketing messaging is developed whereby a consultant creates the art. HandPicked hired MarketWise, a research consulting company, to survey its customers. Rather than relying on one method, an integrated approach is used. The three methods of surveying the HandPicked target market include focus groups, e-mail, and managers asking consumers questions. Results of the data collection reveal that the target market recognizes the quality and value of the merchandise and services provided (Goth, 2009; Hiter, 2009) (Table 7.3).

Survey Composition

If you have ever taken a statistics course, you may have heard the statement, *Numbers are only as good as the interpretation*. I've heard the statement also phrased as *You can fib using statistics*. The numbers from surveys will inform fashion marketers about some attributes, characteristics, perceptions, and behaviors of the target market. If this information is used correctly, meaning if the information is

TABLE 7.3

Results of Consumer Survey Conducted by MarketWise for HandPicked

QUESTION	CONSUMER ATTRIBUTE
Average number of households in the area surveyed	26,000
Number of miles consumers are willing to travel to shop at HandPicked	15 miles
Percent of female shoppers	99 percent
Marital status	64 percent married
Age	37 percent between 25 and 34 years old
Percent who have children	37 percent have children
Race	94 percent Caucasian
Income	37 percent earn $100,000 or more
Education level	51 percent or more have a bachelor's degree

(Hiter, 2009)

interpreted correctly, the fashion marketer can use the information to change, enhance, and improve the next generation of marketing efforts.

There are two important facts to remember when developing and implementing surveys. First, ask the right questions. This statement may seem simple, but all too often the wrong questions are asked. At the beginning of any survey process, the objective of the survey must be identified.

Answer the question, *What information do you need—not want, but need—from your target market?* Examples may include:

- Why did you purchase the "purple passion" lipstick?
- Did you give the "purple passion" lipstick to a friend or use it for yourself? (Remember that because of POS, you know for a fact that the customer purchased "purple passion" lipstick.)
- Did the "buy-one-get-one-free sale" encourage you to purchase the lipstick?
- If sales are dropping, you need to find out why.
  - Was the marketing campaign offered during the wrong season?
  - Was the wrong product featured?
  - Was the pricing incorrect?
  - Did you misunderstand the message?

The second most important aspect of a survey is making sure you are giving the survey to your target market. Fashion marketers promote products regionally, nationally, and internationally. Once you have decided the objective of your survey, it is important to clearly understand which portion of the target market should be providing the feedback. One survey is not necessarily designed for the entire company or for every fashion marketing effort. Segment the surveys and the people answering the survey based on the questions. Sending out a survey to everyone simply because you have a mailing or e-mail list is a waste of time and will make the recipients angry.

WHAT TO ASK

The majority of consumers won't tell you negative aspects of the fashion marketing program; they hit the marketers where it counts—at the profit margins. When a fashion marketing program insults, confuses, or bores the target market, consumers tend to (a) not purchase the product, (b) patronize other fashion retailers, or (c) ultimately become loyal to another brand.

Fashion marketers rarely seek feedback on products that have a good or high product turnover. Fashion marketing efforts are successful when products are selling. Consumers' opinions are sought during the design stage or after an unsuccessful implementation of a product line. Consumer input during a design stage can influence the product's style, design, marketing efforts, or methods of reaching the consumer (e.g., specific magazine to advertise). Questions posed regarding a failed product or marketing effort often reveal why the target market failed to adopt the product or returned the product.

Random Survey of Existing Customers

The random survey of existing customers is a method to keep connecting to the attitudes of shoppers on a continual basis. Using a predetermined series of questions, patrons of the retail operations are asked to provide feedback. Each month different members of the target market are asked to participate in the survey. Typically the store manager will contact the consumers either by phone, in the store, or by e-mail. The sample is small, ranging from 10 to 15 people. The purpose of the monthly survey is to understand consumers' attitudes about the retailer, brand, fashion marketing efforts, and customer service. Each month, the questions posed on the survey may focus on one specific attribute or a wide range of attributes. Regardless of the topic, the survey does not take a long time for the consumer to answer. It is also used to reinforce that their opinions matter.

SUMMARY

The careful selection of the target market is critical to the profitability and long-term success of any company. The target market consists of consumers on whom the company actively focuses its marketing efforts. Companies typically have a primary target market, secondary target market, and a tertiary target market.

Market segmentation is an important part of reaching the target market. There are four levels of market segmentation: (1) mass marketing, (2) segment marketing, (3) niche marketing, and (4) micromarketing. Mass marketing exists when fashion products are targeted to *all* consumers. Segment marketing exists when fashion products are marketed specifically to individual consumer groups (i.e., segments). Niche marketing occurs when subgroups are developed within segment

TABLE 7.4

Consumer Questionnaire

	STRONGLY DISAGREE	DISAGREE	NEUTRAL	AGREE	STRONGLY AGREE
Getting very good quality is important to me.	1	2	3	4	5
Choosing a brand is confusing.	1	2	3	4	5
I frequently purchase well-known national brands.	1	2	3	4	5
I usually buy more expensive brands.	1	2	3	4	5
It is fun to buy something new.	1	2	3	4	5
I monitor the amount of money I spend.	1	2	3	4	5
I usually buy the newest styles.	1	2	3	4	5
Once I find a brand I like, I stick with it.	1	2	3	4	5
There are so many brands to choose from, I often feel confused.	1	2	3	4	5

marketing. Fashion marketers use a micromarketing strategy when they individualize a marketing program.

Regardless of the demographics and psychographics of the target market, the guidelines for marketing to the consumers remain the same. The guidelines are: (1) focus on the primary target market, (2) keep the message simple, (3) repeat the message frequently, (4) communicate your company's name, (5) maintain a consistent corporate image, and (6) don't use the same message for multiple markets.

Target markets continually evolve. Companies' products change as the demographics and psychographics of the market change. As the composition of target markets changes, so does the viability of retailers' profitability and gross margin. To be successful in the long term, fashion marketers must be skilled at adjusting to the changing status of their target market. The quicker and more responsive a fashion marker is at responding to the environmental changes, the better the opportunities the retailer has for reaching the target market's fashion needs and wants.

To have a firm understanding of the evolving target markets, companies frequently obtain feedback from their consumers. Through the use of focus group interviews, paper surveys, and electronic surveys, fashion marketers are able to better understand consumers' perceptions and opinions regarding each aspect of the organization. Companies try to assess consumers' perceptions and opinions regarding the level of customer service, the quality of products, their satisfaction with the products, the breadth and depth of products, the cleanliness of the store, and safety.

REFERENCES

American Heritage College Dictionary (Eds.). (1993). *American Heritage College Dictionary*. Boston: Houghton Mifflin.

Bebe. (2009). Company Web site. Retrieved from www.bebe.com/About-bebe-old-Special-Features.

Burke, K. (2007, April 9). Gucci goo—Meet the latest baby boomers, *Sydney Morning Herald*. Retrieved on December 22, 2008 from www.lexisnesis.com/us/lnacademic/results/docview/.

Clodfelter, R. (2008). *Retail buying: From basics to fashion*. (3rd ed.). New York: Fairchild Books.

Data points: Changing U.S. demographics: Getting older and more diverse. (2008). *U.S. News & World Report*. Retrieved on June 23, 2009 from www.usnews.com/articles/opinion/2008/08/18/data-points-changing-us-demographics.html.

Dunne, Patrick, M. and Robert F. Lusch (2007). *Retailing*. Cengage Learning: Florence, KY.

Goth, S. (2009, March 3). Personal interview with merchandise manager, Hand-Picked, Columbia, South Carolina.

Hiter, K. (2009, March 3). Personal interview with marketing manager, Hand-Picked, Columbia, South Carolina.

Huguenin, Patrick (2009, January 7). The kid stays in the picture. *Daily News*, p. 31.

JCPenney (2009) Company Web site. Retrieved on February 25, 2009 from www.jcpenney.com.

Johnson, L. (2006). *Satisfying the 10 cravings of a new generation of consumers: Mind your X's and Y's*. New York: Free Press.

Juicy Couture (2009). Company Web site. Retrieved July 9, 2009 from http://www.juicycouture.com/press.

Kendall, G. T. (2009). *Fashion brand merchandising*. New York: Fairchild Books.

Korn, A. (2009, March 2). Personal interview.

Kotler, P. & Armstrong, G. (2001). *Principles of marketing* (9th edition). Upper Saddle River, NJ: Prentice Hall.

McMahon, M. (2008, August 17). U.S. melting-pot of nations, *Canberra Times*, p. 14.

New York Times. (2008, December 22). Economic slowdown helps Wal-Mart stores' profit, *New York Times*. Retrieved on December 22, 2008 from www.iht.com/articles/2008/11/14/business/walmart2.php.

Nordstrom. (2009). Company Web site. Retrieved February 12, 2009 from http://nordstrom.com.

Nunes, P. & Johnson, B. (2004). *Mass affluence: Seven new rules of marketing to today's consumer.* Boston: Harvard Business School Press.

O'Donnell, J., & Kutz, E. (2008, April 14). Big retailers seek teens (and parents): Hip fashions seen as key to fighting off specialty stores. *USA Today*, p. 1B.

Ostrow, R. & Smith, S. R. (1988). *The dictionary of marketing*. New York: Fairchild Books.

Sasha Cosmetics. (2009). Company Web site. Retrieved on June 23, 2009 from www.sachacosmetics.com.

Spenceley, A. (2009, March 27). Shopping mecca is teens' weekend home. *St. Petersburg Times*, p. 8.

Strauss, M. (2006). Walmart is trying to chic, by george. *The Globe and Mail*. Retrieved on December 22, 2008 from http://www.lexisnesis.com/us/lnacademic/results/docview/.

Teenagers: Fads and fashions. (2004). *Good Morning TV. The Globe and Mail*. Retrieved December 15, 2008 from http://tvnz.co.nz/view/page/410965.

U.S. Census Bureau (2005–2007). American community survey. Retrieved July 9, 2009 from http://factfinder.census.gov/servlet/DTTable?_bm=y&-geo_id=01000US&-ds_name=ACS_2007_3YR_G00_&-mt_name=ACS_2007_3YR_G2000_B02001.

Wignall, A. (2008, June 2). Media: The pink pound. *The Guardian*, p. 3

Zimbalist, K. (2007). Magical thinkers: They've orchestrated America's current luxury boom, lifting the consumer even higher. Meet Neiman Marcus' leading ladies. *Time Style & Design*, p. 9–92.

KEY TERMS

Define or briefly explain the following terms:

Baby boomer ______

Consumer ______

Disposable income ______

Focus group ______

Generation X ______

Generation Y ______

Gray market ______

Mass market ______

Micromarketing ______

Niche marketing ______

Pop-up ______

Primary target market ______

Profit margin ______

Secondary target market ______

Segment marketing ______

Shopper ______

Shopping ______

Staple product ______

Target market ______

Tertiary target market ______

CLASS OR TEAM DISCUSSION QUESTIONS

1 | Select a generation. Detail the considerations when developing an integrated fashion marketing campaign to this generation.

______

______

2 | Give an example of a fashion marketing effort for each of the following: (a) mass marketing, (b) market segmentation, and (c) niche marketing.

3 | Explain why or why not you, as a fashion marketer, would use the same marketing campaign as you have supplied above for the company's primary and secondary target market. Justify your answer.

4 | Why is it important to obtain feedback from your target market? What are methods of obtaining feedback from your target market?

INTERNET ACTIVITIES

1 | Using the Internet as a resource, find two companies that provide excellent fashion marketing efforts by following the rules regarding reaching the target market. Find two companies that do not follow the rules regarding reaching the target market. Discuss the similarities and differences between these two companies' fashion marketing efforts. As a fashion marketer, provide suggestions for improving the marketing efforts.

2 | Select one company. Using the Internet as a resource, conduct a thorough investigation of the company's target market. Investigate by brands the following: (a) demographics; (b) psychographics; (c) primary, secondary, and tertiary target markets; and (d) messages targeted toward each target market.

STUDY QUESTIONS

1 | What are the characteristics of Generation X?

2 | Why is Generation Y important to fashion marketers?

3 | What are the characteristics of baby boomers?

4 | What are the differences among primary, secondary, and tertiary target markets?

5 | Define market segmentation.

6 | When would mass marketing be successful in the fashion industry?

7 | What is micromarketing?

8 | How is micromarketing different from niche marketing?

9 | What are the guidelines to use when marketing to the target market?

---

10 | What are the methods for obtaining feedback from your target market?

---

11 | What types of questions are asked when obtaining feedback from the target market?

---

12 | What is an integrated survey?

MULTIPLE-CHOICE QUESTIONS

1 | What rule(s) should fashion marketers always follow?

- **a.** Always let the target market know your name.
- **b.** Always keep the company's primary target market in mind.
- **c.** Keep the audience in mind.
- **d.** All of the above (*a*, *b*, and *c*).

2 | What is the ultimate goal of the majority of fashion marketers regarding the target market?

- **a.** To build teen loyalty into lifetime and family loyalty
- **b.** To maximize the number of senior citizens who are loyal
- **c.** To expand the geographic distribution of the secondary target market
- **d.** To expand the size of the tertiary target market that is captured

3 | Which of the following products have, at one time or another, been marketed specifically toward the fashion-conscious consumer?

- **a.** Cell phones, razor blades, and cotton undergarments
- **b.** School binders, PDAs, and Apple computers
- **c.** Automobiles, children's bicycles, and Barbie dolls
- **d.** All of the above products have been marketed toward the fashion consumer (*a*, *b*, and *c*).

4 | What attributes or characteristics typically influence the fashion-marketing message?

a. Demographics
b. Psychographics
c. Marketing budget
d. The competition's marketing efforts

5 | When should fashion consumers start marketing to consumers in order to retain them as lifelong consumers?

a. When the consumer reaches the fashion marketer's target-market age bracket (i.e., can wear the products)
b. When the consumer has a full-time, permanent career
c. After college
d. Between 13 and 17 years of age

TRUE-OR-FALSE QUESTIONS

1 | _____ Demographics are the most important consumer characteristic a fashion marketer should understand about his or her target market.

2 | _____ Technology has significantly influenced fashion marketers' ability to physically reach market segments.

3 | _____ Fashion marketers typically do not actively promote to the tertiary target market.

TABLE 8.1

THE Market Planning PROCESS

step 1 CHAPTER 2 | Be inspired; become passionate regarding a product/service; be driven to succeed and committed to working toward a goal.

step 2 CHAPTER 3 | Intrinsic attributes of the products and services are marketed in terms of value, satisfaction, and quality. Building upon the mission statement, in this step you will make decisions regarding the pricing, communication, value, satisfaction, and quality associated with the purchase or the products and/or services.

step 3 CHAPTER 4 | Identify a comprehensive list of products and services offered by the company.

step 4 CHAPTER 5 | Examine the products and services component of the core marketing concept related to the trickle-down theory, media and celebrities, and the belongingness theory.

step 5 CHAPTER 6 | Examine the buying season in relation to the marketing process.

step 6 CHAPTER 7 | Examine marketing methods of targeting the consumer.

step 7 CHAPTER 8 | **Examine the methods of exchange and relationships with the consumers. This includes making decisions to sell products and services through brick-and-mortar retail operations, direct marketing, and the Internet.**

step 8 CHAPTER 9 | Examine the image and brands of the company in relation to marketing efforts.

step 9 CHAPTER 10 | Conduct a market analysis of how companies are able to successfully cross product boundaries.

step 10 CHAPTER 11 | Examine trends in the fashion industry regarding a) counterfeit merchandise and b) the impact of such merchandise on the industry's sales, profits, product design, consumers' attitudes.

step 11 CHAPTER 12 | Conduct a market analysis of fashions in the global environment in order to determine impact to the company's existing marketing efforts.

8

Cross-Channel Shopping

"All things being equal, people will buy from a friend. All things being not quite so equal, people will still buy from a friend."

—Mark McCormack, chairman and chief executive officer of International Management Group

chapter objectives

After reading this chapter, you should be able to understand Step Seven of the Market Planning Process. This includes being able to:

+ Explain the concept of cross-channel shopping.

+ Examine the implications of cross-channel shopping in relation to a company's marketing efforts.

+ Compare the various fashion marketing strategies that companies employ to increase sales and profits as they relate to consumers' shopping patterns.

Given the opportunity, consumers tend to purchase from retailers whom they trust. The greater the channels of distribution the trusted retailer offers, the greater the probability the consumer will respond to its multichannel marketing efforts. Imagine a time when consumers had limited fashion product information prior to entering the store. In order to find out if a retailer carried a particular product, color, or size—say, a garment in periwinkle blue that fits you perfectly—you, the fashion consumer, were required to drive to each store. The hunt through the various racks began, frantically flipping through garment tags for the right size and style.

The Internet has changed how fashion retailers market their products. Consumers log on to retailers' Web sites 24/7 for shopping tips; to learn about sales, clearance products, new arrivals in the store, and products sold only through the Web site; and to obtain coupons that can be downloaded and printed via a personal home computer.

This chapter addresses the dramatic nature of how fashion consumers obtain general information, comparison shop, decide on a location for future product analysis, and make the ultimate decision to purchase or start the fashion hunt over again.

HOW CONSUMERS SHOP

It is impossible to talk about fashion marketing without briefly addressing the characteristics of retail operations. How consumers shop, where they shop, and why they choose a particular store influence the fashion marketer's overall campaign. Retailers and the fashion marketing team hired to promote the merchandise are faced with three distinct types of selling avenues: brick-and-mortar stores, direct marketing, and e-retailing.

Brick-and-Mortar Retail

Brick-and-mortar stores are the traditional backbone of the fashion retailing industry. Even during the technological age of the Internet, brick-and-mortar stores continue to dominate in annual sales and profits. The synergy of social interactions during shopping activities at brick-and-mortar retailers is a measurable attribute not duplicated by the patronage of catalogs or e-retailers (Mathwick, Malhorta, & Rigdon 2001). For many consumers, the familiarity of the physical shopping activity holds more value than price and quality (Currah, 2003). The convenience and immediate gratification when purchasing from brick-and-mortar stores provide consumers with an outlet when they "need" to purchase a product (Bauman, 2001).

Perhaps the most frequently cited limitation of patronizing brick-and-mortar retailers is the propensity for making impulse purchases (Dittmar, Friese, & Beattie, 1996). The propensity for making impulse purchases is often increased when shopping with a companion due to an opinion and/or perceived or real coercion to purchase. Limitations such as prohibitive distances to a particular store, time allotment for shopping, or geographic or physical travel constraints may encourage patronage of other channels.

Without a doubt, the dominant form of shopping for fashions is at brick-and-mortar retailers. As such, the dominant form of marketing fashions also features brick-and-mortar retailing. Challenges are inherent with this form of retailing. The primary challenge of a brick-and-mortar retailer is bringing consumer traffic into the store. Without consumer traffic, the retailer cannot hope to make sales or profits. A second challenge of a brick-and-mortar retailer is to continually offer consumers discounts, sales, and promotions throughout the store without (a) looking like a discount store (unless you are a discount store), (b) losing your gross margin, and (c) losing your sense of fashion. Brick-and-mortar stores that "splash" sales signs throughout the store can look more like a garage sale than a fashion retailer.

Despite more than 50 percent of its products being soft lines, Sears has long been known as a hard-line retailer. In 1997, the company realized that they needed to focus more heavily on fashions in order to drive traffic into the stores. Sears executives reviewed fashion from Paris, London, and Milan. The trends were then adopted to fit the needs of the Sears target market (e.g., price range). The company's fashion sales rose 4.8 percent compared to the 2.6 percent of a national competitor (Chambers & Davis, 1998).

At times it can be difficult for brick-and-mortar retailers to distinguish themselves from the competitor. Many brick-and-mortar retailers carry nationally branded merchandise or mass-produced merchandise. As such, consumers may find similar, if not identical, items at competitors' stores. Brick-and-mortar retailers have the challenge of distinguishing their entire company from others. It is essential to entice consumers to stay in your store, touch merchandise, and purchase multiple items. This enticement is accomplished through successful fashion marketing efforts.

Giorgio Armani believes his designs should be presented in the round. That is, to truly appreciate his creations, consumers should view his fashions from the front, back, inside, and outside. As the "king of Italian tailoring," Armani designs should be lovingly stroked in order to be fully appreciated. For this to happen, first-time consumers need to visit one of the many international Giorgio Armani boutiques (Watson, 1999/2000).

Think about your favorite shopping mall. On a sheet of paper, list the companies that you know are in the mall, and then either go online

figure 8.1
The Giorgio Armani boutique provides a brick-and-marketing intimate shopping opportunity for the discriminating fashion consumer. Only fashions designed by Armani are sold at the boutique.

or go to the mall (a reason to shop) and look at the mall directory.

- How many stores in total does the mall offer?
- How many stores did you identify on your list?
- What is the difference between the number of stores in the mall and the number of stores on your list?
- Why do you think you did not identify the missing stores?
  - Do the storefronts have poor signage?
  - Are the stores not positioned well within the mall?
  - What type of marketing efforts do the stores use?
- How would you enhance the stores' marketing efforts to encourage consumer patronage?

Direct Marketing Retail

Direct marketing has long been an important part of fashion marketing's efforts. A **direct marketer** is a retailer who "markets through direct mail, telephone retailing, catalog retailing, mail-order advertising, flyers, and inserts in credit card statements and in newspapers (Ostrow & Smith, 1988, p. 74). Direct marketers rely on a quality database. That is, the database must be a mailing list of current consumers, strong prospective consumers, and/or persons who match the demographics and psychographics of the identified target market. Simply having a large database does not make the direct marketing effort successful.

Catalogs remain an important aspect of fashion marketing. Consumers typically save catalogs for future viewing and rip out pages featuring products that remind them of a particular store or brand name. Consumers also like to share catalogs. Discussing the contents of the catalog, the store that published the catalog, and the products inside the catalog helps to ingrain all of the above in the consumer's memory. Long after the discussion, consumers involved in the discussion remember the store and the products. Yet despite all this, consumers still purchase the majority of their products through a brick-and-mortar retailer, typically a mall, or online through an e-retailer (Lueg, 2006).

Motivation to purchase merchandise from catalogs is stimulated by the enjoyment of experiencing a portrayed lifestyle or image (Mathwick et al., 2001). Placing products in unique lifestyle settings and across a two-page layout, catalogs can present a wider variety of merchandise than a brick-and-mortar store can (Ritzer, 1999). Combined with the convenience of placing orders 24 hours a day, 7 days a week, the appeal of catalog merchandise presentation is an incentive for shopping behavior and purchase (Mathwick et al., 2001). Catalog retailers reap benefits from consumers' viewing habits, and consumers spend more money per transaction on each catalog purchase (Mathwick et al., 2001).

Some research reveals a recreational component to catalog shopping, where an intrinsic value is shown in the enjoyment of viewing a catalog. Catalog shoppers may patronize brick-and-mortar stores of the same company, viewing catalogs as an extension of the store. As consumers' familiarity with catalog shopping increases, the importance of uniqueness in product assortment and customization of products become as important as convenience and price, which are important motivators for patronage (Mathwick et al., 2001).

Anyone who has ever cleaned out a mailbox full of unwanted paper clearly understands some of the challenges of direct marketers. Much of the marketing efforts are wasted either by consumers throwing them away or just not reading the copy, or simply because there was so much competition for the consumer's attention that the copy was not effective.

Some direct marketing efforts rely on the consumer acting within a time period. For example, a fashion marketer may offer 20 percent off all merchandise during the first week

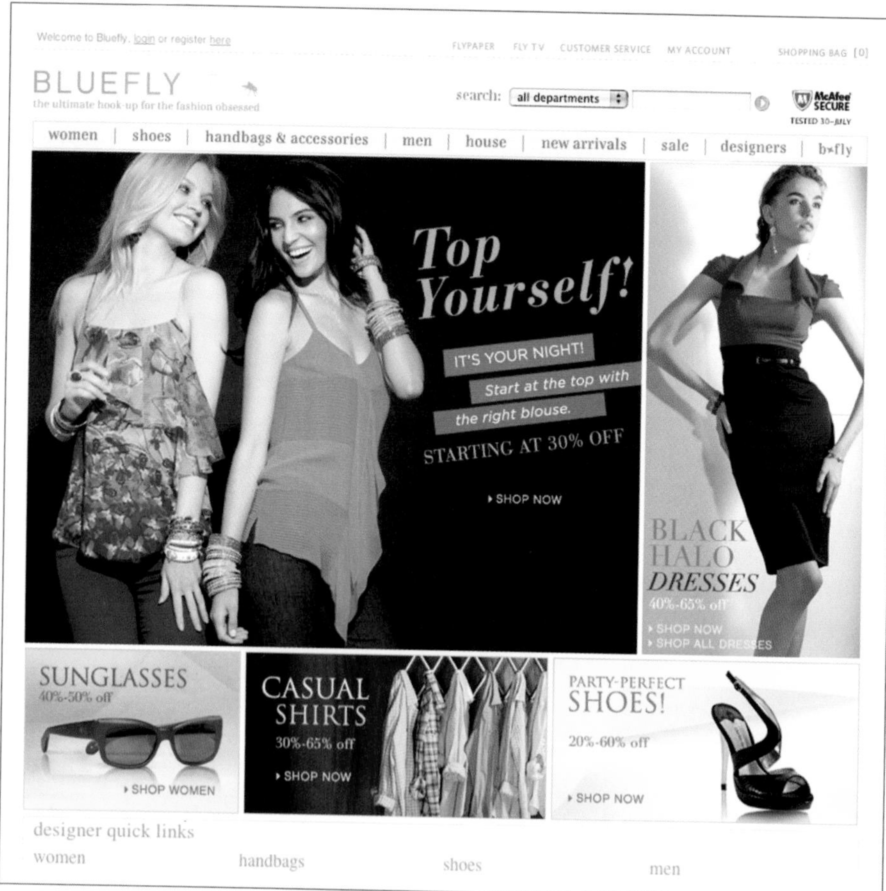

figure 8.2
Bluefly.com is an e-retailer that sells fashions and accessories. The single-channel retailer is able to reach consumers nationally and internationally by marketing and selling to consumers through the Internet.

in October. If the consumer views the marketing piece during the second week in October, a negative perception of the retailer could be formed.

I encourage you to take a challenge. Save your direct marketing flyers, postcards, and catalogs for two weeks. As you receive the direct marketing efforts, read them just like you would during any other occasion. However, instead of throwing them away, place them in an envelope or folder. At the conclusion of two weeks, examine the fashion marketing efforts.

- How did you feel toward the direct marketer? Did you trust the direct marketer? Why or why not?
- Which was your favorite marketing retailer (this doesn't necessarily mean you wanted the product; you could simply have liked the material)?
- Which was your least favorite direct marketing retailer? Why?
- Which direct marketing retailer encouraged you to act? Why?
- Did you purchase any products? If so, describe what you purchased and why.

E-retail

An **e-retailer** is a retailer who sells products and/or services via the Internet. The e-retailer may or may not have a brick-and-mortar location. E-retailing is considered a direct marketing channel. Because this channel has taken on such an important role in fashion marketing, it will be addressed as a separate channel. Many small companies begin solely as e-retail operations. Other companies, such as Banana Republic, use the e-retail channel to offer their smaller secondary or tertiary target markets specialized sizes. These sizes may include *women's tall* and *men's big and tall.* E-retailers who offer specialized sizes provide an expanded target market interest in the overall company. The consumer may then identify products and/or services of interest for family and friends, and ultimately build shopping loyalty toward the retail organization. E-retailers also provide the retail organization with relief from carrying excess inventory within the brick-and-mortar store. The e-retailer does not depend on beautiful (and expensive) physical surroundings that are often required by the brick-and-mortar operation. The cost per square foot of the e-retailer is much lower than that of a brick-and-mortar operation. The gross margin can be placed in fashion marketing efforts.

The online retail channel accounts for 7 percent of the retail industry. With more than $204 billion in annual sales, the online retailer is the fastest growing channel. In 2007, consumer sales through the Internet increased 22 percent (Haberkorn, 2008). Online shoppers tend to be very interactive with the retailer. Twenty-nine percent write product reviews, compared to only nine percent of brick-and-mortar shoppers. The Internet is also a primary source of information for 61 percent of consumers (CanWest News Service, 2007). E-retailers are the channel of choice when consumers need to make a quick purchase decision because of their 24/7 shopping accessibility and the ability to comparison shop among e-retailers with little effort. The more frequently consumers access e-retailers, the more likely they will make a purchase (Park, Lennon, & Stoel, 2005). E-retailers offer information enhancements to the purchase decision (Lee & Lee, 2005). E-retailers' price-and-quality search engines and services allow consumers to obtain product details (e.g., how and where it was manufactured, special features) (Rogers, Negash, & Suk, 2005). The presentation of products in a setting also offers consumers display ideas, provides viewing pleasure, and increases the possibility of purchase (Lee & Lee, 2005). Consumers are more market savvy, knowledgeable about retail channel members, and in some cases better able to negotiate sales, based on information obtained via the Internet (Tinning, 2008).

Bluefly.com is an example of a clothing e-retailer (Figure 8.2). The company has chosen to sell only through this channel. Between 2004 and 2006, the company's net sales have increased 43 percent. Bluefly.com also increased its unique mailing database by 28 percent (Table 8.2).

E-retailers may also be associated with a brick-and-mortar retail operation and/or a direct marketing operation. During 2006, J. C. Penney Company, Inc.'s Internet sales

TABLE 8.2

Internet Clothing Retailer Bluefly.com

MEASUREMENT	INCREASE BETWEEN 2004 AND 2006	2006	2005	2004
Net Sales	43%	$77,062	$58,811	$43,799
Average Order Size (including shipping and handling)	$69.13	$257.64	$220.17	$188.51
New Customers Added During the Year (based on unique e-mail addresses)	50,036 (28%)	177,213	148,975	127,177

(Bluefly.com annual report, 2007)

reached $1.3 billion (Power, 2007). According to *Women's Wear Daily* writer Denise Power, by 2012, approximately 85 percent of U.S. households will have broadband Internet. This is an increase of 30 percent from 2007 (Power, 2007). This has enormous implications for fashion retailers' ability to reach consumers via multiple channels.

Some brick-and-mortar retailers use Web sites solely for information purposes. Sally Beauty Supply is a nationwide hair-care store that targets hair stylists and women who care about grooming. The company features a Web site with hundreds of products, price information, store hours, and locations. Consumers are not able to purchase through the Web site. The Web site is used to drive business into the brick-and-mortar locations.

Internet retailers provide consumers with the ability to purchase merchandise from around the globe. In the past, consumers were limited to purchasing exotic merchandise from other countries while vacationing or while on business trips. Consumers are now able to log on to international Web sites and purchase exotic products 24/7 (Edelson, 2005).

The Internet is an important part of any fashion marketer's efforts. The layout and maintenance of the Web site can be, however, detrimental to the online and in-store sales. The navigational ease, quality, and quantity of information provided, including visuals and shopping links, all provide consumers with an overall image of the company (Jamison, Gold, & Jamison, 1997). Depending upon the quality of the computer system, e-retailers may continue to have challenges with sizing images, confusing internal navigation, presenting accurate color palettes, or maintaining unreliable Internet connections (Nitse et al., 2004). Many consumers may also miss the tactile and olfactory sensory experiences associated with a brick-and-mortar retail shopping experience (Khakimdjanova & Park, 2005).

As college students, you probably use the Internet a lot for research. The library is available online; so, too, is the fashion world. In just one click, I can leave the world of Biology 101 and enter the world of Chanel couture. Sometimes the Internet is so tempting that shopping (or just browsing) online can't be ignored. Tell me I'm not the only one.

I have another challenge for you. This time you will be accessing the Internet to evaluate your likes and dislikes of shopping online. Consider it fashion marketing research. (1) Select your favorite fashion designer brand. This brand must be offered online. (2) Access the brand's home page. (3) Review the product offerings. (4) Examine the various marketing messages.

- What is your overall impression of the Web site?
- What are the strengths of purchasing products through this channel?
- What are the limitations of purchasing products through this channel?
- What are the strengths of the Web site (i.e., the operations of the particular Web site, not the channel in general)?
- What are the weaknesses of the Web site?
- Have you purchased merchandise through this Web site?
- Were you satisfied? Explain.

CROSS-CHANNEL SHOPPING

Fashion-conscious consumers are typically interested in seeking out products at a variety of retail locations. They want to look unique and possess items that are different from those of their friends and neighbors. Unfortunately, everyone cannot always afford and/or have access to high-end retailers. This desire for uniqueness resulted in the evolution of **cross-channel shopping**. Cross-channel shopping is defined as the patronage of more than one retail medium (i.e., brick-and-mortar, catalog, e-retailer) (Murphy, 2000; Pascale, 2000; Scally,

TABLE 8.3
J. C. Penney Retail Net Sales

RETAIL NET SALES	2006 (53 WEEKS)	2005	2004
Department Stores	$16,950,000	$15,943,000	$15,357,000
Change from Prior Year	6%	4%	
Direct (Catalog, Internet)	$2,953,000	$2,838,000	$2,739,000
Change from Prior Year	4%	4%	
Total Net Sales	$19,903,000	$18,781,000	$18,096,000

(J. C. Penney, 2007)

2000; Stores, 2000). Cross-channel shopping is classified into three categories:

1 Visiting stores to evaluate a product or to gather information prior to purchasing online.
2 Using the Internet to locate the product, and then going to the store to make the purchase.
3 Using a catalog in conjunction with the Web site for making the purchase decision (Nitse et al., 2004, p. 2).

In 2005, more than 45 million consumers in the United States cross-channel shopped (Tierney, 2007). These consumers frequently cross-channel-shopped national retailers (e.g., Pier 1 Imports, Target, Bloomingdale's) based on the company's reputation and geographic location (Eastlick & Feinberg, 1999; McDonald, 1993; Noble, 2001). Oftentimes, a consumer will identify a product through one channel (e.g., Internet or catalog) but purchase the product at a different channel (Khakimdjanova & Park; 2005; Sim & Koi, 2002). Reasons for shopping through multiple channels include: a search for information via retailers' Web sites, the psychological need to try on or touch products, and the need for instant gratification (i.e., the desire to obtain the product sooner than if the product was delivered by mail).

Each time a consumer accesses two or more channels of a particular retailer, his or her actions promote longevity in the marketplace and increase the opportunity for multiple sales (Khakimdjanova & Park, 2005). Sensory experience via brick-and-mortar retailers, design examples via catalog retailers, and detailed product information via e-retailers offer consumers a complete retail experience (Nitse et al., 2004; Burk, 2003). Some e-retailers spend millions in their organization to entice consumers' patronage and loyalty through cross-channel shopping (Rose, Meuter, & Curran, 2005). Consumers who cross-channel-shop are significantly more valuable to retailers than those who shop at one channel (Stich & Leonard, 2008). For example, J. C. Penney generated almost $17 million net sales from its brick-and-mortar stores in 2006. The company generated almost $3 million additional net sales from catalog and e-retail operations that same year. It can be assumed that many J. C. Penney customers who shopped through the catalog and e-retail operation were loyal to the brick-and-mortar locations. The multiple channels generated additional net sales, encouraging existing customers to spend additional dollars at J. C. Penney while also attracting new customers (Table 8.3).

Shopping behavior is recognized as consumers' utilizing and combining products from a variety of multichannel retailers. The act of browsing retail channels enables consumers to learn about choices and begin the process of elimination (Ainslie & Rossi, 1998). This shopping activity creates the flexibility to make a unique combination of choices in a national brand marketplace.

Retailers position their multichannel operations as an integrated, value-rich package that generates interest and offers product exclusivity within each channel (Khakimdjanova & Park, 2005). Cross-channel shoppers encounter multichannel retailing as a total shopping experience and purchase items from a variety of retailers in order to differentiate themselves from others (Gullestad, 1995).

Attributes and barriers within each channel reveal the extent to which consumers cross-channel shop; however, little research is published as to why this occurs (Sim & Koi, 2002). For example, attributes of brick-and-mortar shopping include (1) the ability to touch products, (2) an enhanced excitement from the shopping experience, and (3) the ability to communicate personally with the retail associates. Barriers to brick-and-mortar shopping include (1) geographic distance to the store, (2) limited store hours, and (3) the ability to only view products offered at that particular store. Cross-shopping multichannels provide fashion marketers the resources to maximize the positive retailing attributes while minimizing barriers. Understanding which product features consumers prefer and how consumers shop for fashions may benefit multichannel retailers faced with the challenge of identifying the most effective channel (Friend & Walker, 2001). Product attributes include design (i.e., shape, color, and style), rarity, and value (Simonson & Nowlis, 2000). For instance, catalogs offer incentives to order online and the Web site provides coupons for showroom purchases (Borsuk, 1998). An e-retailer may provide product information prior to selecting the information at the local brick-and-mortar retailer. Nordstrom provides four different catalogs, each marketing different messages to its target market. These include the Nordstrom November 2008 Luxe book, the Nordstrom December 2008 Last-Minute Gifts book, the Nordstrom December 2008 Accessories book, and the Nordstrom January 2009 book (Nordstrom, 2009). Each book (i.e., catalog) has a very specific and well-defined marketing message. The repeated and frequent (i.e., monthly) message reminds customers that during the busy holiday season, Nordstrom is available for their shopping needs. Consumers could purchase online, through the book, phone, or in-store.

Multichannel retailers are wise to copy their style, branding, and tag lines throughout all their channels. Consumers need to be reminded of the store where they are shopping, regardless of the channel in which they are shopping. For example, Talbots' trademark red doors are featured on its brick-and-mortar stores, on its shopping bags, and at http://www.Talbots.com. The products and services offered by Talbots' channels are representative of the entire company, demonstrating to its customers that regardless of which channel consumers choose to search for information and/or shop for products, they will receive the same Talbots standard of fashion (*Women's Wear Daily*, 2007, May 24).

Improved technology has enhanced women's willingness to shop on the Internet. The

figure 8.3
Consumers can easily recognize a Talbots store by its red doors. The red doors are used on all brick-and-mortar stores and in most of its promotional pieces.

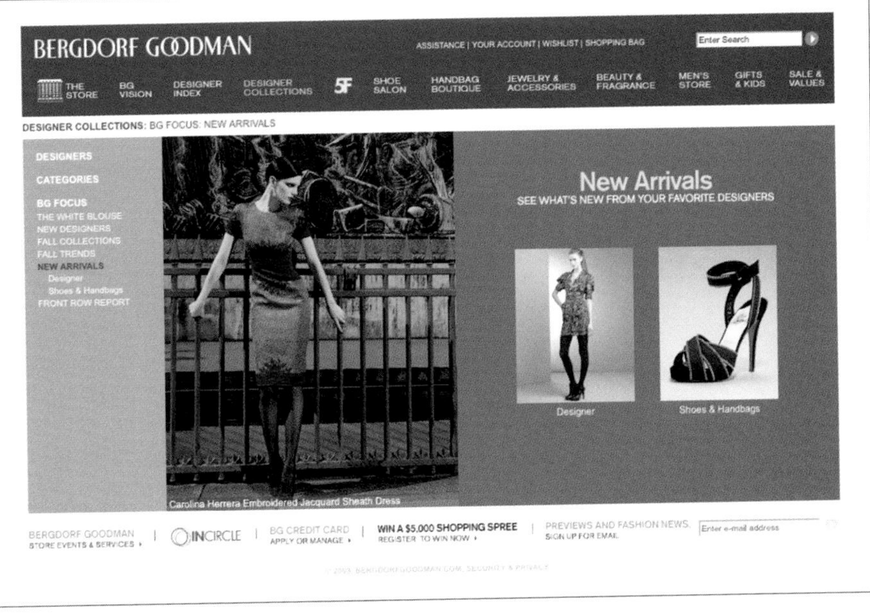

figure 8.4
A store Web site is often used as a marketing tool to inform consumers of new product arrivals. This Bergdorf Goodman Web site features three different product categories: dresses, designer fashions, and shoes and handbags. The merchandise featured is designed to stimulate purchasing interest in any of the retail channels.

visual representation of products has improved significantly. Consumers are able to view products in 360 degrees and in all colors, and read testimonials from consumers. For example, Zappos.com is a single-channel e-retailer. It sells shoes and accessories. The company's primary selling point is its extraordinary services, which include free shipping on all purchases and returns and a 12-month return policy. Products are viewable in all available colors and in 360 degrees. The friendly service policy and easy order procedure has made Zappos.com the largest shoe e-retailer in the United States (Zappos, 2009).

In addition to increasing retailers' overall sales, the Internet has also helped extend the holiday selling season. The day after Thanksgiving has traditionally been the largest in-store shopping day in the United States. After a busy weekend of holiday shopping in brick-and-mortar stores, consumers can now log on to the Internet for additional shopping. The Monday after Thanksgiving has been coined *Cyber Monday* by the National Retail Federation (Marcovitz, 2007).

There are five principal methods consumers can use to cross-channel shop. Four of the methods include two channel members. The fifth method includes shopping among three channel members.

Brick-and-Mortar—Direct Marketing Cross-Channel Shopping

As previously noted, the earliest type of cross-channel shopping is through brick-and-mortar and direct marketing. Brick-and-mortar retailers have long relied on catalogs, inserts, and flyers to entice consumers into the store. Advertisements in weekend local newspapers are used to stimulate interest on special sales, increase traffic, and generate interest in a specific department within the store. Direct marketing has long been known to be beneficial to retailers. Consumers are able to save the advertisements, bring them to the store, and pass them along to other consumers.

Brick-and-Mortar—Internet (Information Only) Cross-Channel Shopping

Not all fashion retailers have the technical capabilities, financial resources, or product demand to warrant offering multiple sales channels. Fashion marketers do, however, need to gain maximum exposure to their target market in order to generate store traffic

figure 8.5
The Salvatore Ferragamo flagship store in New York City is two stories. Men's and women's fashions, shoes, and designer accessories are sold at the high-profile brick-and-mortar retailer.

and market share. Fashion marketers in this category offer brick-and-mortar—Internet (information-only) channels.

Consumers regularly surf e-retailers for fashions during a break at work, during commercials on television, when they are bored, or when they need a "fashion fix." With a click of the mouse, consumers log on to a fashion retailer's Internet site and learn about clearance sales, new arrivals, available sizes, and store hours at the various branch locations.

With many fashion products, consumers use the Internet to gather information and then purchase the product at the brick-and-mortar channel. Reasons for cross-channel shopping even though the Internet offers products for sale include: (a) the desire to try merchandise on for fit, (b) the need to experience the enjoyment of a shopping atmosphere, and (c) discomfort with purchasing online due to credit card fraud.

Brick-and-Mortar—Internet (Information or Purchase) Cross-Channel Shopping

Macy's has been a well-respected fashion department store for more than 150 years. The company operates in over 775 brick-and-mortar stores as well as e-retailer services. Consumers are able to access Macy's Web site for fashion products, purchase items through the Internet, and find information on the Web site and then shop at one of the store locations. Regardless of the channel, the fashion-marketing message emphasizes that Macy's offers consumers fashionable products, affordable luxury, and a special retail environment (Macy's, 2008).

Ferragamo is another company that uses cross-marketing efforts. In 1923, Salvatore Ferragamo opened a boot shop in Hollywood, California. By 1928, he opened his first manufacturing company in Florence, Italy. More than 80 years later, the Ferragamo family continues to bring quality and luxury to consumers. The company has expanded its product offerings to fashions, leather goods, timepieces, and perfumes for men and women. Realizing that its products are highly desirable for consumers throughout the globe, the Ferragamo Company has brick-and-mortar retail stores and a very profitable online store. Regardless of the channel, its fashion marketing efforts are consistent with the company's mission statement, brand, and image (Ferragamo, 2009).

Direct Marketing—Internet Cross-Channel Shopping

Fashion direct-marketing companies have long been able to effectively communicate with consumers. Once the direct-marketing efforts are delivered to the target market, consumers are able to view the company's name, logo, and products repeatedly over an extended period of time. The direct marketers are also able to provide lengthy details regarding styles, sizes, product guarantees, and the company's history. In addition, most direct-marketing companies provide phone service for consumers who require personalized service.

In order to capture a wider target market, decrease printing and mailing costs, and reach out to consumers who are computer users, many fashion direct-marketing companies operate an Internet channel. Whereas the direct marketing efforts are static, the Internet channel offers the retailer and target market opportunities for streaming video of the products in use, extended product displays, movement in product presentations, and speed in ordering. Merchandise can be ordered via the Internet, and within ten minutes the order is confirmed. Many companies will guarantee shipping within four to seven days of payment by credit card. This service results in loyalty, repeat purchase behavior, multiple purchases, and more frequent purchase behavior.

Appleseed's is an example of a women's fashion retailer that sells through catalogs and an e-retail site. The company offers women's, petites, accessories, and shoes. Its rewards program encourages consumers to visit the Web site frequently. The 1-800 phone number allows first-time viewers of the e-retail site to call in questions about sizes, shipping rates, and return policies. The catalog and e-retail site can be branded with the company's logo and image at a much lower cost than a brick-and-mortar store. The lack of a brick-and-mortar location saves the company on expensive retail square footage that must be designed in a visually pleasing manner to the consumer (Appleseed's, 2009).

MISTAKES TO AVOID IN DIRECT MARKETING

Direct marketing efforts, regardless of the type (e.g., catalog, flyers, Internet), are only as good as the database. Companies that take the time up front to identify consumers who are more likely to purchase their products will be significantly more profitable in the long run. These consumers may be persons who have purchased from the company in the past, answered a survey regarding the propensity to purchase their product, or had favorable results after sampling their product (Ballantine Resources, n.d.). Fashion marketing means big business; big business can result in large amounts of marketing dollars spent in an attempt to generate even larger sales and profits. Many hundreds of thousands of dollars in profits can rely on the copy of a catalog, the banners of the Internet, or the colors and images used in the newspaper inserts.

Smart fashion marketers test direct-marketing efforts prior to local, regional, national, and international distribution (Ballantine Resources, n.d.). The most effective method for testing the direct marketing efforts is through the use of focus group interviews. A focus group interview is defined as a form of indirect interview used in market research. In a focus group interview, a small group of consumers is invited to participate in a spontaneous discussion. The purpose of the discussion is to provide consumer insight into products and services (Ostrow & Smith, 1988, p. 100). The results provide the fashion marketer with in-depth, honest opinions from the primary target market. In an effective focus group interview, information surfaces that the direct marketer did not realize was a concern or desire of the target market.

Any fashion product will possess features and benefits. A **feature** is defined as a "distinctive quality or characteristic" of a product, whereas a **benefit** is an advantage of a product (American Heritage College Dictionary, 1993). Consumers can easily identify features of products. For example, the features of a Coach purse include a leather handle, grommet feet, and a logo. Benefits of the Coach purse include its reputation as a status symbol and quality (Ballantine Resources, n.d.).

OFFERING FREE GIFTS THROUGH DIRECT MARKETING

Everyone, even the wealthiest person, likes a free gift. Direct marketing efforts are particularly successful when there is an offer for participating. The offer can be small, typically related to the product. For example, Victoria's Secret offers consumers a benefit when they hand in a card marked with those magic words, *Purchase one item and receive one item at same or lesser value free.* The fashion marketing effort gives consumers the guidelines for receiving the benefits offered by Victoria's Secret.

If you were to ask a room full of fashion-forward men and women, *What is the first thing you do when you pick up a fashion magazine, read the articles or look at the fashion advertisements?*, nine out of ten people would probably say, *Look at the advertisements.* Fashion magazines are funded through their advertisements, not subscriptions. Direct marketers invite themselves into the consumer's home. When using direct marketing, make sure that you present the absolute, positively best information first. **Do you know of anyone who ever saved his or her best or most expensive outfit for a special occasion, and when the special occasion arrived, the outfit either didn't fit or was out of style?** Direct marketing can be a lot like your expensive outfit. If you don't use it or present it up front, the money spent goes to waste. Be large and in charge. State your point in the beginning and state it often.

FOLLOWING UP ON DIRECT MARKETING EFFORTS

Direct marketing often requires **follow-up**. Follow-up is defined as any type of action on the company's part that will connect the company with the consumer. Follow-up can be in the form of a phone call, e-mail, letter, postcard, or text message. Follow-up can be used to thank the consumer for purchasing your product, for calling your direct line, or even for returning a product. The purposes of a follow-up are to keep your company in the consumer's mind, build good will with the consumer, and encourage long-term loyalty.

THE VALUE OF GRAPHICS AND "MAGIC WORDS"

The majority of consumers view pictures before they read text. Direct marketers realize the importance and difficulty in getting and keeping consumers' attention. In addition to selecting the correct graphics, direct marketers must use special, or magic, words. These words grab consumers' attention at a moment's notice. Examples of *magic words* include *new, discount, limited-time offer,* or *expires soon.* Through these words, consumers learn that the fashions featured in the direct-marketing piece are unique. Consumers' interest and attention is drawn into the copy.

ENGAGING THE FIVE SENSES

Finally, fashion direct-marketing efforts should include all five senses—or at the very least two or more. **Have you ever noticed a consumer walking through a store with outstretched arms touching garments on both sides?** She doesn't look at the garments; she simply feels the texture. All of a sudden, the consumer comes to a sudden stop as if she has walked into a brick wall. The reason for the sudden collision is that she has felt a texture that she appreciates. Only then will she consider reviewing the style and design of the garment. In most cases, direct marketing doesn't allow consumers to physically touch the product. The senses, however, can be brought alive, thereby bringing the product into the consumer's home by imagination. For example, perfume sample cards are a popular marketing tool that are attached in magazines. The scent on a sample perfume card allows the consumer to imagine the fragrance on her skin. The scent is designed to create an image in the consumer's mind. **Have you ever opened a sample perfume card and the perfume immediately brought up images of a beautiful dress, glittering jewelry, and a wonderful date night?** SOLD! Not only do you want the perfume, you place the card in your purse and share it with your friends. Or am I the only person who has done this?

figure 8.6
Store windows are an important marketing tool. This Salvatore Ferragamo window includes large signage to attract traffic, brand name recognition by repeating the store's name, presenting a variety of merchandise, and allowing customers to see inside the store from the street.

figure 8.7
Perfume advertisements are marketed heavily in magazines. In order to stimulate the target market's olfactory glands, a sample of the fragrance is provided in the advertisement. The reader can sample D&G perfume while reading the fashion magazine.

Ask yourself:

- What kinds of experiences have you had when you opened a perfume sample card?
- Do you think perfume sample cards are an effective marketing tool?

Another example of a sense used in fashion marketing is sight. Junk mail—we all get lots and lots of junk mail. However, when we see fashions printed on glossy paper and in color—stop the presses.

Ask yourself:

- How many times have you ripped pages out of a catalog or flyer because you liked the garment pictured?
- What is your first action: Read the text, or examine the fashions?
- When you examine the fashions, do you literally dissect every aspect of the garment or accessory? Do you find yourself saying things like, *I like the waist, but I would have made the neckline different?*
- Do you use the photos as a reference for future fashions that you either design yourself or purchase?

Fashion marketing efforts communicate in a very powerful manner by using our visual senses.

TIPS FOR DIRECT MARKETING

Grabbing the fashion consumer's attention in a matter of moments is essential. The following eight points should be revisited throughout your fashion marketing efforts:

1. Use a targeted mailing list.
2. Test the direct-marketing efforts.
3. Stress features, not benefits.
4. Offer a special.
5. Come to the point.
6. Follow up.
7. Say magic words: *free gift, percent off, discount, new.*
8. Appeal to all five senses.

Fully Integrated Cross-Channel Organization

Tri-channel companies—that is, companies that operate brick-and-mortar, direct marketing, and Internet channels—are typically larger in nature. They require significant profits, the distribution of products, and solid operating procedures in each channel. The primary purpose of companies that operate a trichannel fashion marketing business is to maximize the market share (i.e., sales, profits). Multichannel companies maximize the accomplishment of their goals (e.g., sales, profits, and customer traffic) when (a) in-store core strengths are identified and maximized and (b) these strengths are used to enhance the company's Internet presence. The in-store and Internet channels should work together to strengthen the consumer offerings of one another as well as to minimize the weaknesses inherent in each channel (Field, 2006). For example, the in-store operation offers personalized customer service and the ability for consumers to try on apparel. The Internet offers 24/7 shopping and the identification of products at specific branch locations. Consumers are able to identify products via the Internet, locate the branch locations that have their size, and plan a shopping trip during store hours.

The brick-and-mortar operations may include one location or a series of branch locations nation- or worldwide. The largest fashion marketers typically have a **flagship store**. A flagship store is considered the main location of a brick-and-mortar retailer. In many retail companies, the buying staff and corporate management officers are located at the flagship store. Oftentimes, the flagship store is a historical building, located in a predominant part of a city.

Direct marketing and e-retailing are designed to support and supplement the brick-

and-mortar sales. The brick-and-mortar retailer remains the predominant fashion marketing effort in the retailer and consumers' minds. Direct marketing and the Internet are used to continually strengthen consumer loyalty, entice impulse spending at a specific company, and build brand loyalty.

JUSTIFICATION FOR MULTIPLE CHANNELS

As the retailer and fashion marketer increases the number of channels, the complexity of operations increases. The outcomes of fashion marketing efforts may justify expansion. There are two reasons for expanding channels: expanding product lines and expanding the marketing message.

Expanding Product Lines. The addition of a Web site provides the fashion marketer with the ability to (a) offer products that are different than those offered in the brick-and-mortar location (b) offer larger quantities of products than offered in the brick-and-mortar location, (c) offer special sizes that would not sell in the brick-and-mortar location, and/or (d) feature clearance products, thereby providing valuable square footage in the brick-and-mortar location for high-demand products.

If a product is not offered at a store, some companies offer delivery to the retail operation. By doing so, the product delivery draws consumer traffic into the store, thereby encouraging consumers to view merchandise in the store and to purchase additional items before and/or after they pick up the merchandise that was ordered online.

Expanding Marketing Messages. Retailers who use two or more channels are able to expand their fashion marketing messages to the consumer. They may use the exact same messages, use a series of blended messages (i.e., use some of the same messages and some new messages), or use completely different messages in each channel. Regardless of the message, it is vital that the retailer maintain the same store image and marketing message. Consumers must at all times be aware that they are shopping at the same store, regardless of how they are shopping (i.e., brick-and-mortar, direct marketing, Internet) (Stitch & Leonard, 2008).

Consumers have been known to browse a store and not easily recognize the store. Consumers who surf the Internet for fashions click through different Web sites even faster than they walk through different stores at the mall or flip through the pages of catalogs. It is easy for consumers to click through retailers' Web sites and not realize which Internet site they have logged on to. Because many consumers search the Internet for information and then go to the brick-and-mortar location to physically inspect the products, it is vital for fashion marketers to mark each page of their Web sites with the company's name. It is also important to indicate if the product is (a) available in the store, and (b) which branch locations have the product. In any form of marketing, never assume that consumers know the answer or possess the information.

Cross-channel shopping becomes particularly important for retailers and consumers during the holiday season. Consumers often use the Internet for information (e.g., price, location) and then purchase the product at an in-store retailer (Mui, 2009, October 24).

MARKETING METHODS

Three methods of marketing products to consumers exist: push marketing, permission marketing, and pull marketing.

Push Marketing

Push marketing is a form of advertisement that is pushed onto the consumer. Consumers are forced to read the advertisement regardless of their desire (Kotler & Armstrong, 2001). Examples of push marketing used in the Internet include pop-up advertisements and company banners. Push marketing is often

figure 8.8
Multiple pull out cards are provided in each fashion magazine. The pull out card offers the reader a discount on a year's subscription to the magazine as compared to buying the publication at the newsstand.

viewed as annoying, and experts disagree regarding the return on the investment in these advertisements.

Permission Marketing

Permission marketing consists of advertisements that entice consumers to purchase or join a company. This form of marketing is passive, requiring the consumer to take action. In today's increased competition within the fashion industry, permission marketing is not as effective as other forms of marketing (Kotler & Armstrong, 2001). For example, *Vogue* magazine includes a pull-out card inviting readers to subscribe. Readers may pay immediately or request to be billed later. Once the consumer sends in the card, *Vogue* has data on the consumer and can continue to solicit him or her. It is probable that since the consumer initially read the fashion magazine, he or she may eventually subscribe.

Pull Marketing

Pull marketing is used extensively in fashion direct marketing. Pull marketing occurs when consumers purposely seek out the direct marketer (Kotler & Armstrong, 2001). Pull marketing is actively used in cross-channel shopping. Take, for example, the Christmas catalog that Neiman Marcus sends out each year. The catalog features exotic, one-of-a-kind products. The majority of consumers cannot afford the products. The catalog does, however, pull consumers into the store's Web site and brick-and-mortar locations. **What lover of fashion can resist looking at the catalog even if he or she can't afford the products?** An immediate impulse may be to log on to the Web site. Perhaps there are items in a lower price range. An image comes to mind and the question forms, *I wonder what is on sale?* Once browsing the Web site, the next thought that comes to mind may be, *The Web site looks so pretty, I bet the store looks fabulous at this time. I'm going to see how it is decorated.*

Brooklyn Industries is an example of a fashion company that has integrated its cross-channel marketing efforts in order to maximize sales. Based in New York, the company manufactures casual apparel for a female youthful market (Kwon, 2007). During 2006, the company's marketing budget of $201,000 helped the organization realize more than $10 million in revenue. During 2007, the company increased its marketing budget to $15 million. Cross-channel marketing efforts have helped this fashion company aggressively capture the attention and financial resources of its target market (Table 8.4a).

The company emphasizes cross-channel marketing through catalogs, store windows, advertisements, install displays, direct mail, photography, and product placement (Table 8.4b). Brooklyn Industries uses window displays (i.e., brick-and-mortar store) to maintain interest from existing customers and attract traffic from shoppers who have never patronized the store. Increased direct-marketing efforts by the company have two-fold goals: (1) to use the marketing pieces as fashion magazines that remain with the consumer, as opposed to being thrown away, and (2) to promote the Brooklyn Industries brand.

Internet sales are so popular with consumers that on Cyber Monday in 2007, more than $730 million in sales were generated. This sales figure rose 21 percent from the previous year (Ridley & Huguenin, 2007). Due to consumers' diligent online shopping habits, Walmart.com and Target.com reached the Number 2 and 3 spots in terms of the most popular online retailer on that day. Walmart.com's hits increased 103 percent compared to the previous year; Target.com's hits increased 86 percent compared to the previous year (Ridley & Huguenin, 2007). Sephora, an international retail beauty chain, successfully uses multichannel marketing to encourage consumers into its stores and onto its Web site. The company's multichannel efforts are so successful that even in difficult economic times the company realizes double-digit sales growth (Misonzhnik, 2008).

EMPOWERED SHOPPING OPPORTUNITIES

Cross-channel shopping opportunities have changed consumers' shopping experiences (Dolberg, 2007). Consumers are able to search out specific customer services, identify national brands, and shop for the lowest price, all from the comfort of their house, car, office, or the backyard by using an iPod or laptop. Consumers are then able to select the best method of purchasing the products (i.e., in-store, e-retailer, catalog). The multi-channel shopping experiences for a single retailer as well as the retailer's competitor provide consumers with empowered shopping opportunities.

Retailers' profits are often dependent on **multiple sales.** A multiple sale is when a consumer purchases two or more products during one sales encounter. Cross-channel retailers develop multiple sales opportunities through **cross-channel loyalty programs.** A cross-channel loyalty program is a program that spans all channels within a retailer. The program is designed to increase consumers' loyalty to the retailer. In some cases, the retailer will design a program to build loyalty to a company brand (Tierney, 2007).

Loyalty programs encourage consumers to shop frequently at multiple channels. Some programs require consumers to purchase products in order to receive a reward. Other products provide a reward simply by returning documentation of belonging to the cross-channel loyalty program (Tierney, 2007).

Talbots sponsored a loyalty program to encourage summer spending as well as loyal patronage throughout the year. The "Classic Awards" program offered members an opportunity to earn points toward a $25 dividend when a future purchase was made with a Talbots charge card. The program also allowed consumers to earn points when they

TABLES 8.4A AND B
Cross-Channel Marketing Efforts of Brooklyn Industries

A. Revenue and Budget for 2006 and 2007

REVENUE/BUDGET	2007*	2006
Annual Revenue	$15 million	$10.1 million
Marketing Budget	$301,000	$201,000
Marketing Budget as a Share of Revenue	2 percent	2 percent

**projected*
(Kwon, 2007)

B. Marketing Budget Line-Item Breakdown

ITEM	2007*	2006
Catalogs	$100,000	$57,000
Store windows	$60,000	$12,000
Advertising	$40,000	$80,000
Installing displays	$38,000	$30,000
Direct mail	$26,000	$6,000
Photography	$21,000	$12,000
Product Placement	$16,000	$16,000

**projected*
(Kwon, 2007)

Sephora is in Europe and the United States. Sephora products are sold in brick-and-mortar stores, online, and in JCPenney stores nationwide.

BOX 8.1 **Sephora: A Natural Beauty**

Many consumers know Sephora as the leading retail beauty chain in Europe. The company is rapidly expanding its brick-and-mortar stores throughout the United States, and sales on Sephora.com are on the rise. Consumers can cross-channel shop in 515 Sephora stores throughout 14 countries, as well as in Sephora catalogs and online. Sephora also has an agreement with J. C. Penney. A Sephora counter is located inside the J. C. Penney retailer.

What you may not realize is that LVMH is the parent company of Sephora. That's right, the luxury manufacturer, fashion marketer, and retailer also owns Sephora.

Both in the brick-and-mortar stores and online, Sephora offers its customers classic beauty brands as well as emerging brands. Consumers are able to purchase all their beauty-care staples, including makeup, skincare, fragrances, bath and body products, hair care, grooming tools, natural and organic product lines, and gift sets (Sephora, 2009).

open a Talbots charge card. Both programs (a) encourage store loyalty at Talbots, (b) remind consumers to use the Talbots charge card, and (c) provide consumers with a reward (i.e., discounts on future purchases).

UNIQUENESS IN FASHIONS AND NATIONAL RETAILERS

There is a delicate balance with fashion consumers—they want to look unique with their designs without looking out of place. To accommodate this, national fashion retailers need to sell merchandise in mass quantities in order to make a profit. The primary limitation of patronizing national retailers is the lack of uniqueness in product design. The evolution of national channel retailers into multichannel operations creates opportunities for consumers to personalize apparel and accessory fashions with unique products (Murphy, 2000). The combination of products from brick-and-mortar stores, catalogs, and e-retailers enables consumers to display their unique style through product assortment (Noble, 2001). Consumers who desire unique fashions may choose to select products by cross-channel shopping, thereby lessening the possibility of having the same products as their neighbor (Koelemeijer & Oppewal, 1999). The result is an individualized collection of merchandise from brick-and-mortar stores, catalogs, and e-retailers as consumers combine products that are symbolic of their own style (Hartnett, 2001).

Uniqueness Theory

Uniqueness is defined as consumers' desire to differentiate themselves from one another by displaying a compilation of items differently than friends and/or neighbors (Snyder & Fromkin, 1977). Uniqueness theory attempts to explain consumers' purchasing behavior as it relates to product features. The theory postulates that one's sense of uniqueness is projected and perceived by others and motivates an individual to acquire items that reflect a difference relative to others (Snyder & Fromkin, 1977).

Establishing a sense of uniqueness is signified by the acquisition of products and sustained through consumers' behavior and possessions (Lynn & Harris, 1997). For example, acquiring unique, hard-to-obtain items such as one-of-a-kind jewelry is reflected in a desire to own rare items few others possess (Lynn & Harris, 1997). A desire to be admired for uniqueness nourishes the activity of acquiring a variety of possessions (Simonson & Nowlis, 2000).

Consumers display possessions in order to portray their uniqueness (Gullestad, 1995). Studying fashion marketing as an expression of uniqueness is important in the quest to understand why and how often consumers purchase fashion products (e.g., apparel, home décor) (Madigan & Munro, 1996). Some consumers feel pressure to own a home that portrays style and a sense of design. Retailers acquire mass-produced merchandise and promote it to target markets in such a manner that they can identify aspects of uniqueness in the product's design (Madigan & Munro, 1996). For example, marketing mass-produced vases in combination with silk flowers enhances the merchandise, differentiating them from the vases sold by the competing national brand retailer.

Consumers recognize product uniqueness as important; however, standardized design and widespread distribution of large quantities of identical merchandise influence their ability to consistently satisfy their desire for uniqueness (Simonson & Nowlis, 2000). The desire for uniqueness in fashions is viewed by many retailers as an opportunity to (a) differentiate products from one another, (b) differentiate oneself from the competition, and (c) act as the deciding variable when selecting from two or more similar products (Cruesen & Schoormans, 1998). A few studies reveal that consumers have a conceptual idea of a product when they initiate the shopping process for fashion. More often than not, however, consumers are unable to verbalize their preferences until they identify the product (Schmid, 1998).

The level of rarity of fashions and accessories are considered important to consumers with a high need for uniqueness (Snyder, 1992). Mass production tends to lessen rarity, leading to the perception of a diluted marketplace (Kruger, 1998). Although an overlap of products exists among retailers, it is possible for diversity to be offered in the marketplace.

The perceived value of an object is defined as a consumer's internal perspective of its worth. The object may cost very little and be perceived as valuable because it adds significantly to a collection. Likewise, the cost of an item does not necessarily increase a product's value simply because of the price tag (Grace & O'Cass, 2005). Moderate-income consumers acquire items gradually with attention to value rather than style (Madigan & Munro, 1996). Making judgments regarding the value (perceived or actual) of home décor items owned or desired is one of the more complex and important cognitive tasks consumers face. The act of acquiring an object appears to increase its perceived value (Ciarrochi & Forgas, 2000).

Consumers' store and product preferences are influenced by the relationship among (a) assortment composition; (b) availability of specific items, prices, and store ambience; and (c) purchase goals (Koelemeijer & Oppewal, 1999). Shopping behaviors are influenced by such products attributes as the origin of the product, the context of the purchase, and the ways that these influence identification of the most attractive option.

SUMMARY

Cross-channel shopping is classified into three categories: (1) visiting stores to evaluate a product or to gather information prior to purchasing online, (2) using the Internet to locate the product and then going to the store to make the purchase, and (3) using a catalog in conjunction with the Web site for making the purchase decision.

As the retailer and fashion marketer increase the number of channels, the complexity of operations increases. The outcomes of fashion marketing efforts may justify expansion. There are two reasons for expanding channels: expanding product lines and expanding the marketing message.

Cross-channel shopping opportunities have changed consumers' shopping experiences. Consumers are able to search out specific customer services, identify national brands, and shop for the lowest price, all from the comfort of their house, car, office, or backyard, by using an iPod or laptop. Consumers are then able to select the best method of purchasing the products. The multichannel shopping experiences for a single retailer as well as the retailer's competitor provide consumers with empowered shopping opportunities.

REFERENCES

Ainslie, A., & Rossi, P. E. (1998). Similarities in choice behavior across product categories. *Marketing Science, 17*(2): 91–106.

Appleseed's. (2009). Company Web site. Retrieved on June 24, 2009 from http://www.appleseeds.com.

American Heritage College Dictionary (Eds.). (1993). *American Heritage College Dictionary*. Boston: Houghton Mifflin.

Bauman, Z. (2001). Consuming life. *Journal of Consumer Culture, 1*(1): 9–30.

Ballantine Resources. (n.d). "The 12 most common direct mail mistakes . . . and how to avoid them." Retrieved on August 28, 2007 from www.ballantine.com/dmmistakes.html.

Bluefly.com (2007). Annual report. Retrieved on September 3, 2007 from http://biz.yahoo.com/e/070228/bfly10-k.html.

Borsuk, M. (1998). Web sites cast big shadow over real estate leasing strategy. *Discount Store News, 37*(1): 14.

Burk, R. R. (2003). Technology and the customer interface: What consumers want in the physical and virtual store. *Journal of the Academy of Marketing Sciences, 30*(4): 411–32.

CanWest News Service (2007). Online shoppers use Internet more: Study; More likely to blog or post videos. *The Gazette*, p. B3.

Chambers, V., & Davis, A. (1998, April 13). Direct from Paris . . . to the mall. *Newsweek, 131*(15): 64.

Ciarrochi, J., & Forgas, J. P. (2000). The pleasure of possessions: Affective influences and personality in the evaluation of consumer items. *European Journal of Social Psychology, 30*(5): 631–49.

Cruesen, M. E. H., & Schoormans, J. P. L. (1998). The influence of observation time on the role of the product design in consumer preference. *Advances in Consumer Research, 25*: 551–56.

Currah, A. (2003). The virtual geographies of retail display. *Journal of Consumer Culture, 3*(1): 5–37.

Dittmar, H., Friese, S., & Beattie, J. (1996). Objects, decision considerations and self-image in men's and women's impulse purchases. *Act Psychological, 93*: 187–206.

Dolberg, S. (2007, August). The cross-channel advantage. *Direct, 17*.

Eastlick, M. A., & Feinberg, R. A. (1999). Shopping motives for mail catalog shopping. *Journal of Business Research, 45*: 281–90.

Edelson, S. (2005). The 'wi' phenomenon. *Women's Wear Daily, 189*(129), 32.

Ferragamo (2009). Company Web site. Retrieved July 8, 2009 from http://www.salvatoreferragamo.it/en/#folderId=/en/experience/brandhistory.

Field, K. (2006, January). Best clicks: Six grocers with strong on-line presence. [Electronic version] *Chain Store Age*, p. 87.

Friend, S. C., & Walker, P. H. (2001). Welcome to the new world of merchandising, *Harvard Business Review, 79*(10): 133–141.

Grace, D., & O'Cass, A. (2005). An examination of the antecedents of repatronage intentions across different retail store formats. *Journal of Retailing and Consumer Services, 12*: 227–243.

Gullestad, M. (1995). Home decoration as popular culture: Constructing homes, genders, and classes. In T. del Valle (Ed.), *Gendered anthropology* (pp. 128–161). London: Routledge.

Haberkorn, J. (2008, April 8). Web sales may hit $204 billion: Online shopping to rise 17 percent. *The Washington Times*, p. C08.

Hartnett, M. (2001) Logistics consultants see varying needs for multi-channel retailers, *Stores, 83*(1): 111–14.

Jamison, B., Gold, J., & Jamison, W. (1997) *Electronic selling: Twenty-three steps to e-selling profits.* New York: McGraw-Hill.

JCPenney (2007, Dec. 11). Annual report. Retrieved on Aug 30, 2008 from http://media.corporate-ir.net/media_files/irol/70/70528/presentations/InvestorFactBook.pdf.

Khakimdjanova, L. & Park, J. (2005). Online visual merchandising practice of apparel e-merchants. *Journal of Retailing and Consumer Services, 12*: 307–318.

Koelemeijer, K., & Oppewal, H. (1999). Assessing the effects of assortment and ambience: A choice experimental approach. *Journal of Retailing, 75*(3), 319–45.

Korgoankar, P. K. (1984). Consumer shopping orientations, non store retailers, and consumers' patronage intentions: a multivariate investigation. *Journal of the Academy of Marketing Science, 12*: 11–22.

Kotler, P. & Armstrong, G. (2001). *Principles of marketing.* New York: McGraw-Hill.

Kruger, R. M. (1998). Mass appeal. *Discount Merchandiser, 38*(1): 75.

Kwon, B. (2007, January). Sales more than doubled last year. So why are they changing tactics? *Inc. Magazine*, p. 54.

Lee, B-K., & Lee, W-N. (2004). The effect of information overload on consumer choice quality in an on-inline environment. *Psychology & Marketing, 21*(3): 159–183.

Lueg, J. E. (2005). Teenagers' use of alternative shopping channels: A consumer socialization perspective. *Journal of Retailing, 82*(2), 137–153.

Lynn, M., & Harris, J. (1997). Individual differences in the pursuit of self-uniqueness through consumption. *Journal of Applied Psychology, 27*(21): 1861–83.

Macy's (2008) Company Web site. Retrieved January 28, 2009 from www.macys.com.

Madigan, R., & Munro, M. (1996). House beautiful: Style and consumption in the home. *The Journal of the British Sociological Association, 30*(1): 41–57.

Marcovitz, M. (2006, June). Winning on the Web. *Gourmet Retailer, 27*(6), 78–79.

Mathwick, C., Malhorta, N., and Rigdon, E. (2001) Experiential value: Conceptualization, measurement, and application in the catalog and Internet shopping environment, *Journal of Retailing, 77*(1): 39–56.

McDonald, W. J. (1993). The role of demographics, purchase histories, and shopper decision making styles predicting consumer catalog loyalty. *Journal of Direct Marketing, 7*: 55–65.

Misonzhnik, E. (2008, January 1). On and off the Web. *Retail Traffic*, p. 42.

Mui, Y.Q. (2009, October 24). Online spending down as holiday season nears: recession puts breaks on fast-paced growth of e-commerce. *The Washington Post*, p. A10.

Murphy, P. A. (2000). Clicks vs. bricks: Data helps retailers develop multi-channel customer strategy. *Stores, 82*(9): 168–170.

Nordstrom (2009). Company Web site. Retrieved January 29, 2009 from http://www.nordstrom.com.

Nitse, P. S., Parker, K. R., Krumwiede, D., & Ottaway, T. (2004). The impact of color in the e-commerce marketing of fashions: An exploratory study. *European Journal of Marketing, 38*(7): 898–915.

Noble, S. M. (2001). Consumers' channel preferences: an integrated model. Dissertation, University of Massachusetts, Amherst.

Norway, S., Jackson, S., & Moores, S. (Eds.), *The politics of domestic consumption* (pp. 321–35). Hertfordshire, England: Prentice Hall/Harvester Wheatsheaf.

O'Cass, A., & Fenech, T. (2003). Web retailing adoption: Exploring the nature of Internet users Web retailing behavior. *Journal of Retailing and Consumer Services, 10*: 81–94.

Ostrow, R., & Smith, S. R. (1988). *The dictionary of marketing.* New York: Fairchild Books.

Park, H-J., Burns, L. D., & Rabolt, N. J. (2007). Fashion innovativeness, materialism, and attitude toward purchasing foreign fashion goods online across national borders. *Journal of Fashion Marketing and Management, 11*(2), 201–214.

Park, J., Lennon, S., J., & Stoel, L. (2005). On-line product presentation: Effects on mood, perceived risk, and purchase intention. *Psychology & Marketing, 22*(9): 695–719.

Pascale, M. (2000). Online catalogers, spending more, making more, bringing more inhouse. *Catalog Age* (June): 8–13.

Power, D. (2007, June 19). Retailers ready to boost interactivity on the Web. *Women's Wear Daily, 193*(130): 10.

Ridley, J., & Huguenin, P. (2007, November 28). Shoppers click till they drop! Online sales soaring for gifts and gadgets. *Daily News*, p. 2.

Ritzer, G. (1999). *Enchanting a disenchanted world: Revolutionizing the means of consumption.* Thousand Oaks, CA: Pine Forge Press.

Rogers, W., Negash, S., & Suk, K. (2005). The moderating effect of on-line experience on the antecedents and consequences of on-line satisfaction. *Psychology & Marketing, 22*(4): 313–331.

Rose, G. M., Meuter, M. L., & Curran, J. M. (2005). On-line waiting: The role of download time and other important predictors on attitude toward e-retailers. *Psychology & Marketing, 22*(2): 127–151.

Scally, R. (2000). Clicks-and-mortars have right stuff to dominate the Internet. *Design Retailing Today, 39*(8): 13.

Schmid, J. (1998). The eight commandments of design. *Catalog Age, 15*: 57–60.

Sephora (2009). Company Web site. Retrieved July 8, 2009 from http://www.sephora.com/?cm_mmc%3dus_search-_-GG-_-top%20perf%20kw_googleus%20sephora-_-{esvcid}.

Shop.org reports highlights: Multichannel supershoppers. (2001). *Stores, 83*(11), 16.

Short, P. (2007). Does your Internet marketing pull? Retrieved August 28, 2007 from *Marketing Information.* http://emailmarketing-inc.com/6136.php.

Sim, L. L., & Koi, S. M. (2002). Singapore's Internet shoppers and their impact on traditional shopping patterns. *Journal of Retailing and Consumer Services, 9*: 115–24.

Simonson, I. (1990). The effect of purchase quantity and timing on variety seeking behavior. *Journal of Marketing Research, 27*: 150–62.

Simonson, I., & Nowlis, S. M. (2000). The role of explanations and need for uniqueness in consumer decision making: Unconventional choices based on reasons. *Journal of Consumer Research, 27*: 49–68.

Sinioukov, T. (2000). I is for integration. *Dealerscope, 42*(12): 26, 30.

Snyder, C. R. (1992). Product scarcity by need for uniqueness interaction: A consumer catch-22 carousel? *Basic and Applied Social Psychology, 13*(1), 9–24.

Snyder, C. R., & Fromkin, H. L. (1977). *Uniqueness: The human pursuit of difference.* New York: Plenum. 2nd edition (1980).

Stitch, M. & Leonard, J. (2008, March 10). Ring up e-commerce gains with a true multichannel strategy. *Advertising Age*, p. 15.

Stores Eds. (2000). Survey finds gains for retailers in multi-channel shopping. *Stores, 82*(11): 20.

Szymanski, D. M., & Hise, R. T. (2000). E-satisfaction: An initial examination. *Journal of Retailing, 76*(3): 309–22.

The 100 top brands 2006. (2007, August 28). *Business Week* Online. Retrieved August 28, 2007 from http://bwnt.businessweek.com/brand/2006.

Thomas, D. (2001). Leverage today's technologies for successful multi-channel retailing. *Stores, 83*(1): 180.

Tian, K. T., Bearden, W. O., & Hunter, G. L. (2001). Consumers' need for uniqueness: Scale development and validation. *Journal of Consumer Research, 28*: 50–66.

Tierney, J. (2007, February). Courting cross-channel loyalty. *Multichannel Merchant,* 26–27.

Tinning, W. (2008, December 16). Sales up online as shoppers hunt for bargains: Internet sales rice by 16 percent compared with last year. *The Herald,* p. 7.

Tversky, A., & Simonson, I. (1993). Context dependent preferences. *Management Science, 39*(10): 1179–89.

Watson, L. (1999/2000). Twentieth century fashion: 100 years of style by decade & designer. New York: Fairchild Books.

Women's Wear Daily. (2007, May 24). "I thee Web," *Women's Wear Daily, 112,* p. 2.

Wong, N. Y. C. (1997). Suppose you own the world and no one knows? Conspicuous consumption, materialism, and self. *Advances in Consumer Research, 24*: 197–203.

Worzala, E. M., & McCarthy, A. (2001). Bricks-and-clicks: e-commerce strategies for the chain retailer. *Journal of Shopping Center Research,* 7–34.

York, E. B. (2007, October 29). This isn't the holiday catalog you remember; Sears and other retailers use the old-world books to drive shoppers online. *Advertising Age,* p. 4.

Zappos. (2009). Company Web site. About us. Retrieved on June 24, 2009 from http://about.zappos.com.

KEY TERMS

Define or briefly explain the following terms:

Benefit ______________________________

Cross-channel loyalty program ______________________________

Cross-channel shopping ______________________________

Direct marketers ______________________________

E-retailer ______________________________

Feature ______________________________

Flagship store ______________________________

Follow-up ______________________________

Multiple sale ______________________________

Permission marketing ______________________________

Pull marketing ______________________________

Push marketing ______________________________

Uniqueness ______________________________

CLASS OR TEAM DISCUSSION QUESTIONS

1 | Discuss the classifications of cross-channel shopping. What are the classification's strengths and/or limitations for fashion marketing efforts during national economic downturns?

____

____

2 | For a fashion marketer, is there a preference for one particular retail channel? Does the fashion product influence the preference for the channel? If so, explain the advantages and limitations, based on the fashion product category.

____

____

3 | Discuss scenarios (e.g., product categories, seasons, and economy) when a fashion marketer should use the following strategies: (a) push marketing, (b) permission marketing, and (c) pull marketing.

INTERNET ACTIVITIES

1 | Using the Internet as a resource, find an example of fashion marketing efforts from a fashion company. The company should represent a multichannel fashion retailer. Compare the differences and similarities in fashion marketing efforts used in each retail channel.

2 | Using the Internet as a resource, find five retailers that use a cross-channel loyalty program. Discuss the differences and similarities among the fashion marketing cross-channel loyalty programs identified. Select the fashion marketing you believe is the most effective. Justify your selection.

STUDY QUESTIONS

1 | What is cross-channel shopping?

2 | What are the benefits and limitations of operating a brick-and-mortar retail operation?

3 | What are variables that fashion marketers must take into consideration when working with a multichannel retailer?

4 | What are some of the challenges for e-retailers?

5 | What is cross-channel shopping? Why is cross-channel shopping important to the fashion industry?

6 | How can fashion marketers stimulate cross-channel shopping behavior?

7 | What is a focus group interview?

8 | What are the benefits and limitations of a focus group interview?

9 | What is push marketing? In your opinion, is push marketing effective?

10 | What is permission marketing? Provide an example of permission marketing.

11 | What channel of distribution frequently uses pull marketing?

____

____

12 | What is the value of a cross-channel loyalty program?

____

____

MULTIPLE-CHOICE QUESTIONS

1 | What is the most effective method for testing direct-marketing efforts?

a. Sales
b. Profits
c. Focus group interviews
d. Returns

2 | Fashion marketing efforts that entice consumers to purchase or join a company are a type of _____.

a. Push marketing
b. Permission marketing
c. Pull marketing
d. Tag marketing

3 | Consumers who cross-channel-shop are _____ times more valuable to retailers than those who shop at one channel.

a. Two
b. Three
c. Four
d. Five

4 | The *primary purpose* of companies that operate a trichannel fashion marketing business is to _____.

a. Maximize market share
b. Lower fashion marketing expenses
c. Maximize manufacturer discounts
d. Enhance the company's image

TRUE-OR-FALSE QUESTIONS

1 | _____ The success of a marketing campaign is often based on the number of multiple sales a product category generates. This is because a retailer's profits are often dependent on multiple sales.

2 | _____ Since e-retailing only represents 2 percent of all sales, fashion marketers should not spend the marketing budget on this venue.

3 | _____ The primary challenge of a brick-and-mortar retailer is bringing consumers into the store.

TABLE 9.1

THE Market Planning PROCESS

step 1	CHAPTER 2	Be inspired; become passionate regarding a product/service; be driven to succeed and committed to working toward a goal.
step 2	CHAPTER 3	Intrinsic attributes of the products and services are marketed in terms of value, satisfaction, and quality. Building upon the mission statement, in this step you will make decisions regarding the pricing, communication, value, satisfaction, and quality associated with the purchase or the products and/or services.
step 3	CHAPTER 4	Identify a comprehensive list of products and services offered by the company.
step 4	CHAPTER 5	Examine the products and services component of the core marketing concept related to the trickle-down theory, media and celebrities, and the belongingness theory.
step 5	CHAPTER 6	Examine the buying season in relation to the marketing process.
step 6	CHAPTER 7	Examine marketing methods of targeting the consumer.
step 7	CHAPTER 8	Examine the methods of exchange and relationships with the consumers. This includes making decisions to sell products and services through brick-and-mortar retail operations, direct marketing, and the Internet.
step 8	CHAPTER 9	**Examine the image and brands of the company in relation to marketing efforts.**
step 9	CHAPTER 10	Conduct a market analysis of how companies are able to successfully cross product boundaries.
step 10	CHAPTER 11	Examine trends in the fashion industry regarding a) counterfeit merchandise and b) the impact of such merchandise on the industry's sales, profits, product design, consumers' attitudes.
step 11	CHAPTER 12	Conduct a market analysis of fashions in the global environment in order to determine impact to the company's existing marketing efforts.

9

Image and Branding

"You do not merely want to be considered just the best of the best. You want to be considered the only one who does what you do." —Jerry Garcia

chapter objectives

After reading this chapter, you should be able to understand Step Eight of the Market Planning Process. This includes being able to:

+ Explain the concept of brands, branding, and image.

+ Identify differences among types of brands.

+ Analyze strategies used in presenting brands.

+ Compare fashion marketing strategies used by different companies in the marketplace.

As a musician, Jerry Garcia strived to be the absolute best in his industry. His statement regarding "being the best of the best" reveals his passion, ambition, and drive to touch the lives of his fans. Fashion designers, manufacturers, and retailers in the fashion industry also strive to be the "best of the best." They distinguish themselves through their brands.

American, Korean, Japanese, Italian, French, and British consumers all have one fashion characteristic in common. They are passionately—almost to the level of obsession—attracted to brands. The acquisition of a store-brand, manufacturer-brand, or designer-brand product can change a gloomy day into the brightest day of the week. When it comes to fashion and brands, it often doesn't matter to consumers if the product "goes with anything" in one's existing wardrobe. If the brand is desirable and fits one's image, the product must be acquired. That is a huge accomplishment for a fashion marketer: making a brand indispensable to one's fashion wardrobe. Furthermore, most brands have identifying logos, symbols, or designer names printed or embossed on the fashions. Consumers are paying for the brand and paying to advertise the brand—another fashion marketing accomplishment. This chapter addresses Step Eight of the Marketing Process (Table 9.1) and the importance that fashion marketing places on branding as well as the influence that brands have on products, companies, and consumer purchasing behaviors. The importance of accurately communicating the brand and image to the consumer will be addressed. The branding techniques and attitudes of large and small companies will be examined. As we progress through this chapter, the reader will be asked to compare (a) the similarities and differences, as well as (b) the challenges of branding products, in both large and small companies.

THE POWER OF IMAGE

Fashion consumers pay attention to every detail. They examine four different shades of blue used in three different types of silk before deciding on a scarf. A perfume bottle is often more important to a consumer than what it contains. A particular shade of yellow will be examined on four identical rainbow flip-flops before making a purchase. Fashion marketers clearly understand that image is important to fashion consumers. The question remains, however, as to what is the "right" image for each target market.

Image is "a mental perception or impression held by an individual about himself, about others, or about products and services" (Ostrow & Smith, 1988, p. 115). Each company, regardless of its mission, must clearly identify, understand, and implement the desired image. The image must be consistent with the company's mission statement and its target market.

TABLE 9.2
Examples of Company Taglines

COMPANY	TAGLINE
The Athlete's Foot	Athlete, everyday
Benetton	United colors of Benetton
Bloomingdale's	Like no other store in the world
Dillard's	The style of your life
eBay	Love to shop?
Express	Shop now. Shop online. Shop in style.
Fossil	What vintage are you?
H&M	Fashion for the future
J. C. Penney	Every day matters.
J. Jill	Inspired style
JoS. A. Bank	The expert in men's apparel
Kohl's	Expect great things.
Limited Too	It's a girl's world.
Loehmann's	The biggest deal in designer fashions
Macy's	The magic of Macy's
Marks & Spencer	Your M&S
Men's Wearhouse	You're gonna like the way you look. I guarantee it.
Mr. Formal Tuxedos	Tuxedos for all generations
Nike	Just do it! / Be a better athlete.
Payless ShoeSource	Buy one, get 1/2 off everything.
A Pea in the Pod	Maternity redefined
Ross Dress for Less	New brands . . . same low prices
Stein Mart	We can save you.
Zappos.com	Powered by service

In addition, all actions the company takes must present the image in a consistent manner. Any deviations from the image will result in confusing consumers, stockholders, and employees. A tagline, often placed directly under the company's name, is used as a reminder of the company's desired image or reason for conducting business. A tagline is a series of words that presents an immediate impression (Table 9.2). The purpose of this chapter is to demonstrate how companies can use image and related activities to enhance their fashion marketing efforts.

An image is formed through every action, form of communication (e.g., promotion, advertisement, sales), and environmental stimulus. The image presents the company's personality. The more consistent the image (or personality) is presented to the target market, the more effective the desired marketing efforts. The image influences how consumers, employees, and stockholders view the products. For example, part of the Tiffany & Co. image is the blue box. The color of the box was chosen in 1837, the same year the company opened. The decision was made because the founders, Charles Lewis Tiffany and John B. Young, believed the shade of blue represented quality and craftsmanship. More than 170 years later, this color is the image of Tiffany & Co.; it is used throughout the company's marketing and packaging efforts. Words are not required to convey a message. When anyone sees the distinctive blue, they immediately recognize Tiffany & Co. They also expect the product to be of high quality (Tiffany & Co., 2009).

Deciding on an image is often easy; the implementation, however, is far more difficult. Discounters should present an image of value and price savings. High-end retailers should present an image of exclusivity and of a wide variety of services. The difficulty is not in deciding on an image, but in (a) selecting the proper strategy, and (b) consistently implementing the strategy to promote that image. In addition, retailers aren't the only entities

BOX 9.1 Couture Without the Couture Price Tag

Annabelle LaRoque graduated from the University of South Carolina with a Bachelor of Science in retailing. While studying fashion merchandising, she was confident of many things: She thoroughly enjoyed sewing, was passionate about fashions, and consistently identified the current trends. When LaRoque told people her plans to own an apparel brand, some said she was crazy. Confident, positive, and definitely determined, Annabelle opened LaRoque in 2005. Named in honor of her late father, she created the LaRoque brand. The custom-made dresses, skirts, and tops are known for fine-quality fabrics, excellent craftsmanship, and characteristic ruffles and wrap-around designs.

Women are beating a path to the LaRoque doors. The target market receives a couture brand without the couture price tag. Uniqueness and satisfaction are guaranteed. Women provide input regarding the style, design features, and the all-important choice of fabric for the LaRoque fashion. As owner of the LaRoque brand, Annabelle LaRoque's goal is to have every woman confident that the garment fits both her body and her personality (LaRoque, 2009).

Annabelle LaRoque, designer of the LaRoque brand, wanted her designs to be unique, identifiable, and representative of the women from the South. Pictured here is a dress by LaRoque.

concerned with image. Fashion designers and marketers must continually strengthen their desired image. However, once their products leave the manufacturing plant for the retailer, the marketers have less control over how their products are presented and, thus, over how their company image is being perceived by the consumer.

Designers, manufacturers, and retailers may not always be successful in projecting a positive image. Poor design lines may be developed. Manufacturing mistakes may occur. Delivery delays may cause problems at the retail stores. Can companies' images be saved? In many cases the answer is yes. Take for example Alexander McQueen. McQueen's fashions for the most part are readily accepted, loved, and savored by the fashion world. His "bad boy" image adds to the excitement of his collection. Unfortunately, his first collection for Givenchy was received so negatively that even McQueen admitted, "I know it was crap" (Watson, 1999/2000, p. 51). Today, McQueen's image and brand are definitely not crap; he has since been accepted as an internationally successful fashion innovator.

On February 11, 2010, Alexander McQueen was found dead from an apparent suicide.

Although we may never understand the circumstances around his death, McQueen recently suffered a significant loss. His mother had passed away just nine days earlier. Designers, models, and industry professionals expressed their sadness at the loss of such a talented designer (Addley, 2010).

Think about your favorite fashion designer, manufacturer, or retailer. How would you answer the following questions?

- Which adjective would you use to describe the company?
- Why do you like this company more than other companies?
- Which marketing methods do you perceive to be the most effective in the company's efforts to portray this image?
- Does the company's image extend to your personal image when you use its brand(s)? Explain.

BRANDING VERSUS BRANDS

It would be a mistake to think that the words *branding* and *brands* are synonymous. "**Branding** . . . is the corporate science of adding value" (Baldauf, 2004, p. 53). Branding a company, product, and services relies on making the customer emotionally committed to your organization. For various reasons (e.g., how they have been treated, the atmosphere, the color of the shopping bags—all of which are part of branding), the consumer believes that no other retailer provides him or her with the same level of quality products and service (Baldauf, 2004).

Branding a Company

The goal of any fashion company is to brand itself such that any person, regardless of whether or not he or she is in its target market, can state the company's brand in one word. The brand should tell the company's story (Macintosh & Gentry, 1999). Branding a company is a three-step process. The first step is to identify which products and services are essential to the customer and which ones might be relinquished (i.e., preferred by the customer, but not necessary). The second step is to identify the competition (both national and global). The third step is to perform a comparative analysis of the company to its competition. To do this, the company needs to ask questions about itself relative to the competition.

Examples of such questions may include:

- Which aspects of retailing (e.g., customer service, distribution) is the competition doing better than you?
- Why do consumers buy from the competition?
- Do the consumers who buy from the competition also buy from you?

Answers may be in narrative format (i.e., qualitative statements). **Qualitative** differences are illustrated by statements. For example, *Consumers stated that they liked the advertising campaign for the women's casual apparel lines.* As a marketer, it is important that you identify your core strengths. Quantitative and qualitative statements often identify these strengths (Macintosh & Gentry, 1999). Additional answers may appear in the form of financial statements or **quantitative statements.** An example of a quantitative statement is: *My company's marketing sales results are 5 percent higher than my competitors'.* Therefore, these product lines would be carried in order to maintain a balanced retail operation and satisfy the consumer's needs. Your marketing efforts should be focused heavily on the products that are your best sellers and considered the mainstay of the company (Macintosh & Gentry, 1999).

Brands

A **brand** is "a particular product or line of products, offered for sale by a single producer or manufacturer and made easily distinguishable from other similar products by a unique

Hugo Boss brands include fashions for men and women.

BOX 9.2 Hugo Boss: Under the Brand's Umbrella

Hugo Boss introduced the BOSS brand in 1970. BOSS Black represents the men's business wear line. The fashions are classical, elegant, and well-tailored. The second brand under the BOSS brand umbrella is BOSS Orange. This brand is men's casual wear. BOSS Green (sportswear) represents the third BOSS brand. Each BOSS brand offers high-quality fabrics, construction, designs, and fit. BOSS Black and BOSS Orange were eventually added to women's wear. Another Hugo Boss brand is HUGO. Unlike the BOSS brands, HUGO represents less conventional styles.

identifying name and/or symbol" (Ostrow & Smith, 1988 p. 26). The brand and the fashion marketing efforts for the brand are influenced by the consumer's values (Box 9.2). Brands help consumers identify with one another; they act as a bond between individuals, communities, and groups regardless of the level of familiarity they have with each other. A brand is successful when the consumer perceives the brand as the only solution to his or her consumer needs. For this to happen, the company must build the brand from the outside in. That is, brands should be the result of the needs of the target market, not the result of what the company decides it wants to market. The "outside-in" branding approach assists the fashion marketer in successfully identifying with the customer (Baldauf, 2004).

A fashion marketer typically has multiple brands that coordinate with each another. The reason for offering multiple brands is similar to that of offering apparel in multiple colors and lines; the fashion marketer maximizes the breadth and depth of sales to the target market. The merchandise offered is given a wide impact through the various brands.

In order to be successful, it is critical that the fashion marketer offer a complete line of each brand. The brand must be clearly promoted to its target market. While consumers often purchase multiple brands within a company, they should clearly understand the differences among the different brands. Differences in brands may be based on sizing, styling, fabric (e.g., natural vs. synthetic), or use (e.g., evening wear vs. daytime wear).

It is often best to have all brands consistent with the branding (i.e., image) of the company. Inconsistent brands tend to confuse consumers and weaken the image. The Ferragamo company places its name on all of its marketing efforts. The font remains the same throughout its marketing efforts. This continuity provides a sense of security to the target market. When they see the familiar logo, they know that the name represents luxury and quality.

Luxury brands such as Ferragamo, Gucci, and Dolce & Gabbana place a signature logo on their brands. Manufacturers such as Levi's, Candie's, and Coach use their name as the logo.

Ask yourself:

- Do you think the brand's logo enhances the intrinsic value of the brand?
- When is a logo "overexposed"?
- Are all luxury brands equal in how they are perceived?
- Is the Gucci brand as intrinsically valuable as the Yves Saint Laurent brand?

TYPES OF BRANDS

Brands vary based on who manufactures the products and where the products are sold. The brand's ultimate success rests in the fashion marketer's creativity. The more successful the fashion marketer's efforts, the more customers purchase the products; the greater number of customers who make positive comments about the marketing and merchandise, the more loyal the customers become to the brand. The question remains, of course, as to which type of brand customers will prefer—the company's national brand, a store brand, or a combination of both.

National Brands

A **national brand**, sometimes referred to as a manufacturer's brand, is defined as "a nationally advertised brand offered for sale by a producer or retailer." Manufacturers' brands often carry a distinctive and widely recognized brand name or trademark (Ostrow & Smith, 1988, p. 141). Fashion merchandise is often marketed as national brands in order to maximize the profitability of the fashion designs. These brands are not necessarily well-recognized brands; the brand name is provided for product identification. This identification simplifies all levels of the fashion marketing efforts.

How fast can you describe the trademark(s) for the following national and/or international brands? Does the company have more than one trademark? If so, which trademark represents each brand?

- Alexander McQueen
- Calvin Klein
- Chanel
- Dolce & Gabbana
- Dooney & Bourke
- Hugo Boss
- Isaac Mizrahi

- Kate Moss
- Louis Vuitton
- Ralph Lauren
- Stella McCartney
- Yves Saint Laurent

National brands are often used throughout the fashion marketing effort. Fashion marketers sell "security, safety, and confidence" when they promote the concept of national brands. Depending on the company, some national brands also market consumers on the history of the company, products, and the brand. Consumers are assured of the quality, value, and consistency in sizing.

Donna Karan's national brand has been adopted by the mass market and celebrities. One of Karan's most famous clients is Barbra Streisand. Donna Karan has been passionately protective of her image and brands. According to Donna Karan, "I am a woman with a rounded figure. I'm not a model size 8. I won't design clothes that can't be worn by women in a size 12 or 14" (Watson, 1999/2000b, p. 28).

Store Brands

Store brands are brands only sold by a particular retailer. They are very important to any fashion marketer. The brands are less expensive than national and designer brands, but they have a higher markup. As such, the fashion retailer realizes a higher **return on investment (ROI)**. ROI is defined as "a predetermined margin of profit which represents a desired return on investment" (Ostrow & Smith, 1988). As a result, every time a consumer purchases a store brand product, the retailer realizes a greater profit than when a consumer purchases a national brand or designer brand.

When developing a store brand, the company takes into consideration the mission statement, the market, the purpose of the brand, and marketing efforts. According to Warren Buffett, "[i]t takes twenty years to build a reputation and five minutes to ruin it. If you think about that, you'll do things differently." A strong store brand can become a fashion leader for decades. A weak store brand can harm the entire company.

What is your evaluation of the following brands? Look on the Internet. Do you think the brands are marketed effectively? Is the branding effort consistent with the store?

- Aqua by Bloomingdale's
- bebe sport by bebe
- Caslon by Nordstrom

BALANCING THE BRANDS MARKETED

Fashion marketers are continually faced with decisions regarding which brands to market, the number of brands to market, and how aggressively brands should be marketed. The retailer may often have useful input regarding the fashions that are marketed in the advertising campaign, but the marketing should be left up to the professional (i.e., the fashion marketer).

One Brand

The number of fashion brands marketed depends on the breadth and depth of brands offered by the organization. For example, some fashion retailers choose to carry only the brand(s) designed and manufactured specifically for that company. Other companies choose to carry a wide breadth of brands in an attempt to attract a large target market. Companies that design their own products will probably never carry a brand other than their own label. Walk into any Versace, Gucci, Ferragamo, Vera Wang, Burberry, Chanel, or Cole Haan store, and the brand will feature the

figure 9.1
The Cole Hahn grand opening in Las Vegas attracted celebrities into the high-end designer store. Known for its classic styles, quality fabrics, and craftsmanship, Cole Hahn has developed a strong and positive brand.

company's name. This strategy provides the company simplicity in getting its name in front of its target market, consistency in a fashion marketing message, and a decreased risk of confusing the consumer. High-end designers and fashion marketers typically use this fashion strategy when promoting their brands.

Tom Ford has been extremely successful at promoting his image and brand. The designer originally started in fashion and has since crossed product boundaries into the fragrance industry. The marketing and ultimate sales of his fragrance are most successful at Selfridges & Co in London, England. Because of the fragrance's enormous success, Ford visited the store and signed autographs. This marketing effort made a huge impact on the image and branding effort. According to David Walker-Smith, menswear and beauty director at Selfridges, "[Tom Ford] pushed the boundaries of fragrance in the way it is sold and presented —and our customers adored it" (Packing them in, 2009).

Gap Inc. introduced the Gap brand and brought its branding concept to the mass market. Instead of carrying a small portion of its own brand and filling the remaining inventory with national brands, Gap Inc. decided that its fashion marketing strategy would be to fill the entire Gap inventory with the Gap brand. One brand is used for one store. Similar to the designer fashion marketing strategy, Gap believed that consumers would remember the name *Gap*, understand that all the merchandise is branded by Gap (therefore if the consumers liked the merchandise they would shop at the store again), and not need to remember the brand name but simply the name of the store.

Gap Inc.'s fashion marketing strategy proved to be so successful that the company initiated another store and brand under the name of Old Navy. The merchandise is at a lower quality and price, reaching out to a broader target audience. Old Navy's fashion marketing efforts soon became very profitable for the company. This division generated the greatest number of sales in the Gap organization—$5.2 billion net sales during 2008 (Gap Inc., 2009) (Table 9.3).

When a company offers only one brand, the fashion marketer still must decide which products to promote during each advertising campaign. The brand will be consistent (i.e., the only brand carried by the company), but the products, styles, and designs may vary. Many fashion marketing divisions make an overall year-long advertising plan at the beginning of the year. By doing so, the company will have an overview of which products will be promoted each month. For example, fashion marketers rarely give up the opportunity to tie in a sale and/or promotion with a national holiday, season, and/or event. Valentine's Day, St. Patrick's Day, Easter, spring break, and the beginning of the school year are all good reasons to promote a company's brand-name merchandise.

TABLE 9.3

Gap Brands

Doris and Don Fisher opened the first Gap store in San Francisco in 1969. Originally the store carried Levi's jeans and other products to complement customers' easy lifestyle. In 1983, Gap Inc. acquired Banana Republic. This brand offers the company and market a different version of casual and comfort; the theme is more safari, worldly, and travel-oriented. Realizing an untapped need for casual clothing at lower prices, the company opened Old Navy in 1994. Three years later, Gap Inc. introduced its online presence by opening Gap.com. In 2007, the corporation earned $15.8 billion in revenue.

DIVISION	2008 REVENUE GENERATED
Gap North America	$4.2 billion
Banana Republic North America	$2.4 billion
Old Navy	$5.2 billion
International	$1.7 billion
Gap Inc. Direct (online)	$1 billion

(Gap Inc., 2009)

figure 9.2
Tom Ford enhanced the Gucci brand and image through creative and hip designs. Since leaving Gucci, Ford has been extremely busy branding the fashion, accessories, and fragrance line using his name. He is featured here in England promoting the Tom Ford fragrance line.

Target's Xhilaration brand is stylish, inexpensive, and fast fashion. The merchandise is marketed with the expectation of moving the fashions through the stores fast, then bringing in different styles.

BOX 9.3 Targeting the Market: An Insider's View

Brandi Gayle is an executive team leader of apparel at Target. Three weeks before the brands are advertised, Gayle's Target team promotes the fashions within the store. Outfitting the fashions (i.e., store displays) and observing customers' opinions help Target understand which brands should be offered long-term, Gayle says. Store brands that continue to have a huge impact on the company and target market include Xhilaration, Mossimo, and Merona Collection. National brands are also carried and promoted in order to give the target market a well-rounded product offering (Gayle, 2009).

Multiple Brands

Most mass marketers carry multiple brands. Each brand is priced at a different level. The brands may consist of several store brands, national brands, and designer brands. This fashion marketing strategy is designed to provide consumers with the maximum number of purchasing options. Although consumers benefit from familiarity in brands, they also want to view a variety in colors and styles. The variety of brands provides consumers with choices. Offering multiple brands also provides a subtle method of getting consumers to purchase more expensive items than they had planned, thus enhancing the store's profitability. Jackie Scott Howie, owner of Kicks, carries a wide variety of designer shoes. The brands that are featured in the store's advertisements are based on the upcoming season (e.g., holiday vs. beginning of school), trends (e.g., color palette), and customer input (Howie, 2009).

When a retailer carries multiple levels of brands (i.e., store brand, national brand, designer brand), the fashion marketer must identify a strategy for how to promote each brand and how much emphasis to place on each brand. The strategy's ultimate deciding factor is the company's desired image. A company's **desired image** is not necessarily the same as its actual image. Desired image is the image the store is trying to portray to the consumers, employees, and stakeholders. The **actual image** is the image that is *perceived* by the consumers, employees, and stakeholders.

In recent years, the menswear industry has seen a strong focus on brand identification. Instead of venturing out and expanding brands, many menswear companies are placing the majority of their efforts on their core brands. Tommy Bahama (e.g., island shirts) and Phillips-Van Heusen (e.g., dress shirts) are examples of large companies that are marketing their image and brand toward their core products. The companies are focusing their efforts on "what they do best" (Thomas and Palmieri, 2009).

An upscale children's store typically has a large breadth and depth of merchandise. **Merchandise breadth** refers to the number of different products carried. **Merchandise depth** refers to the number of units within one product category. As the breadth and depth of merchandise offerings expand, the fashion marketer must carefully decide how best to inform consumers of the company's merchandise offerings. Jeans are considered the number one product purchased by consumers. While Levi's and Gap jeans are well-known, there are literally dozens of different denim manufactures. The William Rast denim manufacturer is located in Los Angeles. In an attempt to successfully brand the jeans, the company developed a marketing strategy:

> The new strategy divides the William Rast denim collection into three tiers—the opening tier retails from $165 to $175; the mid-tier consists of jeans retailing for $185 to $195; and the top tier, at $195 and up. All jeans are branded the same, with the same packaging and signature logo. The differences in prices stems from the amount of work that goes into the jeans. The opening tier, for example, consists of the more basic styles and washes, while the top tier includes jeans made with intricate details such as destruction, hand-painted details, and heavy washing. . . . The idea is for the company to open the brand up to new distribution channels. . . . Each style has a very clear, distinct personality (Kaplan, 2009, p. 12).

figure 9.3
Sale signs are a successful marketing tool for grabbing the consumer's attention. It is important to make sure the signage style is consistent with the retailer and fashions' branding and image. The sign in this window doesn't take away from the fashions displayed in the store window.

While the William Rast company manufactures jeans and clearly brands a limited line, other companies manufacture and/or carry a large number of brands. For example, Little Lambs & Ivy, a clothing store in South Carolina, carries more than 350 brands. Its merchandise offering is broad and narrow, meaning the company carries a lot of brands but not all styles within each brand. Because of the extensive nature of the brands, the president of the company markets the store and its relationship to the community rather than an individual product. This strategy has worked well for the company.

NICHE BRANDING

In a global market where consumers can access the latest fashion trends from nontraditional promotional marketing tools such as a cell phone, iPod, laptop, or desktop computer, or from traditional tools like television and magazine ads, **niche branding** is becoming increasingly important. Niche branding is defined as branding products that originate from a central brand. The niche brand is clearly identified with the central brand but addresses a smaller, more specific market (Bedbury & Fenichell, 2003).

The progression of niche branding strengthens the central brand and offers opportunities for additional niche brands to other markets. Repeated and effective communication between the fashion marketer and the target market is critical in order for the niche brand to be successful. Products within the niche brand must also continually evolve. The evolution of the brands provides the company with strong financial growth through customer sales. The niche brand evolution also sparks additional niche brands both domestically and globally (Bedbury & Fenichell, 2003).

Estée Lauder is an international skincare organization whose brands have a reputation for elegance. Headquartered in New York City, the company started in 1946 with skin cream (i.e., central brand). Since it began, the company has expanded into makeup, skincare, and fragrances. Estée Lauder's success is based on its technological advances in the industry and on its niche branding. Examples of Estée Lauder's niche brands are *Beautiful* ("the fragrance of a thousand flowers"), *Sensuous* ("Warm, luminous, feminine, every woman wears it her way"), *Pleasures* ("the delightful new spirit in fragrance"), and *Pure White Linen* ("the fragrance to live in all year long; fresh, luminous, pure") (Estée Lauder, 2008).

Niche brands help support the central brand. That is, the more loyal consumers are to a niche brand, the greater propensity the target market will gravitate to purchase niche brands within the central brand (Bedbury & Fenichell, 2003).

For example, the Estée Lauder company has a central brand of Estée Lauder. Within each product division (i.e., skincare, fragrance, makeup, gifts), niche marketing occurs. The marketers specifically target the existing consumers within each niche so that they will purchase within the other product niches of the Estée Lauder company. These efforts maximize the number of products available to customers within each niche brand and the company's brand. The fashion marketer's goal is to entice consumers to purchase products throughout the company line of brands.

Building a Relationship

Fashion marketers attempt to build a strong and long-term relationship between the consumer and the niche brand. The relationship is emotional, passionate, and personal (Bedbury & Fenichell, 2003). While the niche brand may possess tangible qualities (e.g., superior quality, style, sizing), it is the fashion marketer's responsibility to instill the intangible attributes of the niche brand (e.g., freshness, femininity, new spirit). The Estée Lauder Company Web site states that it is "recognized in over one hundred countries for quality maintained and promises kept" (Estée Lauder, 2008). The relationships the fashion marketers at Estée Lauder are building include trust,

figure 9.4
Using a celebrity to promote a product can be very successful. The celebrity's image must match the brand and image of the product. Gwyneth Paltrow is the spokesperson for Estée Lauder fragrances. The celebrity is known to be health conscious, and looks fresh, youthful, and carefree. Her face on marketing advertisements is directed toward younger, polished, wealthier consumers.

understanding, problem solving, sensuality, and self-worth. Review Table 9.4, which lists niche brands sold by the Estée Lauder Company. Compare the intangible relationship terms used by the fashion marketers.

Brand Strength

Brand strength empowers the product, the brand's name, and the company (Bedbury & Fenichell, 2003). As the strength of a brand increases in the consumer's mind, the brand's value to the company increases. It is important to remember, however, that all brands have a weakness or a limitation; that is, a brand cannot be all things to all people. To compensate for a brand's weaknesses, other brands are developed and marketed to spin-off markets. When fashion marketers clearly identify a brand's strengths and play to these strengths, they automatically make the brand stronger, market toward a consumer niche, and, in all likelihood, build a more profitable and longer-lasting brand. Brands become weak when the brand characteristics are diluted, trying to be "all things to all people." Fashion marketers' brand messages become diluted and ineffective when the marketing message is focused toward the mass market. Estée Lauder, for example, offers a wide range of products, some of which include body lotions, lipsticks, and fragrances. These products are used for very different reasons, yet they all carry intrinsic and extrinsic value.

Intrinsic value is value as perceived by the consumer. It brings internal value to the individual consumer. Intrinsic value may be different among consumers, and it may give them a feeling of happiness from wearing the product. Each consumer may view the value of the product differently. An example of intrinsic value is a consumer who purchases her fifth

TABLE 9.4A–C
Estée Lauder Niche Brands and Relationships

A. Body Performance

PRODUCT	EMOTIONAL BIND
Anti-Cellulite/Anti-Fluid Advanced Visible Contouring Serum	Younger
Firming Body crème	Younger
Naturally Radiant Moisturizer	Golden glow

B. Lipsticks

PRODUCT	EMOTIONAL BIND
All-Day	For busy women
Estée Lauder Signature	Seduces your lips
Pure Color	Luxury, power
Pure Color Crystal	Electricity, daring shine

C. Fragrances

PRODUCT	EMOTIONAL BIND
Beautiful	Floral, soft
Pleasures	New spirit
Sensuous	Warm, luminous, feminine
White Linen	Fresh, luminous, pure

(Estée Lauder, 2008)

figure 9.5
So many shoes, so little time. For many women, having at least three different styles of shoes in one color is a necessity. Recently designer and branded footwear has become an important mainstay of the shoe industry.

pair of black high-heeled shoes because "they make her feel pretty." Technically, the other four pairs of black shoes are sufficient. The fifth pair, however, makes her happy. The intrinsic value of the shoes is worth spending $350.

Think about the last time you purchased a fashion item for intrinsic value.

- What product did you purchase?
- Describe the intrinsic value.
- What marketing efforts did the company use to help portray the intrinsic values?
- Did you show the fashion item to your friends? Did this enhance the intrinsic value?
- Does a different brand offer a similar intrinsic value? Why or why not?

Extrinsic value is the value of the product as viewed by others. It exists when value is generated from external sources. According to the Estée Lauder Company, the fragrance *Beautiful* has a soft floral scent. The *Cinnabar* is an exotic, mysterious, and spicy fragrance. The two brands offer very different features. The same woman may use both brands, but for very different occasions. If the Estée Lauder company were to offer only one brand but say the fragrance was a "soft floral scent, yet also warm, luminous, and feminine," the brand would probably be weakened. The fashion marketers would be overreaching expectations. By offering a variety of brands within each product category, the company is able to build long-lasting brand strength, consumer loyalty, and profit growth.

TABLE 9.5

Examples of Cosmetics Companies and Their Brand Values

COMPANY	BRAND VALUE
Bobbi Brown	"Makeup is a way for a woman to feel like herself, only prettier and more confident." A realistic approach to beauty
Erno Laszlo	TranspHuse Surgiceuticals: The use of products instead of plastic surgery
Estée Lauder	"Stringent product testing resulting in luxurious products"
MAC	Products featured in *InStyle*, *Allure*, *Elle*, and *W*. The products are also used in music tours, theater, films, and television.
Smashbox	Insider secrets of the cosmetic industry given to the customer. Personalized attention.

As you once again think about your latest fashion purchase, can you identify the extrinsic value? Specifically:

- What extrinsic value did the fashion item hold?
- What marketing efforts did the company use to help portray the extrinsic values?
- Does a different brand offer a similar extrinsic value? Why or why not?
- What is more important in a brand—intrinsic or extrinsic value?
- Find an advertisement for the brand on YouTube. Identify the marketing message in relation to the intrinsic and extrinsic value.

Brand Extension

Brand extension is defined as "the practice of marketing new products under well-known brand names in an effort to capitalize on the positive image the parent brand has in the consumer's mind" (Ostrow & Smith, 1988, p. 26) (Table 9.6). Brand extension is an effective method of building brand width (Bedbury & Fenichell, 2003). Brand width is defined as the number of lines and styles associated with a specific brand. The wider the brands, the more variety of fashions consumers are able to select and purchase. Brand width also complicates branding efforts. Each design, style, and line should be cohesive with the brand; consumers should readily recognize the brand regardless of the fashion line.

One method of brand extension is to develop a second brand and offer it to a different target market. Gap Inc. successfully extended their brand of Gap clothing to Gap Kids and Baby Gap. All merchandise carried within the stores are manufactured specifically by Gap and sold at Gap stores. The all-inclusive branding efforts ease the fashion marketing efforts because all products are branded and marketed by Gap Inc.

A second method of brand extension is used by high-end fashion designers. The high-end target market consists of only a small percent of the consumer base. While the luxury products are expensive and the profit margin is typically high, the ability to expand the target market is finite. A successful method of building brand width is by extending a brand to a different target market. Luxury designers such as Vera Wang, Donna Karan, and Christian

TABLE 9.6

Examples of Brand Extensions

COMPANY	BRAND EXTENSION
Gap Inc.	Baby Gap
	Gap
	Gap Kids
Vera Wang	Simply Vera (discount)
	Vera Wang (bridal couture)
	Vera Wang LOOK (ready-to-wear)
Limited Brands	Bath & Body Works
	C.O. Bigelow
	Henri Bendel
	La Senza
	The Limited
	The White Barn Candle Co.
	Victoria's Secret
Macy's	Alfant
	American Rag
	The Cellar
	Charter Club
	Club Room
	Columbia Field Gear
	First Impressions
	Greendog
	Haven
	Hotel Collection
	INC International Concepts
	Jenni
	JM Collection
	ML/Material London
	Style & Co.
	Tasso Elba
	Tools of the Trade

Dior have successfully extended their brands into the ready-to-wear and discount markets. Starting in 1990, Vera Wang built the wedding dress brand based on quality, craftsmanship, and originality (Vera Wang, 2008). The Vera Wang LOOK brand is targeted at the mass market. Whereas Vera Wang's wedding dresses are based on high-end custom designs, the LOOK brand provides the mass market with a piece of the famous designer without the exclusive price tag. More recently, Kohl's agreed to carry Vera Wang products, thereby further expanding the Vera Wang brand. The Vera Wang brand offers discount-minded consumers fashion-forward merchandise at discount prices.

The third method of extending a brand is by adding brands under different names and product categories. During the 1980s, Leslie Wexner, CEO of Limited Brands, wanted to extend the company's brands and dominate shopping malls with its products. Wexner knew that having multiple The Limited stores throughout the mall would not necessarily encourage consumers to purchase more products. Instead of increasing the number of identical stores (e.g., The Limited), Wexner extended the types of stores (and brands) the company owned. Within each mall, consumers would be able to shop at multiple Limited Brands-owned stores and purchase Limited Brands-branded products within a single shopping trip. Although the stores are clearly distinct, the brands can be marketed and built upon one another. For example, Limited Brands owns and operates Victoria's Secret, Bath & Body Works, C.O. Bigelow, The White Barn Candle Co., Henri Bendel, and La Senza. The fashion marketing efforts of Victoria's Secret, Bath & Body Works, and The White Barn Candle Co. are distinct and separate campaigns; remember that each fashion marketing campaign cannot be and is not all things to all consumers. Visualize the following scenario, however. Stores are typically in close proximity to one another in a mall; perhaps they are either across the aisle from one another or just a few stores away from each other. Consumers who patronize Victoria's Secret may also patronize Bath & Body Works. After all, what goes better with new lingerie than new bath salts and lotions? To complete the package, a scented candle will make the bathroom smell even more romantic. Subtle fashion marketing efforts delivered through in-store signage, flyers, or coupons are often very successful and profitable.

Store brands are sold exclusively by the retailer. As such, store brands are designed to generate store traffic and customer loyalty. The merchandise is typically lower in quality than national brands but not always. The merchandise caters to the mass market. This strategy allows for large quantities of store-brand merchandise to be sold.

During the early years of store brands (e.g., the 1970s), brands were developed and marketed by the retailer. The designer of the

figure 9.6
Once a designer or company has developed a recognizable and trustworthy brand, product expansion is relatively easy. Vera Wang has expanded into the fragrance industry with LOOK.

figure 9.7
Starting with only $5,000 Leslie Wexner built an empire of retail stores. Each store has a unique brand and image.

products was unknown. During the late 1990s and early 2000s, fashion marketers realized that placing a designer's name on store brands could increase the merchandise turnover to an all-time high. An increasing number of designers and celebrities are either designing or **licensing** their names for store brands. Licensing is defined as "an agreement between the creator of a product or line of products and a manufacturer in which the creator (licensor) gives the manufacturer (licensee) permission to use his name in the marketing of a product in return for a royalty, usually computed as a percentage of sales" (Ostrow and Smith, 1988, p. 134). Store brands that feature a designer's name add prestige to the fashion and the store and stimulate the consumer's desire to purchase in multiple quantities.

A licensed agreement is successful when the licensed product and marketing efforts continue to follow the original designer and/or manufacturer's mission statement. For example, Lacroix licensed its fragrance line to Paris-based Inter Parfums SA. Inter Parfums SA is responsible for manufacturing, marketing, and distributing the Lacroix fragrance line. During 2008, this line generated over $1.4 million. Under the undisclosed licensing agreement, Lacroix earns a percentage of the sales or profits (depending on the contract). Additional beauty licensing agreements by Inter Parfums SA are held with Burberry, Lanvin, Quiksilver, and Van Cleef & Arpels (Socha, 2009).

The beauty industry is an attractive area for designers to become involved in licensing agreements. Beauty products require a significant amount of technical (i.e., chemical) product research and development, which is time-consuming, costly, and out of the designer's area of expertise. Beauty products are, however, a financially lucrative industry and a logical extension of the fashion industry.

The designer who has generated the most licenses—indeed, sold his name—is Calvin Klein. Klein is known for classic fashions (e.g., white shirt, cable-knit sweater, jeans). His licensing agreements range from apparel, fragrances, and accessories. In today's fashion industry, licensing is the norm rather than the exception. Dolce & Gabbana, Yves Saint Laurent, Chanel, and Dior also have licensing agreements. These agreements provide the fashion companies with the ability to generate additional capital without significant effort, present a well-rounded portfolio of fashion product offerings, and generate brand-loyal consumer behavior.

Overexposure through licensing can harm an image or brand. Fashion designers and/or manufacturers must be cautious regarding the quality and type of products the brand name is licensed. The entire marketing concept must be considered prior to completing a licensing agreement.

Questions to ask include:

- Is the licensed product consistent with the image and brand of the company?
- How will the licensed product be marketed?

figure 9.8
The Calvin Klein brand started in women's fashions. Since the early days of the brand, Calvin Klein products have expanded into men's wear, accessories, underwear, and fragrances.

- To what degree does the company (e.g., Dolce & Gabbana) have a say in the marketing of the licensed product?
- What is the product placement for the licensed product? Will the product be located next to a competitor? If so, will the product placement harm or help the company's sales, profits, image, and/or brand?
- Will the licensed product help build customer loyalty regarding other product lines within the company?
- How will the licensed product potentially influence the financial status of the company?

EXCLUSIVITY

A designer's, manufacturer's, or retailer's image can be influenced by the level of **exclusivity** of its products. Exclusivity (also known as **exclusive distribution**) is a form of distribution in which a product or service is offered for sale to only one distributor or retailer in a particular territory. The manufacturer or producer thus gives the exclusive right to resale to a single organization (Ostrow & Smith, 1988). There are a variety of reasons fashion marketers, designers, and retailers decide to use a strategy of exclusivity (Freeman, 2002).

Exclusivity bolsters the customer's perception of individuality. Consumers who desire a fashion garment or accessory that is unique, high quality, and well suited to their personalities are willing to purchase an exclusive product (albeit an expensive product). Fashion marketers often use exclusivity during the introduction of a product line as an attempt to enhance the allure and excitement of the product. Exclusive distribution is typically reserved for large fashion cities such as New York or Los Angeles. Extensive promotion is provided regarding the exclusive distribution of the fashion merchandise. Once the merchandise is rapidly accepted by the consumers in a particular market, the fashion marketer has marketing distribution campaign options. One option is to promote the exclusivity of the product as only being sold in the selected markets. Consumers who desire the merchandise must obtain the merchandise from the selected stores. This fashion marketing strategy enhances the brand's image as selective, special, and possessing both intrinsic and extrinsic value.

A retailer and its fashion marketer may decide to offer the product through exclusive distribution. Exclusive distribution occurs when a brand is offered only through one retailer. The retailer typically features the name of the brand on the product and throughout the fashion marketing campaign. Exclusive distribution generates a strong and loyal target-market following. In addition, the merchandise brands complement one another. The disadvantage of exclusive distribution is the need to maximize marketing efforts, sales, and profits at the selected locations. Examples of exclusive distribution include Gap, Harry Winston, and Burberry.

Temporary limited exclusive distribution is a fashion marketing strategy that is often used to create excitement about a new brand. Temporary limited exclusive distribution occurs when a brand is offered at one retailer for a limited time. The exclusive distribution is marketed heavily, featuring the name of the retailer, the brand, and product qualities. The emphasis of these fashion marketing efforts is placed on the fact that consumers are able to obtain the product only at the particular retailer. The objectives of the temporary limited exclusive distribution are to increase customer traffic in the retail store, encourage high merchandise turnover of the brand being marketed, and ultimately instill a sense of customer loyalty to both the retailer and the brand.

A fashion marketer may also decide to offer exclusivity during a limited time and then offer widespread distribution. The initial promotion of the product's exclusivity builds anticipation and excitement for the product and additional recognition for the brand. This fashion marketing strategy is typically only implemented when the product is designed to be carried by the company long-term. This strategy has been successfully used in the perfume industry.

Exclusivity is being experienced with many online fashion marketers (Boorstin, 2005; Rosenthal, 2006). Online or home shopping networks (e.g., QVC, Home Shopping Network) will often provide merchandise that is either not available in stores or not readily available in a consumer's location. When consumers access some retail Web sites, they will see a meter in the corner of the television screen. The meter displays the number of remaining available fashion products. The number is designed to be an incentive to encourage purchasing behavior and a reminder that once the consumer purchases the item, he or she has purchased one of the few items left (Rosenthal, 2006).

Because a product is limited in distribution, consumers who have access to the product typically pay a high price for the object and make a significant effort to acquire the object. This effort and higher price increase the perceived image. The image may vary among consumers. For example, some consumers may view the purchase as a luxury while others view the purchase as rational because the object is needed. An example of an exclusive product is the Air Max 180 Cowboy by Nike. The limited-edition sneakers feature a hunter-green, lizard-skin design with a light

figure 9.9 Two simple words provide the consumer with an understanding of the brand and image . . . *Harry Winston*. This jeweler serves celebrities, presidents' wives, and the ultra rich. The Harry Winston brand and image was created throughout more than 100 years of craftsmanship and dedication to rare gems.

figure 9.10
Serena Williams is a world class tennis player who designs her tennis outfits. Her passion for fashion crosses over into jewelry. Using her name as a brand, Serena sells her jewelry on QVC.

pink swoosh. The company manufactured 140 pairs and sold them only in its South Miami location. One customer flew from Denver to Miami and waited in line two days prior to the day the shoes went on sale (Hamilton & DeQuine, 2006). Even though the plane ticket cost more than the shoes ($100), the exclusivity of the shoes greatly enhanced his image. Such consumer purchasing behavior enhances the fashion marketing industry.

Longevity

Exclusive fashion products are typically of high quality. Consumers may keep the exclusive garments for years, perhaps even decades. For example, a custom-made jacket in the style of the Chanel jacket from 1960 can still be worn and is considered highly fashionable in the twenty-first century. Burberry's trademark plaid provides the company with an image of quality, tradition, and conservative fashion. During the 1990s, the company realized that they could reach out to a wider group of fashion consumers by changing the color of the plaid on an annual basis. The famous Burberry plaid is available in the traditional camel, pale blue, pale pink, and red. The fabric is made into scarves, the lining of coats, purses, and dog collars. The products will last for years, but consumers can update their fashions with different colors of the highly sought-after design.

Consider the following questions:

- Can you identify fashion designers with long-term marketing prowess? Log on to YouTube and examine the various designer fashion shows. Which designer names have been in existence for more than 50 years?
- What microeconomic attributes (i.e., attributes inside the company) make this company successful?

figure 9.11
The Burberry design is perhaps one of the most easily recognizable plaid designs. This branding feature allows consumers to identify Burberry products from a distance without the use of wording.

- What macroeconomic attributes (i.e., attributes outside the company) make this company successful?

Customer Traffic

Fashion designers and manufacturers typically use exclusivity as a strategy that takes advantage of small retailers and boutiques. Instead of producing large quantities of a design, small productions are made (e.g., 100–500 units are produced). However, fashion marketers then make more frequent design changes and introduce the changes to the consumer sooner and on a more intimate level, using the small retailers and boutiques. Boutiques and small retailers provide fashion marketers with valuable information regarding product knowledge, selling techniques, and customer data. This information can then be integrated in marketing efforts (Hamilton & DeQuine, 2006).

Fashion retailers, large and small, use exclusivity to build customer traffic into their specific stores. Consumers are typically aware of brands. They actively seek out specific brand names based on intrinsic and extrinsic value. Nationwide companies carry their own store brand as a form of exclusivity. For example, Target offers exclusive brands by designers at popular prices. Examples of the brands the company has offered in the past include Isaac Mizrahi and Mossimo (Young, Moin, & Greenberg, 2006). Nordstrom, Neiman Marcus, Saks Fifth Avenue, and J. C. Penney have all been successful in developing exclusivity through the use of store brands.

figure 9.12
Designer fashions such as Mossimo and Isaac Mizrahi changed how consumers viewed the Target brand. The retailer changed its image from a discounter to a fashion retailer offering lower prices.

PRODUCT-ONLY RELATIONSHIP

A **product-only relationship** with your customers exists as a multidimensional connection with the product, company, consumer,

and culture. The branding of the product instills in the customer a desire for the product above other products in the same category. This desire attracts loyal customers to the company, brand, and product. The longing for the product results in positive word-of-mouth advertisement. The ultimate product-only relationship is when a consumer will purchase and wear only one brand.

The consumer wants, and in many cases insists, on the brand. The culture of the company, the marketing, the packaging, and the distribution are as important to the relationship with the customer as the product itself (Bedbury & Fenichell, 2003). Fashion marketers attempt to instill a product-only relationship into the customer's mind through all marketing efforts. They realize the success of their efforts when the branding of the product results in customer loyalty.

Product-only relationships seem simple on the surface: Market the product in such a manner that the consumer wants the product above all other brands. However, if this marketing strategy were simple, all fashion marketers would be successful at the product-only relationship. In reality, not all fashion marketers have the pulse on the culture of their consumers (i.e., target market). Furthermore, not all fashion marketers are equally adept at communicating their message to their consumers. Remember, in today's culture, fashion marketers have a wide variety of media in which to reach consumers. The message must strike a balance between *Purchase this brand, preferably in multiple quantities* and *This product is special.* A form of product-only relationship is often demonstrated by the customer's **signature brand**. A signature brand is a brand that a customer chooses to wear exclusively.

Ask yourself:

- How important is a product-only relationship to a marketing concept?
- Can you give an example of when you responded positively to the product-only relationship as a result of marketing efforts? For example, did you ever flip through a magazine and absolutely STOP when you saw a specific advertisement and say out loud, *I need that purse!*? What attributes about the advertisement made you *need* that purse?

figure 9.13
Sarah Jessica Parker in front of signage for Sex in the City and Manolo Blahnik shoes. Parker wore Blahnik brand shoes in various episodes of *Sex and the City*.

Massclusivity

When exclusivity was originally designed as a fashion marketing strategy, the products were typically expensive (e.g., perfume, designer clothing). Because of its sheer size, however, the mass market is where the majority of fashion profits are realized. The mass market, similar to the upper-class market, appreciates limited-edition fashion items. The mass market, however, is unable or unwilling to pay $6,000 for a handbag. They do, however, appreciate and want exclusivity just like the upper-class market.

To satisfy the mass market's need for exclusive products and stimulate their purchasing behavior, fashion marketers have designed a strategy called massclusivity. Massclusivity refers to a strategy whereby retailers offer limited-edition merchandise. The strategy is designed to stimulate consumer enthusiasm toward the limited-edition item and promote its merchandise turnover (Boorstin, 2005). An increasing number of mass fashion retailers are offering limited-edition products in order to create excitement. High-fashion designers such as Karl Lagerfeld, designer for Chanel, and Stella McCartney created limited-edition lines for H&M. In both cases, the merchandise sold out in a matter of hours (Boorstin, 2005).

Fast Fashion

Fast fashion is a relatively new term, coined during the twenty-first century. Fast fashion is "a strategy to move fashion into and out of the store fast" (Frazier, 2006). Traditionally, fashion retailers ordered the same style of merchandise in quantities that would last three months. Fast fashion is designed to provide new styles every four weeks. Discounters, mass marketers, and luxury retailers all use a fast-fashion strategy (Frazier, 2006). Fast-fashion items may include a $29.99 sweater from Target or a $500 pair of shoes from Neiman Marcus. Price does not dictate the ability of an item to be classified as fast fashion. Fast-fashion items are classified as such based on their identification as a fashion product, ability to draw traffic into a store (i.e., demand for the product), desirability by the primary target market, and limited availability.

Fast-fashion products offer fashion marketers many benefits. One benefit of a fast-fashion strategy is the excitement it generates. The merchandise is typically promoted in print or television spots as a special promotion for a limited time. Consumers realize that the fast-fashion items are "special" and will be sold out soon; restocking is not an option.

A second benefit of fast fashion is the incentive for consumers to purchase multiple items. Once consumers begin shopping, the reminder

figure 9.14
The Stella McCartney brand is redesigned for the H&M store and target market. The original brand is expensive and targeted toward an upper-scale market. The H&M brand is targeted toward a mass market.

that the item is available for a limited time is used by the fashion marketer to encourage the consumer to purchase the item in quantities. The consumer may be encouraged to purchase the fast-fashion sweater in two different colors.

The third benefit of fast fashion is the limited risk of carrying old or stale merchandise. Fast-fashion merchandise typically sells out rapidly. Retailers' merchandise turnover continues at a steady pace, thereby assuring a reliable return on investment.

Finally, fast-fashion merchandise promotes consumer traffic. The steady stream of new fashion merchandise encourages consumers to continually browse the store for new items. Even consumers who "just browse" have a higher likelihood of purchasing one or more items during each visit. The likelihood of consumers becoming loyal customers increases with each successive purchasing visit.

Identity

Identity is defined as how you are viewed by your consumers. Companies continually work to build a strong, positive identity that is tied to the mission statement. The company's products, brands, services, and employees' actions build upon the identity. Ultimately, a successful fashion marketing identity will result in long-term customer loyalty, positive word-of-mouth promotion, increased sales, and increased customer traffic (Hart, 2005).

Consumer who own two or more products from one brand begin to build an identity with the brand. This identity is an important part of their fashion image and statement. As the consumer adds additional products by the brand, loyalty tends to increase. Fashion apparel designers and manufacturers often cross product boundaries in an attempt to further enhance loyal consumer behavior. That is, designers will license their name on non-apparel products (e.g., accessories, stationery, candles). The result is added brand exposure. Meanwhile, consumers are able to further build and strengthen their identity with the brand through the additional purchase of branded products.

As you look in your closet, count the number of items by each brand.

- Do you identify yourself with one designer or retailer?
- Is your identity product specific? For example, a consumer may tend to purchase Coach purses, Dior perfumes, and Ralph Lauren apparel.
- What do the brands in your closet reveal about your shopping loyalty behaviors?

Individuality

Fashion marketers require a sense of **individuality**. Individuality refers to "the sum of qualities that characterize and distinguish an individual from all others" (Merriam-Webster Dictionary & Thesaurus, 2000). Individuality is used to distinguish fashion retailers, brands, products, and levels of quality from one another (Hart, 2005). Fashion designers are known for modifying the images seen on the runway to fit the target market's needs. For example, fashions shown at the New York City, London, and Paris fashion shows are often expertly crafted, made of expensive fabrics, and feature exaggerated silhouettes. These fashions can be modified for the average consumer using different fabric, changing the silhouette, and using mass-production techniques. The individuality of the fashions is placed on each design. Each fashion marketer uses different characteristics or emphasizes different elements of the design.

With the exception of very few exclusive ultra-luxury products, fashion marketing efforts are universally designed to sell the maximum number of products manufactured. Successful marketing efforts result in strong, loyal consumer purchasing behavior, not just positive attitudes toward the marketing efforts. Successful marketing efforts also result in convincing consumers who traditionally purchased from the competition to become loyal purchasing consumers. This goal may seem counterintuitive to the concept of individuality. After all, if a large portion of the marketplace purchases the brand, consumers will not have individuality. Often times, the products are distributed nationally and internationally. This distribution greatly assists the consumer in being able to have individuality (i.e., decreases the chance of "everyone" wearing the same item). Global distribution is addressed in detail in Chapter Twelve.

To offer consumers individuality in the fashion world, fashion designers and manufacturers are required to provide a broad array of product lines. This mix-and-match feature of product lines allows consumers to build a unique and individual fashion statement. In addition, designers may offer a similar product but rarely, if ever, a similar design. Ralph Lauren, Dolce & Gabbana, Tommy Hilfiger, Calvin Klein, and Liz Claiborne all offer a white cotton button-down shirt. Yet, as you look at each designer's shirt, they all offer different styles, fabrics, and fit (i.e., loose versus fitted). Consumers are able to obtain individuality while the designers also sell in mass quantity.

BRAND MANTRA

Being involved in the fashion industry is a lot like being in a candy store. There are always wonderful tempting items surrounding you. Fashion marketers are expected to know the latest trends in colors, styles, and methods of communicating with consumers (Bedbury & Fenichell, 2003). In short, fashion marketers become the **brand mantra** for a company. A brand mantra is a fashion marketer's understanding, implementation, and protection of the brand's soul. To be truly effective as a fashion marketer, the brand mantra must go beyond making slogans for the company and implementing new brands. Fashion marketers must understand the emotional tie the brand holds with the target market. Likewise, marketers must use the brand, sometimes exclusively. They must hire people who understand the brand intimately. This intimate understanding of the brand means being well versed in the company's mission, values, emotional bind, brand value, niche marketing, and purpose. Unless fashion marketers and their teams clearly understand these concepts, the brand will falter. Hence, a fashion marketer must *become* the brand mantra. For example, Nike's brand mantra is authenticity. In every marketing campaign, the company uses a real athlete to demonstrate the authenticity of the apparel (Bedbury & Fenichell, 2003).

Continuity

Today's consumers are more sophisticated, informed, and brand conscious than ever before in history. They expect more from companies in terms of reliability, dependability, honesty, and ethics. Consumers also require companies to maintain continuity in their marketing efforts. The continuity must be in the form of the marketing message, presentation of the mes-

figure 9.15
Nike protects its brand and image by using real athletes in all advertisements.

sage, and actions of the corporate executives and employees.

Marketing Message

In Chapter Two, "The Impact of Fashion," the various methods of marketing were discussed. Fashion marketers now have increased opportunities for reaching the target market and building customer loyalty (Bedbury & Fenichell, 2003). Throughout a season's fashion marketing efforts, the message should be similar, regardless of the venue (e.g., billboard, television, Web site). In the early 2000s, Gap Inc. presented striped knitted products for the holiday season. Fashions were featured on billboards, television, and in-store banners. Consumers immediately knew that the brand was Gap. The continuity of the marketing message gave Gap Inc. widespread store recognition, brand and product exposure, and built consumer traffic to Gap for the holiday season.

BRAND CHAPERONE

Successful fashion marketers act as a strict **brand chaperone**. Being a brand chaperone requires overseeing the actions of marketing a brand for continuity, quality, effectiveness, strength, and longevity (Bedbury& Fenichell, 2003). In order to be marketed successfully, the brand, its message, and its qualities must offer continuity. Consumers seek, perhaps above all else, continuity from companies. They want to know that each time they purchase a product, the size, color, fit, and texture of the product will be the same as the original product purchased. The brand message, regardless of its format (e.g., magazine advertisement, billboard, runway show) must also be consistent. Successful fashion marketers act as brand chaperones when they carefully review marketing efforts to verify that consumers (not just the target market and purchasers) will immediately recognize the brand. A **consumer** is the end user of the product. The **target market** is the population a company selects as a target for its marketing efforts (Ostrow & Smith, 1988). Fashion marketers are effective brand chaperones when consumers, not just the loyal target market, readily identify the brand. The quality of the brand must never be sacrificed for profits. Brand chaperones clearly understand that once brand quality is reduced, the brand itself is altered.

SUMMARY

The goal of any fashion company is to brand itself such that any person, regardless of whether or not he or she is in its target market, can describe the company's brand in one word. The target market is a segment of a population that a company focuses its marketing efforts upon (Ostrow & Smith, 1988). The brand should tell the company's story (Macintosh & Gentry, 1999).

A fashion marketer typically has multiple brands that coordinate with one another. The reason for offering multiple brands is similar to that of offering apparel in multiple colors and lines; the fashion marketer maximizes the breadth and depth of sales to the target market. The merchandise offering is given a wide impact through the various brands. Fashion marketers attempt to build a strong and long-term relationship between the consumer and the niche brand. The relationship is emotional, passionate, and personal (Bedbury & Fenichell, 2003). While the niche brand may possess tangible qualities (e.g., superior quality, style, sizing), it is the fashion marketer's responsibility to instill the intangible attributes of the niche brand (e.g., freshness, femininity, new spirit).

When a company carries multiple levels of brands (i.e., store brand, national brand, designer brand), the fashion marketer must identify a strategy regarding how to promote each brand and how much emphasis to place on each brand. The ultimate deciding factor of this fashion strategy is the company's desired image.

REFERENCES

Addley, Esther (February, 12, 2010). Alexander McQueen's death mourned by fashion world. *Guardian.co.uk*. Retrieved April 21, 2010 from http://www.guardian.co.uk/lifeandstyle/2010/feb/11/alexander-mcqueen-death-fashion-mourn.

American Heritage College Dictionary (Eds.). (1993). *American Heritage College Dictionary*. Boston: Houghton Mifflin.

Baldauf, A. (2004). The brand of freedom. *Radical Society*, 30(3–4), 51–62.

Bedbury, S. & Fenichell, S. (2003). *A new brand world: 8 principles for achieving brand leadership in the 21st century*. New York: Penguin Books.

Bobby Brown Company (2008). Company Web site. Retrieved September 25, 2008, from http://www.bobbibrowncosmetics.com/templates/whatsnew/index.tmpl.

Boorstin, J. (2005, August 22). What's in fashion this fall? *Scarcity*, 152(4). Retrieved June 18, 2009 from http://money.cnn.com/magazines/fortune/fortune_archive/2005/08/22/8270016/index.htm.

Cordell, V. V., Wongtada, N., & Kieschnick, R. L, Jr. (1996). Counterfeit purchase intentions: Role of lawfulness attitudes and product traits as determinants. *Journal of Business Research*, 35, 41–53.

Erno Laslo Company (2008). Company Web site. Retrieved September 25, 2006 from https://www.ernolaszlo.com/flash.asp.

Estée Lauder Company (2008). Company Web site. Retrieved September 25, 2008 from http://www.esteelauder.com/home.tmpl.

Frazier, M. (2006, January 9). The latest European import: Fast fashion. *Advertising Age*, 77(2). Retrieved June 18, 2008 from http://wf2dnvr4.webfeat.org/BP39K164.

Freeman, H. (2002). Fashion industry a costly stitch-up, says designer: Price of catwalk clothes 'set to build image of exclusivity.' *Guardian Newspapers Limited*, Retrieved June 18, 2008 from http://wf2dnvr4.webfeat.org.

Gap Inc. (2009). Company Fact Sheet. Retrieved on June 4, 2009 from www.gapinc.com/public/about/abt_fact_sheet.shtml.

Gayle, B. (March 20, 2009). Personal interview.

Hamilton, A., & DeQuine, J. (2006, March 13). Freaking for sneakers. *Time*, 167(11) Retrieved June 18, 2008 from http://wf2dnvr4.webfeat.org.

Hart, S. (2005). Pretty isn't enough. *Architectural Record*, 193(2), 123. Retrieved from http:wf2dnr4.webfeat.org/BP39K176.

Howie, J. S. (2009). Personal interview.

Hugo Boss. (2009). Brand overview. Retrieved on June 4, 2009 from http://group.hugoboss.com/en/brand_overview.htm.

Kaplan, J. (2009, June 4). Contemporary labels work through tough times. *Women's Wear Daily*, p. 12.

Korn, A. (2009, March 3). Personal interview.

LaRoque, A. (2009, March 2). Personal interview.

M.A.C. (2008). Company Web site. Retrieved September 25, 2008 from http://www.maccosmetics.com/templates/products.

Macintosh, G. & J. W. Gentry (1999, July 25). Decision making in personal selling: Testing the KISS principle. *Psychology and Marketing*, Volume 16, Issue 5, pp. 393–408.

The 100 top brands 2006. (2007, August 28). Business Week Online. Retrieved August 28, 2007 from http://bwnt.businessweek.com/brand/2006.

Ostrow, R & Smith, S. R. (1988). *The dictionary of marketing*. New York: Fairchild Books.

Packing them in at Selfridges. (2009, June 12). *Women's Wear Daily*, p. 7.

Rosenthal, J. (2006, June). Hold the fist-fights. *Fast Company*, 106. Retrieved June 18, 2008 from http://wf2dnvr4.webfeat.org/BP39K198.

Smashbox (2008). Company Web site. Retrieved September 25, 2008 from http://www.smashbox.com/.

Socha, M. (2009, June 1). Lacroix commits to keeping house alive. *Women's Wear Daily*, p. 3.

Thomas, B., & Palmieri, J. E. (2009, June 4). Avoiding distractions: Men's brands retrench, focus on core products. *Women's Wear Daily*, pp. 1, 6.

Tiffany & Co. (2010). Tiffany & Co. website homepage. Retrieved April 21, 2010 from http://www.tiffany.com/?siteid=1&omcid=G36084&iq_id=11154713&utm_source=google&utm_medium=cpc&utm_campaign=01%2BBranded%2BNew%2B-%2BExact&utm_term=11154713-tiffany%2Band%2Bcompany.

Wang, V. (2008). *Vera Wang on weddings*. Retrieved October 14, 2008 from http://www.verawangonweddings.com.

Watson, L. (1999/2000). *Twentieth century fashion: 100 years of style by decade & designer*. Philadelphia: Chelsea House.

Young, V., M., Moin, D., & Greenberg, J. (2006, April 5). Survival of the fittest: Moderate vendors rush to adapt to new world. *Women's Wear Daily*, 191(72), Retrieved June 18, 2008 from http://wf2dnvr4.webfeat.org/bp39k1101.

Zimbalist, K. (2007). Aisles of style: She puts her indelible stamp on the bridal dress industry, then the red-carpet: Now Vera Wang is set to revolutionize mass-market ready-to-wear with her new line for Kohl's. *Time Style & Design*, pp. 96–98.

KEY TERMS

Define or briefly explain the following terms:

Actual image ______________________________

Brand ______________________________

Brand chaperone ______________________________

Brand extension ______________________________

Brand mantra ______________________________

Brand strength ______________________________

Branding ______________________________

Consumer ______________________________

Desired image ______________________________

Exclusive distribution ______________________________

Exclusivity ______________________________

Extrinsic value ______________________________

Fast fashion ______________________________

Identity ______________________________

Image ______________________________

Individuality ______________________________

Intrinsic value ______________________________

Licensing ______________________________

Merchandise breadth ______________________________

Merchandise depth ______________________________

National brand ______________________________

Niche branding ______________________________

Product-only relationship ______________________________

Qualitative ______________________________

Quantitative ______________________________

Return on investment (ROI) ______________________________

Signature brand ______________________________

Store brand ______________________________

Target market ____________________

Temporary limited exclusive distribution ____________________

CLASS OR TEAM DISCUSSION QUESTIONS

1 | Discuss various company activities and actions that influence a brand's image. Give examples regarding an existing company.

2 | Why is branding so important to a company? If successful branding is essential to the success of fashion marketing, what are the reasons some (or many) companies are not completely successful at their branding efforts?

3 | Give examples of niche brands that (a) emanate from a central brand and (b) stimulate greater sales and profits for the company and central brand.

4 | Discuss the strengths and limitations of national and store brands. Is there a recommended proportion of national brands to store brands a retailer should carry?

INTERNET ACTIVITIES

1 | Select a fashion company of your choice. Go online and identify its branding efforts. Categorize its branding efforts (e.g., use of media). Discuss the type of story the company's branding effort is either (a) attempting to tell or (b) successfully telling.

2 | Access the Internet to find fashion marketing efforts that emphasize individuality. Discuss the product(s) and the influence individuality has on the branding and image of the products.

STUDY QUESTIONS

1 | What is the difference between a brand and a brand extension?

2 | What is the difference between a market segment and a market niche?

3 | Can a company offer multiple market niches? Why or why not?

4 | What is the purpose of a brand?

5 | Does a company typically have more then one brand? Why or why not?

6 | Does a company change its brand frequently? Why or why not?

7 | What is the difference between desired brand image and perceived brand image?

8 | How can a company verify that its brand is projecting the desired brand image?

9 | What does it mean for a brand to offer extrinsic value?

10 | What is fast fashion?

11 | Can the same market be attracted to opposing brands (e.g. *Beautiful* and *Cinnabar* perfumes)? Explain. How does your response influence marketing efforts?

12 | How does fashion influence a fashion marketer's efforts?

13 | What does *exclusive distribution* mean?

14 | How does exclusive distribution influence a fashion marketer's efforts?

____

____

15 | How does a fashion marketer build brand strength?

____

____

MULTIPLE-CHOICE QUESTIONS

1 | _____ is a vivid representation or description.

- **a.** Brand
- **b.** Image
- **c.** Product
- **d.** Advertisement

2 | Which of the following is not a stage of the branding process?

- **a.** Document all of the products and services the company offers.
- **b.** Identify the competition.
- **c.** Identify quantitative and qualitative differences in how your company does better than the competition.
- **d.** Identify where your marketing efforts exceed your competition.

3 | _____ is defined as branding a product that originates from a central brand.

- **a.** Mass-market branding
- **b.** Niche branding
- **c.** Fashion branding
- **d.** Central branding

4 | _____ is a strategy to move fashion into and out of a store fast.

- **a.** Rapid fashion
- **b.** Fast fashion
- **c.** Niche fashion
- **d.** Mass fashion

5 | What action is used to build brand width?

- **a.** Brand extension
- **b.** Spin-off markets
- **c.** Niche marketing
- **d.** Central branding

TRUE-OR-FALSE QUESTIONS

1 | _____ The success of brands is influenced by popular brands.

2 | _____ The extrinsic value of fashion products is more important than their intrinsic value.

3 | _____ All companies should have a mission statement.

TABLE 10.1

THE Market Planning PROCESS

step 1	CHAPTER 2 | Be inspired; become passionate regarding a product/service; be driven to succeed and committed to working toward a goal.
step 2	CHAPTER 3 | Intrinsic attributes of the products and services are marketed in terms of value, satisfaction, and quality. Building upon the mission statement, in this step you will make decisions regarding the pricing, communication, value, satisfaction, and quality associated with the purchase or the products and/or services.
step 3	CHAPTER 4 | Identify a comprehensive list of products and services offered by the company.
step 4	CHAPTER 5 | Examine the products and services component of the core marketing concept related to the trickle-down theory, media and celebrities, and the belongingness theory.
step 5	CHAPTER 6 | Examine the buying season in relation to the marketing process.
step 6	CHAPTER 7 | Examine marketing methods of targeting the consumer.
step 7	CHAPTER 8 | Examine the methods of exchange and relationships with the consumers. This includes making decisions to sell products and services through brick-and-mortar retail operations, direct marketing, and the Internet.
step 8	CHAPTER 9 | Examine the image and brands of the company in relation to marketing efforts.
step 9	**CHAPTER 10 | Conduct a market analysis of how companies are able to successfully cross product boundaries.**
step 10	CHAPTER 11 | Examine trends in the fashion industry regarding a) counterfeit merchandise and b) the impact of such merchandise on the industry's sales, profits, product design, consumers' attitudes.
step 11	CHAPTER 12 | Conduct a market analysis of fashions in the global environment in order to determine impact to the company's existing marketing efforts.

10

Crossing Product Boundaries

"Great things are done by a series of small things brought together." —Vincent van Gogh

chapter objectives

After reading this chapter, you should be able to understand Step Nine of the Market Planning Process. This includes being able to:

+ Explain the concept of name dominance.
+ Comprehend the importance of fashion marketers' influence on increasing multiple sales.
+ Analyze the guidelines to be used by fashion marketers when building brand integrity.
+ Explain attributes associated with brand identification.
+ Comprehend differences among fashion marketing campaign messages.
+ Evaluate methods of dovetailing fashion marketing campaigns.

Hermès International began when Thierry Hermès made harnesses for carriage makers during the late 1800s. Today, consumers around the globe seek out the company's fashions, accessories, and scarves in particular (Watson, 1999/2000). Ralph Lauren started his empire by making ties in his kitchen with his wife, Ricky. Today Polo Ralph Lauren is known for its lifestyle marketing techniques (Gross, 2004). The phenomenon over Kate Spade designs was ignited over six simple, structured handbags. Fashion followers of Kate Spade reveled in the fact that they could purchase stationery, shoes, and kitchen items from the designer (Kate Spade, n.d.).Van Gogh's statement regarding great things being accomplished through a series of small accomplishments may be seen throughout the fashion industries. Fashion designers, manufacturers, and marketers all began with inspiration, determination, and willpower. Their fashion empires expanded exponentially when the companies crossed product boundaries.

When you think of the word *fashion*, what immediately comes to mind? Do you think of a particular piece of clothing or accessory? Perhaps you think of a designer? Maybe you think of yourself wrapped in clothing made by a particular fabric? Throughout the 1990s and early 2000s, consumers have focused on fashion for themselves—meaning on clothing and accessories. But their sense of fashion has also been extended to all parts of their lifestyles. For example, try to remember the number of times last month that you purchased a non-clothing product because it was either made by your favorite apparel designer, in your favorite color, matched your *style,* or represented your sense of fashion. If you can think of at least one instance, you purchased a product as the result of fashion marketers crossing product boundaries. You are not alone!

figure 10.1 Regardless of the products and marketing efforts, Ralph Lauren portrays a classic image.

This chapter addresses the influence that fashion marketing has on consumers when they choose to purchase products other than apparel. Consider the following questions in relation to marketing fashion-forward products.

- Have you ever selected a particular day planner or stationery item because it had a designer's name associated with it?
- Does a day planner by Kate Spade look more fashionable than a generic-brand one?
- If you did purchase a product with a designer's name, do you use the designer's name when talking about the product? For example, do you find yourself saying *my Kate Spade day planner*, or *I have a Coach day planner*?
- Does your level of enjoyment increase when everyday products are associated with fashion designers?
- Do you currently own a wallet that costs more than the amount of cash you carry in the wallet? If so, don't feel bad—you are in good company. Besides, you probably look absolutely fabulous as you pull the wallet out of your designer handbag. Someone once said that image is everything.

EXPANDING FROM A CORE PRODUCT CATEGORY

Fashion marketers begin with a **core product category**. The core product category defines the existence of the company. The product should generate the majority of the company's sales. In most cases, this category will generate over 65 percent of the sales and profits for the company. When the target market and even persons outside the target market (i.e., persons who don't purchase the product), think of the company, they immediately think of the core product category. This category is called the *bread and butter* of the company. Regardless of the success of any of the other product lines offered in the company, customers will continue to purchase the core product category.

Many fashion marketers begin regionally. Once their product is accepted, they will expand nationally. The true test of the product's success and longevity is global consumer acceptance. Marketing fashions nationally and globally requires an understanding of different cultures, geographic regions, body shapes and sizes, and distribution channels.

Since the 1980s, the fashion industry has seen a transformation of its goals. Once a company has gained national and/or international success, the marketer *crosses product boundaries*. Crossing product boundaries occurs when a designer or marketer specializing in a core product category designs and/or markets a different product category.

Reasons for Crossing Product Boundaries

Fashion marketers may have very specific reasons for crossing product boundaries. In this portion of the chapter, we will address seven reasons. Fashion marketers may perceive one or all seven reasons as critical to the company's decision to expand its product offerings. The seven reasons include: (1) expanding name dominance; (2) building upon current expertise in the industry; (3) consolidating efforts; (4) increasing merchandise turnover; (5) increasing company profit margin; (6) increasing exposure to a greater target market; and (7) increasing customer loyalty.

EXPANDING NAME DOMINANCE

When it comes to marketing fashions, name recognition is critical. Without the name of the brand, consumers may purchase a copycat brand. This purchase can lead to loss of sales and profits. Worse, it can unintentionally lead to loyalty to a different company's brand.

Once name recognition is acquired, fashion marketers seek to expand name dominance. Name dominance exists when the marketer offers numerous products in categories other than the original product under the same

The Kate Spade brand is known for its simplicity and sense of fun. Originally starting with handbags, Kate Spade has crossed boundaries into china, glass wear, stationary, and shoes just to name a few products.

BOX 10.1 Crossing Over with Kate Spade

The Kate Spade brand is more than just a pretty purse. The line of six handbags designed by Kate Spade in 1993 was the result of her dissatisfaction with the handbag marketplace. Color, simplicity in style and design, and an emphasis on functionality proved to be the trademarks of the Kate Spade handbags.

With the success of the handbags, Kate and her husband, Andy Spade, decided to cross over into other products. Five short years after launching the handbag line, the company offered consumers stationery, personal organizers, journals, classic pencils, and erasers. The target market readily accepted these fashion accessories. By 1999, Kate Spade shoes complemented the Kate Spade handbags. The company also has a signature fragrance, a line of sunglasses and eyeglasses, and textiles. The Kate Spade company hasn't limited its offerings to fashions and accessories. The Kate Spade home collection includes china, glassware, and table settings.

Regardless of the product category, branding of the Kate Spade name and product is carefully protected. Throughout the company's fashion marketing campaigns, the presentation of each product category is clean and elegant without being stuffy. The presentation of the company name is consistent throughout all product categories (e.g., font style, image, branding). Product designs continue to focus on simplified lines, reminiscent of the 1960s (Kate Spade, n.d.).

name. For example, Calvin Klein originally started out designing and marketing women's wear in 1968. His company crossed product boundaries into the fragrance, swimwear, hosiery, and accessory industries during the 1980s. Calvin Klein gained name dominance when Phillips-Van Heusen Corporation bought the company in 2003. The company expanded the brand's lines to include golf shirts, mattresses, luggage, makeup, and new

BOX 10.2 Crossing Product Boundaries: Building Customer Loyalty

Target uses the following methods to increase customer loyalty:

Online Store

- Spend $50 online, save 10 percent, and receive free shipping
- Weekly advertisements listed
- Fashion videos posted
- All categories of merchandise posted
- Sale merchandise highlighted
- Gift cards
- Gift registry
- Store brands
- National brands

Brick-and-Mortar Stores

- Gift registry
- Giving back to the community
- Starbucks and snack area
- Limited grocery aisles
- Store credit card
- Store brands
- National brands

fragrances. In addition, the company is developing a new line of Calvin Klein stores. The stores feature Calvin Klein products, using the lifestyle fashion marketing concept. As consumers enter the store, they are able to mix and match products based on a lifestyle. This concept maximizes the fashion marketing potential for the Calvin Klein organization while also maximizing consumers' shopping benefits. Consumers who have difficulty visualizing the presentation of outfits particularly benefit from the lifestyle marketing concept (McKenna, 2007). Other companies that successful expanded name dominance include Michael Kors, Laura Ashley, Martha Stewart, and, of course, Ralph Lauren.

Ask yourself:

- How do you, as a student of fashion marketing, measure name dominance?
- Do you think consumers measure name dominance the same as a student of fashion marketing? Why or why not?
- If consumers measure name dominance in a slightly different way than students of fashion marketing, how can fashion marketers compensate for the differences in group perceptions?
- Which company do you perceive as having name dominance in each of the following fashion industries: (1) luxury apparel, (2) mass-market handbags, (3) discount shoes, and (4) mass-market cosmetics?

BUILDING ON CURRENT EXPERTISE IN THE INDUSTRY

Once a fashion designer is successful in marketing one product brand, it is significantly easier to design, manufacture, and market additional products. The fashion marketer has learned about the financial, legal, and distribution concepts necessary to building and operating a successful business. Contacts have been established in raw products (e.g., fabrics), banking (e.g., securing additional financing), and advertising. Michael Kors started out designing and marketing women's apparel. His attention to detail, style, and fashions brought him to the forefront of the fashion industry. Michael Kors's expertise in the industry readily allowed him to cross product boundaries, from apparel into fragrances, shoes, and bedding (Michael Kors, 2009). Jennifer Lopez is well-known for her singing, acting, and dancing. The marketing of her fashions makes her millions of dollars annually. When she decided to add a fragrance line to her apparel, her marketing team already had expertise in the industry. The financial, legal, and distribution systems were in place. The loyal target market who adored Jennifer Lopez fashions, particularly her velour warm-up suit, was a captive audience for the marketing campaign for the J. Lo women's fragrance.

A SWOT analysis is typically conducted during the process of adding additional product lines. This analysis consists of an examination of the strengths, weaknesses, opportunities, and threats facing a company (Table 10.2). The company should build upon its strengths, minimize its weaknesses, capitalize on opportunities, and understand its challenges. Strengths may include experience, existing target market, profit margin, marketing expertise, or financial resources. Opportunities may include finances, human resources, logistics, or property. Challenges may include downward changes in the economy or incoming competition to the region.

As you think about companies that have expanded its product lines, consider the following:

- What are the strengths of the product lines?
- What are the strengths of the company and its marketing efforts?

figure 10.2
Michael Kors has gained enormous brand exposure in recent years. In additional to fashion and accessories, he has crossed over product boundaries into the fragrance industry.

TABLE 10.2

SWOT Analysis Regarding Adding Product Lines

ANALYSIS	EXAMPLE OF QUESTIONS TO BE ANSWERED
Strengths	• What are the company's strengths? Include a discussion of finances, product lines, personnel, marketing, market share, and ability to adapt to a changing environment. • What attributes make these strengths work for the company?
Weaknesses	• What are the company's weaknesses? Include a discussion of finances, product lines, personnel, marketing, market share, and inability to adapt to a changing environment. • What attributes make these weakness for the company?
Opportunities	• Are consumers spending more money? • Are there technological advances that can assist the company design, manufacture, and/or sell additional products better and/or faster? • Can product lines be added to complement the existing product offerings? • Can an extension of the brand be added?
Threats	• Which companies are gaining market share? • What is the state of the economy (e.g., are consumers spending money)? • Is the company in a financially sound position? • Does the company have the resources (e.g., financial, personnel, facilities) to expand product lines without diluting its existing product line's marketing efforts?

- Can you identify any weaknesses of the company?
- Are there any opportunities in the marketplace that the company should tap?
- What are the challenges facing the company (e.g., economic, market share)?

CONSOLIDATING EFFORTS

The expansion of product offerings does not necessarily mean that efforts must be duplicated. Some of the operations within a company can be incorporated within existing departments as the company expands and crosses product boundaries. The size of the department, including personnel, may increase, but cost-savings efforts can be made. If desired, centralized management can be used for financial, marketing, and personnel offices.

Marc Jacobs successfully consolidated his fashion marketing efforts. The Marc Jacobs collection includes women's, men's, Little Marc Jacobs, fragrance, home collection, and eyewear. On the Marc Jacobs Web site (http://www.marcjacobs.com), the company's fashion marketers effectively show a variety of pieces from each collection. The Web site is used to remind the consumer that Marc Jacobs designs for the entire family, as well as for their lifestyle. The consumer can click on different icons for specific needs (e.g., men's apparel vs. bedding). This consolidation of fashion marketing efforts also benefits the company in time and resources while assisting the consumer.

Different product categories do not mean that different marketing teams should handle the marketing efforts. An excellent marketing team is able to market any product regardless of the category. The fashion marketing efforts by Ferragamo are extensive. The company sells menswear, women's wear, leather products, shoes, and handbags. Regardless of the product line, the marketing team promotes and advertises all of the product lines as a comprehensive product offering.

INCREASING MERCHANDISE TURNOVER

In retailing, there is a saying that the first product sold helps the retailer break even. The second product sold helps the retailer earn a profit. With each sale transaction, the greater number of products sold, the greater the chance to generate profits. As a fashion marketer's product boundaries deteriorate, the chance to increase multiple sales across products boundaries increases. Companies that market multiple product categories often have the ability to generate excitement in their marketing campaigns. This excitement can lead to an increase in merchandise turnover. That is, the greater the diversity of products marketed, the greater the probability of selling merchandise in large quantities.

Daniel Swarovski started the Swarovski company in 1895. For decades the company created beautiful crystal figurines and home accessories. In 1977, the company crossed product boundaries by designing and marketing jewelry. Additional products include fine-quality pens and crystal-studded handbags and accessories (Swarovski Company, 2009). The company went one step further in crossing product boundaries: the crystal ball that dropped for the 2009 New Year's celebration in New York's Times Square. The Swarovski name was repeated in newscasts weeks before the event. This effort generated free, worldwide marketing as television cameras from around the world watched the crystal ball drop to ring in the New Year.

INCREASING COMPANY PROFIT MARGINS

The financial health of any company is based on the profitability of the company. Fashion marketing companies can be equally profitable with either a small profit margin or a large profit margin. **Profit margin** is defined as the relation of gross profit to net sales. The higher the profit margin, the fewer the products required to sell to break even. The profit margin on product categories may vary. Fine jewelry typically has a high profit margin, at around 200 percent. Apparel, shoes, and costume jewelry typically have a profit margin of 100 percent. Marketing merchandise that offers different profit margins can benefit the company long term.

Tom Ford is world renowned for reinventing Gucci. In April 2005, the designer left Gucci and developed the Tom Ford brand. Product lines include beauty, eyewear, and menswear (Tom Ford Company, 2009). Tom Ford's

figure 10.3 Marc Jacobs introduced his designs through women's fashions. More recently, his line of women's shoes is very popular, sexy and extends his brand.

expansion into various product categories required research and development to take products to market. Prior experiences in fashion enabled Ford to set a profit margin similar to that used in the past. His beauty products (e.g., fragrances) would typically require a higher profit margin. Fragrances require a great deal of research, development, and packaging effort. While the profit margin on apparel may be 50 percent, it may be 70 percent on fragrances.

figure 10.4
Tom Ford fragrances are logical extensions of his successful fashion designs. Consumers who appreciate Ford's fashion designs may be drawn to his fragrances first based on the name then based on the scent.

GROWING TARGET MARKETS

A target market is finite in size. That is, there is a limited number of people within a target market. These individuals typically have a limited amount of disposable income devoted to the company's product category. **Disposable income** is the amount of income available to spend after expenses are paid.

For example, many women believe the statement, *You can never have enough shoes.* If you spend all your money on shoes, how will you purchase clothes? (No, the answer isn't to charge them.)

Todd Oldham started out as a fashion designer. He crossed product boundaries, and increased his target market by designing furniture and home accessories for La-Z-Boy furniture. As the creative director for Old Navy, his fashions are marketed on nationwide television to a large target market (Oldham, 2009).

INCREASING CUSTOMER LOYALTY

The more fashion marketers are able to place the company's name and products in front of their target market, the greater the likelihood of building customer loyalty. Increasing customer loyalty is about making customers understand that the company relates to them. As a multifaceted retailer, Target crosses product boundaries by offering its target market extended services. The services are designed to enhance the customer's shopping experiences and lifestyle. Easy access within the store, discounts on products and services, as well as multiple ways of shopping, are methods of building customer loyalty.

Think about a memorable or favorite fashion marketing piece. This may be a form of promotion, special event, or advertisement. Describe the marketing effort. Ask yourself:

- What feelings does the marketing piece evoke in you?
- Do you talk about this marketing piece to your friends?
- Does the marketing piece encourage you to purchase multiple products?
- Are you a loyal customer of the products or services? If so, does the marketing piece play a role in your loyalty?

MARKETING MULTIPLE PRODUCT CATEGORIES

The purpose of a fashion marketing campaign is to showcase one or more products to stimulate sales and profits. As the number of product categories increases, fashion marketers face the challenge of creating different marketing campaigns for various product categories. Depending on the product category, fashion marketers use different marketing campaigns. This is particularly important if the product categories are significantly different (e.g., women's apparel, furniture).

The guidelines for fashion marketing for multiple product categories are similar to marketing for a single product category. Marketing efforts can be used to inform and educate consumers or stimulate sales and profits. The goal of most marketing efforts across fashion product categories is to stimulate sales and profits. Regardless of how sexy, funny, exotic, or beautiful the marketing campaign is, if sales don't increase based on the campaign, the marketing effort was a failure.

Fashion designers are rapidly crossing product lines. Designers who started out creating women's apparel are venturing into other product categories, such as home furnishings. These efforts are causing the fashion marketers to be extra careful in their efforts. As the product categories expand, it becomes increasingly easy to blur the message, image, and marketing efforts.

Guidelines for Marketing Multiple Product Categories

When fashion marketers are faced with promoting a variety of product categories, there are a wide variety of guidelines that should be followed in order to ensure the fashion marketing efforts maintain the company's image and branding integrity. Five specific guidelines have been identified that are particularly important to follow when marketing fashions. These guidelines include: (1) maintaining a constant brand, (2) including company identification, (3) initiating a call to action, (4) including complementary product categories, and (5) dovetailing ongoing marketing campaigns.

MAINTAINING A CONSISTENT BRAND

Regardless of the product category being marketed, the brand image should be maintained. Consistent placement of the brand on fashion marketing efforts is critical. The brand identification, its placement, and its presentation impact on consumer acceptance of the product being marketed and the brand. Brand identification is typically used in the form of a logo. The marketing team develops the logo. There may be different logos for each product category, or the same logo might be used for all product categories (Box 10.3). The end result of the fashion marketing efforts is the same: the designer and/or manufacturer of the product are immediately reinforced in the consumer's mind. When consumers see the products in a store, on the street, or in a store window, they will remember the designer and/or manufacturer without needing a reminder of the brand.

Fashion marketers must consider the product, message, and medium (e.g., print, radio, television). The company's mission and corporate philosophy may also be brought out in the marketing campaign. Products such as home furnishings, cars, and children's toys are considered part of the consumer's fashion accessories. These products are an extension of the fashionable person's wardrobe. To effectively reach the target market in products other than apparel and accessories, it is essential that the fashion-related marketing image be used to promote nonclothing and accessory products. In addition, the marketing campaign should present a fashion image consistent with that of the company. As consumers view the marketing campaigns, they should readily recognize the quality, style, and presentation as those of the company. The image must remain intact. These fashion marketing efforts will result in consumers believing that the non-apparel products have the same qualities as the apparel products marketed by the company. The consistent image builds trust, loyalty, and security in purchasing different

Hello Kitty was originally a brand targeted toward small children. Over the years, teens and college-aged students enjoyed the Hello Kitty theme. MAC cosmetics teamed up with Hello Kitty to make a fun and trendy line of makeup.

BOX 10.3 The Expanding Brand of Hello Kitty

Hello Kitty! Girls around the world are familiar with the cute and very petite figure with an oversized bow. The Hello Kitty character was born in the 1970s and has captured the hearts of girls and young women worldwide. Hello Kitty and her likeness can be found on clothing, pencil cases, lunch boxes, erasers, shoes, wallets, luggage, clocks, and almost every imaginable product that children and girls use. The truly loyal Hello Kitty user can obtain a Visa credit and debit card with the Hello Kitty image on the front of the card. Hello Kitty embodies a spirit of friendship, fun, sassiness, and innocence. In 2009, MAC cosmetics extended the Hello Kitty product line to include Hello Kitty Color Collection and Hello Kitty Kouture. The Hello Kitty Color Collection consists of affordably priced cosmetics. The Hello Kitty Kouture line is a higher-end brand. The cosmetics represent the fun, sexy, and edgy nature of the Hello Kitty brand (Naughton, 2009).

product categories from a valued designer or manufacturer. Tommy Hilfiger, Gucci, and Dior carefully protect their brands throughout the category expansion process.

INCLUDING COMPANY IDENTIFICATION

Company identification in marketing efforts should be presented in the identical format, regardless of the product category. The identical font and style of the name provides the customer with easy recognition of the company and overall brand. The loyal target market will gravitate toward the name and look at the new product category. Customers who haven't purchased from the company before will recognize the name and understand that product category expansion is occurring. Company identification can be in the form of a logo or the company's name. Regardless of the method of identification, it is essential that the audience clearly understand the company that is sponsoring the marketing efforts.

High-end luxury and mass-market fashion products frequently feature company identification.

Consider the following:

- Describe five luxury company logos.
- Describe five mass market company logos.
- What are the differences and similarities between the logos?
- Are words or symbols more effective in a logo? Explain.

INITIATING A CALL TO ACTION

A fashion marketing campaign, regardless of the product category, is designed to stimulate the target market to act. More importantly, your fashion marketing campaign should specifically encourage the target market to purchase the product featured in the advertisement. Some advertisements are subtle, while others are overt, regarding the purchasing of products. Regardless of how the fashion marketer communicates with the target market, it is essential that there is a **call to action**. A call to action is a written statement, oral comment, or image encouraging consumers to purchase the product. There are thousands of products competing for the consumer's attention. Consumers can purchase through a brick-and-mortar store, direct marketer, and the Internet. Never assume that a consumer doesn't need to be reminded that your product is the best.Target reminds consumers they "gotta have it" in a recent print advertising campaign.

INCLUDING A COMPLEMENTARY PRODUCT CATEGORY

As the target market accepts a product, a **complementary product category** offers the next logical step to growing the company. A complementary product category refers to any product that can logically be associated or marketed in the company's name. For example, as a handbag and shoe designer, it is a natural fit for Kate Spade to lend her expertise to the stationery industry. Crossing over into designing hunting and fishing gear would not be as credible.

Fashion marketers rely heavily on the success of the original product as they begin their campaign to promote a complementary product category. Name recognition, brand acceptance, and loyal customers are emphasized. Unlike when launching an original product category, fashion marketers clearly understand that they already have a loyal target market. That is, loyal purchasers of the brand will probably try the new product category.

As the company expands its product categories, the fashion marketer's efforts become more complex. Continuity in perceived versus actual image, branding efforts, and crossover purchasing efforts must be carefully monitored. The products and marketing efforts must always add value for the consumers. If the efforts are implemented incorrectly, they may become inconsistent with the company's mission statement, image, and brand. Perhaps one of the most successful fashion marketers to cross product categories is Ralph Lauren. The global company maintains its brand and image while expanding across product categories. Products and services offered by the Ralph Lauren company include: (a) menswear—Purple Label, Black Label, Polo Ralph Lauren; (b) women's wear—Ralph Lauren Collection, Black Label, Blue Label, Lauren by Ralph Lauren, Pink Pony, RLX, Tennis, Ralph Lauren Golf; (c) Ralph Lauren Shoes and Accessories for men and women; (d) Ralph Lauren Baby; (e) Ralph Lauren Children; (f) RL classics; (g) Create Your Own; (h) Ralph Lauren Home; (i) RL Restaurant; (j) RL TV; (k) *RL Magazine*; and (l) RL Style Guide (Ralph Lauren, 2009).

DOVETAILING PRODUCT CATEGORIES

One of the reasons that fashion companies expand and cross over into other product categories is because of the success of the primary product offering. As the primary fashion product offering grows, brand awareness builds, and a loyal target market is strengthened; the company realizes that other market opportunities exist. The fashion marketer can capitalize on the synergy opportunity of each product. Depending on the product category, some of the products can be marketed in the same advertising message. Viewers can learn about the variety of products offered, while consistency is maintained in the products' attributes (e.g., quality, versatility, value, and style). This method maximizes the consumer's exposure to the products offered. It also presents an image of fashion dominance in the marketplace.

Complementary product categories such as apparel, accessories, and leather goods can

figure 10.5
Lifestyle store design setting within a store helps consumers understand what it would feel like to wear an entire ensemble. All products featured are designed by Ralph Lauren. In addition to encouraging brand loyal purchasing, the setting stimulates the purchasing of products in other categories.

George Carson (general manager) and "Marty" Carson (owner) don't just market and sell furniture. They market a way of living. All of the products at Marty Rae's are designed to help consumers maximize the enjoyment of their home.

BOX 10.4 Marketing Marty Rae's

The fashion industry is in Martha "Marty" Carson's blood. Marty is a trailblazer and role model for women and a mentor to her son. She started as a bridal consultant in 1958. Marty would go on to own a ladies' apparel store and fashion-forward furniture store named Marty Rae's. The furniture store was incorporated in 1978. During this era, women typically didn't own large retail operations; they certainly didn't actively operate the stores. Today, her son George Carson is the general manager of the furniture store. The furniture industry has changed significantly over the decades. The individualizing of fashion furniture is possible without sacrificing price. Overseas manufacturers, higher-quality products, and individualized fabrics provide customers with unique furniture pieces. Today, customers are looking at furniture similarly to how they look at fashions in their closet. They want their homes to represent their personality. At Marty Rae's, the company slogan, *Beautiful Furniture, Endless Possibilities*, is more than just words. The entire Marty Rae's team works to guarantee that its customers are excited about the furniture pieces purchased, whether it is a small accent piece or an entire room setting. Customer relations, satisfaction with the products, and after-the-sale service makes Marty Rae's marketing efforts successful (Carson, 2009).

comprise an excellent fashion marketing message to a loyal target market. Ferragamo, Ralph Lauren, and Martha Stewart have included multiple product categories in their fashion marketing campaigns. The marketing campaigns feature a lifestyle setting where the various products are used together, emphasizing that the brands fulfill multifaceted portions of the target market's lifestyle needs.

EXAMPLES OF CROSSOVER FASHION CATEGORIES

The health and beauty industry is closely interwoven with the fashion industry. Components of the health industry include hand, foot, and facial care. Manicurists, pedicurists, dermatologists, and plastic surgeons all work for the better living conditions of men and women. While some consumers may say they *need* a manicure, in actuality, a professional manicure is a luxury, not a necessity.

Health Industry

Dermatologists play an important role in consumer's skin health. Taking off unhealthy moles can prevent serious diseases such as skin cancer. The skill level of a dermatologist can minimize scarring, thereby allowing the consumer to maximize fashion options. The need for plastic surgery is situational. Many people get their lips pumped up with Botox as a fashion statement. Botox, or Botulinum toxin type A, is a bacterium that causes botulism. Botox temporarily reduces muscle activity. Many consumers believe that having Botox pumped into their forehead to reduce lines enhances their livelihood. Other forms of plastic surgery, however, truly are necessary. A woman who has a DDD bra size can live a more fulfilling and less physically painful life by obtaining a breast reduction. Her fashion options will be expanded exponentially by having surgery to reduce her breasts to a B or C bra size.

Consider the following:

- Simon Cowell of *American Idol* gets Botox on a regular basis. Do you think you will get Botox, perhaps ten years after graduation —once lines crease your face?
- Have you ever considered plastic surgery to enhance or fix a portion of your body?
- What is your perception of people who have plastic surgery?

Beauty Industry

Think of the fashion industry. What immediately comes to mind? You may think of beautiful wrap dresses by Diane von Furstenberg, stiletto sandals by Jimmy Choo, oversized sunglasses by Dior, or you may visualize wearing a fabulous handbag by Fendi. Think back to when you were in your early teens. **Did your mother ever tell you that beauty was more than just a pretty face? Did your grandmother ever tell you that inner beauty is also**

figure 10.6
There is a saying that says, "Imitation is the sincerest form of flattery." Wearing a Fendi handbag like a model or celebrity can make you feel special, unique, or privileged.

figure 10.7
Dolce & Gabbana cross product boundaries in many ways. The creative duo has retail stores, design men's and women's fashions, shoes, accessories, and fragrances. For the very special client, they also design couture gowns for the Oscars.

important? You have probably been told that inner beauty is more important than outer beauty. Personally, I believe this to be true. Of course, this doesn't stop me from purchasing moisturizer and the best makeup for my skin type. The beauty industry markets fashions from inside and out. The beauty industry strives to make consumers look fabulous and feel confident about its products.

A multibillion dollar industry, the beauty industry is continually made into a powerhouse industry by fragrances, cosmetics, lotions, creams, and hair care products. No one can deny that the high-end fashion marketing efforts from companies such as Estée Lauder, Dior, Chanel, and YSL sell millions of products and generate a healthy profit margin. During 2008 and well into 2009, however, mass-market consumers across the United States adopted lower-end cosmetics and bath accessories to fill their beauty needs. Fashion marketers aggressively promoted lower-end beauty product vendors such as Nature's End, L'Oréal Paris, and AHAVA. Value-pricing strategies were successfully being employed (Nagel & Brookman, 2009). Fashion marketing teams' ultimate goal is to make consumers loyal users of a company's entire line of products. Once the economy improves, marketers hope consumers will continue to use their products even after they have the money to switch to a more expensive brand.

Dolce & Gabbana is internationally known for its exquisite fashions. Its couture gowns grace the Academy Awards and Golden Globe red carpet runway shows. The biggest names in Hollywood and the richest consumers own their fashions. Their designs are, in a word, *divine*. The dynamic designing and fashion marketing duo are crossing product boundaries into the beauty business. Dolce & Gabbana offer makeup to complement its fashions and fragrance brands. The natural environment is used as inspiration for eye shadows and lipsticks. The designers believe that similar to women changing their fashions to accompany their mood, so too should they modify their makeup (Epiro, 2009).

The beauty industry isn't just for the rich and famous. It has expanded into the hip market, younger generation, and alternative markets. In other words, *beauty* has truly become a term that is after all "in the eye of the beholder." Back to the question posed several pages ago. **Did your mother ever tell you that beauty was more than a pretty face?** According to the beauty industry, it may mean spiked hair or nails painted fluorescent blue. The Hello Kitty beauty line began as an alternative to "stuffy" cosmetic lines. The company wanted its customers to have fun with its products.

Ask yourself:

- What is the primary reason you select a beauty line?
- What influences your purchasing decision the most?
  - Price
  - Gift with purchase
  - Advice from a friend
  - Impulse—to make yourself feel better
  - Ability to purchase with a credit card
  - Advertising
  - Other factors

Furniture and Home Accessories

The furniture industry is all about fashion, function, and at times famous names. Consumers are no longer satisfied with manufacturers dictating furniture style and designs. Today's consumers are gravitating toward the marketing concept called **lifestyle collection concept**. Lifestyle collection concept consists of a comprehensive marketing effort from a central brand. The furniture manufacturer provides paint, wallpaper, fabric, bedding, and furniture options revolving around one brand. The colors, styles, and designs coordinate. This marketing system makes it easier and time efficient for the consumer to select items. The lifestyle collection also encourages consumers to select more products from one brand, thereby encouraging loyal purchasing behavior. Brands that use a lifestyle collection concept include Martha Stewart and Ralph Lauren. The Martha Stewart furniture brand is a particularly popular line because the price is lower than comparable quality furniture, the company has excellent brand awareness, and the merchandise is an excellent value (Carson, 2009).

Home accessories are becoming an important part of fashion statements in consumers' lives. Whether dining in alone or entertaining a few friends, the kitchen has become the main focal piece of the home. The marketing of casual yet colorful dishes has become extremely successful. Similar to changing your apparel colors as the seasons change, consumers are using different colors and patterns of dishes for the changing seasons. Consumers are becoming more interested in knowing the designer's background. Umbra home furnishings at Target feature new designers. The designer's biography and inspiration are provided on a promotional board by the product offerings. Part of home accessory marketing efforts is allowing consumers to better understand the designer's inspiration. This knowledge makes the consumer feel a part of the design and more connected to the brand. Other designers who have told their story in conjunction with the marketing of home accessories include Kathy Ireland, Arnold Palmer, and Martha Stewart (Carson, 2009).

Toy Industry

Even in a slow economy, toy sales play an important role in marketers' and retailers' success. During 2008, the toy industry generated $21.64 billion. This same year, some of the most successfully marketed toys included Barbie, Crayola, Star Wars, and Webkinz (NDP Group, Inc., 2009). The Barbie doll has long played an important role in the fashion industry. In March 2009, the Barbie doll turned 50. Women worldwide remember playing with their Barbie dolls. The fashions, pearls, and high-heeled shoes were all part of pretending to be a beautiful woman. Decades later, the Barbie doll evolved, as did her fashion opportunities. Mattel, the international toy

figure 10.8
Many women want to feel special on their birthday. Barbie is no different. For her 50th birthday, Barbie decided to wear couture.

manufacturer that created Barbie, created an integrated global marketing campaign revolving around Barbie's fiftieth birthday (Tran, 2008).

SUMMARY

To cross product boundaries means to market a product different from the core category. The core product category defines the existence of the company. This product should generate the majority of the company's sales. Once a company has gained national and/or international success, the company may cross product boundaries. Reasons for crossing product boundaries include: (1) expanding name dominance, (2) building upon expertise in the industry, (3) consolidating efforts, (4) increasing merchandise turnover, (5) increasing company profit margin, (6) increasing target market, and (7) increasing customer loyalty.

The guidelines for fashion marketing multiple product categories are similar to marketing for a single product category. Marketing efforts can be used to inform or educate consumers or to stimulate sales and profits. The majority of marketing efforts across fashion product categories are aimed at stimulating sales and profits. Regardless of how sexy, funny, exotic, or beautiful the marketing campaign, if sales don't increase based on the campaign, the marketing effort was a failure. Guidelines for marketing multiple product categories include (1) maintaining a consistent brand, (2) including company identification, (3) initiating a call to action, (4) including complementary product categories, and (5) dovetailing product categories.

REFERENCES

Carson, G. (2009, March 25). Personal interview.

Epiro, S. (2009, January 19). Dolce & Gabbana launches first color line. *Women's Wear Daily*, p. 9.

Gayle, B. (2009, March 20). Personal interview.

Gross, M. (2004). *Genuine authentic: The real life of Ralph Lauren*. New York: HarperCollins.

Kate Spade. (n.d.). Company Web site. Retrieved on June 25, 2009 from www.katespade.com.

Marc Jacobs. (2009). Company Web site. Retrieved March 23, 2009 from www.marcjacobs.com/#folder=/specialitems&.

McKenna, B. (2007, March 31). Fashion forward: Not satisfied with its previous expansions into fragrances, jewellery and sunglasses, Calvin Klein will make a play for the home front in the new few years, with a slew of new products and the goal of doubling sales to $8-billion (U.S.). *The Globe and Mail*. Retrieved December 15, 2008 from www.lexisnexis.com/us/lnacademic/results/docview.

Michael Kors. (2009). Company Web site. Retrieved on March 22, 2009 from http://michaelkors.com.

Nagel, A. & Brookman, F. (2009). Heavy promos to capture wary shoppers. *Women's Wear Daily*. p. 10.

Naughton, J. (2009, November 21). MAC saying 'hello' to kitty collection. *Women's Wear Daily*, p. 4

NDP Group Inc. (2009, February 12). U.S. toy industry sales generate $21.64 billion in 2008. Retrieved from ww.npd.com/press/releases/press_090212.html.

Oldham, T. (2009). Old Navy Web site. Retrieved March 22, 2009 from http://oldnavy.gap.com.

Ralph Lauren. (2009) Company Web site. Retrieved July 6, 2009 from www.ralphlauren.com/shop/index.jsp?categoryId=1760781&ab=global_men.

Riley-Katz, A. (2008, November 19). Donna Karan urban Zen store meets Hollywood. Retrieved December 15, 2008 from www.wwd.com/retail-news/donna-karan-urban-zen-meets-hollywood.

Swarovski Company. (2009) Company Web site. Retrieved June 30, 2009 from www.swarovski.com.

Tom Ford Company. (2009) Company Web site. Retrieved June 30, 2009 from www.tomford.com.

Tran, K. T. L. (2008, November 14). Barbie at 50: Fashion marketing blitz for icon. *Women's Wear Daily*, p. 11.

KEY TERMS

Define or briefly explain the following terms:

Call to action ______________________________

Complementary product category ______________________________

Core product category ______________________________

Disposable income ______________________________

Lifestyle collection concept ______________________________

Profit margin ______________________________

CLASS OR TEAM DISCUSSION QUESTIONS

1 | Is there such a concept as *too many* product categories under one company umbrella? Explain.

____

____

2 | Can a fashion marketing team use extremely different profit margins (high versus low) without damaging the company's image? If so, when and what type of promotional efforts would be used in each case?

____

____

3 | Discuss the importance of brand identification. Which steps should fashion marketing divisions undergo to ensure brand identification on the various product categories? Explain.

____

____

INTERNET ACTIVITIES

1 | Using the Internet as a resource, select one company that has crossed product boundaries. Find examples of marketing efforts that you believe do not provide a consistent image with the company.

Describe the strengths and limitations of the marketing efforts.

____

____

Is the company's image tarnished because the company added too many diverse product categories or because the marketing team failed to communicate the message?

How would you improve the situation?

2 | Select a company that offers multiple product categories. Access the Internet. Collect data on the company's progression of merchandise categories. Discuss how the addition of categories included the company's marketing efforts. Provide strengths and weakness of the company.

STUDY QUESTIONS

1 | What is a core product category?

2 | Give examples of companies that have successfully crossed product category boundaries.

3 | What does it mean to have name dominance?

4 | How does a company obtain name dominance?

5 | Define profit margin.

6 | How does a marketer maintain a consistent brand?

7 | What is a complementary product category?

8 | Explain brand acceptance.

9 | When would a company not cross product boundaries?

10 | What are the benefits of crossing product boundaries?

MULTIPLE-CHOICE QUESTIONS

1 | The purpose of a fashion marketing campaign is to ____.

a. Showcase one or more products.
b. Stimulate sales.
c. Stimulate profits.
d. All of the above (*a*, *b*, and *c*)

2 | Which of the following statements is true?

a. With each sale transaction, the greater the number of products sold, the greater the propensity to generate profits.
b. Companies need a large profit margin in order to cover their marketing costs.
c. Brand identification is not important.
d. None of the above statements are true.

3 | Which of the following are not considerations when marketing different product categories?

a. A company's mission statement
b. A company's image
c. A company's short-term and long-term goals
d. All of the above are considerations when marketing different product categories.

4 | _____ is typically used in the form of a logo.

a. Brand identification
b. Sponsorship
c. Product acquisition
d. Name dominance

TRUE-OR-FALSE QUESTIONS

1 | _____ Home furnishings, cars, and office supplies can often be an extension of the consumer's fashion accessories.

2 | _____ Placement of the brand identification is not important.

3 | _____ Fashion marketing efforts can result in consumers believing that non-apparel products have the same qualities and value as the apparel products marketed by the company.

TABLE 11.1

THE Market Planning PROCESS

step 1 CHAPTER 2 | Be inspired; become passionate regarding a product/service; be driven to succeed and committed to working toward a goal.

step 2 CHAPTER 3 | Intrinsic attributes of the products and services are marketed in terms of value, satisfaction, and quality. Building upon the mission statement, in this step you will make decisions regarding the pricing, communication, value, satisfaction, and quality associated with the purchase or the products and/or services.

step 3 CHAPTER 4 | Identify a comprehensive list of products and services offered by the company.

step 4 CHAPTER 5 | Examine the products and services component of the core marketing concept related to the trickle-down theory, media and celebrities, and the belongingness theory.

step 5 CHAPTER 6 | Examine the buying season in relation to the marketing process.

step 6 CHAPTER 7 | Examine marketing methods of targeting the consumer.

step 7 CHAPTER 8 | Examine the methods of exchange and relationships with the consumers. This includes making decisions to sell products and services through brick-and-mortar retail operations, direct marketing, and the Internet.

step 8 CHAPTER 9 | Examine the image and brands of the company in relation to marketing efforts.

step 9 CHAPTER 10 | Conduct a market analysis of how companies are able to successfully cross product boundaries.

step 10 CHAPTER 11 | **Examine trends in the fashion industry regarding a) counterfeit merchandise and b) the impact of such merchandise on the industry's sales, profits, product design, consumers' attitudes.**

step 11 CHAPTER 12 | Conduct a market analysis of fashions in the global environment in order to determine impact to the company's existing marketing efforts.

Counterfeiting, Legislation, AND Ethics

"Making money doesn't oblige people to forfeit their honor or their conscience." —Baron Guy de Rothschild

chapter objectives

After reading this chapter, you should be able to understand Step Ten of the Market Planning Process. This includes being able to:

+ Explain terms associated with counterfeit fashion goods.

+ Comprehend laws associated with counterfeit and knock-off products.

+ Distinguish among the types of counterfeit products.

+ Evaluate the impact counterfeit products have on fashion marketing efforts.

+ Assess the reasons that consumers purchase counterfeit fashions.

The fashion industry is divided between companies that make a profit selling original products and individuals who forfeit their honor or conscience by illegally selling counterfeit merchandise. Consumers worldwide are caught in this vicious cycle. Some consumers consciously choose to purchase counterfeit merchandise for the cost savings. Others would rather have one genuine fashion product than ten low-quality counterfeit items. Regardless of which side you are on, counterfeiters significantly harm the fashion industry, yet they also make millions of dollars. This chapter addresses the impact of counterfeit merchandise, ethics, and the enforcement of the law.

It is the fashion marketer's responsibility to make the company's brand and its products desirable to the target market. Many of the designer products are out of the reach of the designated target market, yet still desired by consumers. There is an enormous controversy rippling throughout the fashion industry and among consumers: Is it better to purchase fewer items of higher quality or many fashion items that are more disposable because of their low quality? The answer is obviously very personal. Not everyone can afford expensive designer fashions. Illegal goods flood the market in search of buyers who either unknowingly or willingly purchase the fashions. Unfortunately, the outcome is enormously detrimental to the fashion industry.

A global trend is occurring whereby consumers who *need* the fashion statement but cannot afford the actual product are purchasing counterfeit items. A counterfeit product is a copy of an original design that attempts to trick the consumer into thinking the product is manufactured by the original company. Counterfeiters specialize in high-end designer handbags, luggage, apparel, jewelry, and highly sought-after national brand merchandise such as Nike footwear (Barnett, 2005). Regardless of the type of merchandise, counterfeit merchandise distribution continues to increase annually, resulting in millions of lost profits to the companies that designed, marketed, and sold the original products (Barnett, 2005).

COUNTERFEIT MERCHANDISE

Regardless of how knowledgeable a person is of fashion, he or she will at one time or another have heard about counterfeit Rolex watches, seen "designer" handbags being sold for $20 on the streets of New York, or perhaps read in the paper about a police raid of stolen merchandise. A **product** is "any industrial or handicraft item, including packaging or graphic symbols, but exclud[ing] computer program[s] (computer graphics and icons aren't expressly excluded)" (Bezzegh, 2004). Fashion marketers attempt to protect the actual design of the fashion product as well as the packaging. As you learned in Chapter Three, packaging is an important component of fashion marketing efforts.

Counterfeit products are typically those that are highly recognizable by consumers. Counterfeit merchandise consists of products that are purposely designed and marked with a company trademark. These features infringe upon the rights of the owner (i.e., company) (Sridhar, 1007). Merchandise may include designer brands, brands with a distinctive logo, and/or brands with a distinctive color combination. The counterfeit products must have a relatively easy design to copy. Intricate designs increase the cost of the production, thereby increasing the cost of the final product. Most consumers who purchase a counterfeit product want the look of the real product but are not willing to pay a high price (Penz & Stottinger, 2005).

Design law exists to help protect fashions from being copied (Bezzegh, 2004). Design law is applicable to products that are manufactured through a company or organization. The law does not protect handicraft merchandise. As you read this, you may think that it is unfair that the law does not cover handicraft merchandise. However, it is very fair. The design law exists to protect companies that design products that are manufactured and distributed in large quantities. Handicraft merchandise is typically produced as a unique item. **Have you ever sewn a top? Did you like the garment so much that you made a second top? Did the top turn out to be identical (and I mean absolutely identical)?** Probably not. Perhaps you changed the color of the fabric or you used a completely different type of fabric. Perhaps you lengthened or shortened the sleeves. You probably didn't make 20 identical tops for yourself. If you did, you may need a fashion overhaul.

The design law is structured to help fashions from being copied. These fashions will be designed, manufactured, and distributed nationally or globally. Counterfeiting is a $200 billion annual industry (Tucker, 2007). Counterfeiting is the production and sale of fake products (Penz & Stottinger, 2005). Counterfeit products, and counterfeiters, are flooding the market. When unemployment rates rise, consumer activism in the products is low, and the legal system is unable or lacks resources to catch and process counterfeiters. Seven percent of the world's trade deals in counterfeit goods (Hilton, Choi, & Chen, 2004). Counterfeit products are saturating the globe, growing by 150 percent. Compared to the growth of 4 percent global trade, counterfeit products are at an all-time high (Smith, 1997).

Consumers often purposely purchase counterfeit products in order to satisfy aspiration or status needs (Sridhar, 2007). Counterfeit high-end handbags are located on Canal Street in SoHo (Barnett, 2005). There is never any question that the merchandise is not genuine. Fashions are sold on folding tables by people who will barter for discounts when a consumer purchases multiple items. Merchandise can be purchased for cash only. MasterCard, Visa, and American Express are not accepted by these vendors. Just a few blocks away, consumers can walk into stores and purchase a real Gucci bag. A consumer can even select the form of payment—cash, credit, or check.

Counterfeit products are classified into four areas: (1) well-known brands that are highly visible; (2) high-tech, high-priced products; (3) prestige products; and (4) high-tech research and development products (Sridhar, 2007). Well-known brands (e.g., Nike) and prestige products (e.g., Gucci) are examples of items that are often counterfeited in the fashion marketing industry. Counterfeit copies can be further classified into four subtypes that impact the marketing of well-known brands and prestige products. These include: vanity fakes, overruns, condoned copies, or copies by the fashion houses (Hilton et al., 2004).

Karen Lear, attorney and senior lecturer at the University of South Carolina. Ms. Lear teaches Law for Retailers and works with practicing attorneys regarding work attire.

BOX 11.1 Karen Lear, Counterfeit Law Expert

Karen Lear, attorney and senior lecturer at the University of South Carolina, is an expert in the law and the fashion industry. Prior to becoming an attorney, Professor Lear was a human resource manager and merchandise coordinator for Belk. Belk is a privately owned department store located in southern regions of the United States. After earning her law degree, she practiced law in South Carolina.

Wanting to combine her passion for the fashion industry and her expertise in law, she joined the Department of Retailing faculty at the University of South Carolina. Here, she teaches upper-division law for retailers courses, training future generations of retailers and fashion marketers to combat the impact that knockoffs, counterfeiting, and blanks have on the fashion industry. According to Lear: U.S. designers have a disadvantage when it comes to the copyrighting of fashions. France and Italy heavily subsidize the fashion industry. Foreign designers have a heavily enforced copyright design for several years after the fashions hit the market.

In the United States, the property laws protect only the logo. Because knockoffs are legal in the United States, fashions are copied without any negative repercussions. Counterfeit merchandise is illegal, yet counterfeiters work overtime to beat the law. They learn new methods of how to cheat the system every day. These illegal products harm individuals, businesses, and the economy. The good news is that the United States is working hard to catch fashion counterfeiters. The reality is that counterfeit products will probably only be stopped when consumers stop purchasing the products. Counterfeit merchandise is driven by consumer demand (Lear, 2009).

Vanity Fakes

Vanity fakes are products that have low intrinsic value and low perceived value. This type of counterfeit product rarely, if ever, harms the genuine brand because consumers are able to distinguish the actual brand from the vanity fake brand. In the long-term, vanity fakes do present a challenge to the brand as they continue to flood the market. Over time, consumers may compare the low quality to the actual brand (Hilton et al., 2004). A large "diamond ring" made of plastic is an example of a vanity fake. Consumers readily know that the ring is a fake.

Think about your last shopping experience.

- How many vanity fake fashion products did you see consumers wearing?
- Are vanity fakes popular in your city or state? If so, why do you think they are popular?
- How are vanity fakes marketed?
- Are the marketing messages significantly different from those of the genuine product? Or does the marketer try to mimic the original's marketing efforts?
- What do you personally like or dislike about vanity-fake fashions?

Overruns

Overruns are copies made from leftover material. The original manufacturer often makes overruns. Overruns are made by the designer's specifications. They are sold at a high gross margin (Hilton et al., 2004). The design specifications provide a better level of quality than vanity fakes and counterfeit fashions from an external source. Overrun fashions will not, however, have the same level of quality or the same design features as the original fashions. Marketing efforts will typically not promote overruns, thereby avoiding customer confusion in the brand's image, quality, and design features.

Condoned Copies

A **condoned copy** is made by other designers or fashion houses. Designers continually reinvent and change their original designs. This is done to (a) encourage consumers to purchase the most recent version of the design, (b) update the design, and (c) thwart counterfeiters. Condoned copies are typically based on vintage designs. Condoned copies keep the designs in the market while the designer's newest versions are selling at higher prices (Hilton et al., 2004).

figure 11.1 Outlet malls are very popular with some manufacturers and many consumers. This Nike Factory Store draws in consumer traffic from great distances.

figure 11.2
Consumers can purchase designer counterfeit products in Chinatown in New York City.

Self-Copies

Self-copies are copies made by the fashion house. Self-copies are used when high-end design houses and manufacturers sell merchandise to a secondary market. This secondary market is typically the mass market. Design rejects, seconds, or product manufacturers for the bridge market provide the designer with a high-profit market, brand-name exposure, and control of the copies. Outlet stores are frequently used as a source for selling self-copies. Marketing efforts are kept minimal in order to keep overhead costs low. In-store signage and newspaper advertisements are used to promote brand names at low prices.

Outlet malls have become extremely popular with consumers throughout the United States (Figure 11.1). The malls act as a destination shopping source, and consumers are willing to drive a greater distance for them than for a traditional shopping experience. Jones New York, Lennox, Nike, and Coach have stores in outlet malls throughout the United States.

As a future fashion professional, how would you answer the following marketing questions:

- Should the in-store promotional efforts of an outlet store be (1) identical to the company's full service stores, or (2) somewhat less glossy, based on the store's outlet status? Explain.
- What is the most effective method of marketing fashions in a specific outlet store in a mall? That is, in an outlet mall, what are some additional methods of generating store traffic into your specific store? Explain.
- In an outlet mall, which attributes should a fashion retailer feature in its advertising campaign (e.g., price, product, place)? Are all attributes equally important? Explain.
- Will the outlet mall detract consumers from purchasing the brand at the traditional mall or online? Why or why not?

DISTRIBUTION OF COUNTERFEIT GOODS

Visualize a man wearing a black trench coat. He is standing on the corner of a busy city street. He opens the trench coat and shows you 20 different watches. He assures you that *every watch is guaranteed to be a solid gold Rolex*. He will sell you the Rolex for only $100, cash only; purchase two and you receive a $10 discount. Thirty years ago, counterfeit goods were sold under "cloak and disguise." Today, counterfeit merchandise is sold out in the open for all to see. Consumers are able to purchase illegal fashion merchandise on the street and through the Internet; counterfeit merchandise is all around us.

Street Vendors

Street vendors set up a table and sell merchandise from the curb. Large cities like New York and Chicago have street vendors on many of the busiest avenues. Merchandise is set up on a table on the busiest corners in the city. The vendors accept cash only. The variety of merchandise varies widely and includes handbags, watches, wallets, sunglasses, scarves, and T-shirts. Most items cost less than $25. Handbags that have a familiar design may sell for as much as $60. As consumers look down other streets, they can typically see a waiting van prepared for a quick getaway in case the police decide that it is time to shut down business. This means the merchandise for sale is either stolen or illegal. Another possible explanation is that the street vendor does not have a license to sell merchandise.

Ways to identify a fake or counterfeit product include:

- Fake animal skin
- Fake leather
- Flawed stitching
- The logo is not on the correct location; the real product has the logo in only one specific place.
- Missing logo
- Misspelled words on hangtags
- Nickel-plated hardware instead of brass
- No credit card payments
- No product guarantee
- Poor-quality dustcover
- Poor-quality workmanship
- Small amounts of stitching (Lear, 2009)

E-retailers

An e-retailer can sound honest, legitimate, and forthright; 86 percent of e-retailers are legitimate and honest. However, approximately 14 percent of counterfeit merchandise is sold though the Internet (Corcoran, 2007). The strength of e-retailing also provides counterfeiters with a perfect avenue for selling illegal merchandise. Consumers can't physically inspect the product in advance; they don't have direct contact with the retailer. Once the product is received, the consumer usually does not return the merchandise (Corcoran, 2007).

Counterfeit merchandise sold through the Internet makes it difficult for consumers to trust independent or small online businesses.

Give some examples of marketing statements to include on a business Web site to assure consumers of the company's legitimacy.

- What images should be located on the Web site to verify its legitimacy?
- What contact information should be located on the Web site to verify its legitimacy?

GLOBAL COUNTERFEITING EFFORTS

Counterfeiting isn't just a U.S. phenomenon. Approximately 6 percent of the world's merchandise is counterfeit (Corcoran, 2007). Counterfeit products are an international problem (Box 11.2). The International Chamber of Commerce and the Organisation for Economic Co-operation and Development (OECD) estimate that counterfeit merchandise is a $200 billion industry (Norquist and Zahourek, 2008). Intellectual property theft in Canada alone is estimated to be as high as $22 billion (Beatty, 2008). In the United States, $197 million dollars worth of counterfeit merchandise was seized in 2006. Of this, 80 percent of the fake illicit products were manufactured in China (Mawson, 2008).

U.S. Customs estimates that more than 5,000 Internet sites sell counterfeit designer handbags. Many Internet sites trick consumers into believing that the products are genuine. A popular technique counterfeiters use is to ship non-branded merchandise from Asia into the United States. Once the merchandise is processed through Immigration and Customs Enforcement (ICE), the counterfeiters

BOX 11.2 Counterfeiting and the Global Marketplace

Counterfeit merchandise is not just big business; it's global business. Between 2004 and 2006, U.S. authorities seized counterfeit merchandise worth an estimated $4.13 trillion. This means that (a) consumers purchased merchandise they thought was real or colluded in the crime, (b) businesses lost sales from legitimate consumers, (c) designers' and manufacturers' reputations were harmed from defective merchandise, and (d) people were involved in the illegal sale of merchandise. China, Russia, Ukraine, Chile, and Turkey are the most prominent areas for generating counterfeit merchandise. In response to the rapidly increasing number of counterfeit products flooding international markets, the International Chamber of Commerce developed the Business Action to Stop Counterfeiting and Piracy (BASCAP). The purpose of BASCAP is twofold: to work with companies in the fight against counterfeiting and piracy and to encourage governments to create and enforce anticounterfeit legislation (de Mesa, 2006).

These "vendors" in Florence, Italy, display counterfeit handbags on blankets. The blankets are used instead of tables so that they can quickly gather up the products when police sirens are heard. The Italian police aggressively prosecute sellers and buyers of counterfeit merchandise.

are able to apply the trademarks, brands, and other identification marks on the products. The purpose of this two-step process is to avoid detection. If the merchandise is confiscated at ICE, the officials simply have unbranded merchandise that looks similar to other merchandise on the market. The counterfeiters use sophisticated equipment to embroider, emboss, and imprint the trademarks and logos (Cocks, 2007). Once the merchandise is on U.S. soil, the counterfeiters act swiftly to process, distribute, and sell the merchandise.

THE IMPACT OF COUNTERFEIT MERCHANDISE

Counterfeit merchandise is detrimental to the fashion marketing industry. Counterfeit merchandise directly harms the brand's status. Creating, developing, and growing a brand takes time, creativity, and a lot of financial prowess. Unfortunately, the brand's status can easily be tarnished through excellent but faulty counterfeit products (Corcoran, 2007). For example, an excellent counterfeit product is one that looks 95 percent similar to the brand;

figure 11.3
The influence of counterfeit products on the industry is significant. As counterfeit merchandise floods the marketplace, the exclusivity of the brand declines.

the faulty characteristic may be a zipper that breaks or a handle that rips.

Counterfeit merchandise also impacts the exclusivity of the brand. Marketers carefully protect the number of SKUs that are produced and distributed nationally and internationally. Many designer fashions depend on the exclusivity of the product. When a counterfeit product floods the marketplace, the brand's exclusivity is harmed (Corcoran, 2007).

Nationally and internationally, employment in the fashion marketing industry is negatively influenced by counterfeit merchandise. Over 750,000 jobs have been lost due to counterfeit merchandise (Doyle, 2009, March 20). More than 300,000 jobs are lost annually throughout Europe due to the effects of counterfeiting (Eisend & Schuchert-Creler, 2006). An estimated $350 million in taxes are lost (Baldauf, 2003).

LEGISLATION

One of the first steps businesses can take to stop counterfeit products is to understand how counterfeit products are manufactured, distributed, and sold. The International Anti-Counterfeiting Coalition provides information for designers, manufacturers, retailers, and consumers. The coalition's Web site is designed to (1) strengthen honest companies' efforts in the marketplace, and (2) weaken counterfeiters' efforts (International Anticounterfeiting Coalition, 2009).

Each time a consumer unknowingly purchases a counterfeit product, his or her trust in the brand decreases. The product is inferior to the genuine product. The consumer believes the product is genuine, but inferior in quality, hence a growing distrust in the brand (Wee, Tan, & Cheok, 1995).

Counterfeit products, often disguised as the real brand, have flooded the supply chain at an unprecedented rate. Reasons for the increased rate of fake products include (a) improved quality of counterfeit goods, (b) sale of merchandise through Internet sites whereby consumers are unable to personally evaluate merchandise prior to the sale, and (c) globalization (Hilton et al., 2004).

Counterfeit merchandise purchased under the real brand name through the Internet is a real threat to designers, manufacturers, and retailers. Consumers often have limited visual acuity when looking at pictures on the Internet. A seller of fashion products may state that a product is genuine but hide incriminating product design features. Only when the product is shipped does the consumer realize that the product is fake. The "shipped from" address and phone number will probably also be fake. The consumer will end up with a very expensive fake product. Scams like this occur throughout the world. They are difficult to track because of fake routing numbers and nonexistent phone numbers.

A reliable method of purchasing brand-name merchandise is through the manufacturer or a retailer. The type of channel selected (i.e., brick-and-mortar store, direct marketer, Internet) should be reliable and legitimate. If the product's price is significantly lower than that offered at other locations, the merchandise is probably not authentic. Not only does fake merchandise harm the fashion industry, it cheapens the company's image.

The Federal Trademark Dilution Act

The Federal Trademark Dilution Act (FTDA) is defined by the U.S. Supreme Court as an "act that describes the factors that determine whether a mark is distinctive and famous, and defines the term dilution as the lessening of the capacity of a famous mark to identify and distinguish goods or services" (H. R. 1295: An Act, 2010). The dilution of a famous mark may be in the form of similar names, logos, or tag lines.

Trade Dress Law

Have you ever thought, *My designer wallet looks real, but something isn't quite right*? The wallet has designer features, but something is not quite the same, though you don't know what. You may have purchased a counterfeit product without knowing it. The **Trade Dress Law** was designed to help consumers from making this mistake. The Trade Dress Law refers to the manner in which a product is "dressed up" to go into the market. This law assists designers and manufacturers in the protection of their product designs. The product designs must satisfy two criteria: They must be distinctive, and they must be nonfunctional (Maldonado, 2002). The nonfunctional aspect of the criteria refers to the embellishments of the product. For example, the lettering, colors, logo, and hardware on a handbag are nonfunctional. These nonfunctional portions of the product must be distinctive. Designers and manufacturers get around the Trade Dress Law by slightly changing the nonfunctional attributes of a product.

For example, consider the following:

- Have you ever noticed a handbag that had *LV* embossed on it? What company's product is being copied?
- A golf shirt with a dog stitched on the left shoulder is patterned after what company?
- Two-toned ballerina flats without any embossing or bows are copied from which famous designer?
- Can you think of other distinctive fashion products?

Since 1979, Coach, Inc., has advertised a line of handbags under the name *Coach Collection*. The common features of the handbags include: (a) a rectangular hangtag with beaded chain, (b) a gloved-leather handle, (c) bound edges, and (d) heavy brass or nickel-plated hardware. The line of handbags have continued to sell well over the years and have brought the company a great deal of recognition, sales, and profits. We Care Trading Co., Inc., featured extremely similar product designs to the Coach Collection line. Coach, Inc., sued We Care Trading Co., Inc., based on the trade dress law. Coach, Inc., won the suit on the grounds that the four features of the collection (listed above) are distinctive and nonfunctional (Maldonado, 2002).

Lanham Act

In 1984, the Lanham Act "subjected anyone who intentionally traffics or attempts to traffic in goods or services and knowingly uses a counterfeit mark on or in connection with such goods or services to a fine of no more than $250,000 and a prison sentence no longer than five years, or both" (Cocks, 2007, p. 523). Unfortunately, the act did little to deter the trafficking of goods. In fact, the trafficking of trademarked goods continued to escalate. In response to this trend, the Violent Crime Control and Law Enforcement Act of 1994 was enacted.

The Violent Crime Control and Law Enforcement Act of 1994

The Violent Crime Control and Law Enforcement Act of 1994 was designed to strengthen the Lanham Act. Regardless of the monetary penalty and threat of going to jail under the Lanham Act, the trafficking of trademarked goods was at an all-time high in the United States. Congress realized that stiffer penalties were needed in order to change the trend. Under the Violent Crime Control and Law Enforcement Act, first-time offenders could be charged as much as $2 million in fines and be sentenced up to ten years in prison. Repeat offenders could receive a $5 million maximum fine and 25 years in prison. This act was designed to get violators out of circulation and deter potential violators from entering the trademark trafficking business (H. R. 3355, An Act, 2010).

INTERNATIONAL EFFECT

In the United States, consumers typically will not be arrested for purchasing counterfeit products from vendors. Consumers brazenly browse over knockoffs as police walk past them on the street. Police officers will rarely if ever stop consumers from purchasing merchandise from the street vendors, but this still does not mean that it is ethical or legal. This scenario is not the same in Italy and France. In 2005, a law was enacted that criminalized the sale and purchase of any counterfeit merchandise. When caught, the seller and purchaser may be sentenced to up to three years in jail (Galloni, 2006). The Italian police are also proactive at deterring vendors who sell merchandise without a license. The vendors typically have their merchandise mounted on a piece of cardboard. The cardboard is lightweight and allows them easy access to run away from the police and into an alley.

CONSUMER ETHICS

The success of counterfeit products is due to an understanding of the consumer target market. Similar to any retail operation, there is a target market for counterfeit fashion products. One theory that may explain why so many consumers across the globe ignore laws regarding the purchase of counterfeit and pirated fashion products is **cognitive dissonance**. Cognitive dissonance is an uncomfortable feeling that arises when a person has two opposing thoughts or actions. For example, consumers may experience cognitive dissonance when they knowingly purchase counterfeit fashion merchandise. The purchase is made for intrinsic and extrinsic value.

Consumers who purchase counterfeit goods have been able to successfully reduce cognitive dissonance to such an extent that they no longer believe their actions are illegal (Eisend & Schuchert-Creler, 2006). Some methods of reducing cognitive dissonance in purchasing counterfeit or pirated fashion products include: (a) not caring enough or not fully recognizing that the merchandise is illegal, (b) helping a small business (i.e., the counterfeiter) grow, or (c) avoiding thoughts about who is being hurt by his or her actions.

The Price Is Too Good to Pass Up

The majority of consumers, regardless of the country they live in, can't afford designer merchandise. If a consumer does decide to purchase a $6,000 Rolex or a $5,000 Gucci handbag, it probably will be the only high-end luxury item purchased that year (or ever). High-end luxury items are purchased by people with enormous incomes, such as celebrities (e.g., Jennifer Lopez, Halle Berry), executives of companies (e.g., Martha Stewart, Donald Trump), and persons born into wealth (e.g., Paris Hilton, Kim Kardashian). Most consumers are required to save their dollars if they want the latest Jimmy Choo shoes or Chanel oversized sunglasses.

Purchasing knockoffs and counterfeit products may seem like a good compromise to some consumers. They often justify the purchase of counterfeit (and, remember, illegal) goods by saying *the price is too good to pass up*. Counterfeiters tempt consumers with deep discount prices; products are offered anywhere from 60 to 80 percent lower than the actual brand (Power, 2007).

This Isn't Illegal

While visiting a big city, the temptation to purchase a fake Gucci handbag for $200 may seem too good to resist. What many consumers don't stop to think about is that the purchase of counterfeit products is illegal and supports criminal organizations (Steele, 2009). As consumers walk down the streets of New York, Chicago, Italy, Paris, and other large cities, street vendors may be seen with counterfeit and pirated fashion products. At any time of day, consumers can be seen flocked around tables looking for the best deal on a counterfeit "Rolex," "YSL" handbag, or "Hermès" scarf. Many consumers knowingly purchase counterfeit handbags, watches, sunglasses, or shoes and tell themselves *this isn't illegal, I'm not hurting anyone*, and *everyone does it*. In actuality, (1) purchasing counterfeit products is illegal; (2) every time a counterfeit product is purchased, the image, sales, profits, and employment opportunities of the fashion industry are irreparably harmed; and (3) everyone does not purchase counterfeit products (Eisend & Schuchert-Creler, 2006). The $6,000 Gucci question is . . . are your fashion purchasing actions legal or illegal?

I'm Not Hurting Anyone

There can be no disagreement that counterfeit merchandise takes profits out of designers' business. For every YSL knock-off purse that is purchased on the streets of Manhattan, there is one less YSL real purse purchased. However, some legal analysts believe that knockoffs have a positive impact on designers (Barnett, 2005).

The success (i.e., adaptation by large group of consumers) of a designer's product line is dependent, in part, on visibility. The more consumers see others using the various products, the greater the success of the line. As consumers see high-end status products (real or counterfeit) being worn by a large population, they, too, will want items by that designer. The products may include handbags, luggage, scarves, watches, or sunglasses.

Designer merchandise is known for quality materials and workmanship. There is also typically a logo that cannot be replicated on a counterfeit product (Barnett, 2005). Once a consumer has an authentic designer product, it is very difficult to accept a counterfeit product. The genuine quality, materials, and fact that the product is from the authentic designer obliterate any aura and excitement of owning the ersatz product. Consumers own the genuine designs for a reason (e.g., quality, status, and style). Whatever the reason, once you purchase the real product, it is difficult to purchase a counterfeit.

I'm Helping Small Businesses

Many cities feature **boutique retailers** that sell fake designer merchandise at deep discount prices. A boutique retailer is defined as a small specialty store or an area within a larger store. The emphasis is on merchandise selected for a specific customer, presented in an attractive and unified manner, and accompanied by individualized attention on the part of the sales staff (Ostrow & Smith, 1988).

Credence goods are "goods whose quality is difficult to assess before or after purchase and use" (Hilton et al., 2004). Consumers who do not regularly purchase high-quality or designer goods may have difficulty in assessing credence goods. The value of the merchandise is based on the credence—statements—of the vendor, friend, or others. The authenticity of credence goods will sometimes not be proven to the consumer before or even after the purchase. Consumers may not know at the time of purchase, or ever, if the product is genuine. Regardless of whether the consumer does not know the truth, credence is a very important concept to the fashion industry. Consumers need to believe that the product, brand, and image of the company are exactly what they are purchasing.

Other types of goods that may be placed in the sentiment category of *I'm helping small businesses* include search and experience goods. **Search goods** are products that have an intrinsic value objectively assessable prior to purchase (Hilton et al., 2004). Consumers who want a designer handbag may ask friends and family for the best street vendors that sell "designer" sunglasses. **Experience goods** are those where the experience of use after purchase reveals quality with a fair degree of certainty (Hilton et al., 2004). New York street vendors that sell "designer handbags" have customers at their tables year round. This popularity suggests that despite their lack of credentials, customers continue to be satisfied with experience goods.

SUPPLY-CHAIN BEST PRACTICES

Fashion marketers understand that consumers' loyalty to the product brand and the supplier (i.e., wholesaler, retailer) is dependent, in part, on trust. Consumers need to trust that the products they are purchasing are genuine. All fashion marketers, regardless of the size of the company, understand that deceiving the consumer of the product features will weaken customer loyalty and ultimately provide the competitors with a portion of their target market.

Fashion marketers at all levels within an organization (i.e., merchandisers, buyers, managers, sales representatives, sales associates, visual merchandisers) are able to play an active role in the minimization of counterfeit products that harm an organization. The following are examples of supply chain best practices for minimizing counterfeit products in an organization: fair trade, legitimate inputs, legitimate distribution, brand integrity, intellectual property, and counterfeit raids.

Practicing Fair Trade

Although the first portion of this chapter addressed the illegal side of the fashion marketing industry, it is important to recognize the **fair trade** side of the industry. Fair trade is a law designed to control the price of merchandise as it is sold along the channel of distribution (Ostrow & Smith, 1988). The essence of fair trade laws is to ensure that employees who are producing the products are paid a fair wage. Costs (typically from the employees' wages) of producing a product are not undercut, thereby passing on the savings to the consumer. Manufacturers that cut costs to the extreme operate sweatshops or employ children. Despite the fact that these practices are illegal, they still occur around the globe.

An increasing number of manufacturers and distributors nationally and internationally are focusing their fashion efforts on fair trade, regardless of the added cost to the consumer. Companies across Europe that support free trade include Marks & Spencer (United Kingdom) and La Redoute (France). Both companies feature merchandise lines that are all cotton. Higher proceeds will go to the cotton growers, ultimately in an attempt to give them better and fairer working conditions (Groves, 2006). Fair trade products are showing up in high-end lines and the mass market throughout the globe. LVMH purchased a portion of the fair trade clothing line EDUN (Bold, 2009). Fashion shows in London feature fair-trade fashions made from organic and

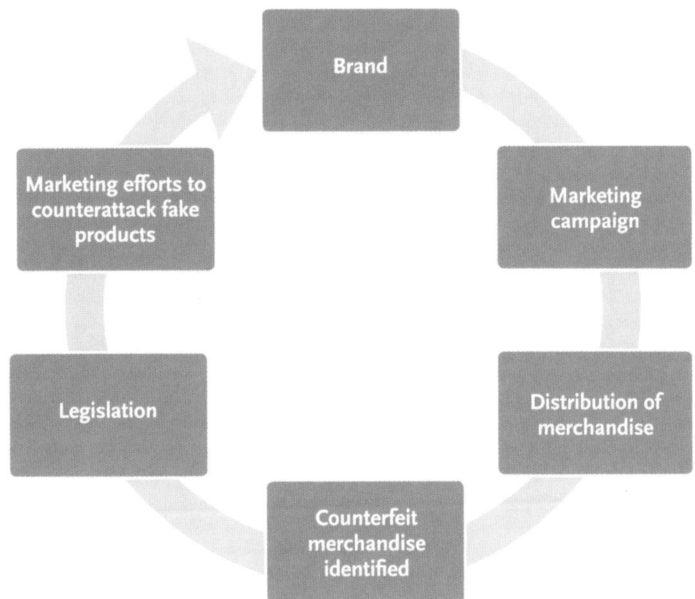

figure 11.4 Counterfeit products ultimately negatively influence the brand and consumers. The brand may be harmed. Additional marketing efforts may be required to counteract the counterfeit products. The additional expenses are then passed onto the consumer.

recycled matters (Hopkirk, 2008). Canberra, Australia promotes fair-trade fashions as part its fashion-related events (Dengate, 2008).

Securing Legitimate Inputs

Within any organization, written guidelines and regulations should be developed regarding where and from whom the merchandise buyers can purchase. A **guideline** is an indication or outline of policy or conduct. For example, a fashion marketing company may have a guideline that 30 percent of the overall products be made in the United States. Notice that the guideline doesn't state which products. The word *overall* also is an indicator that one department—for example, women's designer wear—could be 100-percent imported apparel. The merchandise buyers would still be following the guideline. Here is where regulations come into play.

A **regulation** is a rule that deals with details of procedure, one that company employees might be required to follow. Company regulations regarding securing legitimate inputs include (a) using only legitimate vendors (e.g., manufacturers, wholesalers), and (b) making employees liable for noncompliance with company regulations (Cordova, 2007).

Verifying Legitimacy of Distribution

Counterfeit organizations often target small retailers. They may combine a small percent of real products with the counterfeit products. The lower-priced merchandise is a selling point for the small retailers, who are often struggling to meet their profit margin. The retailer may be told that the supplier has a few products left; the supply is not large enough for larger retailers. As such, the price will be lowered for the small retailer. The small retailer purchases the counterfeit goods with the belief that they are real. In the long run, the counterfeit products harm the store's image (Wee, Tan & Cheok, 1995). Steps for verifying legitimate distributors and consumers include: (a) educating employees to identify real brands from counterfeit brands, (b) tracking high-volume purchases, and (c) tracking frequent purchases by cash (Wee, Tan & Cheok, 1995).

Monitoring Brand Integrity

Counterfeiters prey on the willingness for retailers and/or consumers to be ignorant of **brand integrity**. Brand integrity is the verification or authenticity of the brand. Brand integrity exists when the trademark is (1) registered with the customs authority, (2) possesses identification marks of its actual brand through the use of watermarks on documents, and (3) has barcodes and radio frequency identification (RFID) associated with the specific brand (Kort et al., 2006).

Intellectual Property

When they think of fashions, many consumers are brand, name, and label conscious. These consumers aren't necessarily luxury shoppers. Target, for instance, draws a strong target market for its Mossimo brand. Gap crosses income and age boundaries. Nordstrom offers a traditional department-store selection as well as an exclusive line of merchandise. Brands are an important attribute to fashion marketers and retailers. The characteristics of the brand are an important part of their marketing efforts. They significantly influence consumers' purchasing decisions. As such, companies are careful to protect brands, their designs, and product lines. For example, the start-up cost for Coach products is significant. The last thing Coach wants is another company to copy its brand's design and outsell its products. The **intellectual property** (e.g., design) must be protected if the product is to be profitable. In other words, the term *intellectual property* serves as a legal device to deter designs from being copied in their entirety. Intellectual property refers to the creation of an idea or product. Intellectual property includes: (a) trademarks, (b) copyrights, (c) design patents, (d) utility patents, and (e) trade secrets (Tucker & Caabona, 2006). Trademarks are distinct registered marks. Designers conduct a thorough search through the United States Patent and Trademark Office database in order to verify the company's desired trademark is not currently used by another company. Once verified, the trademark is registered. Fashion designers and marketers trademark their products to protect and build a brand image (Tucker & Casabona, 2006).

Under the intellectual property law, the following designs are considered intellectual property:

- Chanel's double *C*
- Dolce and Gabbana's *D&G*
- Gucci's buckle
- Prada's triangle with its name in the middle
- Pucci's print
- *YSL*

Can you identify other designs, trademarks, or distinctive registered marks that may be intellectual property?

Counterfeit Raids

The *Harper's Bazaar* Anticounterfeiting Summit began in 2005. Sponsored by *Harper's Bazaar* and the Kirkland & Ellis law firm, the annual summit is designed to identify methods for deterring counterfeit fashion products. During the 2006 summit, February was declared Anticounterfeiting Month. The Madison Avenue Blue initiative was revealed during the summit. The blue theme was based on the New York City Police Department (NYPD). Ten percent of all blue merchandise sold at specific retailers was donated to the NYPD Foundation. The foundation assists in undercover anticounterfeiting operations (Casabona, 2006).

Government organizations that organize raids on counterfeit rings include ICE and the U.S. Customs and Border Protection, which is part of the Department of Homeland Security (Tucker, 2007). Over a 24-month period, three separate operations imported over $700 million of fake merchandise. After a 19-month investigation, the counterfeiters, along with $230 million in merchandise, were caught. High-end counterfeit products included Chanel, Cartier, Gucci, and Louis Vuitton. Products replicating the highly sought-after brand, Nike, were also found (Tucker, 2007).

Although vendors on the sidewalk harm retailers, the massive number of counterfeiters and counterfeit products also create serious problems for the industry. A significant number of counterfeiters of fashion goods are produced in Asia and are imported into the United States or sold online (Tucker, 2007). Here's one example of fake products being sold through the Internet. During 2003, a man was selling items on eBay under the name "BurberryWorld." He offered a variety of Burberry products. Burberry's lawyers investigated the seller. They wanted to verify that he was selling actual Burberry products rather than counterfeit goods. The lawyers found out that the eBay seller was selling fake Burberry products as well as counterfeit products representing other luxury companies. Although the seller lives in the United States, he obtained the fake Burberry products in Thailand (Casabona, 2006).

Burberry's eBay monitoring program identified another seller, a person in Germany, selling counterfeit Burberry products on eBay. The fake goods came from the same source in Thailand. The German and American collaborated in BurberryWorld. The American received 27 months in jail. Under a German court, the German received 27 months in jail and the equivalent to $1.7 million in fines (Casabona, 2006).

The North Face and Polo Ralph Lauren are highly sought-after products throughout the United States and abroad. Although the two companies both offer apparel and some may say the same target market may purchase from both companies, The North Face and Polo Ralph Lauren are not considered direct fashion marketing competitors. Most companies, particularly fashion marketing companies, do not collaborate with other companies unless there is a humanitarian cause (e.g., breast cancer awareness) or effort that helps all companies involved. The North Face and Polo Ralph Lauren are an example of companies that collaborated to stop an $8 million annual ring selling counterfeit merchandise, including products from these very companies (Tucker, 2006a).

The counterfeit ring operated under the name of TC Fashions and SDT USA. Located in New York City's Garment District, the apparel looked authentic, with the exception of the labeling. Representatives from The North Face and Polo Ralph Lauren verified that the merchandise was counterfeit upon examining a label that incorrectly read "Made in China/ Fabriqué en Bangladesh." Once the counterfeiters were caught, eight million pieces of counterfeit fashions were found in the warehouse; the value was worth over $400 million retail. The counterfeiters sold 33 million garments annually to retailers nationwide (Tucker, 2006).

SUMMARY

Counterfeit products are typically those that are highly recognizable by consumers. Counterfeit merchandise is any product bearing an unauthorized trademark and thereby infringing upon the rights of the trademark owner under the law of the country of importation. These products may include designer brands, brands with a distinctive logo, and/or brands with a distinctive color combination. Examples of counterfeit merchandise include: (a) vanity fakes, (b) overruns, (c) condoned copies, and (d) self-copies. Legislation to deter the counterfeiting of fashion merchandise exists. The Federal Trademark Dilution Act, the Trade Dress Law, and the Violent Crime Control and Law Enforcement Act of 1994 exist to deter the counterfeiting of merchandise. Unfortunately, consumers willingly purchase the products. Excuses range from *I'm not hurting anyone* to *I'm helping small businesses.*

REFERENCES

Atkinson, N. (2009, June 6). How this jacket got jacked: In which our fashion editor plays the role of Erin Frockovitch. *National Edition*, p. WP6.

Baldauf, A. (2003). The brand of freedom. *Radical Society, 30*(3–4): 51–62

Barnett, J. M. (2005). Shopping for Gucci on Canal Street: Reflections on status consumption, intellectual property, and the incentive thesis. *Virginia Law Review, 91*: 1381–1423.

Beatty, P. (2008, February 1). A $22-billion problem. *National Post*, p. FP13.

Bezzegh, T. (2004). Main features of the harmonized European design law. *European Integration Studies, Miskolc, 4*: 3–8.

Bold, B. (2009, May 19). Bono and wife sell stake in fair trade clothing brand. *Brand Republic News Releases*. p. 1.

Casabona, L. (2006). Counterfeiting attack: Luxury retailers unit in major NYC initiatives. *Women's Wear Daily, 23*: 1.

Cocks, S. (2007). The hoods who move the goods: The examination of the booming international trade in luxury goods and an assessment of the American efforts to curtail its proliferation. *Fordham Intellectual Property Media & Entertainment Law Journal, 17*, 501–553.

Corcoran, C. T. (2007). Brands fight online deluge of counterfeit goods. *Women's Wear Daily, 193*(71): 10.

Cordova, E. B. (2007, August 13). Garment district rezoning plan stalls; landlords balk at new rules meant to save manufacturing. *Crain's New York Business*, p. 1.

Dengate, C. (2008, May 18). Fair traders to parade threads. *The Canberra Times*, p. 10.

Doyle, J. (2009, March 20). Vendor's hostages. *New York Post*. Retrieved November 30, 2009 from http://www.nypost.com/p/news/regional/vendor_hostages_Af3Cdy7MeCfGed2Kc7XyZP.

Eisend, M. and Schuchert-Creler, P. (2006). Explaining counterfeit purchases: a review and preview. *Academy of Marketing Science Review* (12). Retrieved July 3, 2007 from http://www.amsreveiw.org/articles/eisend/2-2006.pdf.

Galloni, A. (2006, January 31). Bagging fakers and sellers: Makers of luxury goods try new legal tactics against those who aid counterfeiters. *The Wall Street Journal*, B1.

Groves, E. (2006). Fair trade fashion takes off in Europe. *Women's Wear Daily, 191*(94), 6.

Hilton, B., Choi, C. J., & Chen, S. (2004). The ethics of counterfeiting in the fashion industry: quality, credence, and profit issues. *Journal of Business Ethics, 55*: 345–354.

Hopkirk, E. (2008, January 23). Green is the new black at London Fashion Week. *Evening Standard*, p. 25.

International Anticounterfeiting Coalition. (2009). The International Anticounterfeiting Coalition Web site. Retrieved July 8, 2009 from www.iacc.org/about/mission.php.

Kort, Peter M., Caulkins, J. P., Hartl, R. F., and Feichtinger, G. (2006). Brand image and brand dilution in the fashion industry. *Automatica*, 42: 1362–1370.

Lear, K. (2009, March 20). Personal interview.

Maldonado, R. T. (2002, September/October). Is that a Coach bag? Product configuration trade dress in the second circuit. The Buffalo State *Bulletin*, 2–5.

Mawson, N. (2008, July 7). On the tail of clothing counterfeiters. *Business Day*, p. 4.

de Mesa, A. (2006, October 16). "Brands fight the clone wars," *Brandchannel.com*. Retrieved February 7, 2009 from http:www.brandchannel.com/features_effects

Norquist, G. & Zahourek, K. (2008, September 28). Protecting our creative core. The Washington Times, p. B03.

103rd Congress, H. R. 3355 (2010). Violent Crime Control and Law Enforcement Act of 1994. Retrieved April 21, 2010 from http://frwebgate.access.gpo.gov/cgi-bin/getdoc.cgi?dbname=103_cong_bills&docid=f:h3355enr.txt.pdf.

104th Congress, H. R. 1295 (2010). Amendment to the Trademark Act of 1946. Retrieved April 21, 2010 from http://frwebgate.access.gpo.gov/cgi-bin/getdoc.cgi?dbname=104_cong_bills&docid=f:h1295eh.txt.pdf.

Ostrow, R., & Smith, S. R. (1988). *The Dictionary of Marketing*. New York: Fairchild Books.

Penz, E. & Stottinger, B. (2005). Forget the *real* thing—take the copy! An explanatory model for the volitional purchase of counterfeit products. *Advances in Consumer Research, 32*, 568–573.

Power, B. (2007, December 30). Imitation fashion if the finest form of value. *The Sunday Times*, p. 16.

Smith, S. (1997). Brand-name pirates plunder open borders. *The European, 19*: 4–5.

Sridhar, G. (2007). Countering counterfeits. *Indian Institute of Management. Conference Proceedings International Conference on Marketing and Society*. Retrieved May 31, 2007 from http://hdl.handle.net/2259/313.

Steele, A. (2009, October 3).Raids net 'designer' items, 3 merchants. *The Philadelphia Inquirer*, p. B02.

Tucker, R. (2006, March 1). Attacking counterfeits: Major ring broken up by Polo and North Face. *Women's Wear Daily, 191*(44), 1, 13.

Tucker, R. (2007, June 27). Busted! *Women's Wear Daily Online*. Retrieved June 27, 2008 from www.wwd.com/article.

Tucker, R. & Casabona, L. (2006, February 1). Fighting knockoffs by protecting a brand. *Women's Wear Daily, 191*(22), 12.

Wee, C-H., Tan, S-J., and Cheok, K-H. (1995). Non-price determinants of intention to purchase counterfeit goods: an exploratory study. *International Marketing Review, 12*(6), 19–46.

KEY TERMS

Define or briefly explain the following terms:

Boutique retailer ____________________

Brand integrity ____________________

Cognitive dissonance ____________________

Condoned copy ____________________

Credence goods ____________________

Design law ____________________

Experience goods ____________________

Fair trade ____________________

The Federal Trademark Dilution Act (FTDA) ____________________

Guideline ____________________

Intellectual property ____________________

Overruns ____________________

Product ____________________

Regulation ____________________

Search goods ____________________

Self-copies ____________________

Trade Dress Law ____________________

Vanity fake ____________________

CLASS OR TEAM DISCUSSION QUESTIONS

1 | One method of verifying that a product is not counterfeit is through brand identity. Discuss the steps you, as consumers, have undertaken to verify that the merchandise you are purchasing is not counterfeit. As a consumer, do you look the other way at counterfeit merchandise in order to get a better deal? Explain why or why not.

____

____

2 | Vanity fakes have low intrinsic value and low perceived product value. Can this type of product be marketed successfully in the fashion industry? If so, list the names of fashion products that are included in the vanity fake category.

---

3 | Despite the laws and regulations designed to deter counterfeit fashion merchandise, consumers nationally and internationally can obtain counterfeit fashion merchandise at a fraction of the price of a genuine product. In your opinion, is counterfeiting a significant problem in the fashion industry?

INTERNET ACTIVITIES

1 | Using the Internet as a resource, find five different examples of self-copies. Provide reasons why these particular companies would market fashions using self-copies.

---

2 | Select a company and fashion product category. Using the Internet as a resource, find documentation of fashion counterfeiting efforts. Discuss the following:

The products involved

The company the counterfeit products negatively affected

Any legal actions that were taken against the counterfeiters

The impact on consumers (e.g., number of consumers purchasing the counterfeit products)

STUDY QUESTIONS

1 | What is a vanity fake?

2 | Explain the design law. How does this law help retailers and fashion marketers?

3 | What are some of the reasons consumers purchase counterfeit fashion products?

4 | What is an overrun?

5 | What is the purpose of the ethics law?

6 | Provide an explanation for buying a knock-off brand.

7 | How does intellectual property influence the fashion industry?

8 | How do the Violent Crime Control and Law Enforcement Act of 1994 influence actions in the fashion industry?

9 | What is a condoned copy?

10 | What is a self-copy?

11 | What is the purpose of the Federal Trademark Dilution Act?

12 | Define *ethics.*

MULTIPLE-CHOICE QUESTIONS

1 | What types of fashion products do counterfeiters prefer?

a. High-end designer names
b. Store brands
c. Unknown brand names
d. All of the above (*a*, *b*, and *c*)

2 | _____ is a law that protects the design of a product or article from being copied.

a. Counterfeit law
b. Design law
c. Copycat law
d. Ethics law

3 | Vanity fakes are marketed products that have _____.

a. Low intrinsic value and low perceived product value
b. Low intrinsic value and high perceived product value
c. High intrinsic value and high perceived product value
d. High intrinsic value and low perceived product value

4 | _____ are products that are similar to the original product but not exactly the same.

a. Vanity fakes
b. Overrun
c. Knockoffs
d. Counterfeit merchandise

5 | A(n) _____ is a copy made by other designers or fashion houses.

a. Condoned copy
b. Vanity copy
c. Knockoff
d. Overrun

TRUE-OR-FALSE QUESTIONS

1 | _____ The piracy of fashion products exists in the twenty-first century.

2 | _____ Counterfeit products can be classified into four areas.

3 | _____ Consumers rarely purchase a counterfeit product as a result of the product's physical attributes.

TABLE 12.1

THE Market Planning PROCESS

step 1	CHAPTER 2	Be inspired; become passionate regarding a product/service; be driven to succeed and committed to working toward a goal.
step 2	CHAPTER 3	Intrinsic attributes of the products and services are marketed in terms of value, satisfaction, and quality. Building upon the mission statement, in this step you will make decisions regarding the pricing, communication, value, satisfaction, and quality associated with the purchase or the products and/or services.
step 3	CHAPTER 4	Identify a comprehensive list of products and services offered by the company.
step 4	CHAPTER 5	Examine the products and services component of the core marketing concept related to the trickle-down theory, media and celebrities, and the belongingness theory.
step 5	CHAPTER 6	Examine the buying season in relation to the marketing process.
step 6	CHAPTER 7	Examine marketing methods of targeting the consumer.
step 7	CHAPTER 8	Examine the methods of exchange and relationships with the consumers. This includes making decisions to sell products and services through brick-and-mortar retail operations, direct marketing, and the Internet.
step 8	CHAPTER 9	Examine the image and brands of the company in relation to marketing efforts.
step 9	CHAPTER 10	Conduct a market analysis of how companies are able to successfully cross product boundaries.
step 10	CHAPTER 11	Examine trends in the fashion industry regarding a) counterfeit merchandise and b) the impact of such merchandise on the industry's sales, profits, product design, consumers' attitudes.
step 11	**CHAPTER 12**	**Conduct a market analysis of fashions in the global environment in order to determine impact to the company's existing marketing efforts.**

12

Marketing Fashions Globally

chapter objectives

After reading this chapter, you should be able to understand Step Eleven of the Market Planning Process. This includes being able to:

+ Grasp the importance of global fashion marketing efforts.

+ Comprehend the sequential steps associated with the decision to enter a global marketplace.

+ Understand the influence that cultural, social, and environmental factors have on global fashion marketing efforts.

+ Examine methods of entering a global marketplace.

+ Apply various methods of entering a global marketplace.

+ Discriminate between correct and incorrect global fashion marketing campaign guidelines.

+ Integrate important phases of human nature into the global fashion marketing efforts.

+ Evaluate the success of global fashion marketing efforts.

"Being powerful is like being a lady. If you have to tell people you are, you aren't." —Margaret Thatcher

Margaret Thatcher was the first female prime minister of the United Kingdom. She demonstrated her power every day as she ran the country. Like Thatcher, fashion companies that market products globally demonstrate their power through their actions. Public relations, promotions, and advertising efforts throughout the nation and in different portions of the globe demonstrate the company's (1) ability to adapt to different regions and cultures, (2) financial well-being, and (3) ability to gain consumer acceptance for its products and services.

By 2015, China is expected to exceed the United States in sales of luxury goods. This prediction is based on China's growing population and wealth (Lertora, 2007). Twelve percent of all luxury goods are sold in China; this makes the country the "world's third largest consumer of luxury goods" (Lertora, 2007, p. 109).

Consumers enjoy designer brands as a form of recognition of wealth (i.e., conspicuous consumption). The status symbol of designer brands provides an acknowledgment of wealth, success, and power (Lertora, 2007). An example of companies responding to the growing fashion target market in China is Dior's expansion to Beijing. During 2008, Dior marketed its brand and fashions in Beijing. An art exhibit of Chinese history was blended into the history of Dior's fashions (McLaughlin, 2008). By incorporating China's history, Dior was paying tribute to the country and its heritage and thanking the country for its hospitality. This form of promotion and marketing goes a very long way in building long-term relationships with new global business ventures. It also tells Chinese consumers that Dior cares about their country.

Fashion has become an important part of the culture in Latin America, Africa, and Asia, as well as in the West (Hansen, 2004). The United States and Europe dominate the fashion industry. Key cities include New York, Los Angeles, Tokyo, London, and Paris (Nurchai, 2002). The globalization of fashion markets will have a definite impact on the future trends of fashion marketing in the luxury market. The United States, Italy, Europe, and Japan are established luxury fashion markets. Russia, India, and China are emerging as important fashion markets (Betts, 2007).

Consumers will increasingly want the "new-and-improved" version as well as the "one-of-a-kind" fashion, style, or design. Separating themselves from other consumers through products, fashions, and experiences will become yet another way to express value and importance. The new version of luxury will be defined as a one-of-a kind experience where money is no object to have fashion that only you possess (Betts, 2007). Men and women throughout the world spend billions on fashion. Teens and children, most of whom are not gainfully employed, significantly influence how much their parents purchase. The fashion industry sells in excess of $750 billion of retail globally. As the desire for fashions grows, so does the intensity of fashion marketing efforts. At no other time in history has there been a greater number of fashion marketers working on an international scale. Fashion merchandise is being promoted in creative ways that adapt to the cultural and regional differences of each country (Box 12.1). The products may remain the same; however, the method in which the marketing message is delivered is carefully crafted to ensure successful delivery and acceptance to the global market. It would be an enormous financial mistake to assume that all fashion marketing efforts can be duplicated regardless of the country and product. Likewise, not all marketing efforts need to be reinvented simply because the market in that venue (i.e., country) has expanded.

DECISIONS ASSOCIATED WITH THE GLOBAL MARKET

The U.S. market is the largest consumer (i.e., developed) market in the world. Yet it is unrealistic to believe that one fashion marketer can capture the entire market. That is, it is highly improbable that 100 percent of all consumers within the United States in a specific demographic and psychographic target market will purchase a manufacturer's fashions and stay loyal to that manufacturer's fashions for their lifetime. Fashion marketers have a predetermined goal regarding the amount of the target market they try to obtain from their efforts. The goal may range from 2 to 50 percent depending on their existing market share. Regardless of the success of their marketing efforts, obtaining 100 percent of the U.S. market is unrealistic. **Can you think of any fashion product that 100 percent of consumers will purchase?** Capturing some of the global market is, however, very realistic.

A **global organization**, one that operates in more than one country, earns multiple benefits. The obvious reason for operating and marketing products is to expand the company's brand, category, and/or corporate dominance. As the company expands throughout the globe, its goal is to capture an increasing amount of the global market share.

Domestic fashion marketing—marketing fashions in your home country—is undertaken to stimulate product recognition and sales in your home country. **Global fashion marketing**

figure 12.1
Designers are expanding the size of the target market throughout the globe.

Karen Hiter (marketing manager) and Sonya Ingram (general manager) at HandPicked work with Mexico to bring unique products to their consumer.

BOX 12.1 HandPicked's Global Model for Artisans

Karen Hiter (left), marketing manager, and Sonya Ingram (right), general manager, of HandPicked realize the value of making global connections. For the past 20 years, the company has developed a deep connection to Mexico. Gifted silver jewelry artisans were discovered, yet they had few opportunities to export their crafts. HandPicked's merchandising team has continued to work with the same artisans. These artisans and their families make unique, one-of-a-kind jewelry. The fashions are in such high demand that the company has evolved from showing their merchandise solely at trunk shows to operating 13 stores in three states. The working relationship between the artisans in Mexico and HandPicked has evolved into an appreciation for the artisans' livelihood, families, and culture. They have become part of the HandPicked extended family. As Hiter explains, "Because so much of our products are handcrafted, and we have a long-term relationship with our artisans, it is not like a traditional international buying situation. We protect our artisans. They are part of our team" (Hiter, 2009).

occurs when manufacturers and/or retailers expand their efforts to other countries. These efforts provide global exposure and increased sales and profits. Prior to undertaking global fashion marketing, social and cultural characteristics should be taken into consideration. Marketing activities that are undertaken domestically cannot automatically be used globally. Marketing messages used in one country may be misunderstood in a different country. The risk of misinterpretation of marketing efforts must be considered prior to the implementation of the marketing message.

Globalization of the fashion industry is not a new concept. During the late twentieth century, the globalization of the fashion industry accelerated at a frenzied pace. Technology linked the fashion industry and consumers throughout the world. As the ability to reach areas around the world grew, the smaller companies within the fashion industry realized they could grow through marketing to other countries.

figure 12.2
The steps required to enter the global fashion marketing environment are sequential in nature. The time required a company stays at each step is dependent upon the company's size, resources (e.g., employees, funds), and adversity to risk.

Nine sequential steps should be taken when entering the global marketplace. They include: (1) review the global market environment, (2) decide to enter the global marketplace, (3) select the global marketplace, (4) decide how to enter the market, (5) select a global marketing plan, (6) select a global marketing organization, (7) implement the global marketing plan, (8) evaluate results of the global marketing plan, and (9) make decisions on further global plans based on current results.

The speed in which a company makes these decisions is dependent on a number of variables. Make no mistake, each decision is very important; the outcome can result in winning or losing the company millions (and perhaps billions) in profits. The outcome can also influence how the target market and the competition view the company. Mistakes may be made. It is up to the company to verify that the mistakes are minor and not recognized by the public.

Step One: Review the Global Market Environment

The first step consists of the company reviewing the global marketing environment. In order to successfully conduct business in any country, a company must have a comprehensive understanding of the governmental regulations involved in that particular country's **trade system**. Tariffs, quotas, and exchange controls must be identified in advance. A **tariff** is a tax imposed by the foreign government. **Quotas** identify the limit of merchandise imported into the foreign country. **Exchange controls** limit the foreign exchange; they are a "method used by a government to regulate foreign trade" (Ostrow & Smith, 1988, p. 90). These three types of government regulations—tariffs, quotas, and exchange controls—are common aspects of global marketing. It is, however, imperative that the domestic company have all the information identified during the first step.

The cultural and social characteristics of a country are an important part of the global marketing environment. Regardless of the fashion category, cultural and social implications will influence the decision to enter the global marketplace. Companies that have mind-sets like *Fashion is alike around the world*, or *We don't need to change the way we do business to fit the environment* will probably fail in the global marketplace. Global marketing messages may be similar and in some cases identical to the domestic marketing campaigns. How companies conduct business on a global business scale is completely different. When a business enters a global marketplace, it must respect and respond to the cultural and social values, beliefs, and needs of the host country. If these cannot be met, the best and brightest marketing campaign will not be effective.

As you think about international companies wanting to enter the United States, how would you answer the following questions?

- Are the cultural beliefs throughout the United States the same or even similar? If not, how are they different? How would the different beliefs influence fashion marketing efforts?
- Can you identify social values that are (1) similar and (2) different in different regions in the United States? If social values throughout the United States vary, do you believe that social values vary throughout other countries? How would you, as a fashion marketer located in the United States, learn about these social values?
- An important part of fashion marketing consists of understanding the needs and wants of a target market. What are some methods of clearly and accurately assessing a global market's needs and wants? How can you be sure you aren't being biased because you are fond of the country as a tourist?

Step Two: Decide to Enter the Global Marketplace

Throughout the second step, the company decides whether expanding marketing efforts on a global basis is in the company's best interest. Earlier in this chapter we discussed the rapid pace at which companies are expanding globally. **As you think about your favorite fashion designer or manufacturer, can you identify any that haven't expanded globally?** With the advent of the Internet, it seems like fashion marketers are expanding globally so fast that there are no longer any solely domestic fashion marketers. In actuality, it is acceptable to *just say no* and stay domestic. Not all companies are ready financially, logistically, or perhaps even emotionally, to expand globally. You may ask what emotions have to do with expansion. Technically, emotions should *always* stay out of the equation when making business decisions. However, small domestic fashion companies may wish to stay small based on emotional, rather than financial or logistical, reasons.

Let's say your company is emotionally ready to take the global leap. Your organization also realizes that you are unable to capture a larger portion of the domestic market share. In addition, an increase in the number of domestic competitors (both through brick-and-mortar stores and the Internet) continues to challenge marketing results. If sales and profits are to grow substantially, expanding globally is the logical choice.

Once the decision is made to take the company global, an assessment of the company's personnel should be made. Employees at a variety of levels with the following skills will be needed: (a) expertise in international marketing, (b) knowledge of exporting, (c) knowledge of the specific cultural and social environment(s), (d) knowledge of the specific political environment(s), and (e) the ability to work with foreign nationals.

Step Three: Select the Global Marketplace

Specific global markets are selected during the third step. In Chapter One, Introduction to Fashion Marketing, the importance of the company's mission statement is addressed. Regardless of which marketing activities, domestic or global, a fashion company undertakes, the mission, goals, and objectives must always be considered. The company's mission rarely changes. Goals and objectives can be set in different time frames. Typical time frames include goals for one, five, and ten years. Marketing goals for the domestic company are not necessarily identical to the global marketing goals. Individual goals are based on marketing criteria such as current market share, prior sales, and consumer spending patterns.

The number of global markets to enter is chosen during this stage. A company can choose to market broad and narrow, broad and deep, narrow and deep, or narrow and shallow. The fashion marketing efforts may vary depending on the fashion products, the composition of the target market within a country, and potential impacts on consumers' purchasing behaviors.

Marketing broad and deep is the result of a company marketing intensely across multiple countries. This type of global effort requires strong logistical, financial, managerial, and marketing efforts. Companies that successfully market broad and deep on a global basis are large, well-established organizations. Examples of such companies include Ferragamo, Gucci, Hermès, Prada, and Versace.

Narrow and deep fashion marketing can be used successfully when a company first attempts to enter the global marketplace. A narrow and deep strategy emphasizes a few countries. The deep strategy includes an integrated method of marketing to a narrow number of countries. The marketing campaigns are continually focused on this narrow region. For example, Baby Phat is sold throughout the United States. However, the company's Web site offers the information in six different languages. The global nature of the Web site provides the fashion marketing efforts expansive opportunities beyond traditional geographic borders.

A narrow and shallow marketing strategy exists when one or a few countries are chosen. The marketing campaign is limited. This method of globalization typically results in wasting the company's money. The marketing effort does not reach enough of the target market. The frequency and timing of the efforts are not effective or strong enough to make an impact on purchasing behavior.

As you select a global marketplace, it is important to conduct a SWOT analysis of the region. As discussed in Chapter Six, "The Buying Process," a SWOT analysis is the examination of strengths, weaknesses, opportunities, and threats facing the company. Access the Internet and identify information to answer the following questions:

- Which fashion companies (regardless of their country of origin) have a significant global presence?
- Does length of time in business influence global presence?
- Does the product offering influence global presence?

Step Four: Decide How to Enter the Market

After a company has decided that marketing its fashions globally is in its best interest, a

figure 12.3
The Prada store combines the elegance of the brand with the international architecture of the culture. Infusing itself into the international culture, Prada is able to expand its brand into new international markets.

decision must be made regarding how to enter the market. Three popularly used methods for entering the global market include: (1) exporting, (2) licensing, and (3) direct investment. The decision is typically based on the amount of risk the company is willing to take.

EXPORTING

Exporting occurs when a company sends its products to another country and sells them through an intermediary. **Indirect exporting** exists when the company hires an independent international organization to complete the transaction. Indirect exporting is often a beneficial method of operation for small companies or organizations that are new to global fashion marketing efforts. The independent international organization is responsible for hiring and coordinating overseas employees. Because the independent international organization is an expert within the international market, it brings a wealth of information, skill, and talent to the exporting company. The expenses associated with paying the independent international organization are often outweighed by the risks avoided.

A second option with exporting is **direct exporting**. Direct exporting occurs when the fashion marketing company is responsible for exporting, global distribution, sales, and promotion. Direct exporting gives the exporter greater control over its activities. However the company also assumes the risk associated with the global environment. A variety of agencies exist to assist businesses with exporting and importing. Each agency oversees a different set of activities. A summary of the agencies is provided in Table 12.2.

LICENSING

Licensing is a popular method of marketing fashions globally. Licensing is "an agreement between the creator of a product or line of products and a manufacturer in which the creator (licensor) gives the manufacturer (licensee) permission to use his name in the marketing of a product in return for a royalty, usually computed as a percentage of sales" (Ostrow & Smith, 1988, p. 134).

DIRECT INVESTMENT

The most popular method of entering a global market is **direct investment**. Fashion marketing companies involved with direct investment are physically located in the global marketplace. The company has global distribution, sales, and marketing operations. Direct investment has the greatest amount of risk associated with global marketing. Changing exchange rates, government interactions, cultural and societal nuances, and the enormous financial requirements associated with a direct investment may deter fashion marketers from choosing this method of entering the global marketplace.

Step Five: Selecting a Global Marketing Plan

The global marketing plan is identified in the fifth step of the global marketing process. Two global marketing strategies exist. Companies can use a **standardized marketing mix** or an **adapted marketing mix**. A standardized marketing mix is identical to the marketing mix used for the domestic market. Advantages of this program are that it is cost efficient from a creative standpoint, it provides continuity, and it eases implementation. Technology, specifically the Internet, is used in standardized marketing mixes. The Internet allows the company to compensate for differences in language yet maintain content and context.

A standardized marketing mix may not work in all global marketplaces. The specific country may influence the marketing mix's (a) effectiveness, (b) quality, (c) cost, and (d) implementation. When a standardized marketing mix is not deemed appropriate, companies use an adapted marketing mix. As the name suggests, this marketing mix is adapted to fit the needs of the target market. Changes in the mix are made in order to

TABLE 12.2

Export Assistance

ORGANIZATION AND WEB SITE	FEATURES
ATA Carnets http://www.atacarnets.org	• Acronym for *Admission Temporaire—Temporary Admission* • Allows the company to import merchandise duty free and tax free temporarily up to one year • International customs documents
U.S. Customs and Border Protection http://www.cbp.gov	• Part of the Department of Homeland Security. • One division assists in securing and faciliting trade and travel.
U.S. Department of Commerce http://www.commerce.gov	• Provides information and training on exporting
Export-Import Bank of the United States http://www.exim.gov	Offers: • Small business portal • Country Limitation Schedule • Seminars & symposia • Information for domestic exporters and international buyers
Office of Textiles and Apparel (OTEXA) http://www.otexa.ita.doc.gov	Offers information on: • Trade data • Federal register notices • Earned import allowances • Free trade agreements • Webinars • Labeling requirements
International Trade Administration (ITA) http://www.ita.doc.gov	• Ensures fair trade • Promotes trade and investment
U.S. Small Business Administration http://www.sba.gov	• Assists and protects small businesses • Strengthens the economy through the promotion of small businesses
U.S. Department of State, http://www.state.gov	• Conducts the U.S. Agency for International Development • Explains trade policy and programs • Provides business support

capture a broader and deeper number of the market share. Profits generated from the results of these marketing efforts are perceived to be worth the costs incurred from making the changes to the mix.

Step Six: Select a Global Marketing Organization

During the sixth step of the global marketing process, a global marketing organization is selected. The amount of time, expertise, and experience a company has in the global environment will influence the type of organization selected. Three types of global marketing organizations exist: (a) an **export department**, (b) an international division, and (c) a global organization. An export department consists of an export manager and several personnel. This department is responsible for coordinating exporting efforts. Implementing an export department is the logical extension once exporting efforts are successful.

As the size and intensity of a company's exporting activities increase, the resources of the export department may be stretched. The export department may realize that it is not able to serve the growing global needs of the company. An **international division** is another type of global marketing organization to consider. An international division consists of company personnel from each unit working together in an effort to operate global efforts more effectively and profitably. Marketing, distribution, finance, and research are examples of the areas represented by personnel in the international division.

The largest type of global marketing organization is a global organization. Global organizations have entire global operations in multiple countries. Their brand and marketing efforts are implemented on a global basis. Rather than thinking of the company as being based in their national country, the company is viewed as being dominant in multiple countries. Examples of global organizations include Burberry (Box 12.2), Ralph Lauren, Dior, and Chanel.

Step Seven: Implement the Global Marketing Plan

Once a global marketing organization has been selected, it is time to implement the global marketing plan. The implementation of the global marketing plan is similar to that of a domestic marketing plan. That is, the marketing team prepares (1) a time line of when each promotional piece is to be distributed, (2) a geographic distribution of each marketing piece, and (3) a detailed plan of how and who will implement each marketing piece. In essence, the implementation of the global

figure 12.4 Chanel is a global organization. Regardless of the country the store is located or the marketing effort, Chanel maintains a consistent brand and image.

BOX 12.2 Globalization of Burberry

As a luxury brand known around the world, Burberry's red, black, beige, and white plaid pattern has become synonymous with classic styling, quality craftsmanship, and functional apparel design for men and women. The Prorsum horse is recognizable as the icon logo for the brand. Begun in England in 1856 by Thomas Burberry, the company's first product was the trench coat. The trench coat continues to be one of the company's best-selling products around the globe. Other fashions offered by the company include menswear, women's wear, children's wear, accessories, fragrances, and gifts.

In order to stay competitive in an increasingly challenging global market, Burberry maintains four marketing initiatives; these include: (1) capitalize on existing positioning, (2) maintain brand momentum, (3) rebalance the product portfolio in order to create design innovations, and (4) maintain leadership in the outerwear industry. Focusing on these four marketing initiatives helps Burberry maintain global fashion dominance in a rapidly changing market (Burberry, 2009).

The classic Burberry trench coat is a best seller. The coat is available in men's and women's styles and sized for European and American fit.

marketing plan is a carefully crafted time line of when and how global consumers will be introduced to marketing efforts.

Step Eight: Evaluate Results of the Global Marketing Plan

At the end of a fashion marketing campaign, the effectiveness of the efforts is evaluated. The evaluation is based on goals determined in Step Two, "Decide to Enter the Global Marketplace." The number and degree to which the goals were achieved and the mistakes made are examined. Throughout this stage of the global marketing effort, the team examines which actions to repeat and which actions to change. Regardless of the level of success, the team always looks to how to improve efforts.

The importance and methods of marketing fashions were addressed throughout

figure 12.5
The Giorgio Armani Corporation realized the impact of international travel on marketing and sales. The company operates retail stores in the Hong Kong airport.

Chapter Three, "Product, Price, Distribution, and Placement"; Chapter Four, "Public Relations, Promotion, and Advertising"; and Chapter Five, "Fashion and the Entertainment Industry."

As you view international fashion marketing efforts on the Internet, how would you evaluate the following?

- How easy is it to locate and examine international fashions using an international designer's or manufacturer's Web site? Give an example.
- What are the challenges of placing international fashions on a Web site?
- Effective communication in a marketing campaign is essential if consumers are to act upon the message (i.e., purchase the product). Identify an advertisement that clearly communicates its message. Describe the message. Explain why the advertisement is a success.
- Identify an advertisement that does not communicate its message well. How would you change the marketing message?

Step Nine: Make Decisions on Further Global Plans

The evaluation of forthcoming global plans is a process. The company must continually examine the economic climate of existing global markets, potential global markets, competition, and the company's resources, as well as its long and short-term goals. A careful examination of these issues will help the company decide if expanding global marketing efforts is in the company's best interest. Companies such as Kenzo, Gucci, and Armani are expanding throughout the globe. Gucci is entering into the Munich and Budapest markets (Zargani, 2008). Armani is marketing to travelers by opening shops in Hong Kong's airport. The designer anticipates strong sales by weary travelers waiting for delayed planes (Zargani, 2009).

GLOBAL FASHION MARKETING GUIDELINES

Global fashion marketers' actions are significantly different than they are for domestic marketing campaigns. Unlike when working on a domestic marketing campaign, global fashion marketers must carefully examine cultural and symbolic meanings of colors, shapes, and symbols. Global fashion marketers cannot automatically assume that the global market will understand the visual or written messages of the public relations, promotions, and/or advertising campaign. Differences between countries or regions may result in significant marketing errors or, conversely, the satisfaction of consumers.

A global market does not automatically accept a marketing campaign simply because (a) the product is needed, (b) the company is successful, or (c) the marketing efforts are successful in the home country. Following global marketing guidelines will help the fashion marketer's campaign.

Guidelines for developing a global marketing campaign include:

- Market globally; act locally.
- Don't assume you are an expert on the country.
- Cross-translate messages.
- Acknowledge national holidays.
- Work well in advance with all government agencies.
- Identify any promotional methods not allowed.
- Remember you are a guest in their country.

Market Globally; Act Locally

The phrase *market globally; act locally* means exactly that—cultural, social, geographic, and political considerations must be taken into consideration when planning a fashion marketing effort.

Rule number one when planning a global fashion marketing effort: Take the local community into consideration. Rule number two when planning a global fashion marketing effort: Take the local community into consideration. This may sound redundant, and it is.

What is amazing is how many marketing plans fail because fashion marketers either ignore or forget the rules.

Don't Assume You Are an Expert on the Country

Assumptions can be dangerous. Unless you have lived your entire life in the country and are an expert in the fashion marketing industry in that particular country, don't assume you have all the answers. The president of the United States has an advisory board for a reason—to gain insight from other learned persons. Even the smartest persons in any industry seek out advice. So, too, should fashion marketers when entering global markets. The person or persons providing assistance should ideally be foreign nationals. A foreign national is a citizen of that particular country. He or she is extremely knowledgeable of the country's cultural, societal, and political background. Information and advice can be provided regarding marketing messages and visuals.

Cross-Translate Messages

Do you remember playing a game where you would tell a friend a message and the friend would pass on the message? By the time the secret was passed on to 20 people, the message was completely distorted. Now think of a $20 million fashion marketing campaign in China. After a careful survey, the marketing team is confident that the Chinese market will readily accept the fashions. Billboards, fashion shows, and print advertisements have been designed and implemented. Expensive marketing mistakes may harm the brand. Hiring an interpreter to cross-check the written and verbal portions of the marketing efforts are well worth the time and effort.

Gucci is very familiar with cross-translating fashion marketing messages. The company has stores in New York, Rome, Munich, Hong Kong, London, Shanghai, and mainland China (Kaiser, 2009). The fashion marketing efforts and their messages are adapted to the different cultures.

If you are marketing fashions primarily in the United States but have a Web presence internationally, accurate translation of your marketing message is vital. The translations are always important; what makes them even more important, however, is the fact that the company doesn't have a physical location in the international location. The Web presence is representing your entire company.

figure 12.6
Originating in Italy, Gucci has expanded into an international fashion designer, manufacturer, and retailer.

Acknowledge National Holidays

Various holidays of the host country may not be obvious to the fashion marketer. It is important to understand the holiday's purpose, its symbolic meaning, and how the citizens celebrate. Throughout the United States, fashion marketers use national holidays as a reason for marketing during a specific day, week, or month. This may not be the case in other countries. Indeed, in some countries the citizens may believe it is vulgar to promote the fashions based on a national holiday. Always know when to introduce a fashion to the market and when not to introduce a fashion to the market. Likewise, countries may use products and/or colors as symbolic meanings. It is important to have a clear understanding and respect for the country's beliefs. Positive beliefs may be incorporated into the fashion marketing efforts.

Work Well in Advance with All Government Agencies

Expanding marketing efforts globally takes time, money, effort, and a lot of interaction with government agencies. Companies don't accomplish this within a few months. The planning can take years. The more countries involved, the more complex the planning. The marketing rewards are also greater. Recall our discussion at the beginning of the chapter on the limited number of viable market shares that a company can obtain in the United States. Companies continue to remember this during the global expansion process. It takes time, but the rewards can be enormous.

Identify the Most Applicable Promotional Methods

Different cities are well suited for different marketing efforts. For example, Times Square in New York is filled with electric billboards. The flashing lights encourage consumers to purchase from Target, New Balance, Skechers, Swatch, and Foot Locker. Now some people may say that Manhattan, Kansas, is just as fashionable and exciting as Manhattan, New York. However, you won't find the same level of fashion marketing efforts. There aren't the same number of electric billboards; millions of people don't walk past the marketing efforts 24 hours a day. In fact, the only thing the same about Manhattan, Kansas, and Manhattan, New York, is their names. Different marketing venues are accustomed to promoting fashions in each city. This is also true when marketing fashions globally. Some countries may respond better to print efforts, whereas others respond better to electronic efforts. Understanding the host country's preferences for learning about fashions is essential to the success of the fashion marketing efforts. Learn what magazines

figure 12.7
Times Square is internationally known for its massive billboards.

the consumers read, if they are technologically savvy (e.g., Do they use YouTube? Do they text message their friends?), how much television they watch, which shows they watch, and the influence U.S. culture has on their purchasing behavior.

Remember That You Are a Guest in Their Country

When a fashion marketing team goes global, multiple entities benefit. The fashion designer, manufacturer, and retailer benefit through global expansion. Additional fashions will be marketed and sold; brand loyalty will be strengthened. Long-term profits will be generated nationally and globally. Consumers in the global market will have access to new fashions. The host country generates income from the marketing and sales revenue. In short, all parties benefit from global expansion of the fashion industry. With all the hype about fashion and business, it is very important to remember that the fashion marketer is a guest in the host country. Regardless of the amount of money being generated and the demand for the fashions by consumers, respect for the host country's laws, culture, and society should be maintained. Marketing U.S. fashion in a host country does not mean changing the host country into the United States, nor does it mean disregarding the host country's beliefs, culture, or societal structure. It does mean that regardless of the country's laws, the fashion marketer does not make statements against the state. If the fashion marketer has a problem with the state, then the fashion marketer should not market to the country. Double standards aren't good in any walk of life.

Implications of Marketing Fashion Globally

Marketing fashion globally has a hierarchical perspective. Certain characteristics must be taken into consideration in a sequential order. Unlike the nine rules to fashion marketing, these perspectives are not rules or guidelines. Perspectives are considerations; they include attributes, beliefs, stereotypes about your company and/or country, and perhaps even problems your company has encountered by entering global markets in the past.

The triangle in Figure 12.8 represents the three phases of human nature. The model has

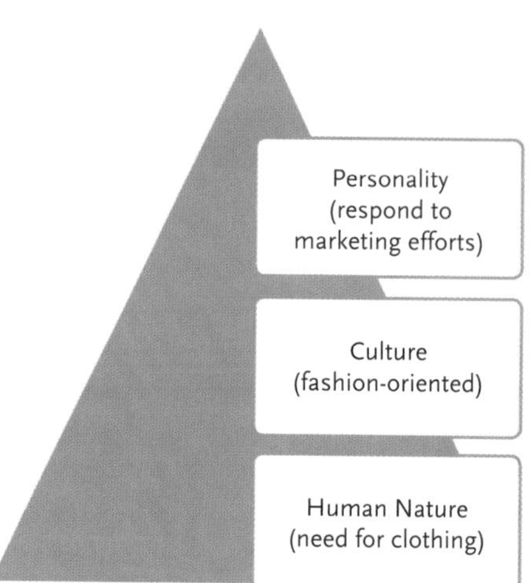

Adapted from "What is Culture," http://blue.butler.edu/~jfmcgrat/culture.htm

figure 12.8
Phases of Cultural Marketing Efforts.

been modified to represent implications of global fashion marketing. In the first phase, *Human Nature*, all persons require clothing. Clothing provides us with protection from the elements. It can be said that not everyone cares about fashion, nor does everyone understand fashion. Fashion marketing efforts do not influence everyone. In the second phase, *Culture*, fashion-oriented consumers may read *Women's Wear Daily*, attend fashion shows, and search the Internet for international designers' latest creations. *Personality*, phase three, occurs when marketing efforts stimulate the fashion-oriented consumer to act. Purchases are made; product and brand loyalty is generated.

Now think about the implications of marketing fashions globally. The world is filled with consumers who wear clothing. Granted, not everyone will want or need your fashions, but even a small portion of the market can significantly impact the financial and historical implications of your company. Also think about the culture. In Chapter Seven, "Targeting the Fashion Consumer," the importance of target markets, demographics, psychographics, and market segmentation was addressed. Level Two, "Culture," is similar, but with an expanded emphasis. Additional information is required because you are working in a global environment—specifically, a host country where you may not be as familiar with the target market. Learn as much about the culture as possible. Personalities of the consumers in the host country may differ from those in the United States. That doesn't mean they won't respond to fashions or fashion marketing efforts. It simply means it is important to understand the personalities. Once you understand them, you, as the fashion marketer, can reach them.

figure 12.9 Target's Go International concept featured fast fashions with an international flair.

DESIRE FOR INTERNATIONAL FASHIONS

Prior to the 1970s, consumers had limited access to international fashions except through fashions shown in magazines or on television. International fashions for the mass market were typically from Mexico, China, or Hong Kong. The inexpensive garments were not necessarily fashionable, nor did they properly fit the U.S. body-sizing standards. As such, fashion marketers had difficulties promoting the fashions in favorable ways. During this same time, Italian and French designers had not yet begun to market to different market segments. They stayed close to their existing target market segment.

Over the past three decades, fashion marketers realized that travel significantly influenced both the products they could obtain and the number of international market segments. Advanced modes of travel have allowed fashion marketers to gain marketing inspiration and a wider target market.

Fashion-conscious consumers of all ages also learned about and adopted international fashion styles. Whereas marketing efforts were originally targeted toward a domestic group, international visitors are now an important

figure 12.10
Here is a dress from Alexander McQueen's Target line. The international designs were marketed and sold by the retailer for approximately six weeks.

component of many fashion marketing efforts. Target's Go International fashion marketing campaign promotes up-and-coming international designers.

Use of Technology

The use of technology has significantly influenced global fashion marketing efforts. Companies are able to track the success of marketing efforts by sales, as well as purchases by a target market and responses to specific marketing messages.

YouTube has promoted international fashion marketing efforts. International fashion shows were once restricted for retail buyers, fashion photographers, celebrities, and wealthy clients. Now anyone with access to the Internet can watch international fashion shows. Savvy fashion marketers are placing their company's fashion shows on YouTube after the show has concluded. The number of hits (meaning, the number of viewers) provides fashion marketers with an overall idea of general interest in the site. The purpose of placing the fashion show online is not necessarily to increase sales of the fashions shown. The purposes are to continue to showcase the company's brand and label, build consumer interest in the merchandise, and stimulate purchasing behavior in any category of the company's products.

Video cameras, high-speed cameras, streaming video, and the Internet enable consumers throughout the world to view exclusive designer fashion shows, the latest international designs, and interviews with designers. Technology allows consumers into the intimate recesses of the fashion world. Information gleaned from Web sites make consumers better informed about (a) the fashion industry, (b) fashion differences among cultures, and (c) designers' sources of inspiration. The advent of multiple forms of communication has assisted in the blurring of fashion boundaries. Mass markets are provided access to images of international fashion runway and trade shows. Fashion magazines and television shows analyze designer and mass-market fashions and discuss how to obtain similar products worn by international celebrities for half the price (Hansen, 2004). For example, Alexander McQueen had focused his fashions predominantly in England. In 2009, his brand was offered at Target throughout the United States (Figure 12.10).

SUMMARY

Global fashion marketing occurs when manufacturers and/or retailers expand their efforts to other countries. These efforts provide for global exposure and increased sales and profits. Marketing activities that are undertaken domestically cannot automatically be used globally. Marketing messages used in one country may be misunderstood in a different country. The risk of misinterpretation of marketing efforts must be considered prior to the implementation of the marketing message.

Companies entering the global market for the first time undergo a nine-step sequential process. The steps include: (1) reviewing the global market environment, (2) deciding to enter the global market, (3) selecting the global marketplace, (4) deciding how to enter the global marketplace, (5) selecting the global marketing plan, (6) selecting a global marketing organization, (7) implementing the global marketing plan, (8) evaluating the results of the global marketing plan, and (9) making decisions on forthcoming global plans.

As the fashion industry expands, the global marketing guidelines may assist fashion marketers in better understanding and adopting their communication efforts around the globe. While consumers who prefer fashionable apparel may be attracted to similar designs and styles, they may not necessarily understand the same method of promotion or advertising message. Global marketing guidelines can assist fashion marketers in avoiding financially expensive mistakes. In addition, it is becoming increasingly important for designers, manufacturers, and retailers to continually examine consumers' desire for international fashions. The rapid evolution of technology enables consumers to obtain fashions from across the globe simply through the click of a mouse. The globalization of the fashion industry brings excitement to consumers, as well as expanding designers' target markets.

REFERENCES

Agins, T. (1999). *The end of fashion: The mass marketing of the clothing business.* New York: William Morrow.

ATA Carnets for Temporary Exports (2009). ATA Carnets for Temporary Exports Web site. Retrieved July 7, 2009 from www.atacarnets.org

Betts, K. (2007). Luxury's first ladies. *Time style & design*, p. 12.

Burberry (2009). Company Web site. Retrieved on March 3, 2009 from www.burberryplc.com

Butler University. (2008). What is culture? Retrieved on January 28, 2009 from http://blue.butler.edu/~jfmcgrat/culture.htm.

Ellsworth, S. (2009, February 15). Personal interview with Shirley Ellsworth, Lambspun.

Export-Import Bank of the U.S. (2009). Export-Import Bank of the U.S. Web site. Retrieved July 7, 2009 from www.exim.gov.

Ferdows, K., Lewis, M. A., & Machuca, J. A. D. (2004). Zara's secret for fast fashion. *Harvard Business Review,* 82(11), Retrieved on December 1, 2008 from http://hbswk.hbs.edu/archive/4652.htm.

Garment Industry Development Corporation (2007). GIDC services & NY apparel industry. Retrieved on July 3, 2007 from www.gidc.org/enter.html.

Gayle, B. (2009, March 20). Personal interview.

Hansen, K. T. (2004). The world of dress: Anthropological perspectives on clothing, fashion, and culture. *Annual Review Anthropology,* 33: 369–392.

Hiter, K. (2009, February 15). Personal interview.

International Trade Administration (2009). International Trade Administration Web site. Retrieved July 7, 2009 from www.ita.doc.gov.

Lertora, J. (2007). Global luxury survey: China, India, Russia. *Time Graphic,* pp. 108–114.

Kaiser, A. (2009, June 2). Gucci opens Shanghai flagship. *Women's Wear Daily,* p. 2.

Kotler, P., & Armstrong, G. (2001). *Principles of marketing.* Upper Saddle River, NJ: Prentice Hall.

McLaughlin, K. E. (2008, November 18). Dior fuses art and fashion in Beijing. *Women's Wear Daily,* p. 4.

Office of Textiles and Apparel (2009). Office of Textiles and Apparel Web site. Retrieved July 7, 2009 from http://otexa.ita.doc.gov.

Ostrow, R., & Smith, S. R. (1988). *The dictionary of marketing.* New York: Fairchild Books.

Nurchai, S. A. (2002). Style piracy revisited. *Journal of Law & Policy,* 10, 489.

Research and Markets (2008). Profile of H&M: A pioneer of fast fashion. Retrieved on December 1, 2008 from www.researchandmarkets.com/reports/568624.

U.S. Customs & Border Protection (2009). U.S. Customs & Border Protection Web site. Retrieved July 7, 2009 from www.cbp.gov.

U.S. Department of Commerce (2009). U.S. Department of Commerce Web site. Retrieved July 7, 2009 from www.commerce.gov.

U.S. Department of State (2009). U.S. Department of State Web site. Retrieved July 7, 2009 from www.state.gov.

U.S. Small Business Administration (2009). U.S. Small Business Administration Web site. Retrieved July 7, 2009 from www.sba.gov.

Zargani, L. (2008, December 16). Gucci grows footprint. *Women's Wear Daily,* p. 13.

Zargani, L. (2009, May 18). Armani opens Hong Kong airport shop. *Women's Wear Daily,* p. 12.

KEY TERMS

Define or briefly explain the following terms:

Adapted marketing mix ______________________________

Direct exporting ______________________________

Direct investment ______________________________

Domestic fashion marketing ______________________________

Exchange control ______________________________

Export department ______________________________

Exporting ______________________________

Global fashion marketing ______________________________

Global organization ______________________________

Indirect exporting ______________________________

International division ______________________________

Licensing ______________________________

Quota ______________________________

Standardized marketing mix ______________________________

Tariff ______________________________

Trade system ______________________________

CLASS OR TEAM DISCUSSION QUESTIONS

1 | Use the Phases of Cultural Marketing Efforts model (Figure 12.8) as a guideline to discuss a company's global marketing efforts. Your discussion should specifically address the relationship between culture and personality. How do demographics and psychographics influence global marketing efforts?

____

____

2 | As a fashion marketer, discuss the strengths and limitations of using a standardized marketing mix. Address the suitability of attributes when using this strategy. Include a discussion of culture, geography, environment, company, and marketing mix.

____

____

3 | Debate the following statement: *All fashion companies should expand globally or else they will become extinct*. You should include a discussion supporting and opposing the statement.

INTERNET ACTIVITIES

1 | Using the Internet as a resource, find an example of three fashion companies, one representing each type of global marketing activity: (a) exporting, (b) licensing, and (c) globalizing. Discuss the differences between the companies' marketing efforts. What type of opportunities, strengths, and risks does each company face in the global efforts?

2 | Select a company and fashion product category. Access the Internet. Collect data on a company's global marketing efforts. Examine and discuss whether the company used: (a) a standardized marketing mix, or (b) an adapted marketing mix. Address where the marketing efforts are conducted (i.e., countries).

STUDY QUESTIONS

1 | Which attributes make a company global?

2 | Discuss the differences between domestic fashion marketing and global fashion marketing.

3 | Which aspects of a country are considered when reviewing the global marketing environment?

4 | What level of expertise is required in employees when expanding globally?

5 | Define *licensing.*

6 | What is a standardized marketing mix?

7 | Explain the difference between indirect exporting and direct exporting.

8 | When should a company be involved in a direct investment?

9 | Describe the three types of global marketing organizations.

10 | What does it mean to *market globally and act locally*?

11 | How has travel influenced consumers' desire for international fashions?

____

____

12 | How has technology influenced consumers' desire for international fashions?

____

____

MULTIPLE-CHOICE QUESTIONS

1 | Which of the following methods of globalization occurs when an organization receives royalties?

a. Direct investment
b. Exporting
c. Indirect marketing
d. Licensing

2 | _____ exists when the global marketing mix is adapted to fit the needs of the target market.

a. Adapted marketing mix
b. Generalized marketing mix
c. Regulated marketing mix
d. Standardized marketing mix

3 | When a company is globalized, _____.

a. The company markets globally and acts locally.
b. International efforts are integrated throughout the entire company.
c. Marketing efforts transcend the globe to carry a consistent image.
d. Statements *a*, *b*, and *c* are accurate when a company is globalized.

4 | _____ defines the limit of merchandise brought into the foreign country.

a. Exchange control
b. Quota
c. Tariff
d. Trade system

5 | _____ is a tax imposed by the foreign government.

a. Exchange control
b. Quota
c. Tariff
d. Trade system

TRUE-OR-FALSE QUESTIONS

1 | ____ With the advent of technology, language barriers have been completely eliminated when marketing in different countries.

2 | ____ Not all cities throughout the globe offer the same marketing opportunities/benefits.

3 | ____ An international division consists of an exporting agency hired from outside the company to assist in globalization efforts.

Glossary

ACTUAL IMAGE The image that is perceived by the consumers, employees, and stakeholders.

ADAPTED MARKETING MIX A marketing mix that is adapted to fit the needs of the target market.

AMERICASMART-ATLANTA The largest wholesale buying mart in the United States.

ARMCHAIR FASHIONISTA Person who is not in the fashion business, but thoroughly enjoys watching and critiquing fashion.

ARTIFACTS Objects of importance.

APPAREL MART A mart attended by manufacturers and merchandise buyers for retailers to sell and buy products.

BABY BOOMERS Consumers born between the years 1946 and 1964.

BELONGINGNESS THEORY Theory that states people need social acceptance.

BENEFIT An advantage of a product.

BETTER PRICING ZONE A pricing zone that offers affordable and stylish fashions in national and store-brand names to a target market.

BILLBOARD ADVERTISING Advertising that is used exclusively as an outdoor form of marketing.

BOUTIQUE RETAILER A small specialty store or an area within a larger store.

BRAND A particular product, or line of products, offered for sale by a single producer or manufacturer and made easily distinguishable from other similar products by a unique identifying name and/or symbol.

BRANDING The corporate science of adding value.

BRAND CHAPERONE The person charged with overseeing the actions of marketing a brand for continuity, quality, effectiveness, strength, and longevity.

BRAND EXTENSION The extending of a brand into another brand. Brand extension is an effective method of building brand width.

BRAND INTEGRITY The verification or authenticity of the brand.

BRAND MANTRA A fashion marketer's understanding and implementation of a brand's soul.

BRAND STRATEGY The plan employed to create, introduce, and promote a particular brand.

BRAND STRENGTH The strength a brand provides to the product, the brand's name, and the company.

BRICK-AND-MORTAR STORE A physical retail operation.

BRIDGE FASHIONS Fashions that feature a designer label with a 30 percent lower price tag than that of the original line. Bridge-line merchandise is made at a lower quality and features fewer design features than couture-line merchandise.

BRIDGE PRICING Pricing that represents a bridge between designer and better-priced merchandise. High-end designers may offer a bridge label, extending the brand to a secondary market.

BRITISH FASHION COUNCIL, THE (BFC) The council that promotes and stimulates the British fashion industry.

BUDGET PRICING ZONE The least expensive pricing zone. Merchandise in this zone is specifically targeted to the mass market. Merchandise offered in the budget pricing zone is not necessarily a staple or fashion insensitive.

CALENDAR SALE Promotional method whereby during a particular month, a sale is offered every day. Each day, something different is on sale.

CALIFORNIA MART A mart specializing in fashion, textiles, gifts, and the home market.

CALL TO ACTION A written statement, oral comment, or image encouraging consumers to purchase the product.

CENTRALIZED BUYING OFFICE (also known as a *central merchandising plan*) An office (or plan) in which the buying for an entire company is conducted from the company's headquarters.

CHAMBRE SYNDICALE DU PRÊT-À-PORTER The association that supports the French ready-to-wear industry.

CHANNEL OF DISTRIBUTION A distribution channel consisting of designers, manufacturers, wholesalers, retailers, and ultimate consumers. The route along which goods and services travel from producer/manufacturer through marketing intermediaries.

CHAPTER 11 A legal claim of bankruptcy.

CHICAGO APPAREL CENTER A mart that provides wholesalers and retailers with a complete line of services.

CLASSIC MERCHANDISE Apparel that is considered timeless and popular throughout the years.

CLASSIC PRODUCT LINE A product line that is offered consistently over a period of time.

COGNITIVE DISSONANCE An uncomfortable feeling when a person has two opposing thoughts or actions.

COGS The cost of goods sold.

COMPLEMENTARY PRODUCT CATEGORY Refers to any product that can logically be associated or marketed in the company's name.

CONDONED COPY A copy made by any other designers or fashion houses.

CONSUMER The end user of a product.

CONTEMPORARY PRICE ZONE The price zone targeted for quality, yet affordable, fashions. This price zone allows for marketing to a large target market.

CONTINUITY OF PATRONAGE A model whereby a product is disposable and the consumer is automatically replenished with a new one on a monthly basis.

CORE PRODUCT CATEGORY A product category that defines the existence of the company.

COUTURE FASHIONS Custom-made, handmade designs made with master craftsmanship.

CPT Cost of advertising involved in reaching one thousand potential customers with a specific target market.

CREDENCE GOODS Goods whose quality is difficult to assess before or after purchase and use.

CROSS-CHANNEL LOYALTY PROGRAM A program that spans all channels within a retailer. The program is designed to increase consumers' loyalty to the retailer.

CROSS-CHANNEL SHOPPING The act of shopping at multiple retail channels.

DALLAS MARKET CENTER The largest mart in the United States.

DECENTRALIZED BUYING OFFICE (also known as a *departmentalized merchandising plan*) An office (or plan) in which a company uses different buying offices based on geographic region, merchandise category, and/or divisions.

DEMANDS Specifications that consumers require in a company.

DEMOGRAPHICS Vital statistics of a population, including the size of the group and its age, sex, birth and death rates, location, income, occupation, race, and education.

DEPARTMENT STORES Stores categorized based on the type of merchandise sold. They offer a wide variety of soft lines (i.e., apparel for the entire family) and hard lines (e.g., home furnishings).

DESIGN LAW Law to help protect fashions from being copied.

DESIGNER The person responsible for creating the fashions.

DESIGNER SIGNATURE FASHION PRICE ZONE The highest fashion price zone.

This zone is reserved for high fashions that are created from quality fabrics, and have impressive styling, designs, and craftsmanship.

DESIRED IMAGE The image that the store is trying to portray to the consumers, employees, and stakeholders.

DESTINATION PLACEMENT Placement of merchandise requiring consumers to walk through the area, thereby maximizing the breadth and depth of products offered by the retailer.

DIRECT EXPORTING A term describing when the fashion marketing company directly takes on exporting, global distribution, sales, and promotion responsibilities.

DIRECT INVESTMENT A term describing when the fashion marketing company, physically located in the global marketplace, invests in global distribution, sales, and marketing operations.

DIRECT MARKETER A marketer who utilizes a database specifically to target consumers, bypassing traditional channels of distribution.

DISCOUNT STORE A store that operates on a low profit margin.

DISPOSABLE INCOME The amount of money you have to spend after you pay all your bills.

DOMESTIC FASHION MARKETING The marketing of fashions in your home country.

E-RETAILER A retailer that sells products and/or services via the Internet.

EXCHANGE CONTROL A control that limits the foreign exchange.

EXCLUSIVE DISTRIBUTION A distribution model in which a brand is offered through only one retailer.

EXCLUSIVITY Exclusivity resulting from the limited distribution of a product.

EXPERIENCE GOODS Goods where the experience of use after purchase reveals quality with a fair degree of certainty.

EXPORT DEPARTMENT A department that consists of an export manager and several personnel. This department is responsible for coordinating exporting efforts.

EXPORTING The action of a company sending their products to another country and selling them through an intermediary.

EXTERNAL NEWSLETTER A newsletter that is published and distributed to persons outside the company.

EXTRINSIC VALUE The value of a product as viewed by others.

FACEBOOK An online venue for sharing photos, information, news, and sales; it allows marketers to have an interactive Web presence with their existing clientele, as well as to encourage prospective customers to try their products.

FAD MERCHANDISE Apparel that is typically popular for a short amount of time.

FAIR TRADE Law designed to control the piece of merchandise as it is sold along the channel of distribution.

FASHION BEHAVIORAL THEORY A theory that helps explain the reason why consumers adopt or reject fashions.

FASHION INTELLIGENCE The ability to identify or track trends—an important part of merchandise buying and fashion marketing.

FAST FASHION A strategy to move fashion into and out of a store fast.

FEATURE A distinctive quality or characteristic of a product.

FEDERAL TRADEMARK DILUTION ACT, THE (FTDA) Act that describes the factors that determine whether a mark is distinctive and famous, and defines the term *dilution* as the lessening of the capacity of a famous mark to identify and distinguish goods or services.

FÉDÉRATION FRANÇAISE DE LA COUTURE The association that supports the promotion of French couture designers.

FLAGSHIP STORE The main location of a brick-and-mortar retailer.

FLYER Method of fashion marketing using paper, text, and images to promote fashions.

FOCUS GROUP A group of consumers who are asked questions about a product and/or marketing effort.

FOCUS GROUP INTERVIEW A form of indirect interview used in market research.

FOLLOW-UP Any type of action on the company's part that will connect the company with the consumer.

FREQUENCY The number of times an audience is exposed to a message.

GENERATION X Persons born between 1965 and 1979.

GENERATION Y Persons born after 1979. Also referred to as *echo-boomers*.

GLOBAL FASHION MARKETING The expansion of marketing efforts to other countries.

GLOBAL ORGANIZATION An organization that has entire global operations in multiple countries.

GRAY MARKET A term referring to consumers who are retired.

GUIDELINE An indication or outline of policy or conduct.

HANGTAG An informational tag generated by the manufacturer and attached to the product.

HARD LINES A term referring to functional products. Examples of hard lines include home furnishings, cell phones, luggage, cars, and school supplies.

HONG KONG TRADE DEVELOPMENT COUNCIL, THE A council providing national and international buyers with information regarding designers from Hong Kong and Asia.

IDENTITY How you are viewed by your consumers.

IMAGE A mental perception or impression held by an individual about himself, about others, or about products and services.

IMMEDIATE-RESPONSE MARKETING MESSAGE A marketing message designed to encourage viewers to purchase a product immediately.

IMPULSE PLACEMENT How low-priced, high-profit margin products are placed within the immediate vicinity of the cash register.

IMPULSE SHOPPING Shopping without forethought.

INDIRECT EXPORTING A type of exporting whereby the company hires an independent international organization to complete the transaction.

INDIVIDUALITY A term referring to the sum of qualities that characterize and distinguish an individual from all others.

INFOMERCIAL A commercial that is programmed for thirty or sixty minutes.

INTELLECTUAL PROPERTY Refers to the creation of an idea or product; serves as a legal device to deter designs from being copied in their entirety.

INTERNAL NEWSLETTER A newsletter that is published solely for the company's employees.

INTERNATIONAL DIVISION A division consisting of company personnel from each unit in an effort to operate global efforts more effectively and profitably. Marketing, distribution, finance, and research are examples of the areas represented by personnel in the international division.

INTERNET RADIO Radio stations that stream live through the Internet.

INTRINSIC VALUE A value that is internal and unique to each individual consumer.

KNOCKOFF A product that looks remarkably similar to a genuine product.

LICENSING The act of agreement between a creator of a product or line of products and a manufacturer in which the creator (licensor) gives the manufacturer (licensee) permission to use his name in the marketing of a product in return for a royalty, usually computed as a percentage of sales.

LIFESTYLE COLLECTION CONCEPT Comprehensive marketing effort from a central brand.

LIFESTYLE CONCEPT A marketing approach that presents products in a group setting based on a set of behaviors, activities, interests, opinions, or attitudes.

LOGO Generally one or more letters worked into some distinctive typographic or calligraphic design.

MANUFACTURER A company that produces fashions.

MARKET A set of actual and potential buyers of a product.

MARKET-PENETRATION PRICING STRATEGY A pricing strategy whereby the product's initial price is set low, thereby enticing consumers to purchase.

MARKET SEGMENTATION The subdivision of a population (frequently, ultimate consumers) into smaller parts, or demand segments, having smaller characteristics.

MARKET-SKIMMING PRICING STRATEGY A pricing strategy designed to generate a larger-than-average gross margin.

MARKETING Managing markets to bring about exchanges and relationships for the purpose of creating value and satisfying needs and wants.

MARKETING CONCEPT A concept that assists the marketing team in organizing, arranging, and delivering products and services. These actions focus on two objectives: (1) to satisfy consumer's wants and needs, and (2) to fulfill the organization's primary goal.

MASS MARKETING Marketing to all consumers.

MASSCLUSIVITY A term referring to a strategy whereby retailers offer limited-edition merchandise to a mass market. The strategy is designed to stimulate consumer enthusiasm toward the limited-edition item(s) and promote merchandise turnover.

MEMBERSHIP PRICING A pricing strategy whereby consumers sign up for a retailer's membership.

MERCHANDISE BREADTH The number of different products carried.

MERCHANDISE DEPTH The number of units carried within one category.

MERCHANDISE LINE A group of products that are similar in style and design, and that coordinate with each other and are by the same designer and/or manufacturer.

MERCHANDISE TURNOVER The number of times a particular merchandise category is sold.

MICROMARKETING Marketing by individualized program.

MISSION STATEMENT A written statement of the company's purposes—the reasons for being in business and their overarching mission or goal.

MOBILE ADVERTISING Advertising through a PDA, BlackBerry, or other handheld wireless device.

MODA PRONTA Italy's ready-to-wear industry.

MODERATE FASHION PRICING ZONE A zone of pricing targeted to the mass market. Fashions priced in this zone are typically items that the majority of the population wears.

MULTIPLE SALE The sale of two or more products during one sales encounter.

NATIONAL BRAND A nationally advertised brand offered for sale by a producer or retailer. Sometimes referred to as a *manufacturer's brand.*

NATIONAL CHAMBER OF FASHION, THE The organization charged with increasing the number of fashions exported from Italy annually.

NEEDS Absolute requirements needed to be met in order for the target market to purchase.

NICHE BRANDING The further branding of a product(s) that originated from a central brand. The niche brand is clearly identified with the central brand but addresses a smaller, more specific market.

NICHE MARKETING Marketing that occurs when subgroups are developed within segment marketing.

OPEN-TO-BUY (OTB) The amount of money a merchandiser has to spend during the buying season.

OVERRUNS Copies made from leftover material. The original manufacturer often makes overruns.

PACKAGING The bags, boxes, gift wrap, tissue paper, plastic bags, and any other form of material used to hold the consumer's purchases.

PERCEIVED COST The amount a consumer perceives he/she pays for a product.

PERMISSION MARKETING Advertisements that entice consumers to purchase or join a company.

POP-UP An electronic advertisement that pops up on a Web site automatically while the user is logged on.

POSTCARD A card typically 4 ¼ inches × 6 inches in size, that allows full advertising on one side and partial advertising on the second side.

PRIMARY TARGET MARKET The majority of the consumer market who patronize your store.

PRODUCT Tangible objects that satisfy consumers' wants and needs.

PRODUCT-LINE PRICING A pricing strategy whereby a price point indicates the quality level within a merchandise line.

PRODUCT-ONLY RELATIONSHIP A multidimensional connection with the product, company, consumer, and culture. The branding of the product instills in the customer a desire for the product above all other products in the same category.

PROFIT The amount of money remaining after the cost of goods and services sold.

PROFIT MARGIN The amount of profit a company makes for every dollar.

PROMOTION Short-term non-recurrent efforts to increase buying response on the part of the consumers or to intensify sales efforts by the firm's sale force.

PROMOTIONAL PRICING A pricing strategy whereby a product is introduced at a lower-than-normal price. The product's price is raised after the promotional time line ends.

PSYCHOGRAPHICS Consumers' interests, behaviors, and attitudes.

PSYCHOLOGICAL PRICING A pricing strategy used as the basis of making consumers feel more favorable about a product.

PUBLIC RELATIONS Activities aimed at enhancing the public image of an organization, individual, or public (Ostrow & Smith, 1988).

PUBLICITY Unpaid, nonpersonal public notice in the print or electronic media, which may stimulate the sales of a product or service (Ostrow & Smith, 1988).

PULL MARKETING Marketing that occurs when consumers purposely seek out the direct marketer.

PUSH MARKETING Marketing that occurs when advertisements are pushed onto the consumer. Consumers are forced to read the advertisement regardless of their desire.

QUALITATIVE A term referring to information provided in a statement format. For example, consumers may state that they like the advertising campaign for a women's casual apparel line.

QUANTITATIVE A term referring to numerical differences. For example, a company may report sales results that are 5 percent higher than those of its competitors.

QUANTITY DISCOUNT A discount provided when merchandise is purchased in bundles or multiple units.

QUOTAS A number defining the limit of merchandise imported into a foreign country.

REACH The number of readers or viewers who are exposed to a medium.

REGULATION A rule that deals with details of procedure that one might be required to follow.

RELATIONSHIP MARKETING Marketing efforts designed to build long-term relationships with stakeholders.

RESIDENT-BUYING OFFICE (RBO) A purchasing agent located in a national or international market center whose representatives shop the market daily in order to provide their clients or member stores with information and to select and buy merchandise for them.

RETAILER A company that sells merchandise to an ultimate consumer.

RETURN ON INVESTMENT (ROI) The amount of money generated (i.e., returned) on an investment.

SALES The amount of money generated from goods or services sold.

SEARCH GOODS Products that have an intrinsic value objectively accessible prior to purchase.

SEASONAL DISCOUNT A pricing strategy used to sell merchandise that is out of season.

SECONDARY TARGET MARKET An additional 10 percent of the market targeted after the primary target market.

SEGMENT MARKETING Marketing specifically to individual consumer groups.

SELF-COPY Copies made by the fashion house.

SERVICES Activities and benefits that enhance the shopping experience.

SHOPPER A person looking at merchandise.

SHOPPING Activities that include browsing, interacting, and purchasing in/on various channels (i.e., Web sites, physical stores).

SIGNALS Form of communication regarding the company. Signals may be given through product offerings, press releases, changes in leadership, or the enhancement of store interiors.

SIGNATURE BRAND A brand that a customer chooses to wear exclusively.

SKU A stockkeeping unit.

SOCIAL MARKETING Marketing that encourage consumers to interact with the company.

SOCIOECONOMIC A term describing attributes regarding the consumer's socio- (e.g., age, education, marital status) and economic (e.g., income) status.

STAKEHOLDER A person who has an interest or a stake in a company.

STANDARDIZED MARKETING MIX A global marketing mix that is identical to the one used for the domestic market.

STAPLE An item that is used frequently and that is fashion-insensitive.

STORE BRAND A brand sold by a particular retailer.

STRATEGIC PLAN A series of goals and objectives identified by a company.

STYLE Characteristics of a garment that distinguish it from other types of the same garment. A style is also a way consumers associate themselves with a brand, designer, or way of life.

SWOT ANALYSIS Analysis of the company's strengths, weaknesses, opportunities, and threats.

TARGET MARKET A population selected by a company to target its marketing efforts on.

TARGETABILITY Ability to reach the right customer at the right time for the right cost.

TARIFF A tax imposed by the foreign government.

TEMPORARY LIMITED EXCLUSIVE DISTRIBUTION A type of distribution in which a brand is offered at one retailer for a limited time.

TERTIARY TARGET MARKET The remaining 5 percent of the market, after the target market and the secondary market are identified.

TESTIMONIAL A statement from a consumer regarding the qualities, benefits, and attributes of using a product and/or service.

TIVO A brand and model of digital video recorder.

TRADE DRESS LAW Law designed to verify that consumers clearly comprehend the brand they are purchasing. The law attempts to minimize copycat brands.

TRADE PUBLICATION A publication that provides valuable information regarding the overall status of the industry.

TRADE SHOW An event where meetings, conferences, and seminars are held regarding the industry.

TRADE SYSTEM Governmental regulations in conducting business in a particular country other than the company's host country.

TRICKLE-DOWN THEORY The theory that posits that fashion trends are set by upper-income consumers. After widespread adoption at the top level, designer modifications are made to the fashions to appeal to the mass market.

TRICKLE-UP THEORY The theory the posits that lower-income consumers influence fashion trends.

UNIQUENESS The difference consumers wish to portray and express about themselves —say, by displaying a compilation of items differently than would friends and/ or neighbors.

VALUE-BASED PRICING Form of pricing strategy whereby the consumer perceives the value of the product to be worth the price.

VANITY FAKE Products that have low intrinsic value and low perceived product value.

WANTS Consumers' preferences.

WHOLESALER A middleman who collects merchandise in large bundles. Merchandise is then broken down into smaller quantities and sold to retailers.

YOUTUBE A social marketing medium whereby videos, television commercials, and photos are posted on the Internet.

Credits

CHAPTER 1

1.1 no credit
1.2 courtesy of the author
1.3 WWD
1.4 Condé Nast Digital Studio
1.5 Courtesy Bergdorf Goodman
1.6 WWD/Thomas Iannaccone
1.7 WWD/Robert Mitra
1.8 WWD
1.9 Ronald Asadorian/Splash News
Box 1.1 WWD
Box 1.2 WWD

CHAPTER 2

2.1 WWD/Steve Eichner
2.2 Jeff Vespa/WireImage
2.4 Evan Agostini/Getty Images
2.5 Lipnitzki/Roger Viollet/Getty Images
2.6 The Metropolitan Museum of Art, New York, NY, U.S.A. Photo Credit : Image copyright © The Metropolitan Museum of Art/Art Resource, NY.
2.8 Courtesy of Barneys New York
2.9 Reggie Casagrande
2.10 WWD
2.11 Anonymous, 16th century. Portrait of a Noblewoman. Oil on wood, 44½ × 34¾ in. (113 × 88.3 cm). Gift of J. Pierpont Morgan, 1911 (11.149.1). The Metropolitan Museum of Art, New York, NY, U.S.A. Image copyright © The Metropolitan Museum of Art/Art Resource, NY.
2.12 John Chillingworth/Getty Images
2.13 © The Granger Collection, New York
2.14 © Dyson
2.15 WWD
2.16 © Kevin Galvin/Alamy
2.17 TM Go Red trademark of AHA, Red Dress trademark of DHHS. Photo ©2009 Paul Schiefer.
2.18 WWD
2.19 WWD
2.20 Josh Olins/United Colors of Benetton
2.21 WWD
2.22 © Eric Thayer/Reuters/Corbis
2.23 STAN HONDA/AFP/Getty Images
2.24 courtesy of the author
2.25 Condé Nast Digital Studio
2.26 © Caro/Alamy
2.27 Istockphoto
2.28 The Metropolitan Museum of Art/Art Resource, NY
2.29 WWD

CHAPTER 3

3.1 courtesy of the author
3.2 © Sonderegger Christof/Superstock
3.3 WWD/Steve Eichner
3.4 Oli Scarff/Getty Images
3.5 MARKOS DOLOPIKOS/Alamy
3.6 Stephen Lovekin/Getty Images for 20th Century Fox
3.7 Courtesy of Barneys New York
3.8 Courtesy Victoria's Secret
3.9 Courtesy of Nordstrom
3.10 © Michael Willis/Alamy
3.11 (EXCLUSIVE ACCESS) Mat Szwajkos/Getty Images
3.12 Magnus Magnusson/COPYRIGHT ©2009 FAIRCHILD FASHION GROUP. ALL RIGHTS RESERVED.
3.13 Courtesy Target
3.14 AP Photo/H&M
Box 3.1 Courtesy Saks Fifth Avenue

CHAPTER 4

4.2 © Avital Aronowitz
4.3 Courtesy of True Religion
4.4 Charles Eshelman/FilmMagic
4.5 © Avital Aronowitz

4.7 © Bettmann/CORBIS
4.8 COPYRIGHT ©2009 THE CONDÉ NAST PUBLICATIONS. ALL RIGHTS RESERVED.
4.10 Joe Kohen/WireImage
4.11 Courtesy of Bebe
Box 4.1 WWD
Box 4.4 WWD

CHAPTER 5

5.1 Jeffrey Mayer/WireImage
5.2 WWD
5.3 Maury Phillips/WireImage
5.4 WWD/Robert Mitra
5.5 WWD
5.6 Splash News/Paul Hadfield
5.7 © Avital Aronowitz
5.8 Jayne Fincher/Getty Images
5.9 WWD
5.10 James Devaney/WireImage
5.11 Chapple/Tsui /Splash News
5.12 WWD/John Aquino
5.13 WWD
5.14 courtesy of the author
Box 5.1 © Warner Bros./Courtesy: Everett Collection
Box 5.2 WWD/John Aquino
Box 5.3 Jean-Paul Aussenard/WireImage

CHAPTER 6

6.1 WWD/Robert Mitra
6.2 COPYRIGHT ©2009 FAIRCHILD FASHION GROUP. ALL RIGHTS RESERVED.
6.3 © Avital Aronowitz
6.4 © KIM/Alamy
6.5 WWD
6.6 WWD
6.7 WWD/Steve Eichner
6.8 WWD
6.9 WWD
6.10 WWD/John Aquino
6.11 Hulton Archive/Getty Images
Box 6.2 Courtesy of Stein Mart

CHAPTER 7

7.1 WWD/John Aquino
7.2 Sara Jaye/AbacaUSA.com
7.3 no credit
7.4 Barry Brecheisen/WireImage
7.5 WWD/John Aquino
7.6 WWD
7.7 © Avital Aronowitz
7.8 © Inti St. Clair
7.10 Condé Nast Digital Studio
7.11 Courtesy JCPenny
7.12 David Rohmer/X17agency.com

CHAPTER 8

8.1 Robert Mora/Getty Images
8.2 Courtesy Blue Fly
8.3 © Avital Aronowitz
8.4 Courtesy Bergdorf Goodman
8.5 WWD/John Aquino
8.6 © Peter Horree/Alamy
8.8 © Avital Aronowitz
Box 8.1 WWD/Kyle Ericksen

CHAPTER 9

9.1 Ethan Miller/Getty Images for Cole Haan
9.2 Nick Harvey/WireImage
9.3 © Jeff Greenberg/Alamy
9.4 Stephen Shugerman/Getty Images
9.5 Howard Berman/Getty Images
9.6 WWD/Thomas Iannaccone
9.7 Charles Eshelman/Getty Images for Henri Bendel)
9.8 © Avital Aronowitz
9.9 Marsaili McGrath/Getty Images
9.10 John Parra/WireImage for HSN
9.11 © Avital Aronowitz
9.12 Courtesy of Target
9.13 Janet Mayer/Splash News

9.14 AP Photo/Bernd Kammerer
9.15 Courtesy of Nike
Box 9.1 Courtesy of Laroque, photo by Travis Teate
Box 9.2 WWD/John Aquino
Box 9.3 Courtesy of Target

CHAPTER 10

10.1 WWD/Steve Eichner
10.3 WWD
10.4 Condé Nast Digital Studio
10.5 WWD/John Aquino
10.6 Ahmad Elatab-SaleemElatab/Splash
10.7 WWD
10.8 Victor Chavez/WireImage
Box 10.1 WWD/Kyle Ericksen
Box 10.3 COPYRIGHT ©2009 FAIRCHILD FASHION GROUP. ALL RIGHTS RESERVED.

CHAPTER 11

11.1 Martin Thomas Photography/Alamy
11.2 Steven Georges/Press-Telegram/Corbis
11.3 courtesy of the author
11.4 courtesy of the author
Box 11.1 © Frank Miller/Corbis
Box 11.2 © LA PHOTOTHEQUE SGM

CHAPTER 12

12.1 YOSHIKAZU TSUNO/AFP/Getty Images
12.2 courtesy of the author
12.3 © SuperStock
12.4 © Avital Aronowitz
12.5 COPYRIGHT ©2009 FAIRCHILD FASHION GROUP. ALL RIGHTS RESERVED.
12.6 © Bartek Wrzesniowski/Alamy
12.7 © Avital Aronowitz
12.9 Courtesy of Target
12.10 Courtesy of Target
Box 12.1 YOSHIKAZU TSUNO/AFP/Getty Images
Box 12.2 Courtesy of Burberry

Index

Page numbers in italics refer to figures or tables.